MEDIEVAL CIVILIZATION

MEDIEVAL CIVILIZATION

MEDIEVAL CIVILIZATION

SELECTED STUDIES FROM EUROPEAN AUTHORS

TRANSLATED AND EDITED

BY

DANA CARLETON MUNRO

AND

GEORGE CLARKE SELLERY

Enlarged Edition

NEW YORK

THE CENTURY CO.

D118
M96m
co.2

Table of Contents

v

Table of Contents

vi

Table of Contents

vii

Preface to First Edition

THIS book is offered as a partial solution of the problem which confronts every instructor in medieval history. Pressing library needs usually prevent him from securing an adequate supply of duplicate books for supplementary readings. In the rare cases in which the instructor succeeds in securing books, many works of great value still remain inaccessible to the average student because he cannot use the continental languages. This book has been prepared in the belief that it will enable the instructor to assign and to quiz all members of the class upon the same supplementary readings, and that it will at the same time permit the students to utilize, in a fuller measure, the results of European scholarship in the medieval field.

It is not a source-book. In making it we have, with two or three exceptions, drawn upon modern authors, making selections on topics which are not adequately treated in English. We have translated and adapted what we have chosen in order to make the selections more useful to students. Often the translations are very free; at times whole pages are omitted. We believe, however, that in no case have we made any change which is not in accord with the author's point of view. It is scarcely necessary to add, what is very apparent from

ix

Preface

the opposing views furnished, that we do not always agree with the authors. But each selection is worthy of careful study and thorough consideration.

Our thanks are due to the publishers who have so kindly allowed us to employ their books. We hope that the selections will cause teachers and the more advanced students to use the originals for further guidance; we know that our little book will have only a partial success if it does not lead many to go to the fountain from which we have drawn.

DANA CARLETON MUNRO
GEORGE CLARKE SELLERY

UNIVERSITY OF WISCONSIN,
October 24, 1904.

Preface to Enlarged Edition of 1907

THIS enlarged volume is designed for the use of the general student of medieval history. The greater number of the selections will, it is confidently believed, prove useful to beginners in the subject; some of them are specially interesting to the more mature; all of them should prove valuable for class use in the hands of the skillful teacher.

Medieval Civilization

MEDIEVAL CIVILIZATION

❦

Victory of the Latin Language

Adapted from G. Bloch, in Lavisse: *Histoire de France,*
Vol. I, Part II, 1900, pp. 388–398.

THE Latin which gave birth to the Romance languages was vulgar Latin, that is, the Latin of the common people. It accompanied the soldiers of the legions, the colons, and the emigrants of every kind, from Italy into the provinces, and thus became the language of the people of all Western Europe—the spoken, not the written, language. We can reconstruct this language to a certain extent, with the aid of the hints let fall by different writers, but only in a most general way. It is well-nigh impossible to follow the alterations which it underwent through contact with the native dialects in Gaul and elsewhere. The essential fact to remember is that it differed from the literary Latin of the educated classes. It gained undivided sway over the lower classes, to the exclusion of the speech of their fathers, and after a long and determined struggle with the literary Latin of the upper classes, it won recognition, when at length the decay of higher learning delivered to it the whole of society. It could now expand everywhere, develop freely according to its own inner law, and finally, under the form of the Romance tongues, usurp the place of the older Latin.

The complete victory of the popular Latin, in fact, only slightly preceded in point of time its own submission to these new idioms which it carried in the germ. It was in the fifth century that it definitely took possession of Gaul, throughout the whole extent of its territory, and from the highest to the lowest classes of the population. Only old Aquitaine, between the Pyrenees and the Garonne, successfully resisted complete conquest. There, in the Basque country, the Iberian speech, more tenacious than the Celtic, raised for itself an impregnable citadel. As for Brittany, it seems well proven to-day that the Celtic dialect, still current in its most remote districts, does not date back to the age of Gallic independence, but is merely an importation of the insular Britons who fled before the Saxons, from the fifth to the seventh centuries A.D.

Thus, by a kind of paradox, it is when she is about to succumb that Rome wins this last triumph. But it is only a seeming paradox. We must not be deceived by the division of history into convenient periods. The prestige of Rome survived her material power. She still remained, for the different peoples, the mistress of the world and the benefactress of the human race. She had just been captured by Alaric when Rutilius sang her immortal destiny, and it is about the same epoch that there appears for the first time in our texts the newly coined *Romania,* so happily conceived to designate, in one word, her empire and her civilization. It is not a matter for surprise that the victories of Latin were prosecuted in the midst of events which destroyed Roman unity.

Victory of the Latin Language

The Romans did not make war on Celtic, the language of the Gauls. They undoubtedly knew that their rule would gain greatly through the diffusion of Latin, and they neglected nothing to extend its use. But in the furtherance of their object, they did not have recourse to any tyrannical measures. In the course of the third century, they even authorized the making of wills in Celtic.

Celtic disappeared before Latin because Celtic was barbarism and Latin was civilization. Latin attracted, therefore, all minds eager for culture; and it possessed the additional advantage of being the official language, without which it was impossible to get along.

It was the official language of the Roman government and of its agents of every grade. The Romans did not have the same respect for the rough dialects of the West as for Greek. They did not have their public acts translated into the Western languages. It was the business of the natives to understand these acts or to have them explained to them.

Latin was also the official language of the city governments. This point is clear in the case of the colonies, although there may be some difficulties with regard to the other kinds of cities. Unfortunately, the inscriptions which alone could settle the question conclusively are insufficient in number, and belong in general to a late epoch, about which there is no longer any question. Nevertheless, it is worthy of note that none has been found which is not in Latin. And at Bordeaux and at Saintes, there are inscriptions, written in Latin by the magistrates, which date from the first century. Is it likely that the Romans were less tolerant toward the language of their subjects than they were toward their institutions? In leaving them their self-government, is it conceivable that they required the rulers of the city to speak Latin? We do not know absolutely, but nothing justifies us in saying yes. In any case, the governments of the cities were entirely aristocratic, and aristocracies do not require to be forced to adopt the language of the conqueror.

Latin, then, was indispensable to the fraction of the aristocracy which claimed to monopolize senatorial or equestrian functions. It was no less necessary for those who restricted their ambitions to the practice of municipal law. The emperor Claudius withdrew the right from a deputy of a province of the East who could plead only in Greek. Even the lower classes had to use Latin in their law-court quarrels and in their appeals before the imperial treasury. And there can be no doubt that they were obliged to make use of it in their dealings with Italian merchants.

Latin crept into use by the most varied paths. It was spread not only by the immigration of freemen, but also by the importation of slaves. The slaves came from all parts of the world, and if they were to understand one another and their masters, they must have a language common to all. Old soldiers, going back to private life, brought it to their homes and taught it to their neighbors. The Church, in the third century, abandoned Greek and adopted as its official language the language of the government. Henceforward its great weight was thrown into the scale. Finally, the school, without being for Rome the brutal instrument which it has become for modern conquerors, exercised a decisive influence, all the more powerful because it embraced the whole man. It did not limit itself to teaching him a new language, but created in him, so to speak, a new spirit, and fundamentally transformed his sentiments and ideas. It was the school which really made the Gaul a Roman.

We know, unfortunately, very little about the elementary education. We can only judge, from various indications, that it was by no means neglected. The total number of illiterates cannot have been very great. The humblest inferior officers were expected to read the Latin watchword from the tablet on which it was written. There were schools for the sons of veterans. An inscription has been discovered at Aljustrel, in Portugal, which contains the regulations for the working of a mine, and it shows that schoolmasters were to be found even in the village which had sprung up about the mine. These elementary schools, the regimental schools perhaps excepted, were private. It had taken the Romans a long time to get the idea that instruction could be given by the State, and when at length they did get it, they appear never to have extended it to the education of the masses. But the search for knowledge was very active in this society, and the initiative of private individuals was sufficient.

We are better informed as to the establishments of a higher grade of education, for the use of the upper classes, and we find here some slight intervention of the public authority.

When Agricola was called to govern Britain, in 78 A.D., he was very zealous in introducing Roman customs. He was not content with inviting the people to build cities with temples, forums, and porticos. He saw to it that the

Medieval Civilization

children of the nobles were instructed in Latin. In this he merely followed the policy adopted a century before in Gaul. There, also, and to a greater extent than elsewhere, schools had been multiplied immediately after the conquest. Strabo, at the beginning of the first century, notes the fact and does not restrain his admiration. It is certain that these schools did not lack the encouragement of the Roman officials. But though the State favored, and, if need be, solicited, the initiative of the cities, it did not in the beginning venture to supplant it. Vespasian was the first to think of paying the teachers out of the public funds. Hadrian, Antoninus, and Alexander Severus had the same thought. It is rather difficult to say just what measures these different emperors took. It appears, from all the facts, that the State ordered the expenditures but did not assume them. It endowed a very few chairs in some famous centers, for example Rome and Athens, but elsewhere it left the municipalities to bear the expense. And what at first was only a benevolent, even if not an absolutely spontaneous, expense on their part, became obligatory. As this occurred precisely at the time when their financial embarrassments began, it is not hard to understand that they did not always acquit themselves of this duty with all desirable alacrity. To put an end to the abuse caused by their niggardliness, Emperor Gratian in 376 A.D. promulgated from his residence at Trèves, and transmitted to the prefect of the diocese of the Gauls, an edict fixing once for all the emoluments which each municipality should assure to its teachers. These varied with the importance of the city and the grade of the teacher.

Victory of the Latin Language

When the State imposed upon the curias the burden of paying the salaries of the teachers, it left them, quite logically, the right of choosing them. That did not, of course, prevent its interference, even in cases where it had not founded or endowed the chairs. The cities, far from being displeased at the emperor's interference in their affairs, were proud of such a mark of interest. Their felicitations were perhaps less warm when they learned the largeness of the salary which the emperor sometimes assigned to the teacher he sent them. Under the emperor Julian the respective rights of the State and the curias were regulated by a law, in accordance with which the curias were to continue to name the professors, though their choice was to be submitted to the imperial approbation. It was a special law, meant to exclude Christians from teaching. But there is no evidence that it was revoked after the death of its author.

Among the schools which flourished in Gaul at the opening of the Christian era, those of Marseilles and Autun held the first rank. Marseilles had lost its political and commercial importance, and had turned its activities into another channel. It had always been one of the hearths of Grecian culture in the West, and more and more devoted its energies to education when other ambitions were vain. Like Athens, whose example it imitated and whose renown it hoped to rival, it sought consolation for its misfortunes in becoming a great university center. Varro called it the city of the three languages. At Marseilles the Gallic students and youths from Italy were educated together. The great Roman families willingly sent their sons thither. They could obtain at Marseilles the same instruction as in a Greek country, with the advantages of nearness to home and of an atmosphere reputed to be more moral. One of the glories of Marseilles was its scientific tradition. There is no evidence that it produced astronomers and geographers, as in the time of Pytheas, but its physicians were illustrious and made great fortunes. One of them, a contemporary of Nero, was rich enough to rebuild, at his own expense, the city walls, which had been destroyed by the siege of 49 B.C.

The school at Autun was very different. It was a real Gallic school and was highly prized by the youth of the land, who had escaped but yesterday from the discipline of the Druids. So great was the attendance about 21 A.D. that a rebel leader, a Sacrovir, desiring to secure the support or at least the neutrality of the whole Gallic nobility, believed that he had attained his object when he seized the students as hostages. The Roman government had not made an unwise choice in selecting Autun as the seat of a great school. It thus rewarded the Æduans, its faithful allies of old, and secured very generally the approbation of the Gallic people. Lyons would not have served so well. It was exclusively Roman, and the young Gauls would have felt that they were in a strange land. They were at home, on the contrary, in this fundamentally Celtic city, Autun, a place which was, at the same time, profoundly devoted to Rome. We do not hear anything more about the school of Autun until the second half of the third century. At that time, its great prosperity was ruined by civil war, and its beautiful buildings fell a prey, with the rest of the city, to the flames kindled by hostile soldiers. It partially recovered, however, from this sad blow, and the Cæsar, Constantius Chlorus (293–306 A.D.), gave it a striking proof of his favor when he sent the rhetorician Eumenius to direct it.

Eumenius was one of the great personages of Gaul, and the most illustrious son of Autun. He was not all Gallic, for he had Greek blood in his veins. His family came from Athens, which his grandfather had left in order to teach rhetoric at Rome. Thence he had passed to a chair in the school of Autun, attracted by its renown and no doubt by the advantages which it assured to its teachers. His grandson inherited his aptitudes and followed for a time in his footsteps. He was born at Autun, and lectured there, in his turn, with striking success. It was this success which changed the course of his life. For Constantius Chlorus heard of his talents and attached him to his person, making him his *magister memoriæ*. This was the name given to one of the state secretaries whose business it was to draw up the documents which were issued from the imperial chancery. There were only a few higher offices in the administrative hierarchy. To abandon it and return to his professor's place was to sink in the social scale. But the emperor was unwilling that it should be considered a disgrace. Not content with maintaining his salary at its existing high level, he doubled it, and to make his object more clear he wrote him the following letter, which he invited him to read publicly on taking possession of his new post:

" Our Gauls, whose sons are instructed in the liberal arts at the city of Autun, and the young men themselves who have so cheerfully served as our escort, assuredly deserve that the cultivation of their natural abilities should be looked after carefully. And what better could be offered them than those riches of the mind which are the only riches fortune can neither give nor take away. Accordingly, we have resolved to place you at the head of this school, which death has deprived of its chief, you whose eloquence and high probity in the conduct of our affairs we have learned to appreciate. It is our wish, then, that you should, without losing any of the advantages of your rank, resume your chair of rhetoric in the aforesaid city, which we desire, as you know, to reëstablish in its former splendor. There you will mold the minds of the young men and give them the taste for a better life. Do not believe that these functions are derogatory to the honors with which you have been invested. An honorable profession increases, rather than diminishes, a man's renown. In conclusion, it is our will that you receive a salary of 600,000 sesterces ($30,000) from the city treasury, so that you may clearly know that our clemency treats you according to your merits. Farewell, most dear Eumenius."

Eumenius was generous enough to consecrate all this income to the restoration of the buildings. Unfortunately, these great efforts were only half successful. The heyday of city and of school had passed away forever.

It was not because the Gallic schools were in decay. They were never more alive than in this fourth century, which was a sort of resurrection for Gaul. The government never lavished more favors upon them, and if the municipalities in parts of the empire were found wanting, there is no trace of their negligence in Gaul. The current had merely been diverted into other channels.

The current followed the displacement of political life and moved toward the North. As early as the time of Marcus Aurelius (161–180 A.D.), Rheims is spoken of as another Athens. But it was Trèves, above all, which aspired to become a great educational center. The Cæsars installed in this new capital had the highest ambitions for the place. They endeavored to attract thither the most celebrated masters by offering them a remuneration one fifth higher than their colleagues elsewhere received. Trèves, nevertheless, never had, from the intellectual point of view, more than a secondary importance. Life was too unsettled upon this frontier, and German barbarism was too near and too menacing for the students to give themselves over, unreservedly, to the labors of the intellect. They found a more favorable center, a safer asylum, at the other extremity of Gaul.

Aquitaine was advantageously situated at this time. It had had its part in the calamities of the preceding century, but, since the strengthening of the empire, it had enjoyed profound peace. Sounds of war which rang across Belgium and the Lyons country echoed only feebly here. Its uninterrupted leisure, the inviolate riches of its fields and cities, marked it out as the last refuge in the Occident for the ancient learning. The happy genius of its people did the rest. The reputation of its rhetoricians became universal. It supplied them to Italy and to the East. It introduced them, as preceptors, into the imperial household. St. Jerome gives them a place in his *Chronicle,* and Symmachus, the most illustrious representative of Latin eloquence at the end of the fourth century, tells us in pompous phrases all that he owed to their lessons.

The most striking thing about these university professors is the place they held in society. They were generally rich, and had not always inherited their wealth, but frequently acquired it in the exercise of their profession. Their fixed salaries were often less than the revenues they derived from the liberality of families, and especially from the registration fees of their students, which naturally increased with the renown of the teacher. And it is to be remembered that they were free from all the taxes and charges which at that time weighed so heavily upon private fortunes. In addition, one must not forget the honor which attached to their position as teachers. As members of the curia, decurions and magistrates, they were in the first rank of the local aristocracy. Some, as we have seen, attracted the attention of the emperor, became provincial governors and pretorian prefects, and even attained the lofty though barren honor of the consulship.

The students were numerous. They had their organizations, their banners, and their meetings for conviviality and noise. The students belonged almost exclusively to the nobility or the middle class, although the emperor Alexander Severus had conceived the idea of bursaries for brilliant but poor youths. The upper classes were shut out from trade, which was left to freedmen, and from the army, which was becoming more and more the property of the barbarians. Accordingly, they threw themselves with ardor into the administrative career, the only one open to their ambitions. And it was through the portal of the liberal studies that the civil service was entered.

Victory of the Latin Language

High intellectual culture was in those days not only the indispensable mark of a well-born man: it was also the best ground for public office and advancement. An advocate of the fisc, a secretary of the chancery, or a pretorian prefect had to be, first of all, a man of letters. If the emperors took such a zealous interest in the prosperity of the schools, if they claimed the right to control rigorously the studies and behavior of the students, their reasons, it is plain, were not purely disinterested: it was because they saw in these youths their future civil servants. No society ever loved and honored learning more than this one. But it is open to the reproach of having pushed the worship of learning to the point of superstition.

We touch here the weak side of this brilliant and much-esteemed education. It has a double claim to our attention: it reveals, in several ways, the weaknesses of this declining civilization; and, in the second place, it does not completely perish with the society which it helped to destroy, but passes several of its features on to the medieval schools, through which, in some degree, it is perpetuated in the schools of to-day.

A school like that of Autun, for instance, was not a university in our sense of the word. It taught both the secondary and the higher subjects, *i. e.*, it embraced grammar as well as rhetoric. It will be remembered that this is still the sacred division of courses in the French colleges. Grammar was not interpreted, any more than at present, in its narrower sense. It was made up of two parts: the art of speaking correctly, and a commentary upon the authors. These were the Greek and Latin authors, and the students began with the Greek. Homer and Menander were the favorites. The young Latins did not always take kindly to this strange tongue, but Greek none the less held its place of honor. It represented the most delicate and elevated side of this glorious civilization, which was already menaced and impaired by Christianity. The only non-Gallic teachers in Gaul of whom we know were of Greek origin. Among the Latin authors most enjoyed was, first of all, Vergil, the most popular of poets, already almost the god he was to become several centuries later. After him, with a long interval between, came Horace and Terence. The Latin prose writers were less appreciated, and the absence of their strong food had its consequences. But the greatest evil was the lack of positive knowledge, systematically taught. Undoubtedly the commentary upon the authors was not purely verbal, and involved a variety of explanations which touched geography, history, philosophy, and even science. But these came in only as the texts gave occasion for the commentary; they were not presented as separate wholes, and they did not lead to investigation. It is this sterile exegesis, this devotion to the book and to the letter, which continued to weigh upon the world even in the age of scholasticism.

The same objections apply to the studies of the higher grade. The narrowness of the program of study is astounding. There was no real study of the sciences; men were swept away from it by the progress of mysticism, and, moreover, the Romans never had esteemed the sciences save for their practical applications. There is the same absence of philosophy; the Romans had always distrusted it as vain babbling, and had left the monopoly of

Victory of the Latin Language

it to the school of Athens. Even law, the peculiar creation and most durable legacy of Rome to the world, had renowned masters only in Rome, Constantinople, and Beyrout. Rhetoric alone remained. A text to be commented upon and a theme to be developed—that was the whole of the higher education. Eloquence, the virile art of the society of antiquity, had become a frivolous and empty diversion. It had occupied such an important place among the ancients that the people of this age did not think of discarding it. But they reduced it to formal, conventional exercises, where the chief thing was to hide under elegance of expression the dearth of ideas. This discipline, which we ourselves have not entirely given up, had its value. It could supple and refine the intellect. But practised for itself, as an end, not as a means, and isolated from all solid study, it was sterile and dangerous. It accustomed the youth to value words above things, to emphasize form rather than content; it pauperized, it enervated the intellect. When a student examines its fruits in the most admired works of this time, the discourses of Himerius, the panegyrics of Eumenius, and the most of the poems of Ausonius, he finds them almost entirely lacking in substance and in thought, and he will be almost compelled to attribute to this teaching a large share in the general decay and ruin of the empire.

The Landed Aristocracy and the Beginning of Serfdom

Adapted from G. Bloch, in Lavisse: *Histoire de France,*
Vol. I, Part ii, 1900, pp. 436–451.

I N the fourth century most of the land in the Roman Empire was in the possession of the senatorial nobility. This nobility had its rise from the practice of conferring the office of senator without requiring the recipients of the honor to take their seats in the senate, or even to reside at Rome. Many of them lived in the provinces, and there were not a few who had never been away from home. They were senators, nevertheless, in the full enjoyment of the titles and privileges of their high station, and with the right of transmitting them to their children. Appointment to certain governmental posts or the mere will of the emperor would also confer it. Hence this nobility was more than a mere hereditary caste; it was an order to which all ambitious men might aspire.

The strength of this aristocracy, which, because of its advantages, swallowed up the lesser nobility, lay in its possession of the land. Landed property was in this era the chief source of public wealth and the most honorable sort of riches. It was, therefore, the source of all consideration and power. We shall examine the methods by which this nobility got possession of the soil and drew wealth from it, and in so doing we shall discover the causes of its power and gain an insight into the condition of the rural population.

The peculiarity of the Roman organization of landed property was its conception of the *fundus* or domain. This word had several synonyms: *ager,* meaning field, *villa,* the home of a master, and *cortis,* the court or yard of a farm. *Fundus* was, however, the strict legal term. The Romans carried the idea of the *fundus* with them into the provinces. The distinctive attribute of the *fundus* was its indestructible unity. It almost always bore the name, from generation to generation, of the man who had owned it in the far-off time when it had first been placed upon the tax-register. It might be broken up by sale or inheritance, but in the eyes of the law it remained undivided, and the coöwners merely possessed parts of it. If one man acquired several contiguous *fundi,* each retained its individuality and its name. The explanation of this peculiarity is undoubtedly the simplification of the work of taxation which resulted.

We must avoid confusing the *fundus* with a modern village. The Romans had no village in our sense of the word. The nearest approach to it was their *vicus,* a group of dwellings. Most European villages have a council or government of some sort of their own; the *vicus* had nothing of the kind. The smallest area which had, under the Romans, a right to make municipal regulations of its own was the *civitas,* which was composed of a town portion and a country portion dependent upon the former. The *vicus,* then, was not a division of the soil. All the soil was divided as follows: first the *civitas,* then the *pagus,* which was a subdivision of the *civitas,* and, finally, the *fundus,* which was a subdivision of the *pagus.* These were the only divisions known to the tax-officials. It should be clear that a *fundus* could not be part of a *vicus,* though there might be several *vici* on one *fundus.*

These *vici* were inhabited by tenants more or less unfree. There was another sort of *vicus,* dwelt in by freemen, but it was unusual, and toward the end of the empire it sank into insignificance before the onward march of the large estate. The growing importance of the large estate did not, of course, affect the permanence of the *fundi.* The joining of one *fundus* to another did not disturb its individuality, and, furthermore, the large estate was not necessarily composed of contiguous *fundi.* In Gaul the large estate of many a rich proprietor was scattered over a wide area, although there was a constant tendency to increase the size of the adjacent portions.

The struggle between the proprietors of large and of small domains has always been an unequal one. It was still more unequal in the period we are discussing. A large domain was more than so many acres of meadow, vineyard, forest, and cultivated land. It was a little world sufficient to itself and provided with agricultural toilers and artisans of every sort. How could a small proprietor compete with such an accumulation of resources? His expenses were relatively greater and his profits smaller. If his small capital gave out he could not borrow, for there was little money in circulation, and the rate of interest was exceedingly high. If political catastrophes prevented the cultivation of the soil and caused famine, he

Aristocracy and Serfdom

was ruined. That is what happened in the second half of the third century. And the vices of the system of taxation heaped to the full his cup of woe. We shall see below how the land-taxes fell with all their crushing weight on those least able to bear them. The small proprietor was compelled to abandon the struggle.

The enslavement of the rural population took place in a variety of ways.

One of the most usual was that of *patronage*. This was not a novelty. The Romans had always been familiar with it, and the Gauls had practised it before the Roman conquest. It did not involve any inconvenient personal subjection so long as the government of the State remained strong. But it became dangerous under the weak sway of the later Roman Empire. The empire at this time had little hold upon the senatorial aristocracy, which was powerful through its riches, its local attachments, and its independence, which the State itself had fostered. Its members were subject to the jurisdiction of the provincial governor in civil matters, but in criminal matters they had been exempted from responsibility to any one save the emperor or his immediate representative, the pretorian prefect, and these were too distant to be any real check. This practical immunity from external control explains adequately the lawlessness of the nobility. Their commonest breach of justice and the laws was perhaps the seizure of land, by fraud or force. The emperors in vain directed their functionaries to oppose such lawlessness, for they had, as we have just seen, rendered them powerless in advance. Is it surprising, then, if the weak landholders more and more fell into the habit of seeking from the strong that support which they could not get from the law? Such an one would apply to a powerful man, would *commend himself* to him, to escape the land-tax, gain a lawsuit, secure protection against an injustice, or obtain the means of perpetrating one. Patronage, or *commendation,* accordingly, spread like a huge net over the whole social body. The State, moreover, saw the peril. It declared all such agreements void, and threatened with severe punishments those who made them. It was useless. Then the State thought that it could compete with these private agreements by offering similar public ones. It offered to become a patron, against itself, in the person of the *defensor* of the city. It failed again. The mere idea of such a system was virtual abdication.

This *commendation* was generally completed by the *precarium,* which was also a very ancient usage. This was the name given to a grant of land which was made to an individual, free of cost, in response to his request, or prayer. Hence the name *precarium.* The *precarium* did not involve any abandonment of ownership by the giver. It was revocable " at will," whenever he wished, in accordance with the legal doctrine that no one could be bound by his own generosity. Moreover, the grant was of necessity a gratuitous one, for any obligation imposed upon the receiver would have violated the essential nature of the *precarium* and made of it a species of legal contract. That was the theory. In practice, it is fairly certain that the receiver of a *precarium* was not satisfied to be a tenant at will, and that the landowner obtained some compensation. There had to be something to make the *precarium* advantageous to both parties, and, as a matter of fact, the proprietor did impose a rent upon his *precarious* tenant. The threat of eviction would, without any legal sanction, insure the payment of it. As long as the tenant paid his rent, he could be morally certain of keeping the use of the land and transmitting it to his children. The *precarium,* then, was nothing but a disguised method of renting land, in which the proprietor was not legally bound and the tenant-farmer had to rely upon usage for his possession and possessory rights.

The transformation of the small proprietor into a tenant of this sort might result from a loan. The lender would prefer a more profitable kind of security than the ordinary mortgage. The borrower accordingly *sold* him his land for the amount of the loan, it being understood that he could buy it back by repaying the loan with interest. Until repayment he enjoyed the use of the land under a *precarious* title. If he never made repayment, which was generally the case, he remained a *precarious* tenant all his life long, and at his death his children could, with the consent of the creditor, take his place. Another method of constituting a *precarium,* apparently the most usual of all, was the extension of the *commendation* from the man to his land. After all, the protection of the man, unless his property were protected, would not suffice. But this protection, too, must be paid for. The small proprietor accordingly gave his land to the large one by a fictitious sale, which the law in vain condemned, and became the *precarious* tenant of his protector. After all, it was better to have a well-defended *precarium* than an estate liable to be pillaged by the first robber.

Commendation combined with the *precarium* was one

of the most potent means of developing the large estate.
But it was more than that. It contained in the germ the
two institutions which are an epitome, or almost an epitome, of feudalism: vassalage and the fief. Another factor in this society paved the way for a new era: the advent of servitude of the glebe, which was not feudal but
was the foundation upon which the whole feudal edifice
rested.

A large estate was made up of two parts, the one cultivated directly by the proprietor, the other indirectly.
The latter grew more and more at the expense of the
former. The part directly exploited was not cultivated
by free day-laborers,—they do not seem to have existed,—
but by slaves who lived in common and worked in gangs
under overseers who were also slaves. This system had
its disadvantages. The slaves got no personal profit from
their toil, and were consequently poor workers. In order
to interest them in their work the proprietors adopted the
idea of picking out the best workers and renting them
bits of land to cultivate on their own account. These were
the hut-slaves, so called because they had their own separate huts for homes. They enjoyed special advantages,
but they still remained slaves and all their possessions belonged to their master. At the end of the third century,
however, their situation grew more stable, and was therefore improved, when the government conceived the plan
of inscribing them on the tax-register as a separate class,
in order to secure an increase of the land-tax. These hut-
slaves, who were also called, after this enrolment, *enrolled
slaves* (*ascripti*), were considered, for tax purposes, to
belong to the soil, of which they determined the value.

Aristocracy and Serfdom

The law, accordingly, forbade a proprietor to sell the land without them. As to selling them and keeping the land, there was no reason for that so long as they kept it productive.

The slaves of this class, the enrolled slaves, were, however, in a decided minority even at the close of the empire. But the freedmen, who were very numerous, as one can see from the place they occupied in the recruiting of the army, were in a similar position. Enfranchisement gave liberty, but not necessarily independence. It was the right of the patron, as the liberator was called, to fix the nature and extent of the duties owed to him by his freedmen by a definite convention, which was recognized and sanctioned by the laws. These duties generally consisted in material services, and more precisely in the master's right to a prior share in the earnings of the freedman. If the freedman had been an agricultural slave, it was the custom to establish him on a bit of land as a tenant. The condition of a freedman tenant was no doubt superior to that of a slave tenant. He had rights and the slave had none, for the prohibition against selling the land without the slave tenant was not made in his interests but in the interests of the land, or rather of the imperial treasury. On the other hand, the condition of the freedman tenant was much inferior to that of the free tenant. He could not, like the latter, free himself from the services he owed his patron or from other restrictions, which varied according to the quality of his enfranchisement. The so-called *Latin* or *Junianus* freedman could acquire property outside of the plot assigned to him, but all such acquisitions went, after his death, to his patron. The freedman who was given citizenship could transmit his acquisitions to his children, but his patron had a right to the share of a child, and if there were no children, he took all. This, of course, is virtually the same as the *mortmain* of the feudal era. So much for the part of the large estate which was directly cultivated by the proprietor.

The part which was cultivated by the proprietor indirectly was intrusted by him to farmers of free birth. But while the slaves rose, little by little, to a condition in certain respects like that of the farmers, the farmers met them, so to speak, half-way down, by their transformation into colons. The names remain the same, but their meanings change. The serf of the Middle Ages is very different from the Roman slave, but he is only this slave in a new situation, and the name of both is always the same— *servus*. The man that we call a colon bears the same name as the free farmer he was originally, *colonus*. The problem is to find out how this free farmer became a colon, how his condition changed while his name remained unaltered. First of all, however, we must determine what this condition was.

The colon was not a slave. He was a freeman, of free birth. He had civil rights, of which the slave was completely destitute and of which the freedman possessed only a part. He could marry; he could found a family. He inherited property from his father and transmitted it freely to his children. True, he was not the proprietor of the land he cultivated as tenant, but he might have other lands in full ownership. He could sue his master, while a freedman could not bring suit against his patron at all. He was bound, chained, only by the land he held as tenant.

Aristocracy and Serfdom

He could not free himself from it. Neither could his children. His condition was not one of servitude in the strict sense of the word, for servitude is the condition of a *person* and his person was free. He was bound, nevertheless, to the soil by the bond of a colon, the *nexus coloniarius*. He did not have a master, but his land did; his land alone had a slave, and he was the slave. Hence the restrictions upon his liberty. Not only was he riveted to this land forever, he and his, but he could not leave it for even one day, and if he married he had to choose a woman from his master's estate and from his own class—otherwise the woman, and any children she might have, would be lost to the master of the estate from which she came. Here again we see a characteristic of the later feudalism, the restriction on *formariage*.

The bond which attached the colon to the land did not, however, impose duties on the colon alone. The proprietor as well had strict duties to perform. He could neither send away his colons nor sell the estate without them. In case of a sale, the new proprietor could not install new colons to the prejudice of the old.

There were general causes which produced this institution of the *colonate* throughout the empire.

The lot of the farmers was a difficult one from the period of the Antonines on. The documents of this time are unanimous in representing their affairs as in a very bad condition, and as keeping them continually behind with their rent. Their situation could only grow worse as time went on. The proprietor could, to be sure, seize their goods, and finally evict those who did not pay. But what good would that do? The seizure of the farmer's chattels would only have completed his ruin, and another put in his place would not have been more fortunate. It was more profitable not to seize or evict, but to take advantage of the embarrassment of the farmer and modify, to his detriment, the conditions of his holding. According to the Roman law, a farmer was obliged to pay a money rent fixed in advance. But farming on shares, although not recognized by the law, was a very common practice. If the parties abandoned the rent system for the share system, the change would be to the advantage of the proprietor alone. For the man who cultivated on shares had no rights the law would enforce, and the proprietor to whom he was indebted could exercise greater pressure upon him than before, by the threat of instant expulsion. In this way, there arose at an early period a whole class of tenants enslaved to their holdings.

The *colonate* arose in other ways also. Laborers in search of work would be installed upon uncleared lands. It was not necessary to pledge them to payment. They offered to the proprietor what they had to give—day-labor for the present and part of the crops for the future, when there should be crops. Meanwhile they remained upon the land of their choice, and when by their labors they had increased its value the proprietor no more thought of sending them away than they thought of leaving it. They were voluntary colons, and they did not differ, essentially, from those who had become colons from necessity.

A third class of colons was made up of the barbarians who were forcibly transplanted, or admitted, upon their request, within the empire. From these vigorous races, Rome demanded cultivators as well as soldiers. They were established upon the State domains or parceled out among individual proprietors. This sort of thing was common in Gaul at the end of the third century upon the territories devastated and depopulated by invasions.

There is no doubt that it was this latter sort of *colonate* which gave rise to the first legislative recognition of the practice. Hitherto, the *colonate* had been a private custom. But the law could not continue to ignore it after it had become a public institution. And the financial reform, which had, as we have seen, caused the fixing of the tenure of the slave, now affected, in a similar way, the lot of the colon. His name was inscribed upon the tax-register, and the same fiscal cause which attached him to the soil made it impossible for the proprietor to evict him.

The difference between the lot of the colon and that of the slave was, after all, chiefly theoretical. As a matter of fact, the colon had a master because his land had one, and because he was enslaved to this land. This is so true that the law which distinguished him from the slave more often distinguished him from the freeman, and as time went on he more and more came to differ from the free-man and resemble the slave. In fact, the *precarious* tenant himself was not a freeman in the full sense of the word.

The development of the large estate through *commendation* and the *precarium,* together with the development of serfdom of the glebe through the assimilation of the condition of the colon, and to a certain extent of the *precarious* tenant also, to that of the slave, were the means by which Roman society was transformed. Through them, there grew in strength, upon the ruins of the State, the landed aristocracy, which, with the exception of the

Medieval Civilization

Church, was the only institution which remained standing after the fall of the empire. Gradually, from this on, the senatorial nobility usurped sovereign powers. The large estate more and more became an organism distinct from, but analogous to, the *civitas,* and independent, if need be, of the State. The proprietor acted as magistrate for his tenants. He represented the State on his domain, and was able either to oppose or to substitute himself for it. The State determined the amount of his taxation ; he levied it on his tenants and turned over the proceeds —provided he consented to turn them over and did not begin by driving off the tax-gatherer. The State again determined how many soldiers he had to furnish to the army ; he picked the men and sent them to the muster. He handed over to the public authorities the wrong-doers who were pointed out to him, and it was not until he refused to deliver them up that the authorities ventured to send soldiers after them. He had a right of police and jurisdiction over his " men," as they were already termed in Roman law, over his freedmen and colons, as well as his slaves. He could beat them with rods, like slaves. The colon and the freedman might, it is true, under some circumstances, bring him before the magistrate, but they were afraid to do it. The *precarious* tenant, who had given himself up wholly to his patron, could not, of course, attempt to do anything of the kind. All that the proprietor lacked, at this time, was military command, and, later on, when need arose he assumed that. Ecdicius, who is said to have fed four thousand poor men during a famine, raised at his own expense a troop of horsemen to repulse a Visigothic incursion.

Aristocracy and Serfdom

The nobles resided almost exclusively upon their estates. It had not always been so. True, they had never completely abandoned the rural life they had led before the Roman conquest, although they had been beguiled by the attractions of the urban civilization of the Romans. But since the end of the third century the cities had undergone great changes. Behind their somber walls, in a restricted space, with their narrow, cumbered streets, their huddled and stuffy dwellings, and their public buildings reduced to petty proportions, they had lost all their charms. Under such circumstances, it would be a matter for surprise if the nobility had not abandoned the city for the country, their first love. Henceforth they went to the city only for infrequent and short visits, on the occasion of religious festivals, or public ceremonies. The remainder of their time was spent in princely fashion in the country.

The writings of the time give us a very good idea of their residences and of their life. On reaching the estate, one would have to pass through the villages of the serfs and the colons before coming to the villa proper, to the lord's residence, the *prætorium,* as it was now called. This name is significant, for it always suggested to the Romans the idea of authority and command. The villa was composed of two distinct parts, the urban and the rural. The rural contained all the things needful for cultivating the soil, the buildings for housing, feeding, and for imprisoning, if necessary, the slaves, the stables, barns, granaries, oil- and wine-cellars, the mill, bake-house, wine-presses, workshops, and smithy. All these were grouped around a large courtyard, the *curtis* of the Middle Ages.

31

Medieval Civilization

The urban part of the villa, located quite close at hand, was the dwelling which the master preserved for his personal use. It was a large, roomy residence, completely furnished and richly decorated, a real palace provided with all the refinements of comfort and luxury—with baths, porticos, inclosed promenades, spacious dining-rooms, special winter and summer apartments, picture-galleries, libraries, and gardens formally laid out and beautified with statues and artificial lakes. These sumptuous residences were to be found by the hundred in the empire, and numerous ruins enable us to reproduce their form.

A noble had many ways of spending his time. To say nothing of the public duties, which he could not escape, the administration of his domains and the cares of superintendence consumed a good portion of his time, although the pleasures of château life still held a very prominent place. The nobles paid visits to one another, they rode horseback, they played dice and tennis, and, above all, they hunted. The Gauls, for example, were ardent hunters, and the well-stocked forests of their country gave them every opportunity to indulge their passion for the chase. Hunting scenes are a favorite subject in the mosaics with which they ornamented their apartments. They had packs of dogs with carefully kept pedigrees; they chased the stag, the wild boar, the wolf, and the aurochs; they used the crossbow and loosed the falcon like twelfth-century lords. In the midst of their diversions, literature was not forgotten. Never, in fact, were the upper classes more devoted to it. They wrote witty and pretentious letters, full of mannerisms, and with the secret hope that they would be widely read and might one day form a collection

like Pliny's. They doggedly wrote verses. To excel in
this mental exercise was equivalent to an honorary title.
They took pride in excelling in verse as later generations
did in wielding deep-biting swords. It is in this particular
that this aristocracy differed from its successor. Although
fond of all physical exercises, it had no taste for the business of arms, which it regarded as unworthy, and from
which it had been weaned by the imperial policy. In a
similar way the inviting and peaceful villa is distinguished
from the *castellum* of the Middle Ages. Between this
pleasure-house and the fortress of feudal times, one cannot help but feel that a world has crumbled.

And yet the feudal château already begins to appear,
the fortress which is to throw its heavy shadow over the
country-side for centuries to come. The first invasions
and the appearance of robber bands had left a feeling of
insecurity, which the ever-recurring evil of brigandage
kept alive. The days of the Roman peace, the *pax romana,*
were gone forever. Every one felt it more or less clearly,
and sooner or later took precautions against sudden attacks. The villa was transformed, as the cities had been,
since the days of Aurelian and Diocletian. A wall sprang
up around it. The beautiful residence of Pontius Leontius, close to Bordeaux, is to this day fortified with ramparts and towers capable of braving a siege. It is the
burgus Pontii Leontii, Leontius's fortress, and undoubtedly it is not the only one which from that time bore a
warlike name. Thus, on all sides, and from all points of
view, we see multiplied symptoms which announce the
end of a great historic period and the advent of a new
society.

Taxation in the Fourth Century

Adapted from G. Bloch, in Lavisse: *Histoire de France,*
Vol. I, Part ii, 1900, pp. 280–289.

THE reigns of Diocletian (284–305) and Constantine (306–337) were marked by great financial innovations. Of the many causes producing these changes, the principal one was the distress occasioned by the disasters of the preceding century. To meet the expenses of the reorganized empire, it was necessary to wring from taxation all it could be made to yield. Indirect taxes were relatively unimportant. The tax upon manumissions had fallen with the numerical decline of the slaves. The succession tax which Augustus had placed upon citizens, as a set-off to their immunity, lost its *raison d'être* with the universal extension of citizenship. Both of these taxes were abolished. The customs-duties, town dues, transit tolls, and taxes upon sales were retained, as were also the monopoly of salt and the exploitation of mines and imperial lands. But by far the most fruitful sources of revenue were the direct taxes upon land and persons.

The assessment of the land-tax was altered. Hitherto its basis had been the *jugerum,* and each proprietor had been taxed according to the number and the quality of the *jugera* which he possessed. Diocletian devised the scheme of dividing the land into portions of equal value,

Taxation in the Fourth Century

which consequently varied in extent according to the quality of the soil. Each of these portions, whether owned by one man or several, formed the unit which bore the tax. The number of these units in the whole empire, in each city, and in each province, being known, and the total amount of the tax to be levied being determined, miscalculation and loss were out of the question. The same method was applied to the direct tax upon persons. It, also, rested upon a taxation unit (*caput*) made up of one or several persons. It is a question still to be decided whether or not this human capitation tax was superadded to the land-tax just discussed. The question is purely theoretical, for the small proprietors who paid this tax disappeared little by little.

A single principle determined the organization of personal taxation. This was neither to lighten the burden of the poor nor to increase that of the rich, but simply to seize, in every case, the point where each class of the population laid itself open to fiscal attack.

The result of this principle was that the capitation tax became a plebeian capitation tax. It fell upon the plebs alone, that is to say, upon every one who was not at least a curial, or, in other words, who was not a landowner, since there was scarcely a landowner who was not a member of the municipal nobility, at least. And, by a new restriction, the urban plebs, the plebs of the cities, ceased to be liable for it. In place of it, they were required to pay a special tax, the *chrysargyrus,* so called because payable in gold and silver, while other taxes could, in general, be paid in kind. The *chrysargyrus* was a tax levied on industry and commerce—upon every form of labor save agricultural labor. Thus the plebeian capitation tax was restricted to the workers in the fields, the colons, or, what amounted to the same thing in the end, to their masters, who were compelled to advance the tax for them.

If the noble classes were freed from the capitation tax, they were none the less bound to make certain personal contributions over and above their land-taxes. The curials paid the tax of coronary gold which, from a voluntary gift of provincials to victorious generals, had become a regular state tax. The members of the senatorial order paid an analogous tax, the *aurum oblatitium,* as well as a supplementary land-tax, the *gleba senatoria.* Senators who attained the pretorship were heavily taxed; they had to provide the public spectacles in the capital of the East or of the West. The municipal magistrates of the various cities bore a similar burden. In general, there was no high functionary who had not to pay the price of his elevated rank.

Payments in kind held such an enormous place in the system that it would almost seem as if they represented the heaviest part of taxation. There were the corvées for the maintenance of the roads and other works of this sort, provisions for the post-service and the army,— horses, food, clothing, and raw materials for the manufacture of arms,—and also the furnishing of conscripts, together with the lodging of the troops and the entertainment of the emperor and his suite, and of every one traveling at his command. All these payments in kind rested upon the land, which was the principal form of wealth, and which was thus subject to a disproportionate burden

Taxation in the Fourth Century

There were also services due from certain industrial and artisan corporations. The corporation of watermen, for example, was bound to provide the necessary water transportation in matters of public utility.

The expenses of government were light compared with those of to-day. To be sure, it was necessary to support the excessive luxury of two courts, and to maintain the plebs of the two capitals. It was also necessary to scatter gold among the barbarians. On the other hand, the army was small compared with those of the present day, and the government officials, though numerous, were not proportionately more numerous than at present in France. There was no diplomatic service, no staff of teachers to be maintained, and no public debt upon which interest had to be paid. If the budget of receipts corresponded to the budget of expenditures it cannot be said to have been too heavy, and yet contemporary writers assert that it was. Various causes aggravated the weight of the burden.

First to be mentioned are the troubles caused by the invasions and the economic distress which they produced. Constantine, in 311, remitted to the Æduans five years of tax arrearages and gave them a reduction of one quarter for the future. The Æduans had just gone through a terrible crisis. Forty years previously they had waged a desperate struggle for the unity of the empire. Many other peoples had undergone the same disasters and secured the same remedy of tax remission. Gratian (367–383) remitted the taxes of all Gaul. Favors of this sort became more frequent, and they bear witness to the evils they were vainly intended to correct.

Medieval Civilization

Another fiscal sore, for which the weakness of the central power was wholly responsible, was the rapacity of the officials. When Julian came to Gaul in 356 he found the country crushed and "panting" under the pressure of official rapacity. When he left Gaul, four years later, after four years of glorious government, the work of recovery was much advanced.

The chief cause of the intolerable weight of taxation was the manner in which the amount was determined and collected. The contemporary complaints refer to this almost exclusively. It should be noted, however, that the subjects of the empire who paid the tax had not, like modern peoples, the satisfaction of settling the amount of the taxes, and the purposes for which they should be used, and of supervising the expenditure. The taxes appeared to them not as a just debt, but as a tyrannical exaction. They were, therefore, the more inclined to complain since they could not appreciate the extent to which the taxes were devoted to useful objects. A large proportion of the taxes were paid in kind. Nowadays the State asks its subjects for money alone. The Roman State asked something more. It demanded that its subjects should help to furnish directly the commodities it required, or aid directly in the public works. It asked of the farmers a portion of their crops and of their cattle; it demanded of the artisans a part of the products of their industry, and of others the assistance of their hands and their substance for its building operations, and the conveyance of its goods. The scarcity of money had produced the system, and the government clung to it more tenaciously as the detestable practice of falsifying the coinage developed.

Taxation in the Fourth Century

The value of the coins often fell very low, while the usefulness of the commodities and of human labor remained the same, and the difference meant a gain for the State and a loss for the individual. The corvée had another inconvenience which was peculiar to it. It was vexatious as well as burdensome; it took men away from their own affairs and exposed them to official abuse of power. And as payments in kind involved corvées for transportation, they pressed upon the populations with redoubled weight.

The obligation to make a declaration of one's property set at loggerheads the tax-payers and the fiscal agents, the former trying to depreciate its value, the latter striving to estimate it at its proper value, and, too often, to give it an excessive valuation. In this duel the officials were at an advantage by reason of the harshness of the Roman laws, which authorized them to resort to torture to secure declarations agreeable to them. And they did employ it, if not against proprietors, against the lower classes. Especially in matters of direct taxes, which bore heavily upon the urban and rural plebs, they made use of it, and the operation of the tax levy became the occasion of odious scenes, which do much to explain the hatred it aroused.

There were two causes for the harshness connected with the collection of taxes. One was the abuse which shifted the main burden of taxation upon the classes least able to bear it; the other, the laws which made the tax-collectors themselves responsible for the amount of the taxes.

The great landowners sought in every way to escape taxation. The incessant crises which placed the empire in jeopardy, and the frequency of the struggles for the im-

Medieval Civilization

perial crown, rendered their assistance most valuable. In return, they were granted collective or individual immunities, which increased with time and dried up a good part of the revenues of the State. In cases where it appeared that the levy of the taxes was imminent they resorted to high-handed measures. They raised small armies from their vast domains and drove away the tax-officials. This was rarely necessary, for they were generally able to come to an understanding with the officials, and the tax-registers became a tissue of frauds. If fresh taxes were imposed, they arranged that the burden should fall upon others. If the emperor granted a remission of taxes, they saw to it that they monopolized the benefit. The governors and functionaries of every grade did not dare to enter into a struggle with these personages, who were eminent in their own districts, and who had often held high places in the government service or at court. Moreover, the governors and functionaries themselves belonged to the senatorial class, of which the great landowners were members, and were therefore only too willing to shut their eyes to such misdeeds.

The result was that the poor paid for the rich, and as it was absolutely necessary to make up from the one side what was lost on the other, the easier it was for the one class to escape, the more pitilessly was the other class exploited. And this was not the least important of the causes of the disappearance of the small landowners. The small proprietor who gave his land to a great proprietor and cultivated it in his name, as a colon, freed himself from land-taxes; and as for the personal capitation tax which now fell upon him as a colon, the intervention of his master rendered that more supportable. The worker in the city had not this mode of escape, although he, also, willingly resorted to patronage to defend himself against the demands of the fisc. That is why the *chrysargyrus* was perhaps the most execrated of all the taxes.

Below the senators of the empire, the *clarissimi,* came the members of the municipal senates, the decurions or curials, who were middle proprietors, or owners of moderate quantities of land. They were the peculiar prey of the fisc. They not only paid, each for himself, the coronary gold tax and the land-tax, but, as assessors, collectors, and guarantors, they bore the weight of the latter for their fellow-citizens of the municipality. When the amount of the taxation of the municipality, as a whole, was settled, their first care was to apportion it among the taxpayers. Then, from the curia itself, they chose exactors, charged with the duty of collecting it. Finally, they were, as a group, bound to turn over the whole amount to the government. In placing these obligations upon the curials, the government saved itself much trouble and expense, and, above all, secured a pledge for the amount of the tax. It did not see that these advantages were slight compared with the resultant evils. For the system of curial taxation undoubtedly inflicted one of those wounds through which the living material and moral forces of Roman society ran out.

There was an initial danger in allowing one group of the taxpayers to determine the share of all. The temptation was too strong to ease their own burdens at the expense of the others. The curials lightened their own loads, not at the expense of the great proprietors, the senators, but at the expense of the small proprietors. The worst phase of the system was that they were responsible in case of deficit,—the exactors first; then, in case of their failure, their sureties; and, finally, the whole curia. Thus it resulted that, in pursuing the debtors of the State, they were protecting their own property from levy, and one can easily understand the ardor of the pursuit. Salvian says that there were as many tyrants as curials, and assuredly it could hardly have been otherwise, human nature being as it is. But the very bitterness which they carried into the task turned to their own destruction. When the smaller landowners were exhausted under the blows of the curial taxation, then it was the turn of the curials themselves. To escape this impending ruin there was but one plan—escape from the curia. Some few succeeded in doing this through exceptional favors, the emperor advancing them to senatorial rank. For the great majority, the curia was a jail whose doors did not open.

The interest of the fisc was too manifest. It had not put its hand on these hostages to let them escape. Hence those laws which weighed so heavily upon the curials— prohibition to live outside the city, to dispose of their property by sale or by will, obligation of the son to succeed to his father's duties, etc., etc. And the curia, as well as the State, saw to it that the laws were observed. The curia intervened energetically to drag back to his chains the colleague whose defection meant an increase of the burden of each remaining curial.

The curials were not the only ones who were riveted to their hereditary condition. The State, in placing a special tax upon each class of citizens, had undertaken the

Taxation in the Fourth Century

graceless task of keeping its hand upon them so that each class might be in a position to pay its share. And as, in addition to the ordinary taxes, it demanded from certain groups services which nowadays are let out to contractors, it was compelled to maintain at the same level not only the fortunes of, but the numbers in, these groups. The watermen who conveyed public property, the workers in the arsenals and in the imperial manufactories, the bakers, the provision-merchants who supplied the bread and meat for distribution at Rome and Constantinople,—these composed hereditary castes, from which neither men nor money were to be withdrawn. Reasons of a similar nature held the soldier to the army and the colon to the soil. Men, imprisoned in a destiny without exit, felt their energies flag, their labors slacken; their mental horizon narrowed, and they lost that regard for general interests without which patriotism ceases to be. They no longer sought to improve their condition. A deadly poison permeated the body social, swallowing up intelligence and will. The evil had many causes, but when one wishes to explain the general stagnation which marked the end of the empire, it is well to remember that it was due in part to a wrongly conceived system of taxation.

Influence of the Migrations

Adapted from F. Martroye: *L'occident à l'époque byzantine;*
Goths et Vandales, 1904, pp. i–ix.

BY the middle of the fifth century, the ruin of the
Roman Empire was consummated in the West. Its
provinces, devastated by a long series of invasions, presented a spectacle of the most frightful distress and the
most complete disorganization. "If the whole ocean had
swept over this country," says a contemporary, "it would
not have made more horrible ravages. Our stock, our
fruits, our harvests have been taken from us. Our
houses in the country have been ruined by fire and water.
The small remnant left to us is deserted and abandoned.
This is only the most petty of our woes. For ten years
the Goths and Vandals have been making a horrible
slaughter among us. Castles built upon rocks, villages
situated upon the highest mountains, even cities surrounded by rivers, have not been able to protect their inhabitants against the fury of these barbarians. Everywhere they have been exposed to the last extremities. If
I cannot complain of the indiscriminate massacre of so
many persons eminent by their rank, and of so many
peoples who may have received only a just punishment
for the sins which they had committed, may I not, at
least, ask why so many young children, still incapable of

sin, were swallowed up in the same carnage? Why did God allow his temples to be consumed by fire? Why did he permit the profanation of the sacred vases, of the sanctity of virgins, of the religion and piety of widows? Why have the monks in their grottoes and caverns, who had no other occupation than praising God night and day, experienced no better fortune than the most profane among men? The tempest has swept away indiscriminately the good and the bad, the innocent and the guilty. The dignity of the priesthood has not exempted the clergy of God from suffering the same indignities as the lowest of the people. They have been thrown into chains, torn by scourges, and condemned to the flames like the worst of men."

These complaints were not at all exaggerated. The author of this poem had himself shared the misfortunes which he describes. He had been led away into captivity and constrained to march on foot, bearing a burden, in the midst of the chariots and weapons of the barbarians, with the sad consolation of seeing his bishop, a holy and venerable man, and all the people in the same condition. To so many ills were added the sufferings caused by the troublesome and greedy administration, by the rapacity of the treasury, by the shameless avidity of the magistrates and officials. The Roman administration, pretending to regulate people, things, and beliefs, had suppressed all individual initiative, and permitted activity only amid a labyrinth of laws and regulations. Constantly it drew tighter and tighter the bonds which enveloped the entire society, prescribing what it was necessary to think, under penalty of chastisement, ordering when and how it was necessary to get married, at what age and under what conditions a man could enter a monastery or become a member of the clergy, where and how he ought to live. The imperial power took away from its subjects all freedom to dispose of their own persons and their own property, crushed them with burdens from which no asylum could liberate them, and left to them no hope except the destruction of the empire, rendered odious by so many persecutions, constraints, and exactions.

This system of government, together with the invasions and the religious and political struggles, had finally dried up the sources of prosperity and diminished fortunes already acquired. A contemporary wrote: " As to the magistrates, they do not govern those who are delivered over to them; like ferocious beasts, they devour them. They are not content with plunder, as is the custom with bandits; they tear them to pieces, as it were, and feed upon their blood. Thus it has come to pass that some, strangled and murdered, have become vagabonds because they could live in no other way. They have become what they would not, because it has not been possible for them to be what they would. After having lost all liberty, they have been compelled to defend their very lives. Moreover, what could the unfortunate do who were continuously ruined, without any respite, by the treasury, and were always threatened with proscription? Forced to desert their dwellings in order not to be tortured in their own houses, reduced to exile in order to escape punishment, the enemy appeared to them more merciful. They fled to the enemy in order to escape the rigors of Roman exactions. Where, among what people other than the Romans, are such evils seen? A like injustice exists only among us. The Franks are ignorant of these crimes; the Huns have none of this rascality; nothing like it exists among the Vandals or the Goths; among the Visigoths such proceedings are so entirely unknown that neither these barbarians nor the Romans who live among them have to suffer them. It is for this reason that, in the countries which the barbarians occupy, all Romans pray never to pass under Roman rule. In this country all Roman people desire to be allowed to continue to live among barbarians. It is not astonishing that our fathers did not conquer the Goths, since the Romans preferred to live with them rather than with us. Not only have our brethren no wish to leave them in order to come to us, but they leave us in order to take refuge with them. The only fact which can rightly cause us to wonder is that all Roman tributaries, impoverished and reduced to misery, do not act in the same manner. The only thing which prevents is their inability to transport to the barbarians their dwellings, their property, and their families."

The facts revealed by this gloomy description are testified to by the law, dated at Ravenna the eighth day before the ides of November, under the consulship of Leo and Majorian (November 6, 458). "We must," writes the emperor, "consider the curias, which the ancients rightly called 'little senates,' as the souls of the cities and the sinews of the republic. Nevertheless, they have been so oppressed by the injustice of the magistrates and by the venality of the tax-gatherers that most of their members have resigned their offices, expatriated themselves, and sought an obscure asylum in the distant provinces."

Medieval Civilization

Thus, after having accustomed the people to bear passively a tyranny which extended to every act of life, the imperial administration had finally worn out the patience of the people and prepared them, according to Salvian's statement, to prefer to live free under the rule of barbarians rather than as slaves under the Romans. The exasperation and disgust of the population explain why the Vandals first, and later the Goths, were able for years to devastate the West and to establish separate kingdoms in Africa, Spain, and Italy. As early as 429, when the Vandals invaded Africa, whole populations of the proscribed awaited them as liberators, and forming a party devoted to them, facilitated the establishment of the first barbarian kingdom.

In Italy, especially at Rome, there could be no thought of separation, such as existed in the provinces; but like causes produced like results. The exactions of the treasury, its continual demands, which exhausted the people; the ever-increasing insecurity, which ruined and destroyed commerce; the abolition of the ancient religions, which had divided the population into two hostile parties; the absolute authority of the emperor, which gave to the citizens no share in public affairs, and permitted to them no effort to remedy the evils of which they were the victims; the organization of the imperial court, which made of the emperor the puppet of ambitious intriguers and cabals,—all these causes for discouragement had produced in every class of society weariness and indifference, and had debased the public character and public morality.

At Rome, misery and the departure of the court had depopulated the city, henceforth all too vast for its inhabi-

48

Influence of the Migrations

tants. The second sack of Rome, captured by the Vandals under Gaiseric in 455, had given the fatal stroke to the unfortunate capital of the West. It did not recover again. A great number of the inhabitants had perished, others had been led away into slavery; those who had been able to escape did not return, but continued to drag out a wretched existence in the provinces of the empire. Rome, depopulated, encumbered by remnants and ruins, commenced then to take on its aspect of majestic desolation.

Germans in the Roman Empire

Adapted from E. Lavisse: *Études sur l'histoire d'Allemagne
Revue des Deux Mondes,* July 15, 1885, pp. 401-408.

AT the end of the fifth century the Burgundians
were masters of the whole Rhone valley; the Visigoths, of southern Gaul and Spain; the Ostrogoths, of
Italy. Before the latter had established themselves, a
great event had taken place. Odoacer, chief of the mercenaries who occupied the Italian peninsula, had taken
the imperial insignia from Romulus Augustulus, the last
of the phantom Cæsars who had succeeded one another in
Italy for half a century, and had sent them to Constantinople. The envoys of the senate, who gave them to the
emperor in 476, told him that a single master was sufficient
for the government of the world. Zeno was obliged to
believe it, and the empire withdrew from the West. Although in theory it maintained its rights, in reality it left
the field free to the barbarian kings. It might have
seemed probable that they were going to introduce a new
mode of life into the old Roman world; but this expatriated Germany survived for only a few generations, and
has left only a memory.

These barbarians, moreover, had settled without violence. The terms of their settlement had been arranged
by the last defenders of the empire. Constantius had

placed the Burgundians, in 413, on the left bank of the Rhine, and thirty years later Aëtius had transported them to Savoy. The Visigoths, ever since they had entered the empire as suppliants, had certainly been unsatisfactory servants. They had departed from the banks of the Danube, had pillaged Greece, Asia Minor, and Italy, had visited Athens, had captured Rome, and then wandered into southern Gaul and Spain. Although they often revolted, they always returned to their obedience, and Constantius, in 419, gave to them as a dwelling-place the *Aquitania secunda.*

Accordingly, the Burgundians and Visigoths were, properly speaking, portions of the imperial army stationed in the provinces ; for the Roman soldiers in the last ages of the empire were lodged in the houses of the landowners, and the law assured to them the use of a portion of the house in which they were guests. It is true that amid the distress of the fifth century it was no longer possible to distribute food to the barbarians ; therefore it was necessary to give them a part of the house and of the estate, and thus they became proprietors. It is true, also, that these armies were tribes commanded by kings who had a government and policy of their own, which could not be harmonized with military obedience ; therefore they obeyed very badly. The Burgundians had spread over the valley of the Rhone without violence, and with the good will of the inhabitants ; the Visigoths, on the other hand, were more enterprising and had to be checked by force. But when the Huns invaded Gaul, the emperor wrote to the king of the Visigoths, " Come to the aid of the republic to which you belong," and Theodoric went to

meet his death in the great battle against Attila. The
Burgundians obeyed without hesitation the summons sent
to them by the Roman general Aëtius. Even after the
withdrawal of the imperial power had left the barbarian
kings independent, the Visigoths lost none of their respect for the imperial majesty, and the Burgundians continued to be its humble servants. The last of their kings
wrote to the emperor, early in the sixth century: " My
race is your servant; my people is yours. I am less proud
of commanding it than of obeying you. My ancestors
always felt that they received their most illustrious titles
from the hands of your Highness. They always prized
the gifts received from the emperor more highly than
their ancestral inheritance."

The Ostrogoths were even more devoted to the empire
than the Visigoths and the Burgundians. After they had
been forced into the service of the Huns, in which they
remained for eighty years, they went to the Danube frontier, as the Visigoths had done seventy-five years before.
They might have seized the land, but " they preferred to
ask the Roman emperor for it." When the emperor had
given them some portions, they demanded better ones, and
ravaged several provinces. After that, they cried for relief from famine. They were without food and without
money when the emperor sent them to Italy, or at least
permitted them to go there. After Theodoric, their king,
had conquered and dispossessed Odoacer, he left the imperial statue standing in the Roman forum, placed the
imperial effigy upon his coins, wrote the emperor's name
on the monuments which he restored, and had the consuls
at Rome confirmed by the emperor. Although he consid-

ered himself both the king of his nation and a sort of colleague of the emperor, he never ventured to express himself freely as to the nature of the office which he held, nor did he obtain a definition of it from Constantinople. As long as he lived, he professed to have the most profound respect for the " very pious and serene " emperor.

The barbarians were, therefore, neither strangers nor enemies to the Roman inhabitants, and they governed them as well as they could. In studying the government of Theodoric, nothing seems changed in the Italian peninsula, except that there were more Romans. The senate, the magistracies, the administration, the schools, and the monuments remained or were restored. Roman Italy, in the hands of the Ostrogoths, was a ruin undergoing restoration. The barbarians had no especial privileges in this state, of which their king was chief, and Theodoric's policy was to make Goths and Romans live in peace, under the same law, so that at some time in the future it would not be possible to distinguish one from the other. The Burgundians and the Visigoths were farther away from Constantinople. Gaul, their new country, was Roman land, to be sure, but it had not been the cradle of the empire, and it had neither senate, consuls, forum, nor the immovable rock of the Capitol; therefore they did not imitate imperial customs so closely. They did not attempt to fuse the two races. The Visigoths followed this remarkable course: they wrote out their own law and, at the same time, drew up a Roman law suited to the novel situation and circumstances in which they were living. All the customary law passed from the Theodosian code into the code of Alaric. But a number of subjects which had been in the Theodosian code were omitted, as useless; dignities, offices, the private treasury of the prince, the privileges of the imperial family, charges, honors, taxes—all these things which had been crushing the empire were lessened or abolished. The two laws, the Visigothic and the Roman, existed, side by side, until the end of the seventh century, and then were fused into a single law, no longer personal, but territorial, common to the two races. Surely, they could not have done better, and as the kings and the people among the barbarians showed no race hostility, no parvenu pride, and none of the wonted severity of the conqueror to the conquered, they may be said to have deserved success.

Undoubtedly they were opposed and disdained by individuals who were inspired by all sorts of feelings, some puerile, others worthy of respect. The Roman patriotism of an Apollinaris Sidonius, for instance, was worthy of respect. Sidonius was born, as he himself said, of a pretorian family. His father and grandfathers had been pretorian prefects; his father-in-law was Avitus, who was proclaimed emperor in 453. In honor of Avitus, he wrote a poem in which he expresses eloquently the fidelity of Gaul to the empire.

This patriotism was ennobled in certain men by an intellectual and moral dignity which makes them seem very great men in the last days of the Roman decadence. Symmachus, who lived in the time of Theodoric, was the fourth representative of an illustrious house. His great-grandfather, according to Ammianus Marcellinus, had held all the magistracies, and had been one of the chief lights in the senate. His grandfather, consul in 391, had defended the altar of victory, which the Christians wished to have removed from the senate chamber. He was not a fervent worshiper of the ancient gods, for he knew full well that they had departed never to return, but he defended the ancient religion, " which had profited the republic so long "; and he said to the emperor Valentinian: " Allow us, I beg you, to transmit to our children the inheritance of our fathers." The glory of Rome was his religion, and he reëdited Livy, in order to popularize the historian of this glory. He was a type of the enlightened Romans who despised those two novelties, which they considered equally fatal to Rome: Christianity, because they were philosophers, and the barbarians, because they were patriots. The third Symmachus followed the family traditions. Meanwhile, times changed, Christianity spread everywhere, and Theodoric reigned at Ravenna. The fourth Symmachus was a Christian, but he had a filial regard for the memory of ancient Rome. He admired Cato of Utica, he reëdited the *Dream of Scipio,* and he composed a *History of Rome* in seven books. He did not refuse to advise and serve Theodoric, who had asked him to supervise the restoration of the Roman monuments. He was no courtier of the Ostrogoth, and he sought to console himself for the present by contemplation of the past. His son-in-law, Boethius, was like him. He, too, was a Christian, but, like the old Romans, he had studied at Athens. He translated Ptolemy, Euclid, and Plato, and he was, standing on the threshold of the Middle Ages, the first of the great disciples of Aristotle. He, too, served Theodoric. But what could the father-in-law and the son-in-law think of the prince who did not love what they loved, who did not know what they knew, and who used a metal plate in which the letters were cut for signing his name? Undoubtedly they despised him, or at least they honored in him only the representative of the emperor. Their eyes were turned toward Constantinople. Theodoric knew it, and they paid with their lives for their fidelity to their native Roman land.

The party of opposition and disdain included, also, a number of those senatorial personages whom Sidonius depicted as living, after the Roman fashion, on villas, where the master's house was already called a *castellum,* because it had been necessary to fortify it. These great lords, who kept in the *atrium* the silver statues of their ancestors, worked a part of their estates by troops of slaves, distributed the remainder to colons, and divided their leisure time between hunting and literature. There were some disdainful ones among these pseudo-learned orators, poets, rhetoricians, grammarians, and jurists, to whom Sidonius applies without shame the names of Plato, Horace, Vergil, and Appius Claudius; they displayed in all branches their pretentious mediocrity,—old pupils of great masters, unable to do anything except imitate, but swollen with pride at their borrowed knowledge and at their adornment of faded rhetoric.

Venerable or ridiculous opponents were not dangerous to the barbarians. The first formed a very small minority, who paid to the memory of Rome the homage of some martyrs. The others gave no cause for uneasiness. That kind of frivolous opposition is encountered every time a revolution brings new men upon the scene. The dispossessed grumbled in their castles; they took ven-

geance in epigrams and consoled themselves by viewing
their own perfection: they did not eat garlic; their perfumes were refined; they used correct language and they
washed their hands—that was enough. Thus the Greeks
found consolation under the government of the Romans,
the Romans under the government of the barbarians, and
the French émigrés under the amnesty granted by the First
Consul. It was inoffensive, and did not hinder the new-
comers from possessing the world. Moreover, the barbarian kings found their most assiduous courtiers among
the Romans. These were not merely traitors who sought
wealth at their courts, and paid rhetoricians who wrote
panegyrics of the king with such a refinement of art that
their heroes could understand them still less than we can;
but there was also at the courts of all these kings honorable men, who served them honorably. In Italy, Cassiodorus may be contrasted with Symmachus and Boethius. Cassiodorus, like Symmachus, belonged to a great
family: one Cassiodorus, a rich landowner in Bruttium,
had defended southern Italy and Sicily against the Vandals; a second was the friend of Aëtius, the last politician
and the last soldier of the Western Empire; but the third
yielded to the course of events: from Romulus Augustulus he passed to Odoacer, from Odoacer to Theodoric.
The last and the most illustrious was the principal minister of Theodoric and his successors. He directed the
old and recently repaired administrative machine. He
placed his learning at the service of Theodoric; he made
of the latter, in the letters which he composed in his
name, a scholar who discussed the history of architecture from the time of the Cyclops, when he wrote, to an

architect; the history of music since Orpheus, when he wrote to a musician; he lent to him the words of an artist who felt and enjoyed all the refinements of art. Thus he made this parvenu venerable; he did the same for the royal family and the race of the Goths, for he demonstrated the identity of the Goths and the Geti, he transformed the Amazons into Gothic women, and made Theodoric a successor of Zalmoxis and Sitalkes. That was some consolation for the descendants of Romulus, who had to obey him; and Cassiodorus said so in fitting language. Such a good servant more than made up to Theodoric for the disdain of Symmachus, Boethius and men like them.

How long would this opposition have lasted, even among the best men? The example of Sidonius shows that very few of them were irreconcilable. He is one of the heroes of the resistance against the Visigoths in Auvergne. As bishop of Clermont, he defended his episcopal city with the energy of despair. When the province was finally surrendered to the Goths, he was indignant at the bishop of Marseilles, who had negotiated the treaty; how could they deliver to the barbarians these noble men of Auvergne who were descended from the Trojans just as fully as the Latins themselves? And he sighed, in his writings, for those years of strife when the swords were fat with blood and the stomachs pinched by famine; he said that he wished that he was still besieged, still fighting, and still starving. But he ended by yielding to the force of events. Before the Visigoths had become enemies of Auvergne he had not disdained to court their king; he had even played dice with him, and, to put him

Germans in the Roman Empire

in a good humor, had let himself be beaten. "I had a request to make; I let him beat me; fortunate defeat!" When those odious Visigoths had taken his province he went into exile for a time; but when he returned he went to salute Euric at Bordeaux. The king kept him waiting two months for an audience. Sidonius consoled himself with a little poem: "Was not the whole world waiting as well as he?" And he described the whole train of suppliants: the Saxon, accustomed to the sea but trembling on land; the Sicambrian, letting grow again his hair, which he had cut after his defeat; the Burgundian, who knelt in spite of his seven feet of stature; even the Roman, who came to beg aid against the dangers from the North.

Thus was extinguished, little by little, this opposition of disdain; after a few generations none of it was left. Moreover, the immense majority of the provincials had gone over to the new order of things. A change of masters made little difference to those of servile condition, the most numerous class of all. The survivors of the middle class, those victims of the imperial taxation, had only one desire: not to be exploited any longer by the Romans. It was then to be expected that barbarians and Romans would come together, the first becoming more civilized, the second more barbarous; they would fuse and find a new mode of life, neither Roman nor German.

Faith and Morals of the Franks

Adapted from E. Lavisse: *Études sur l'histoire d'Allemagne, Revue des Deux Mondes,* March 15, 1886, pp. 366–395.

THE backwardness of the Church in the Merovingian lands is well attested, and one of the chief causes was the poor organization of the clergy. In this particular the Western Church, as a whole, compared very unfavorably with the Eastern Church, where the Christian communities had been grouped together by their bishops in the course of the storms of persecution and heresy which scourged the Church of the second and third centuries. Naturally, this grouping followed the lines of the state organization, and the bishops in each province of the empire established the custom of meeting together at the principal place in the province, the metropolis, and conceded to the metropolitan bishop, who presided over their councils, the seniority of rank of a *primus inter pares*. In the third century the Roman Empire was divided into dioceses, each made up of several provinces. In the East three of the diocesan capitals, Constantinople, Alexandria, and Antioch, became the capitals of ecclesiastical areas known as patriarchates, and to these a fourth, Jerusalem, was added, because of its holy associations.

While the East was thus provided with great churches, regularly organized, the Christian communities of the

Faith and Morals of the Franks

West long remained few and obscure. This was partly due to the small number of cities of marked preëminence in the West. The church at Rome rose to the first rank, but there were no great metropolitanates under it, except in Italy, and the West really never had any patriarchates; Gaul, for instance, which formed a diocese, never possessed a patriarch.

Gaul, moreover, was rent by civil and social wars in the third century, and suffered invasion in the fourth. As a result, the imperial framework began to break down just when the Church might have made use of it, and in its place the clergy accepted that offered by the barbarian kingdoms. The bishops of Gaul did keep in touch with one another, and thus secured the strength necessary to defend orthodoxy against their heretical masters, but the bishops were forced to group themselves by kingdoms, and not by ecclesiastical provinces. A bishop followed the destiny of his city; he changed his sovereign when he passed from one kingdom to another, broke off regular relations with the bishops who remained the subjects of his former king, and ceased to sit in the same councils with them. After Clovis had made himself master of a great part of Gaul, he called all the bishops in his dominions together, at Orleans. This was the most striking manifestation of his power, and if the unity of the kingdom had endured, the church councils would have been the most visible expression of that unity. Perhaps a Gallic Church would have arisen, like the Spanish Church under the Visigoths, with the bishop of the capital city as its chief. But the Church in Gaul followed the fortunes of the ever-changing kingdoms, and the churches of the

Medieval Civilization

different sections had no chiefs but the kings, who were always hostile to one another. In the sixth century a complete transformation took place in the personnel and manners of the clergy. When the Franks first established themselves in the land, the bishops were by custom drawn from Roman families, and the bishop resided in the chief town of the *civitas*. Soon, however, men of the Frankish race obtained episcopal offices. They loved them for their prestige, and especially for their wealth. This wealth grew through gifts, acquisitions, and usurpations. The episcopal churches became great landed proprietors and governed whole rural communities, while the bishops, imitating the lay lords, took up their residence in the country. The more important the bishop's local interests grew, the more he was inclined to concentrate his attention upon them. As a result, the imperfect hierarchy of sees which had begun to spring up in Roman times withered away. To be sure, this very disorder gave the bishop of Rome the opportunity to make his authority felt. He strove to maintain the metropolitans, and to keep a regular representative of the Holy See in Gaul. But, though the authority of the pontiff was recognized in matters of faith, and the primacy of the See of Peter respected, the pontifical monarchy was not yet founded; the pope had not acquired the regular machinery of a government, and many weighty circumstances stood in the way of such a consummation. The Gallo-Frankish Church was abandoned to anarchy; even provincial councils ceased to meet, and in the general confusion discipline was utterly lost.

The Merovingian Church lacked a body, the point of departure from which the soul might seek tasks and set itself duties, of which the most visible and the most urgent was to carry the Gospel to " the neighboring peoples, still plunged in the barbarism of natural ignorance." But it is not always the strength of an organism which produces its force, and powerlessness does not necessarily result from anarchy. The Roman Empire was never weaker than in the days when its administrative machine was perfect in action, and the Church was never more active than it was at the beginning, when people and clergy together formed the holy priesthood spoken of by the apostle Peter, and when the spirit blew where it listed. Did the Merovingian Church, which lacked laws and government, possess vital energy? Was it capable of producing volunteers, pioneers of faith? Had it preserved the spirit of proselytism and propaganda? These are the questions for which an answer must now be sought.

The greatest ecclesiastical personage of Merovingian times was Bishop Gregory of Tours (died 594). The dignity of his life, his charity and goodness, were almost divine, and yet there were pettinesses in his spirit and an undeniable disorder in his conscience. Gregory had good sense and even acuteness; his judgment was good, but his education deficient. General education, which is so fruitful, and which causes intelligent minds to reflect the age in which they live, was, in his day, detestable and injurious. Gregory had no philosophical and very little literary culture; he knew nothing of the Greek language, and his knowledge of Latin was very faulty. He consoled himself, it is true, for his " rusticity," with the thought that it made him intelligible to rustics, and we willingly condone his solecisms and his barbarisms. They are,

however, significant; they reflect the disordered institutions and manners of his time. This man, who did not
understand the logic of syntax, saw the interrelations of
ideas confusedly and lost the proportion of things. At
another epoch he might have been a writer of taste and
wit; and if he stumbles in his books, if he leaves off when
he should continue, and runs on when he should stop, if
he virtually resembles a blind man trying to pick his way
with his cane, the reason is that the good sight which nature gave him was ruined by the surrounding darkness.
History knows many such cases.

Gregory was able to distinguish one luminous point,
but only one, and that was orthodoxy. He concentrated
the strength of his intellect upon it. He never had a suspicion of the history of the formation of dogma and the
marvelous adaptation of Christianity to the intellectual
condition of the Greek and Roman world; all that was
lost in the darkness of night. He did not regret his ignorance, for he failed to perceive it; orthodoxy satisfied
him; it was to him the absolute rule and the supreme law.
This narrow and tranquil faith exercised over his reason and conscience the pernicious sway of a fixed idea,
and, joined to the disorders of a period when the frequency of heinous crimes blunted the sensibilities, it
warped his natural uprightness. The evil influence of his
environment did not lead him to commit immoral actions,
but to pass immoral judgments. He was a good man, with
much delicate tenderness of soul, and when one reads in
his book, full as it is of perfidies, villainies, and murders,
of the ravages of the pestilence which carried off " the
sweet little children who were so dear to him, whom he

had warmed in his bosom, borne in his arms, and fed with
his own hands," one is profoundly touched to come upon
a man and humanity amid such bandits and brigandage.
None of the manifestations of Christian charity were
lacking in the life of Gregory; he was the protector of the
poor and the helpless; he forgave his enemies: the bishop
who slandered him, and the thieves who wished to stop
him on a highway, and whom he recalled from their flight
that he might offer them a cooling draught. He was mild
toward the humble and proud before the great. King
Chilperic could not move him with commands or with
fawning, when he wished to obtain his consent to the condemnation of Pretextatus, bishop of Rouen, and threatened to raise the people of Tours against him. Gregory
made answer to Chilperic that the judgment of God was
suspended over his head, because he wished to violate the
canons. Chilperic, desiring to mollify him, invited him to
dinner, and offered him a dish of fowl and chick-peas
which he had specially prepared for him; but Gregory replied with that solemn naïveté which the consciousness of
his high dignity and the use of ecclesiastical language
often instilled into his words, " It is my food and drink to
do the will of God, and not to please myself with such
delicacies." He knew full well the danger he ran, but
between martyrdom and disobedience to the laws of God
and the Church he would not have hesitated a moment.
And yet this man with the tender heart and sensitive conscience relates terrible crimes without flinching, and often
apparently with approbation. Take the well-known example where Clovis, in order to gain the kingdom of Sigibert, committed or inspired a series of atrocious murders.

Medieval Civilization

Gregory, in commenting on the success of Clovis in gaining the kingdom, remarks sententiously, " For God caused the king's enemies to fall each day under his hand, because he walked with an upright heart before the Lord, and did that which was pleasing in His sight." Gregory enumerates other murders, committed by Clovis, as calmly as if he were reciting a litany. How is this apparent contradiction to be explained? According to Gregory's criterion, the answer is simple. All are of upright heart who acknowledge, all are perverse who deny, the Trinity, " recognized by Moses in the burning bush, followed by the people in the cloud, contemplated with terror by Israel upon the mountain, prophesied by David in the Psalms." Gregory never wearies in repeating that heresy itself insures punishment in this world and the next, and in proof he cites the Arian Alaric, who lost at the same time his kingdom and life eternal, while Clovis, with the aid of the Trinity, conquered the heretics and extended the boundaries of his kingdom to the confines of Gaul. Gregory does not say that Clovis enjoys the eternal glories of Paradise, but assuredly he never dreamed that this confessor of the Trinity could be relegated to hell, with the multitude of those who have blasphemed.

Next to orthodoxy, the principal virtue in the eyes of Gregory was respect for the orthodox Church, its ministers, rights, privileges, and property. Woe to him who violates the right of sanctuary in a church! The saint to whom it is consecrated does not tolerate such sacrilege! A man pursued his slave into the basilica of St. Loup, seized the fugitive, and railed at him, saying: " The hand of Loup [wolf] will not come out of his tomb to snatch

Faith and Morals of the Franks

you from my hand." Immediately the tongue of the bad jester was bound by the power of God; he ran howling through the whole edifice, no longer able to speak the speech of man, and three days later died in atrocious torments. Woe to him who touches the property of the Church! Nantinus, count of Angoulême, appropriated ecclesiastical lands; fever seized him, and his blackened body looked as if it had been roasted over burning coals. A tax-official took possession of some rams belonging to St. Julian; the shepherd strove to protect them, and said that the flock was the property of the martyr. "Do you really believe," said the facetious official, "that the ever-blessed St. Julian eats ram's flesh?" Fever at once fastened upon him, and so fierce was the heat of it that water which was thrown over him turned to steam on contact with his body. Woe to him who disobeys the commands of the Church! A peasant going to church saw a herd destroying his crop. "Alas," he cried, "there's a whole year's labor lost!" He seized an ax, but it was Sunday, and the hand which broke the law of Sabbath rest suddenly stiffened with a terrible grip upon the ax, and a miracle, vouchsafed in answer to tears and prayers, was necessary to open it.

In all his writings Gregory celebrates the power of the saints, propitious to the good and formidable to the wicked. A laborious writer, and busy upon his history of the Franks, which is his principal work, and one of the most curious monuments of the history of civilization, Gregory had always upon his table some manuscript in which he was narrating an inexhaustible series of miracles. He had a particular veneration for St. Martin, a predecessor in the see of Tours, and in zealous naïveté strove to exalt him to the highest ranks of the celestial hierarchy. The renown of St. Martin had filled the whole world. Already Sulpicius Severus had written a history of Martin's preaching and miracles. Gregory continued it, adding chapter after chapter, according as miracles were added to miracles. From Martin's sacred tomb, Gregory viewed the world; after the fashion of Christian writers, he prefixed to his history of the Franks a universal history, which begins with the creation and ends with the death of St. Martin. The first words are, " In the beginning God created heaven and earth," and the last, " Here ends the first book, which contains 5546 years, from the beginning of the world to the passage into the other life of St. Martin the bishop." Through-out the recital of wars and crimes, Gregory follows the miraculous activity of the saint. It was near Tours that Clovis, after having forbidden, as the gravest of crimes, any offense to St. Martin, won his greatest victory; it was there that he received the proconsular insignia, and celebrated his triumph. Even the worst of the kings had some regard for St. Martin. One day Chilperic asked counsel of him through a letter deposited on his tomb, with a blank leaf for the answer, and his envoy waited three days in vain for a response; the leaf remained blank, for the saint reserved his favors for those who honored him with sincere devotion. Gregory did not doubt that his patron was interested in all things, great and small, and he asked of him protection, counsel, and aid against all evils, especially sickness. He was cured of a deadly dysentery by drinking an infusion of dust gathered from the saint's tomb; thrice the mere touching of the tapestry before the tomb cured him of pain in the temples; a prayer, made while he was kneeling on the ground, with mingled tears and groans, followed by a touch given the tapestry, dislodged from his throat a fish-bone, which had prevented him from swallowing even his saliva, and caused the bone miraculously to disappear. One day his tongue swelled so that it filled his mouth; Gregory licked the railing of the tomb, and his tongue resumed its natural size. Nor did St. Martin disdain curing even the toothache, and Gregory, marveling, cried out: " O unspeakable theriac! ineffable pigment! admirable antidote! celestial purgative! superior to all the skill of physicians, more fragrant than aromatic drugs, stronger than all ointments combined! thou cleanseth the bowels as well as scammony, and the lungs as well as hyssop; thou cleanseth the head as well as camomile! "

Such was the religion of Gregory of Tours. To be sure, he was superior to this religion which dominated his spirit. At times it required an effort to break free and raise himself to God; but with the aid of the saints he succeeded. He had a very beautiful conception of the rôle of the saints in the world, and he expressed it with eloquence that burns with sacred inspiration: " The prophet-legislator, after relating how God with his majestic right hand unfolded the heavens, added: And God made two great lights, and the stars, and placed them in the firmament of the sky that they might preside over the day and the night. God also gave to the sky of the soul two great lights, Christ and the Church, to shine in the darkness of ignorance; also the stars, which are the patriarchs, prophets, and apostles, to teach us their doctrines, and enlighten us by their marvelous deeds. In their school are formed these men whom we see, like unto stars, shining in the light of their merits, and resplendent with the beauty of their teaching; they have enlightened the world with the rays of their preaching, going from place to place preaching, building, and consecrating monasteries, teaching men to despise earthly cares and to turn from the darkness of concupiscence to follow the true God." By virtue of his birth and education, Gregory knew and loved some of the successors of the patriarchs and the apostles. He belonged to a family of saints. His mother's great grandfather was St. Gregory, bishop of Langres, who "had for son and successor Tetricus," doubly his successor, since he was both bishop of Langres and saint. St. Nicetius, bishop of Lyons, was Gregory's maternal uncle, and Gregory, when a child and learning to read, slept with the venerable old man. At his uncle's death, Gregory received a precious relic, a napkin from which detached threads were sufficient to work great miracles. On his paternal side, Gregory was related to four saints: St. Gall, bishop of Auvergne, who on the day of his burial turned on his bier so that he might face the altar; St. Lusor, who, one night when the clerks were leaning against his tomb, shook it to remind them of the reverence due to him; Leocadius, citizen of Bourges, who, while still a pagan, welcomed in his house the first missionaries of Berry; and Vettius Epagathus, one of the martyrs of Lyons in the second century. Thus Gregory could trace back his ancestry by an uninterrupted chain of saints to the day when Chris-

tianity was preached in Gaul. Through them, he touched
the apostles, the patriarchs, the prophets, and the creation. The " world of the soul," as he called it, appeared
to him under exact forms; his faith required these quasi-
material representations; but, however crude his faith
may have been, it transported him beyond the miseries
which he saw around him; it caused him to live in an en-
chanted world, all-pervaded by the divine, and it was but
right that, after his death, this companion of celestial beings was recognized as a saint, for the Church in beatify-
ing him only left him, where he had lived, among the saints.

Gregory was an exception in the Merovingian Church,
and to study the action of this Church upon the peoples of
Gaul, it is necessary to strip away from the religion of the
bishop of Tours the features which embellish it. It is
needful, also, to place beside him, and some good and
saintly bishops like him, those uncouth ecclesiastics whose
vices and crimes he narrates: men like Æonius, bishop
of Vannes, a drunkard who, one day, in the midst of the
mass, roared like a beast, and fell bleeding at the mouth
and nose; men like Bertram and Palladius, who quarreled
at the table of Gundobald, and taunted each other with
their adulteries and perjuries, to the great joy of the banqueters, who laughed till they choked; men like Salonius
and Sagittarius, who went to war with helmet and cuirass,
and followed, during times of peace, the trade of highwaymen, attacking even churchmen. These incorrigible
brigands were deposed by a council, but were reinstated,
were imprisoned by Guntram in a monastery, and then
liberated, so great was the indulgence for the crimes of
bishops. They played the comedy of penitence, scattering

alms, fasting, psalm-singing night and day, then returning
to their habitual ways,—that is to say, drinking the night
long, while matins were being sung rising from the table
at dawn to break the seventh commandment; rising about
nine o'clock to bathe, they again sat down to the table,
which they did not leave until evening. We must compare with Gregory men like Badegysil of Mans, who
"never allowed a day or even an hour to pass without
some act of brigandage," and Pappolus of Langres, whose
iniquities were so monstrous that Gregory, who was not
fastidious, refused to commit them to paper. By the
side of these princes of the secular church, one might
name this or that abbot who was an assassin and adult-
erer, a hermit who received from the faithful a gift of
wine, and, deep in his cups, played havoc with sticks and
stones until chained in his cell; and, finally, Chrode-
childis, a Merovingian princess, who had become a nun
of the convent of St. Radegundis, and now rose against
her abbess. In vain did Gregory remind her that the
canons struck with excommunication the nun who left
the cloister. She went to her uncle, King Guntram, and
secured a commission of bishops to examine her griev-
ances. On her return to Poitiers, she found the convent
in great disorder, and several of her companions married.
Fearful of episcopal condemnation, she armed a band of
rascals. The bishops came and excommunicated the mu-
tineers, but they were at once besieged in a church by the
latter, and only escaped after receiving many hard blows.
In turn, the abbess, who had been driven away, armed her
servants. Poitiers fell a prey to civil war; "not a day
without a murder, not an hour without a quarrel, not a

minute without tears." At last the two kings, Childebert and Guntram, took joint action against the women, and a count captured the convent by storm; a church council condemned the insurgents to do penance, but Childebert obtained their pardon. Such scandals show the sort of associates Gregory had, and explain, in part, the inability of the Merovingian Church to reform the morals of Franks and Romans. It would, however, be a superficial judgment to attribute the moral disorder of Merovingian society to the unworthiness of the clergy, for this unworthiness was not a cause, but rather a consequence of the corruption of Christianity by a gross and ignorant people.

But the divine spark survived in the Gallic Church as in the conscience of Gregory. Unworthy as many of the ecclesiastics were, the Church none the less exercised high jurisdiction on behalf of humanity. She was the legal protector of unfortunates. The bishop had charge of the cases of widows and orphans; he clothed and fed the poor; he had the archdeacon visit prisoners every Sunday, and gave asylum to the outcast lepers. Church councils protected the slave, whose lot was worse in sixth-century Gaul than it had been in ancient Germany, or in Rome under the beneficent imperial legislation. The Church forbade the Frankish barbarians to kill their slaves, to sell them outside the province in which they lived, or to separate the man and wife whom she had joined together in the name of God. She did more. She proclaimed the equality of master and slave in the sight of God. Developing the idea of the later Roman law, which ordered that enfranchisement might take place in a church, she included the liberation of the slave among the

Medieval Civilization

works of piety, and the laws themselves assured the master who freed his slave that he should receive his recompense in the future life in the presence of the Lord. The Church treated her own serfs humanely and, good proprietor that she was, made their lot endurable, and the number of the unfortunates who sought shelter with her proves their appreciation of the truth which a later age embodied in the proverb, " It is a good thing to live under the cross."

True, the Church accepted many barbarous customs like the ordeal and the judicial duel, and justified their use from Holy Writ (Lot saved from the fire of Sodom, Noah from the waters, and David's duel with Goliath). On the other hand, her humanizing influence checked the miseries of private war, and taught the barbarians unknown ideas through her horror of bloodshed: *Ecclesia abhorret a sanguine.* To criminals or unfortunates menaced with just or unjust punishment she offered sanctuary, defending them, not against a regular trial, but against immediate violence. If slaves fled from the fury of their master, she bound him to forgive them. Two slaves of Rauching, threatened with punishment for marrying against his will, took refuge at the foot of the altar. Rauching demanded that they be delivered to him, and received them only on his promise never to separate them. He chained them together and gave them living sepulchre in the trunk of a tree, exclaiming: " I keep my word; behold them forever united! " The priest heard of it, and demanded their liberation. He saved the man, but the woman was already dead.

Thus the Church spoke words of gentleness and com-

passion, preserved the sentiment of pity in an age of violence, wiped away many a tear, and saved human flesh
from torture. She reminded the barbarians that they had
souls which sin imperiled. *Remedy of the soul* is the
beneficent phrase to be found in the charters of donation.
The method generally employed to make the remedy sure
was liberality toward the Church. But what of that?
The Church alone knew how to employ wealth, and the
fact that the remedy was often the freeing of slaves, or
the endowment of a charitable foundation, of itself secures the gratitude of humanity for those who discovered
the words *remedium animæ*. But these words also reveal
the secret of Merovingian religion—its selfishness and
self-interest, its calculation, its ready satisfaction with external practices, and its confusion of the pious act with
piety. The Frankish nation had the idea that it was
bound to God by a contract which established reciprocal
duties. "Long live the Christ who loves the Franks," is
in a prologue of the Salic Law. The Franks believed
themselves possessed of rights by virtue of their love for
Christ, because they were the people who "recognized the
sanctity of baptism and adorned sumptuously the bodies
of the martyrs with gold and precious stones." To be
baptized, to provide tombs and shrines for the relics of
the saints, to build and enrich churches, made one a
creditor of God, and such an one might, without fear,
present himself at the last judgment and say, as we may
read in a sermon attributed to St. Eloi: "Give, Lord,
since we have given! *Da, Domine, quia dedimus!*"
Men believed that there was for sins a fixed compensation, comparable to the *wergild*.

Medieval Civilization

The greatest mark of the impiety of these pagans, dressed in the externals of Christianity, was their reduction of God and His saints to the level of forces which man might subjugate and employ as desired. They made continual offers of exchange. The wife of a sacrilegious man who had been struck with a terrible disease for blaspheming a saint asked the saint to cure him, and placed presents in his church. The sick man died, and the widow took back the gifts, for they had been conditional. A child died. The grandmother carried the body into a church dedicated to St. Martin, in which were relics brought by her family from Tours. She explained to the saint why her relatives had made such a long journey to procure the relics, and she threatened that if he did not bring back the dead to life, she would never more bow head before him, or lighten the darkness of his church with tapers. Even the priests assumed to constrain their saints. One of King Sigibert's officers had seized property belonging to the church at Aix. The bishop addressed his patron saint as follows: " Most glorious one, there will be no more burning of tapers or chanting of psalms here until you avenge your servants upon their enemies, and recover for Holy Church the property stolen from you." Then he placed thorn-bushes on the saint's tomb and on the portals of the church. Saints brought to the bar of justice in this way yielded: St. Martin brought the corpse to life, and St. Metrias punished the despoiler with death. The Church related these miracles from the pulpit, and priestly pens preserved the memory of them. Was it strange that simple souls believed that the venal power of celestial beings might be employed for evil purposes? Mummolus, a

Roman, learned that an old Syrian merchant at Bordeaux, Euphronius by name, possessed relics of St. Sergius. It was commonly believed that an Eastern king who had fastened a thumb of this saint to his right arm could put his enemies to flight merely by raising his arm. Mummolus went to Euphronius and, despite the old man's prayers and offer of one hundred and then two hundred pieces of gold to be left in peace, had a deacon, whom he had brought along, open the reliquary, and with a knife he took and broke, in three pieces, a finger of the saint. Then, after praying, he carried off one piece. " I do not think," Gregory says, " that the deed was pleasing to the ever-blessed one." That, however, was the least of the cares of Mummolus; he believed that he had made compensation to the saint with his genuflections and prayers, and never doubted the efficacy of his talisman. Chilperic had the same idea when he seized Paris, notwithstanding his promises to his brothers; when he entered the city he caused relics to be borne before him to shelter him from all evil consequences. Fredegundis did still better. When she hired two assassins to murder Sigibert, she said to them: " If you return alive, I shall honor you and yours; if you perish, I shall scatter alms on your behalf in the places where the saints are honored." In either case their reward would be secure.

Gregory acquaints us with a number of personages whose words he repeats and whose least actions he relates; thanks to him, we know them intimately. Was there among them one man whom we can call a Christian? Was Guntram, that man " of admirable sagacity," who looked " not only like a king, but like a priest of the

Lord?" Even in his lifetime he performed miracles. A poor woman, whose son was dying, one day stole through the crowd to Guntram, detached some of the fringe from his clothing, steeped it in a cup of water, and gave it to the sick one, who was healed. What sort of Christian was this miracle-worker? He took pleasure in the society of concubines, and committed some atrocious deeds. At the death of one of his wives, he killed the two physicians who had bled her in vain. One day, while hunting in the Vosges, he came across a slain animal; he interrogated the game-keepers, and they charged the chamberlain, Chundo, with the deed. The latter denied the deed, and a judicial duel was ordered. Two champions were chosen, and Chundo, seeing that the day was going against his champion, fled toward the sanctuary. Guntram divined his intentions, and cried out that he should be stopped before he reached the sacred portal. He was caught, and at once stoned to death. This prince frequently committed perjury, and no one's word was less to be relied on than his; but, all in all, he was less wicked than the other kings, and he had ecclesiastical tastes. He enjoyed the company of bishops, and visited and dined with them. He loved religious ceremonies, upon which the Church relied to captivate the barbarians, who, in the dazzling splendor of the lights, breathing full breaths of the perfumes, hearing the chants of the priests, and buried in meditation by the celebration of the mysteries, believed themselves transported to Paradise. The "good king" Guntram had another virtue, respect for the person of a bishop. And it is not surprising. Among other experiences, once, when he shut up two bishops in a convent, that they might do penance, his son immediately fell sick, and his servants begged him to liberate the bishops lest his son should die. " Let them out," he cried, " that they may pray for my little children." To be sure, he knew full well that the bishops were bandits, but he feared the sacred character with which they were clothed; he experienced that species of terror inspired by priests of every age in simple people of every land. This was the Guntram who passed for a good Christian, priest, and saint.

Why were not these men Christians? They were not Christians because the Gallo-Frankish Church was no longer able to transmit Christianity. Shut up in an unyielding literal orthodoxy; ignorant, and at the same time sure of herself, she no longer knew how to penetrate into the soul of the pagan, study it, analyze its beliefs and religious sentiments, and discover the instruction needful to its condition. How could a man like Clovis have been transformed into a Christian? It would have been necessary to recover the idea of the supreme God in the religion of the Germans from out the crowd of genii, and above the great figures which represented the ideas of love, the fruitfulness of the earth, and the powerfulness of the sun; it would have been necessary to emphasize the German feeling of the fragility of this life placed between the day and the night, to employ the popular myths of gods who have lived among men, and thus to start with Odin and arrive at Christ. In this way, the Church might have wrought such a change in a warrior, a son of warriors and of gods, a haughty man who loved force alone, a violent man who could but hate and for whom the right of vengeance was a regulated institution, that he would bow his head before the God who chose to be born among the wretched, and to die an ignominious death in order to teach, by the example of his charity toward humanity, the duty of every man to be charitable.

To offer Clovis Christianity was really to demand the transformation of his whole being. If we may accept Gregory's statement, when Clovis hesitated to recognize the Crucified as the Master of the world, and reproached his wife with " adoring a god who was not of the race of gods," Clotilda charged him with venerating idols and adoring Jupiter, who had besmirched human beings with his love and had, according to Vergil, married his own sister. Clovis had no idols; he did not know Jupiter or Juno, and consequently did not understand the superannuated dialectic which had formerly served against the pagans of Athens and Rome, and which the Church had not taken the trouble to renovate. Clovis's answers show that he did not grasp his wife's meaning. When his troops were giving way on the field of battle, he thought of Clotilda's god, not to recall the childish theology which she had taught him, but to invite the Christ to exhibit His strength : " Clotilda says that Thou art the Son of the living God, and that Thou dost give victory to those who put their trust in Thee. I have besought my gods, but they gave me no aid. I see well that their strength is naught. I beseech Thee, and I will believe in Thee, only save me from the hands of my enemies ! " Clovis instituted a sort of judicial duel between the Christ and his gods, and when Christ showed Himself the stronger, he adored Him, not because He was born in a manger and

Faith and Morals of the Franks

died upon the cross, but because He had broken the head of his (Clovis's) enemies.

It matters little whether Gregory's account of the conversion of Clovis is strictly accurate or not; the account makes it plain that one of the best and most enlightened bishops of Gaul did not even dream that it was needful to create a special method of preaching for pagan Germans. This is, in itself, the clearest possible proof of the intellectual inertness of the Church at this time. And this inertness was the main cause of its powerlessness, just as the intellectual energy of the first centuries had been the main cause of its victories over Greek and Roman paganism. Alertness of mind persisted during the struggle against heresies, for heresy struggles are a species of civil war; and as civil war withdraws attention from exterior foes, so the war against the heretic caused the pagan to be forgotten. When the Church had won the battle against heresy, did she recall the continued existence of the Gentiles and her mission to carry on the work of the apostles? She did not, for in the struggle against heresy she had suffered severe losses. She had lost those instruments of ancient wisdom which had enabled her to raise the edifice of dogma. The edifice remained, but it was isolated and gloomy in the night which descended upon the world after the extinction of ancient civilization. The priest no longer sought free acceptance of the faith by the intellect, but imposed a doctrine reduced to formulas, whose history he did not know, which he did not comprehend, and which he did not strive to have comprehended by converts. While the intellect of the Christian was thus made void, his conscience was weighed down with the

81

grossest superstitions. He was so busied with a multitude of small duties, so tied down by the bonds of a complicated devotion, that he did all that could be expected of him when he attended to his own salvation and set himself right with the priests and the saints. Church and church members, arrested on the field of their first victories, were powerless to make conquests outside of Greek and Roman lands. The bishops called themselves the successors of the apostles, and still repeated, from time to time, the words of the Evangelist, " Go and teach the nations," but they were powerless to obey, for their intelligence was no longer high enough and their hearts were not pure enough for the task.

The Merovingian clergy, far from spreading Christianity beyond the Roman frontiers it had attained in the fourth century, did not even win back all the territory it had lost through the German invasions. The north and east of Gaul, the cantons of the Rhine, Meuse, and Scheldt, were full of pagans. In vain did the kings of Austrasia call themselves sons of the Church and proscribe paganism in their laws. They were themselves constrained to recognize it. One day, St. Waast went with King Chlotar to a banquet given by a Frankish warrior. He saw on the table vessels full of beer which had been blessed for the Christian banqueters, and others which had been made ready for the pagans. King Theudebert is praised by Gregory for his piety, and he posed as a champion of Catholicism, and from time to time spoke like a crusader; and yet, when he marched into Italy against the Goths and Byzantines, and his army came to the banks of the Po, the soldiers threw the bodies of

Faith and Morals of the Franks

women and children into the river, in order to win, by human sacrifices, the favor of the gods of war. Dagobert honored the saints and the martyrs, and filled the monastery of St. Denis with his gifts; but on an expedition into Germany he was accompanied by pagans. If paganism thus showed itself in the intimacy of kings who were always surrounded by bishops, it must have been much more living and active among the people, for the churches were then very few in number, and peasants might live and die without ever setting eyes upon a priest.

In the sixth century there was a sort of renaissance of Christianity along the banks of the Rhine. Bishops rebuilt the churches at Trèves, Mainz, Cologne, and Metz, and the poet Venantius Fortunatus praises them for restoring the temples of God. Thus the ancient frontier was touched, but beyond it paganism ruled. The Frankish Church was not disturbed or offended at its proximity. The only missionary work attempted was by St. Eloi and St. Amand, who preached between the Scheldt and the Meuse in the middle of the seventh century. A few leagues from the royal villas of Neustria these missionaries encountered men who were struck with the novelty of their discourses on the one God, creator of heaven and earth.

The conclusive demonstration of the powerlessness of the Merovingian Church is this, that the first great missionaries to Germany came from distant Ireland, and not from neighboring Gaul. The history of the Irish Church is the antithesis of that of Gaul. Christianity was preached in Ireland in the fifth century by St. Patrick, and spread rapidly among a homogeneous population inhabiting a narrow territory. Ireland was never a Roman province, and therefore the Irish Church did not adopt the Roman state organization. The patriarchal government of the clan chiefs had nothing in common with the complex, confused, and care-encumbered government of the Merovingians, and the Irish prelates did not compromise their morals and their authority in the corruptness of courts. The victory of Christianity was a purely moral one, and so there was no rupture or antagonism between past and present; the Irish Celts brought with them, in their conversion, their natural poetry, their legends, imaginativeness, and taste for distant adventures. In the fifth century the conquest of Britain by the heathen Anglo-Saxons cut them off from the continental churches and left them to their own natural genius. It is not true that they ever claimed to live apart in Catholicity, or believed that their Church was to be traced back directly to the apostles and to Christ, or that they denied respect and obedience to the See of Peter; but it is true that the Irish Church had more independence and liberty than the other churches, and that it kept and defended with energy certain peculiar usages of its own. It had not the discipline of the Western Church which, however imperfect, distinguished between the secular and the regular clergy, and made the bishop the chief of his clergy, the protector and supervisor of the monks, and the principal personage of the Church, clothed with all the attributes of official authority. In Ireland, secular and regular clergy were blended; the abbots of the large monasteries were also bishops; laymen and clergy were scarcely to be distinguished from one another, for many whole families lived in the monasteries, which were real cities, inhabited by several thousands of souls. Lastly, while ancient learning was perishing in Gaul, the monasteries of Ireland were great schools, in which the Scriptures and profane letters were studied with equal zeal.

For all these reasons the Irish Church had a very free and active life, and a force of expansion which exhibited itself in missions to Germany. The most illustrious of these missionaries were St. Columban, founder of the monastery of Luxeuil in Burgundy, St. Gall, founder of the monastery of St. Gall in Allemania, St. Kilian, who achieved martyrdom at Wurzburg in Thuringia, and Virgilius, who was bishop of Salzburg in Bavaria. These were veritable apostles and benefactors of the countries in which they preached the Gospel. They possessed singular originality. Columban was an ascetic, who was very hard on himself and others. He wrote a very strict rule for his monasteries. The same man sent a friend pretty little verses, which he had composed " in the measure which Sappho, the illustrious poet, employed for her melodious poems." In them he sings of the vanity and danger of riches, attested by the golden fleece which caused so many woes, by the apple of gold which disturbed the banquet of the gods, the golden rain which corrupted Danaë, the collar of gold for which Amphiaraüs was sold by his wife, and so on; for Columban knew his mythology as well as he did the Scriptures. This disciple of Sappho had the grandeur of a saint in the desert, certain of his virtue, confident in God, and scorning all the magnificence of the world. In correspondence with the bishops of the Frankish Church, he repelled the accusation of error and

Medieval Civilization

heresy which they had made against him, and exhorted them, as one fitted so to do, to obey the canons and perform the duties of their office. He reproached King Theuderich of Burgundy with his debauchery, and urged him to put away his concubines and take a lawful wife. He was not listened to. One day Brunhildis, grandmother of Theuderich, asked his benediction for Theuderich's illegitimate sons. "Know well," he answered, "that these sons will never wear the royal insignia, for they were begotten in sin." Columban was as bold in speech to the pope as to kings, although he appreciated the dignity of the Roman Church. He wrote to the pope: "Every one knows that our Saviour gave to St. Peter the keys of the celestial kingdom." But he added: "Hence arises the pride which causes you to lay claim to more authority than others; but be sure that your power will be less before the Lord if you so think in your heart—" This monk, who instructed all and asked counsel and took orders of none, seems like a prophet in the midst of Israel, captive in a Babylon of iniquity.

The Irish missionaries coming into an unknown world, without the aid of king or prince, and without money or weapons, boldly inaugurated the work which the Merovingian Church was powerless to undertake. They were only a handful of men for all Germany, but they laid broad foundations for this work, and through their monasteries, which were schools of intellectual and agricultural labor, they produced better priests and monks than the contemporaries of Gregory of Tours, strengthened Christianity in Austrasia, and rendered it secure against every pagan assault.

The Hippodrome at Constantinople

Adapted from Ch. Diehl: *Justinien et la civilization byzantine au VIᵉ siècle*, 1901, pp. 439–466.

ATMEIDAN PLACE is in the heart of modern
Stamboul. Down to the present day it has preserved
the name and kept the form of the gigantic circus, the
Byzantine Hippodrome. It was 370 meters long, and 60
to 70 meters wide. On the sides were 30 or 40 rows of
marble seats, where more than 30,000 men could be
seated. The broad aisles and walks were decorated with
a host of statues. Some of the most dramatic scenes in
the history of the empire of the East have been played in
this Hippodrome; the struggles there bring out one of
the most curious sides of the Byzantine civilization. Although we no longer believe, as people formerly did, that
the rivalries of the circus, the famous quarrels of the
Greens and the Blues, make up, together with the theological controversies, the whole empire of the East; nevertheless, we must admit that the Hippodrome represents
one of the most characteristic aspects of the Byzantine
world. It has been well said that at Constantinople " God
had St. Sophia, the emperor had the sacred palace, and
the people had the Hippodrome."

Medieval Civilization

I

AFTER imperial absolutism had effaced in the monarchy every trace of the ancient Roman liberties, the Hippodrome had become the true forum of Byzantium, the hearth and center of all the public life which still survived. There, in the presence of the assembled people, the most important festivals of the national life were celebrated; there, before the eyes of the Byzantine loafers, the trophies which bore witness to the victories of the basileus were exhibited. There, in honor of the successes of Belisarius, Justinian revived all the pomp of the ancient Roman triumphs. That day, for hours, the throng which filled the seats of the circus saw passing before them the spoils of conquered Africa: thrones of gold, precious vases, heaps of gems, costly plates and dishes, magnificent vestments, sumptuous carriages, a hoard of money—all the treasures which the Vandals had accumulated in a hundred years of pillage. Here, it was the insignia of the empire and the vases of Solomon, which had been seized by Gaiseric in the sack of Rome, and which, after eighty years of detention at Carthage, were at length restored to the hands of their legitimate owners. There, behind the victorious general, were the captives, whose lofty stature and tawny locks filled the people with astonishment and admiration; and among them, in particular, was Gelimer, his shoulders covered with a purple mantle. He viewed the seats filled with spectators, and Justinian seated in the imperial box, with a firm glance filled with melancholy irony. Across the circus the long procession

passed until it reached the space before the imperial
throne. There the Vandal king, brutally despoiled of his
purple, was thrown as a suppliant at the feet of the sovereign; and while from the mouth of the conquered fell the
words of Ecclesiastes, " Vanity of vanities, all is vanity,"
Belisarius in his turn knelt before the master. Then the
pompous procession again passed on, while the victor distributed to the people the spoils of the barbarians: golden
girdles, silver vases, and precious objects of every kind;
and a last ray of the vanished Roman glories seemed to
descend upon the Hippodrome in its festal array.

It was in the Hippodrome, also, that a new emperor
first came in contact with his people. There Justinian and
Theodora, consecrated in St. Sophia by the hand of the
patriarch, received the enthusiastic acclamations of their
new subjects, when, in the midst of the pompous procession of patricians and body-guards, they came to seat
themselves in the imperial box upon the golden throne
and, amid the acclamations, the vows for their prosperity, and the rhythmic chants of the factions, they made, for
the first time, according to the accustomed rite, the sign of
the cross above the heads of the assembled multitude.
There, some years later, other and more tragic scenes
were enacted between the basileus and his people, when
those amazing dialogues took place between the master
and his subjects, in which the people questioned Justinian
directly, and hooted at him and insulted him. Indeed, for
the Byzantines of the sixth century, the Hippodrome was
the asylum of the last public liberties. Long before, this
mob, which called itself the heir of the Roman people, had
abdicated most of its ancient rights. It no longer voted

in the forum, it no longer elected tribunes or consuls; but it always retained in the circus the liberty of cheering, railing, hooting, and applauding, the right of addressing to the emperor its petitions and complaints; more frequently still, its sarcasms and insults. In the Hippodrome, in fact, the prince and his people met face to face —one in the pomp of his imperial splendor, surrounded by his patricians, chamberlains, and soldiers; the other in their formidable numerical power, in the fury of their strong but fickle passions; and more than once, in the presence of the clamors of the circus, the all-powerful basileus had to yield.

Lastly, the Hippodrome performed another function: it was the most admirable of museums. Upon the narrow terrace, or the *spina,* which divided the arena into two tracks, along the broad canal which ran in front of the lowest seats, upon the façade of the imperial box, in the marvelous promenade which covered the upper terraces, and from which there was a splendid view over the whole city and beyond the Bosphorus as far as the distant mountains and the green trees on the Asiatic coast, under the colonnaded porticos—everywhere, there was placed a multitude of statues. They were the masterpieces of ancient art, which Asia, Greece, and Rome had been compelled to give up for the embellishment of the new capital of the empire. By the wolf of Romulus stood the Hercules of Lysippus, and that admirable statue of Helen, whose " mouth half open like the calyx of a flower, whose enchanting smile, liquid eyes, and charming figure " were destined to leave the rude companions of Villehardouin unmoved. Above the imperial box stood the four horses

The Hippodrome at Constantinople

of gilded bronze which were carried in the fifth century from Chios to Byzantium, and at the present day adorn the façade of St. Mark's at Venice. In the Hippodrome were all the glories and all the works of art, torn from the shade of their sanctuaries; some of these inspired the superstitious Byzantines with strange and formidable terrors. But, above all else, the Hippodrome was for the people of Byzantium the usual scene of their amusements, the place where their favorite tastes and most ardent passions found satisfaction.

II

NEVER did any people, unless it was the Roman people, take a greater interest in the pleasures of the circus than did the Byzantines of the sixth century. A contemporary wrote: " At this spectacle more than any other the ardor which enflames the soul with an unheard-of passion is prodigious. If the Green jockey gets ahead, part of the people is disconsolate; if the Blue passes him, immediately half of the city is in mourning. People who derive no profit from the affair yell frantic insults, people who have suffered no evil feel grossly injured; and thus, with no cause, they begin fighting as if it were a question of saving their native country." The grave Procopius himself, who shows in general little taste for these sports, says somewhere that without the theater and the Hippodrome life is really joyless.

With much greater reason, the common citizens of Byzantium were madly fond of these pleasures. Two anecdotes, selected from a thousand, will show how far

Medieval Civilization

this passion went in the days of Justinian. At the time when the emperor was building St. Sophia, one owner had refused to be forced to sell a piece of land which the architects needed. He had been offered enormous sums and had refused them all. He had been put in prison and had been obstinate in his resistance. He had been deprived of food, and had suffered hunger without complaining or yielding. The prefect of the city then had an idea: he got the emperor to announce races at the Hippodrome; it was too much for the courage of the prisoner; at the thought that he would not see the sight he let his house go at a low price. Another owner was more accommodating. He declared that he was ready to sell at once the property which was desired, but on the condition that he should have for himself, and for his heirs, a place of honor at the Hippodrome, and that people should pay to him when he entered the same honors as to the emperor. This ridiculous and vain Byzantine was a shoemaker by trade. Justinian was amused and consented to the man's demands, but with this reservation: that the imperial honors should be paid to him from behind. This is the reason why, many centuries later, the people made ironical acclamations and grotesque genuflections before the descendants of Justinian's shoemaker.

Thus Byzantium was passionately fond of everything that had to do with the races, not only the horses, but especially the drivers. The jockeys of the Hippodrome were privileged persons; nothing was lacking to their glory—neither applause nor statues nor honors nor little poems, nor even exemption from taxation. The emperor in person gave them their patents as licensed jock-

The Hippodrome at Constantinople

eys, and caused to be delivered to them the cap embroidered with silver and the scarf with the colors of the faction. The wits of the capital set to work to celebrate their talents, as in the following quatrain: " When nature at the end of time gave birth to Porphyrios, she took an oath, and with her mouth, which cannot lie, she said: It is ended, I shall have no other child; I have endowed Porphyrios with all the grace I had." To a greater extent than successful generals or illustrious victors, the circus jockeys excited the applause and inflamed the passions of Byzantine society. The people divided according to the colors of the jockeys' jackets, and the ardent rivalry of the Greens and Blues filled for many centuries the history of Byzantium. Particularly in the reign of Justinian, it caused so much agitation, so many revolts and so great ruin in the capital, that perhaps it is not at all superfluous to explain briefly here what these two famous parties were.

Since the time of the early Roman Empire, the jockeys of the Hippodrome wore jackets of four colors—green, blue, red, and white; and people who knew some mythology took pleasure in attributing to those colors a symbolical meaning: green signified the earth, blue the sea, red the fire, white the air. The red jackets and the white jackets never became very famous; but, from the first century of the Christian era, the Greens had zealous partisans, among whom they boasted of emperors, like Caligula and Nero; the Blues had champions no less illustrious; and the passion which each party felt in supporting its color more than once caused trouble and led to bloodshed. Naturally, this fashion passed to Constantinople, with the other institutions of the early empire, and there the rivalry of the factions seems to have become even sharper; in the sixth and seventh centuries, more than once, the very history of the empire was mixed up with the struggles between the Greens and the Blues.

Generally, the factions of the Hippodrome are represented as formed from several different elements. In the first place there was a kind of racing society, a jockey-club, containing several hundred and sometimes more than a thousand members; its object and reason for existence was the maintenance of the horses, chariots, jockeys, and all the equipment intended for the shows in the circus—in short, as has been stated, "to organize in some fashion the pleasures of the people." This was really the official faction, which was a regular institution of public utility, and had its place in all the great official ceremonies, its rank at court, its special privileges, its elected chief, and its members who paid dues to the treasury of the society. But to this nucleus were attached naturally the many persons necessary for the celebration of the games. "Poets were needed to compose verses, which were sung on certain occasions in honor of the emperor, composers to set these to music, orchestral leaders to present them, organists to accompany them, painters and sculptors to make imperial images, guards to maintain order, keepers of the barriers to drop them at the start, chiefs of the wardrobe who looked out for the preservation of the jackets and crowns of the jockeys, and, in addition, dancers, mimes, acrobats, and buffoons for the interludes, stable-boys, keepers for the beasts, etc., and above all the jockeys, who wore the jackets with the col-

The Hippodrome at Constantinople

ors of the faction." The party also included a third element. Each Byzantine felt it an honor to enroll himself in one of the factions, to take sides for the champion which it backed at the races; he wore a scarf of the color of his choice, he sat at the circus in the section of seats reserved for the people of his faction, he got excited or grieved over the success or the misfortune of his party. Thus the whole population of the capital was divided into two great parties, which existed in just the same manner in the other cities of the empire; and as among all these associations a feeling of solidarity had quickly grown up, a sort of free-masonry, Blue or Green, was established throughout the monarchy, and finally became a real source of danger.

It may well be, however, as has been suggested recently, that the factions were at times something more. It seems certain that in the sixth century they had a political and military organization which imposed upon the population of the capital certain duties and conferred on it in exchange certain rights. That is the reason that, outside even of the affairs peculiar to the circus, the people often intervened in the political and religious activities of the monarchy. That is the reason, too, since these parties had weapons and constituted a kind of urban militia, that their agitations were really dangerous to the State. And, beyond a doubt, it is true that the emperor, like his subjects, was passionately fond of the pleasures of the circus, and took sides for the Greens or the Blues, and that, when a new prince was present for the first time at the races, it was a weighty matter, a real affair of state, to know to which side his

Medieval Civilization

sympathies inclined. Since the time of Theodosius II the Greens had occupied the place of honor at the left of the basileus, but more than once they had lost the imperial favor. Justinian and Theodora, in particular, accorded to the Blues their special protection, and it is incontestable that the friendliness of the prince ordinarily had the effect of carrying beyond the circus the rivalry of factions; while, in fact, the court party received all the profits and all the privileges, the other party, not as favorably regarded—sometimes even excluded from public affairs, and persecuted—necessarily joined the opposition. This explains the particular severity of the strifes between the Greens and the Blues, and the political consequences which often followed. If we are astonished that the emperor did not maintain a strict and prudent neutrality between the two hostile factions, the reason was that he, too, was a Byzantine and that he was a man of his time and of his country. This is all true, and Justinian appears to have had a very passionate love for the pleasures of the Hippodrome; but all this does not explain fully the peril involved in the conflict which so many times set the government and the factions together by the ears. It seems as if, on the one side, in the popular groups, something of the old democratic spirit of the Greek cities still existed, and that, on the other side, in the government councils, there was an increasing tendency toward an unlimited absolutism. Between these two opposite principles strife was inevitable; the circus was its theater; but the games were not the only cause; they were perhaps not even the principal cause of the strife.

The Hippodrome at Constantinople

III

HOWEVER that may be, the whole population of Constantinople was excited when there were to be games in the Hippodrome. The evening before, the whole city was in motion. In the private amphitheaters of each faction there was a final rehearsal of the troupe. In the Hippodrome the last preparations were made; over the arena they extended great awnings of silk and purple to protect the spectators from the heat of the sun; on the ground they spread fresh sand mixed with fragrant powdered cedar; they tested the barriers behind which the contestants awaited the signal to start; and through the great gates opening upon the Forum Augusteum a multitude of people was already hastening to occupy the best places. When the time came all Constantinople was assembled upon the benches which ran along the sides of the Hippodrome and around the semi-circle at the end; upon the benches nearest the arena were the official members of the factions, girded with scarfs of the rival colors, holding in their hands a short baton surmounted by a cross. Elsewhere in reserved seats were placed the ambassadors of foreign nations, and in the decorated boxes arranged along the straight side of the circus were seated generals, senators, and high dignitaries of the palace and even of the Church. There also was the imperial box, elevated several stories above the level of the arena, so that the basileus, while in the midst of his people, was not at all at their mercy. For that reason, in the Hippodrome no stairway led from the circus to the

Medieval Civilization

official tribune, and on the projecting terrace, slightly below, detachments of the guard were placed all ready to protect the master against the sudden pranks of the populace; for that reason, too, behind the prince's box there was a direct communication with the palace, and solid bronze doors closed the tribune against every unforeseen assault. There, among his eunuchs, courtiers, and high functionaries, the emperor came to sit upon his throne with his crown upon his forehead and his scepter in his hand. Over the bowed heads of the people he made the solemn sign of the cross, while applause, hymns, and the songs of the factions burst forth from every side. The empress did not sit in the imperial box. In this Oriental court it was contrary to etiquette that she should appear frequently in public. But, like the true Byzantine woman that she was, the empress was no less interested in the circus than her husband and his subjects. Procopius says, somewhere, that the women, although they never went to the circus, were as passionately interested as the men in the factional strifes; and how could Theodora have been indifferent to the theater of her first exploits, her first triumphs, and her first hatreds? Accordingly, she witnessed the games—invisible, but present. She sat with her court of ladies in the upper galleries of the church of St. Sophia, which overlooked the circus, and the spectacle began when the people became aware of the presence of their sovereign lady behind the grilled windows of the basilica.

When the signal was given by the basileus, four doors opened on the ground floor of the imperial box; four chariots of the four different colors rushed forth, each

The Hippodrome at Constantinople

one drawn by four horses. Amid cries and acclamations they raced along the track, encouraged by the applause, accompanied by the vows of the rival factions, attempting to pass one another, risking a smash-up at the difficult turn which marked the end of the *spina*. Then the passion for the races, that " mental malady," as Procopius called it, took complete possession of the whole people. They forgot everything,—relatives, friends, laws divine and human,—and thought only of the triumph of the faction. Then were the perils of the State and the cares of private life forgotten; each one would have given joyfully his fortune, his very life, to secure the victory to the jockey of his party. Leaning forward, panting for breath, the spectators followed the fortunes of the race with a fierceness which was still more exasperated by the sight of the rival faction triumphing over its opponent's defeat, replying by insults or jeers to its uneasiness or grief. Then from one side to the other they shot glances charged with hatred; they challenged one another; they dared one another with voice and gesture; they exchanged sarcasms and insults; and if the guards, with their batons in their hands, had not kept the spectators back, more than one of these excitable people would have leaped into the arena, without exactly knowing why, as a contemporary said, and would have gone to punch the heads of the men in the other party. At last the race was finished, and the winner proclaimed; afterward, the same spectacle was repeated three times in the leveled arena. The first part of the program was over.

Then was the time for the interludes—pantomimes, exhibitions of strange animals, feats of acrobats, and

Medieval Civilization

tricks of the clowns. We know the way in which, according to report, Theodora, in her youth, charmed the crowd during this part of the show. On other occasions the show, though less piquant, was no less amusing to the people. A trick dog, yellow, and blind in one eye, was, in the time of Justinian, the particular favorite of the amphitheater. It was a very remarkable animal! It could classify the medals of the emperor as well as a professional numismatist; when rings were mixed up in a vase, it carried each one back to its rightful owner; in a circle of spectators it could designate without error the most miserly person, the most generous, and the most vicious; it could even pick out women who behaved badly; and the witty loungers of Byzantium said that this dog certainly had in his body the prophetic spirit of a witch.

Thus the morning passed. Then the emperor retired with the high officials to the dining-room of the palace of Kathisma, near the imperial box. The people got out their own provisions, unless the prince, in order to do the thing handsomely, gave his subjects this meal. Generally, it was very modest; the fare was made up of vegetables, fruit, and salt fish; but these were enough to make the people happy. The emperor, however, had to be as moderate as his subjects. If he sat too long at table the crowd very soon became impatient. One day, when the emperor Phocas, a successor of Justinian, took too long in dining, the crowd began to sing, respectfully at first: "Rise, O imperial sun, rise and appear." But as the basileus kept them waiting, the cries soon became more lively and the tone more insolent: "You have kissed the bottle too often; you will get into more trouble!"

The Hippodrome at Constantinople

Generally, the emperor did not have to be called to order. Of his own accord, he returned to give the signal for more races. As in the morning, there were four in the afternoon. But when the show ended, the passions which had been excited did not cool down. When they went out, the victors marched, proudly waving the winning colors in the midst of the crowd. The defeated were pursued with jokes and insults. Accordingly, rows were frequent, and these often became bloody battles, which the imperial guard did not always succeed in stopping.

IV

BUT this was not all. Not only on the days of the races did the party which enjoyed the imperial protection follow out all their caprices; they did it every day. Since his inauguration, and even before, Justinian, like his uncle Justin, had shown a particular liking for the Blues, and Theodora had encouraged and increased this partiality. She did not forget that in her youth she had belonged to the Blue faction, and her vindictive nature never pardoned the injustice which she pretended that she had received from the Greens. Thus, being sure of the imperial favor, the Blues soon gave themselves up to all kinds of excesses. Naturally, in this sporting and theatrical world the company was very mixed. Many adventurers or rakes were enrolled in the factions, in the hope of finding some chance for pleasure or profit. They were the especial ones who gave themselves free rein. They adopted a distinctive costume and eccentric manners. They wore long beards, like the Persians. They shaved the hair on the front of the head like the Huns, and let it grow at the back in long curls. They wore coats with sleeves very tight at the wrist and very full at the shoulders, large mantles richly embroidered, breeches and shoes made after the fashion of the Huns; and thus dressed, they strolled about Constantinople at night, attacking and robbing peaceful people, especially those of the Green faction, assassinating their private enemies or having them murdered, even in the churches, forcing their creditors to give them receipts, violating women, and doing all this without any interference by the police or the courts. Naturally, the Greens, constantly maltreated and finding no protection, organized bands on their side, and they too abandoned themselves to all kinds of excesses. As, in addition, many of them were still in favor of the dynasty of Anastasius, their former protector, whose nephews, Hypatius and Pompeius, lived in Constantinople, the opposition of the Green faction very soon took a political form. Against these anti-dynastic tendencies, and those people who were suspected and disliked by the emperor, the public administration necessarily acted without any consideration, and the courts forgot all equity in matters which concerned the Greens. " In these controversies," wrote a contemporary, " the judgment did not depend upon justice and law, but upon the factions' hostility or favor to the parties concerned. If a judge neglected the orders of the factions, it was his death sentence." If Procopius does not exaggerate, it was a regular Terror on a small scale, from which peaceful people of all parties suffered equally. At all events, the result was a formidable state of ferment in

the early years of the reign, which was still more aggravated by the bad administration and the exactions of the
principal ministers, especially Tribonian and John of
Cappadocia. All of these motives combined, in the
month of January, 532, to produce the dangerous rebellion known under the name of the *Nika* riot, which began in the circus, soon spread over the entire city, and
came near driving Justinian from his throne. It deserves
to be recounted at length, because it is very characteristic
of the Byzantine manners: it shows very clearly the passions which agitated the Hippodrome, it is a very famous
episode in the quarrels between the Greens and the Blues,
and, finally, it had very important consequences for the
development of the government.

V

SUNDAY, January 11, 532, the races were taking place,
as usual, in the Hippodrome. The emperor was present
in great pomp; but that day the crowd was very boisterous. Upon the benches where the Greens sat, the racket
was incessant and the hooting continuous; the faction
believed that they had reason to complain of an official
of the palace, the grand chamberlain Calopodios, and at
every opportunity they gave vent to their bad humor.
At last, Justinian became impatient, and ordered a herald
to speak to the people. Then between the spokesman
of the Greens and the emperor's herald there was a most
astonishing dialogue, in which the complaints were at
first respectful, but very soon changed into violent in-

vectives, and anger mingled with irony. This debate must be quoted almost completely, as it is so characteristic of the Byzantine manners in the sixth century.

The Greens: " Long live Emperor Justinian! May he be ever victorious! But, O best of Princes, we are suffering all kinds of injustice. God knows we cannot stand it any longer. Yet we are afraid to name our persecutor, from fear that he may become more angry and that we shall incur still greater dangers."

Herald: " I do not know of whom you are speaking."

Greens: " Our oppressor, O thrice August! lives in the shoemakers' quarter."

Herald: " No one is doing you any injury."

Greens: " A single man persecutes us. O Mother of God, protect us!"

Herald: " I do not know this man."

Greens: " Oh, yes, you do! You know very well, thrice August, who is our executioner at present."

Herald: " If any one is persecuting you, I do not know who it is."

Greens: " Well, Master of the World, it is Calopodios."

Herald: " Calopodios has nothing to do with you."

Greens: " Whoever it is will suffer the fate of Judas, and God will very soon punish him for his injustice."

Herald: " You did n't come here to see the show, but only to insult the officials."

Greens: " Yes, if any one annoys us he will suffer the fate of Judas."

Herald: " Shut up, you Jews, Manicheans, Samaritans!"

The Hippodrome at Constantinople

Greens: " You call us Jews and Samaritans ; may the Mother of God protect us all equally ! "

Herald: " I want you to get baptized."

Greens: " All right, we 'll get baptized."

Herald: " I tell you, if you don't shut up, I 'll have your heads cut off."

Greens: " Each one seeks to have power, in order to be safe. If our remarks hurt you, we hope that you will not be at all irritated. He who is divine ought to bear everything patiently. But, while we are talking, we shall call a spade a spade. We no longer know, thrice August, where the palace is or the government ; the only way we know the city now is when we pass through it on an ass's back. And that is unjust, thrice August."

Herald: " Every freeman can appear publicly where-ever he likes, without danger."

Greens: " We know very well we are free, but we are not allowed to use our liberty. And if any freeman is suspected of being a Green, he is always punished by public authority."

Herald: " Jail-birds, don't you fear for your souls ? "

Greens: " Let the color which we wear be suppressed, and the courts will be out of a job. You allow us to be assassinated, and, in addition, you order us to be punished. You are the source of life, and you kill whomsoever you choose. Truly, human nature cannot endure these two opposites. Ah ! Would to heaven that your father, Sabbatios, had never been born ! He would not have begotten an assassin. Just now a sixth murder took place in the Zeugma ; yesterday, the man was alive, and in the evening, Master of all things, he was dead."

Medieval Civilization

Blues: "All the murderers in the Stadium belong to your party."

Greens: "You do the killing, and you escape punishment."

Blues: "You do the killing, and you keep on talking; all the assassins in the Stadium belong to your faction."

Greens: "O Emperor Justinian! They complain, and yet no one is killing them. Come, let's discuss it; who killed the dealer in wood in the Zeugma?"

Herald: "You did."

Greens: "And the son of Epagathos, who killed him, O Emperor?"

Herald: "You did that, too, and you accuse the Blues of it."

Greens: "That will do. May the Lord have mercy on us! Truth is getting the worst of it. If it is true that God governs the world, where do so many calamities come from?"

Herald: "God is a stranger to evil."

Greens: "God is a stranger to evil! Then why are we persecuted? Let a philosopher or a hermit come to solve the dilemma."

Herald: "Blasphemers, enemies of God, will you not keep still?"

Greens: "If your Majesty orders us we shall keep still, thrice August, but it will be against our will. We know all about it, but we are silent. Adieu. Justice, thou dost not exist any longer. We are going away; we'll become Jews. God knows, it is better to be a pagan than a Blue."

The Hippodrome at Constantinople

Blues: " Oh, horrors! we don't want to see them any longer; such hatred frightens us."

Greens: " We hope the boxes of the spectators will be thrown into the sewer some day."

With these words the Green faction left the Hippodrome in a body; it was the worst insult they could inflict upon the emperor.

While the exasperated mob went out of the circus and spread through the streets, Justinian returned to the palace thinking that as usual the rivalry of the Blues would very quickly allay the fury of the other party. Unfortunately, a troublesome accident united the two parties. The prefect of the city had been too zealous; he had had several rioters arrested and condemned to death. But the executioner bungled his job; twice the rope broke under the weight of the condemned. Then the mob got angry and rescued the victims, whom the monks of St. Conon received into a neighboring church. Now, by chance, one of the prisoners was a Blue and the other a Green; thus the two factions found themselves brought together by a common danger. Two days later, January 13, it was very evident in the Hippodrome; again there was a violent uproar, and instead of the loyalist cry, " Victory to the Emperor Justinian! " they shouted on all sides, " Long live the Greens and the Blues, united for mercy! " and with the cry of *Nika* (victory)—from this rallying-cry the insurrection got the name by which it is handed down in history—the rioters rushed through the city. They attacked the prefecture, demanding the release of the guilty who were still in prison; the guards were massacred; the prefect's palace was burned, and during the whole night the seething mob filled all the streets in the capital. With the union of the two parties, the riot assumed a more serious form. The next day, January 14, the flood of people was beating against the palace gates, demanding the dismissal of the grand chamberlain and of the prefect of the city, and in addition the discharge of the two detested ministers, Tribonian and John of Cappadocia. Justinian yielded, but already it was too late. The emperor's yielding merely encouraged a furious mob; the revolt became a revolution.

Up to that time, however, the sane portion of the people had taken no part in these events and all was not lost. Justinian believed that he could take vigorous action; on the fifteenth, he let loose upon the insurgents his barbarian soldiers, with Belisarius at their head. Unfortunately, in the conflict these mercenaries maltreated the priests of St. Sophia, who had brought out the sacred relics and had intervened to separate the combatants. Then there was a general row. From the windows and the terraced roofs a hail of tiles and stones fell upon the sacrilegious, and the women, who were particularly enraged, engaged actively in the battle. Before this tempest the disconcerted soldiers had to beat a retreat to the palace, and to hasten their flight the victorious people set fire to the public buildings in the neighborhood. The senate-house and the approaches to the palace became the prey of the flames; for three days the fire, driven by a strong wind, continued its ravages, destroying, in succession, St. Sophia, the approaches to the Augusteum, the baths of Zeuxippus, St. Irene, the

The Hippodrome at Constantinople

Xenodochion of Eubulus, the great hospital of Sampson with all its patients, a large number of palaces and private houses, and the whole quarter, one of the most beautiful in the city, which extended from the sacred palace to the Forum of Constantine.

"The city," said an eye-witness, "was left a mass of blackened mounds; as at Lipari or Vesuvius, it was full of smoke and cinders; the smell of the burning spreading everywhere made it uninhabitable, and the sight filled a spectator with mingled terror and pity."

Justinian was frightened. He had shut himself up in the palace, with those who stood by him; means of defense were almost entirely wanting. The guard was a body of ornamental troops, intended to be shown off in ceremonies, and he was not sure that he could trust them. The barbarian troops of Belisarius and Mundus were the only ones that he had confidence in, and they were not very numerous. So the basileus was very uneasy, thinking that he already saw conspirators and assassins all around him, and he became more and more excited and confused. The nephews of Anastasius had come to the palace to protest that they were loyal; he commanded them, in spite of their prayers, to return home, without realizing that he was thus furnishing for the insurrection the leaders which as yet it lacked.

January 18, the sixth day of the riot, Justinian made a last attempt. He appeared in the Hippodrome, holding the Gospel in his hand, and addressed the assembled people: "I swear by this sacred book that I pardon all your offences. I will have no one of you arrested, provided that all trouble ceases. You are not at all responsible for what has happened. I am the sole cause of everything. My sins led me to refuse what you demanded in the Hippodrome." These words were received with a little scattered applause, but from all sides they responded to the prince: "You lie, ass; you are swearing a false oath." And this time Theodora does not appear to have escaped the insults. So Justinian, without waiting for anything more, went back very hastily to the palace.

What might have been expected, happened. The people, in a hurry to give themselves a new master, went to find Hypatius, the nephew of Anastasius, whom they had been applauding on every occasion for several days. In spite of his own unwillingness and the tears of his wife, they dragged him to the Forum of Anastasius, raised him on a shield, placed a golden chain on his forehead in place of a diadem, and gave him the insignia of the empire and the imperial robe, which they had carried off from the part of the palace which they had invaded. Then the crowd hastened to the Hippodrome; they hoisted the new sovereign into the imperial box, and the chiefs of the rebellion began to discuss the best way of storming the residence, which they said Justinian had just left in great haste.

It was the afternoon of January 18. The insurrection, which now included all the discontented and also a considerable number of senators and nobles, assumed more and more the form of a political movement. Events were moving rapidly, and the decisive moment had come. "The empire itself," as Lydus said, "seemed on the eve of its fall." Justinian, without resources, and without

The Hippodrome at Constantinople

hope was thinking of abandoning everything, when Theodora's energy aroused the courage of the emperor and his counselors. At last they took some measures to defend themselves, while Narses attempted to detach the Blues from the revolt, and succeeded in doing so by bribery; and while, because of this division, discord arose among the insurgents, and some loyalists were again heard shouting, " Long live Justinian! O Lord, protect Justinian and Theodora! " Belisarius and Mundus were preparing for a decisive attack upon the Hippodrome. Belisarius succeeded, with some difficulty, in penetrating through the burning débris into the arena, while the soldiers of Mundus broke in at the opposite gate, called the Gate of the Dead, and from the lofty promenades of the amphitheater the imperial troops poured upon the crowd a hail of arrows. Then in the multitude crowded in the circus there was a frightful panic, which became greater when the soldiers pushed mercilessly across the arena, giving no quarter. All who came in their way were massacred without pity, and at night, when the slaughter ceased, more than thirty thousand corpses, according to some,—according to others, nearly fifty thousand,—were strewn on the bloody soil of the Hippodrome.

Hypatius was arrested, with his cousin Pompeius, and brought before Justinian. Both threw themselves on their knees, imploring mercy, swearing that they were innocent, and that they had been forced to do what they did. They added that in getting all the rebels together in the Hippodrome, they had planned to deliver them defenseless to the blows of the emperor. And it was the truth; but unfortunately for Hypatius, amid the disorder of the palace the message which he had sent to Justinian had not reached the basileus. The latter, accordingly, having now recovered his *sang froid,* responded to the suppliants with cruel irony: "Very good; but since you had so much authority over these men, you ought to have exerted it before they burned my city." And early the next morning he had them both executed. Justinian, as Gibbon said, "had been too much terrified to forgive."

Moreover, some senators compromised in the uprising were executed or exiled, and, to justify the severity, an official account of the event was made public, stating that Hypatius and his cousin had planned, and voluntarily carried on, the rebellion to which the imperial authority had almost succumbed.

The frightful bloodshed which terminated this six days' battle calmed the factions of the Hippodrome, and completed the foundation of the imperial absolutism. Justinian was able, without protest, to restrict, and even for some years to suppress almost entirely, the games of the circus. Undoubtedly the parties regained their courage later in his reign; factional disputes and struggles again appeared in the amphitheater; outcries and insults against the emperor were again heard, and Justinian resented these the more deeply because a foreign ambassador was present at this inglorious episode; and more than once, as in 532, Constantinople again witnessed tumult and battle in her streets and flames swept away her public buildings. But the imperial authority was stronger, and always repressed these seditious manifes-

The Hippodrome at Constantinople

tations promptly and energetically; and, becoming more equitable, it was not afraid even to punish the Blues when, on several occasions, confiding in the protection of the prince, they gave the signal for riots. " Thanks to this timely severity," says a contemporary, " order was restored in the city, every one enjoyed freedom from this time on, and all could go about their business or pleasure without fear." Although the capital was sometimes disturbed, these riots were really of little importance compared with the great uprising which, but for Theodora's energy, would have deprived Justinian of his throne.

Such were, fourteen hundred years ago, the tumultuous scenes which filled the Hippodrome and Byzantium with massacre and conflagration. But if the insurrection was put down, its traces were everywhere present. The fire had spread its ravages over the old city of Constantine; everything had to be rebuilt—churches, palaces, and public monuments. It is one of the most meritorious and striking of the tasks of Justinian, that he made his capital veritably in his own image, and attached his name indissolubly to the splendors of St. Sophia.

Christian Missions in Gaul and Germany in the Seventh and Eighth Centuries

Adapted from A. Berthelot, in Lavisse et Rambaud: *Histoire Générale,* Vol. I, 1893, pp. 285–296.

THE work of converting the heathen was carried on with great success in the century and a half which preceded the advent of Charles the Great to the kingly throne. Not only was the knowledge of the true God carried into regions which had never known Him, but territories which had lapsed from Christianity to paganism were reclaimed.

The northeastern portion of the Frankish dominions was the scene of the activity of St. Amand, one of the first great missionaries. St Amand was born in Aquitaine, and became a monk against the wishes of his parents. After visiting Rome he returned to Gaul, in order that he might evangelize the peoples of the Scheldt basin, around Tournay and Ghent. These cantons lay almost waste, and were divided between the Salian Franks and the Frisians. The pagan inhabitants still adored trees and idols in the sacred groves. The saint effected much by his miracles, but more by the authority of the king, who compelled the unbelieving to accept Christianity.

Dagobert ordered that those who refused baptism should be forced to accept it. St. Amand founded the monastery of Elnon, which afterward took his name and became a center of propaganda for the entire region, and a medium of agricultural and all other knowledge. St. Amand was compelled to accept the bishopric of Maestricht. In the valley of the Meuse he preached not only to the pagans, but also to those who were Christians only in name. The opposition of wicked priests impelled him to abandon his see (649). In vain Pope Martin I, who loved the man and was much interested in his labors, wrote and entreated him not to be discouraged. He wished to go as a missionary to the Wends and Slavs. He had his wish, but little success crowned his efforts, and he returned to Aquitaine. There he founded monasteries, but incurred the jealousy of other clerics, and enjoyed little genuine support except from Sigibert II, the pious king of Austrasia.

The relations of Pope Martin I with St. Amand are interesting, for the pope had adopted the policy of Gregory the Great, and sought to find a real prop in the Franks. He had just launched his anathemas against the monothelitic heretics, and wished to show the emperor that he was the head of the Church in the West. He wrote letters to St. Amand, to Clovis II, king of Neustria and Burgundy, and to the bishops of Neustria. He sent them the acts of his council, and demanded that the bishops of the Frankish kingdom should come and form a part of the delegation which he planned to send to the emperor, and which should bear to his imperial majesty, in the name of the Christianity of the West, the

Medieval Civilization

decisions of the council and the anathema launched against heresy. This very significant move was not followed up; it was unique in the seventh century; the anarchy and powerlessness of the Frankish kingdoms dissuaded the popes from leaning upon them. It was not until the triumph of the Carolingian house that relations were renewed between the Austrasian chiefs and the Church of Rome. The first step in this renewed intimacy was the letter of Gregory II, recommending the priests whom he was sending into Bavaria (710). From this time the relations were intimate.

While Gallo-Romans, like St. Amand, strove to convert the infidels, the most active of the missionaries of this age were from the western islands, from Ireland, and, later, from Great Britain.

From Ireland, the island of the saints, came Columban, with twelve other monks of Bangor. He entered France in 585, and preached with prodigious success. King Guntram begged him to reside in his land. He was a true monk of the early times, of the ascetic age, and his austerity won for him general admiration. The rule which he imposed upon his followers was harsh, for he desired blind obedience. After some time he retired to the border-land between the kingdoms of Burgundy and Austrasia, in the Vosges mountains. There, in a semi-desert land, he founded four monasteries, Luxeuil being the principal one. Disciples flocked to him, in spite of his severity and his obstinate adherence to the peculiar practices and ideas of the Celtic Church. He was an ardent zealot, aflame for the work of the Lord. The burden of his preaching was the reformation of morals, and it embroiled him with the great men of the land, the bishops and the princes, for he " scattered the divine fire on all sides without care for the conflagration." He quarreled with Brunhildis and her son Childebert, and his inflexibility won for him expulsion from the land. He took ship at Nantes, but directed his course to Neustria, to the court of Clothair II. Clothair showed much deference to the saint and sought, in spite of his remonstrances, to retain him at his court. Columban passed into Austrasia, and received an equally cordial welcome from Theudebert II. At the request of the king he journeyed to the pagans of Alemannia. He interrupted the sacrifices to Odin, and after the death of Theudebert was driven from the land by its pagan duke. Entering Italy, he founded the monastery of Bobbio, and there died, in 615, in the midst of universal veneration. His disciple, St. Gall, had previously withdrawn to the mountain fastnesses near Lake Constance. The latter's reputation for sanctity brought him many companions, and his hermitage became a monastery, which was enriched with gifts and was one of the most celebrated of the Middle Ages.

Another disciple of Columban, Sigibert by name, founded the abbey of Disentis, near the source of the Rhine. In the high valleys of the Alps, Christianity had preserved some faithful ones ever since the Roman occupation. And so the missionaries found the soil of these regions better prepared, and made more rapid progress here than in North Germany. Alemannia and old Rhætia were brought back to the Christian faith, in the seventh century and the first part of the eighth. The two

Medieval Civilization

principal monasteries of this territory were Hornbach, to the north of the Vosges, and Reichenau, situated on an island in Lake Constance. These communities, and several others which were organized in the valley of the Rhine, brought under cultivation a vast extent of territory, and soon became flourishing.

Bavaria was entered in the middle of the seventh century by the monks of Luxeuil. The dukes of Bavaria, who were probably of Frankish origin, and had intermarried with the Christian Lombards, showed favor to the religion of civilized Europe. St. Emmeran obtained at Ratisbon the general conversion of the Bavarians, and his work was finished by St. Rupert. Coming from the city of Worms, St. Rupert made many journeys and became thoroughly familiar with Bavaria, preaching and baptizing the people, ordaining priests, and dedicating churches. In 696 he baptized the duke, Theodo I, at Ratisbon. He it was who built, on the ruins of the Roman city of *Juvavium,* the new city of Salzburg, in later times the religious metropolis of the land; he established an abbey there, and obtained its first monks from Worms; the abbot bore the title of bishop. About this time (730) Corbinian made a journey to Rome. He had prepared himself for this undertaking by fourteen years of asceticism, and the pope gave him the pallium and sent him into Bavaria, where he founded the church of Freising. Monasteries multiplied around the lakes and in the Alpine valleys of Bavaria. In 716, Duke Theodo II went to Rome in order to acquire the pure faith for himself and his people. He and his successors, Theudebert, Hubert, Odilo, and Tassilo, gave great gifts to the

Missions in Gaul and Germany

churches and established many monasteries, around which cities grew up.

North of Bavaria, in that part of Thuringia which the Franks had conquered in the fifth and sixth centuries, the Celtic monk Kilian carried Christianity to the dwell-ers on the banks of the Main. He was murdered by a Frankish duke, and the origin of the church of Wurz-burg is attributed to him.

All through this zone the missionaries encountered many obstacles. Unlike the valleys of the Rhine and the Danube, it had never been under Roman rule, and the paganism which survived was of an active type. The Frisians and Saxons were converted only by force, and the work demanded atrocious wars and methodical mas-sacres. The Anglo-Saxon monks, protected by the con-quering Austrasians, brought to the work of conversion an inexhaustible devotion. It was through the collabora-tion of the Frankish princes with the monks sent out by the popes that the relations between Rome and the Caro-lingian family multiplied, and ultimately resulted in the alliance which was so momentous for both. Even while they were personally inaccessible to religious ideas, the Austrasian princes perceived the advantages which flowed to them from the work of the missionaries. Conversion to Christianity softened the manners of the Germans, located them around the centers of civilization created by the monks, and caused them to submit them-selves to the ascendancy of their ecclesiastical leaders. Furthermore, the missionaries explored the wooded and little-known districts, and served as excellent gatherers of information for a proposed expedition. So long, too, as the conversion of a people was only partial, the Christian portion of the population necessarily leaned for support upon the neighboring Christian nation.

In the seventh century the archbishop of York and other missionaries undertook to lead to Christianity the Frisians, a race kin to the Anglo-Saxons, and with whom the Anglo-Saxons had commercial dealings. The results appear to have been slight before the coming of St. Willibrod. Taking advantage of the victories of Pepin of Heristal and Charles Martel, and of the consequent loss of strength of the Frisians, he succeeded in converting all of southern Frisia. Here he founded a bishopric, and at the solicitation of Pepin (690) was invested with it, and Utrecht was his episcopal seat. Until his death, in 739, he continued to overturn the idols and combat paganism.

The history of the mission of St. Winfrith is much more important. This Anglo-Saxon, whose ecclesiastical name was Boniface, was, by virtue of his submissiveness to the pope, his apostolic zeal, his politic mind, and his organizing genius, one of the best of the artisans of Roman greatness. He was in a very real sense, although indirectly, one of the chief founders of the Carolingian Empire. He was born in 672, and went as a missionary to Frisia in 716. The moment was not auspicious: Rathbod was at war with Charles Martel; he had expelled the worshipers of God, and reëstablished the worship of idols in the very territory where it had been proscribed after the victories of Pepin of Heristal. Boniface had an interview with Rathbod, but the whole result of this first journey was that he found no place open to his preaching. He returned to England in 717, to his monastery of Nutsell, near Southampton; in 718 he departed for Rome. The pope gave him the task of reconnoitering Germany. He journeyed to Frisia, passing through Bavaria and Thuringia.

He found Rathbod dead (719), Charles Martel victorious over the Frisians, and southern Frisia handed over to the Franks, and during three years he aided archbishop Willibrod. The archbishop offered him the see of Frisia, but he declined it. He now went to the country of the Chatti, that is to say, to modern Hesse, and there established monastic stations and built churches. In 722 he paid a second visit to Rome.

At Rome Pope Gregory II consecrated him as a missionary bishop, gave him a writing which revealed the papal ideas on the subject of ecclesiastical government, and bade him teach them. Boniface swore (we have his oath) absolute obedience to the Roman Church; he swore to have no communion with prelates who to his knowledge professed contrary doctrines, to restore them to the papal obedience, and if he failed in this, to denounce them to the pope, his master. Thus Boniface is the apostle of Catholic unity in faith and discipline. He did not make a distinction between the Catholic faith and obedience to the Holy See, after the fashion of the Anglo-Saxon ecclesiastics. In a letter to Pope Zacharias (742) he unites the two. All the hearers and disciples whom God gave him in his legation he ceaselessly strove to incline to obedience to the Apostolic See. When in 722 he returned to Germany, he carried a letter of recommendation from the pope to Charles Martel: " Knowing that you have on many occasions demonstrated your affection for religion, we recommend to you Boniface, who goes to convert the peoples of German race, and others, dwelling east of the Rhine." In the spring 723 Boniface presented himself at the court of Charles Martel, and received a document placing him under the protection of that prince. This protection was indispensable to the missionary. In a letter to Daniel, bishop of Winchester, Boniface says clearly that without the patronage of the prince of the Franks he could not govern the faithful children of the Church, could not protect the priests and clerks, the monks and the nuns, nor in any way interdict pagan rites and idolatry. He went to Hesse first. Near Fritzlar he overthrew Odin's oak and employed the wood in the construction of a chapel, around which a monastery soon rose. He entered Thuringia and established thirty parishes, which the Saxons soon destroyed, and the monastery of Ordruf, south of Gotha. He recognized that the Germans were capable of comprehending the sanctity of women. He established monasteries of nuns, and to these the German women went to learn the virtues of their sex.

The speed of Boniface's missionary work was so great that in 732 Gregory III sent him the pallium and raised him to archiepiscopal rank, thus adding to his episcopal power to consecrate priests and deacons the authority to ordain bishops.

In 738 Boniface journeyed to Rome to confer with the pontiff, and remained in the Eternal City for over a year. The matter under discussion was the organization of the Church of Germany. In his earlier missionary labors Boniface had found the clergy of Bavaria and Alemannia—countries which had long been Christianized by Irish and Frankish missionaries—little disposed to recognize the authority of the Apostolic See. Intelligent and energetic men like Vergil of Salzburg had offered resistance, and Boniface had found it impossible to apply the instructions given him in 722. Latterly, however, the success of Boniface's missionary efforts and the ascendancy of his protector, the prince of the Franks, had increased his authority. When he left Rome he carried letters inviting the bishops of Bavaria and Alemannia to meet twice a year in synod, and to make submission to the authority of the *vicar of the Holy See,* Boniface. Hubert, duke of Bavaria, had just died, and his successor, Odilo, the protégé and son-in-law of Charles Martel, was favorably disposed.

With his assistance, the envoy of Rome prevailed and organized the Church of Bavaria. He established the four bishoprics of Ratisbon, Salzburg, Freising, and Passau, and the pope approved and confirmed his work. His letter of approval concludes with this recommendation: "Do not cease to teach them the holy Catholic and apostolic tradition of the Roman Church."

Boniface continued his labors. He organized eastern Austrasia, the later Franconia. Here he founded the bishoprics of Wurzburg, for the valley of the Main; Buraburg, to the south of Fritzlar, for Hesse; Erfurt, for Thuringia; Eichstädt, on the border of Bavaria, for the cantons north of the Danube, which were soon to be detached from Odilo's duchy. At the head of these bishoprics he placed his disciples, men who were absolutely trustworthy. One of them, Willibald, was really a remarkable man. He made a pilgrimage to the Holy Land, lived two years at Constantinople and ten years at Monte Cassino, where he studied the rule of St. Benedict. Carolman protected these bishoprics, endowed them with rich lands and privileges, and had churches built for them.

In 744, Sturmi, one of Boniface's disciples, founded the abbey of Fulda. His master had charged him to find a monastic retreat in the forests between the Main and the Weser. He finally chose Fulda. Carolman made him a gift of land 4000 feet square, and invited the leading men of the neighborhood to do likewise, and in a few months the soil was cleared and the monastery built. Sturmi went to Monte Cassino to study the rule of St. Benedict, and was the first abbot of this model monastery. The pope conferred upon him the precious privilege of holding directly from him (753). Fulda was the first *exempt* monastery, the first monastery to be withdrawn from the jurisdiction of the bishop. Ten years later, it had over four hundred monks. Boniface lived there, by preference, and chose it as his burial-place. Fulda was one of the most venerable monastic foundations in Germany, and one of those which contributed most to German civilization and Christianity.

In 741, "thanks to the aid of God and the suggestion of Boniface," as Willibald puts it, a council was assembled for Austrasia. Boniface wrote Pope Zacharias a letter in which he told him that Carolman, duke of the Franks, had earnestly besought him to call together a council for the half of the kingdom which he held. He

had promised the duke, said Boniface, to reform the
Church, which for sixty or seventy years had been in a
pitiable condition. For eighty years no synod had met,
the canons had been disregarded, and the churches and
monasteries plundered. Strictly speaking, we should call
it an assembly rather than a council, for it was really a
meeting of the nobles of Austrasia, in which the bishops
sat as counselors. The bishops nominated by Boniface
were confirmed, and Boniface was recognized as the
archiepiscopal envoy of St. Peter. It was decided that
annual synods should be held, that the priests should be
under the authority of the bishop, and that the property
which had been stolen from the churches should be restored, and punishments were decreed against clerks mis-
conducting themselves. Clerks whose conduct was too
immoral (adulterers or fornicators) were to be deprived
of their ecclesiastical character, and a general prohibition
was laid against ecclesiastics bearing arms or hunting.
Rules were also laid down for the extirpation of pagan
customs.

In 745 a general council was called for the whole
Frankish kingdom. This council exhibits the progress
made by pontifical authority under the labors of Boniface. The evidence is supplied by two very important
letters which the pope wrote, one to Boniface and the
other to the ecclesiastics and laymen of the Frankish
realm. We learn from the first letter that the council
met in Frankish territory, at the command of the pope.
Pepin and Carolman served as intermediaries; it was
they, the lay authority, who "procured" the meeting.
Boniface, as the representative of the pope, presided.

Medieval Civilization

The pope sketched his program to the council: measures against false bishops, schismatics, all those who violated the canonical rules or the Catholic and apostolic faith, and measures to gain restoration of the property of the Church. The pope desired Boniface to hold a council every year, in his name. Cologne was designated for Boniface's metropolitan seat. This gave his title of archbishop a territorial basis, and his organization of the hierarchy was now complete. However, in the following year, political motives led to the transfer of the metropolitan seat to Mainz, which thus fell heir to the precedence which Cologne had hitherto enjoyed. The bishoprics of Germany and, also, Cologne, Tongres, Worms, Spires, and Utrecht were under the jurisdiction of the metropolitan. But Boniface can scarcely be said to have occupied the primate's seat himself; one of his disciples administered the archbishopric as adjunct, while the master pursued his work of converting pagans and introducing ecclesiastical reform.

The Roman discipline was not established in Gaul without opposition. Boniface says, in one of his letters to Pope Zacharias, that he had been exposed, in the course of his labors, to many injuries and persecutions. Two of the false priests of whom he speaks—Adelbert, a Gaul, and Clement, a Scot—were particularly objectionable. The first was nothing but a dreamer and charlatan, performing miracles in the highways and byways, and gathering around himself naïve folk who regarded him as an apostle. The Scot was more dangerous. Boniface says that he waged war on the Catholic Church and scorned the decisions of the councils, and that although he had

a son born in adultery (this is the name Boniface gives
to the marriage of a priest), he still considered that he
could be a bishop. More than once these two insurgents
had been condemned; they had even been put in prison,
but they were liberated and resumed their old practices.
They were cited before the pope and condemned at a
synod in Rome. Two years later, the pope complained of
their persistence in wrong-doing. Such defiance was unusual in a later day, when the papal power was firmly
established.

In 748 Boniface presided over one of the annual councils, and caused the bishops to swear to a formula of
entire submission to the See of Rome: " We have declared and decreed that we would maintain and protect
until the end of our life Catholic faith and unity, and
submission to the Roman Church, St. Peter, and his
vicar; that we would meet together each year in synod;
that the metropolitans should apply to the See of Rome
for the pallium, and that we would canonically follow all
the precepts of St. Peter, in order that we might be numbered among his sheep. And we have all consented and
subscribed our names to this oath, and have sent it to be
deposited on the tomb of St. Peter, prince of the apostles;
and the clergy and the pontiff of Rome have received
it with joy. . . . If any bishop is unable to correct or
reform any matter in his diocese, let him bring it up in
the synod, before the archbishop and all the assistants;
for we have ourselves promised the Roman Church with
an oath, that if we should see priests or peoples departing from the way of God, and should be unable to correct them ourselves, we would faithfully report the affair

to the Apostolic See and the vicar of St. Peter, so that the reformation in question might be accomplished. It is in this manner that all the bishops should report to the metropolitan, and the metropolitan to the Roman pontiff, all the reforms which they do not succeed in carrying out among their peoples. In this way the blood of lost souls will not be upon their heads."

The government of the supreme pontiff, which had been established in the new countries of England and Germany, was henceforth accepted by the old Church of Gaul. The Gallic Church was purified, disciplined, and subordinated to one commander, and the great part it has played in Gaul is well known.

The founder of the Church of Germany, the restorer of the Gallo-Frankish churches, was above all an apostle. It was his desire to end his life in missionary labors, and he deliberately sought the crown of martyrdom. In 755 he went to Frisia, and on the banks of the Bourda was surrounded by infuriated pagans. He forbade his companions to repel force by force, and the pagans, "by a beneficent murder, caused the blood to flow from their sacred bodies." In the abbey of Fulda the body of Boniface, the tireless missionary, was laid at rest.

The Economic Influence of Monasteries

W. Cunningham: *An Essay on Western Civilisation in its Economic Aspects (Mediæval and Modern Times)*, pp. 35-40.

IN the four preceding sections an attempt has been made to show how Christian teaching and ecclesiastical authority were brought to bear in favour of securing law and order throughout Western Europe, and thereby helped to provide the conditions essential for material progress. When we turn to another side of religious life, and consider the results of the founding of monasteries, we find influences at work that were plainly economic. These communities can be best understood when we think of them as Christian industrial colonies, and remember that they moulded society by example rather than by precept.

We are so familiar with the attacks and satires on monastic life that were current at the Reformation period that it may seem almost a paradox to say that the chief claim of the monks to our gratitude lies in this, that they helped to diffuse a better appreciation of the duty and dignity of labour. By the " religious," manual labour was accepted as a discipline which helped them to walk in the way of eternal salvation; it was not undertaken for the sake of reward, since the proceeds were to go to the use of the community or the service of the poor; it was not viewed as drudgery that had to be gone through from dread of punishment. There was neither greed of gain nor the reluctant service of the slave, but simply a sense of a duty to be done diligently unto the Lord. It may be said that this side of the monastic life was specially accentuated as early as the fifth century, because of excesses and irregularities that had even then brought scandal on the religious profession.[1] S. Augustine insisted on the duty of honest labour; and this element of disciplined life found a prominent place in the rule which S. Benedict drew up for the guidance of his monks.[2] The practice, which crept in later, of regarding writing or illuminating as manual industry, tended to the preservation of ancient learning, but it introduced a disastrous division of employment within the community; and the example set by monastic institutions, as Christian colonies, became much less telling after the tenth century.[3] Till that time it may be said that they were living testimonies to the duty of labour, and set forth the true character and dignity of honest work.[4]

The wickedness of the Merovingian rulers was so gross and palpable, that we can scarcely help feeling that their nominal Christianity was an added offence. Nevertheless, the fact that they made a profession of

[1] S. Augustine, De op. monach., c. 36.
[2] Reg. S. Benedict, cap. XLVIII. De opere manuum quotidiano.
[3] Levasseur, Histoire des classes ouvrières en France, I, 144.
[4] Cunningham, Modern Civilisation, 201. This conviction about labour, together with the inculcation of respect for life and property, are the fundamental principles in Christian economic teaching.

Economic Influence of Monasteries

Christianity had real importance. There was at least this difference between the Frankish monarchs and their Saxon or Danish neighbours, that the former encouraged the planting of these Christian colonies,[1] while the latter continued to destroy them. Whenever and from whatever motive a Benedictine monastery was founded in France, a little territory was reclaimed, and a new centre of civilisation was established. Much good work was accomplished by the monks in the keeping a love of learning[2] alive through the Dark Ages; and it is easy to show that their manual activity had great influence as an element in material progress, and that they did not a little to disseminate the industrial arts, to improve agriculture, and to develop more regular commercial intercourse.

Considerable tracts of Gaul had reverted to mere forest[3] under the combined pressure of Roman misgovernment and barbarian invasion; there was hard work to be done in reclaiming land for tillage, and frequent danger from the brigands, and even the wild animals that had come to haunt the secluded neighbourhoods where monasteries were planted. Each of the Benedictine houses was primarily a model farm, preserving the external aspects of a Roman villa,[4] and prosecuting agricul-

[1] By endowments of land, and by immunities which gave freedom from toll, rights to the profits of jurisdiction and rights to take toll. Berthelot, in Lavisse et Rambaud, Histoire générale, I, 339.

[2] S. R. Maitland, Dark Ages, 172.

[3] Montalembert, Monks of the West, II, p. 316.

[4] Paillard de St. Aignan, Changements de l'État social en Belgique in Mémoires de l'Académie royale de Bruxelles (1844), XVI, p. 68. For a description of the Roman Villa, see Meitzen, Siedelung und Agrarwesen, I, 352.

ture according to the recognised methods. It may be impossible to distinguish the improvements in cereals or breeds which were due to the monks, from those that were introduced by the Romans into Gaul and Britain, but at least we may say that the religious colonists maintained the practice of tillage in places where it was in danger of being forgotten altogether.

The monastery perpetuated the traditions of the Roman villa, not merely in regard to the cultivation of the soil, but in its industrial activity as well.[1] It was essential for the prosperity of these establishments that they should be, so far as possible, self-sufficing, and that the monks should be able to provide necessary clothing and to repair the implements of husbandry without relying on outside help. The abbot was, therefore, bound to organise the available labour so as to obtain the best results for the community—he might set an artisan to work at his own trade; but the conception of personal reward was rigidly excluded, and the skilled labourer was discouraged from taking a pride in his work:[2] all was to be done as part of the service of God, and for the advantage of the community, in strict subordination to the directions of the abbot.[3] The Celtic tradition, as we find it in S. Columbanus, is equally strict in enjoining the duty of assiduous manual labour,[4] and the founders of the reformed orders—the Cistercians and Carthusians

---

[1] Levasseur, I, 136, to which I am indebted for many of the subjoined references.
[2] Reg. S. Benedict, cap. LVII.
[3] J. Cassianus, De coenobiorum institutis, IV, cap. XII.
[4] See authorities in Levasseur, I, 138.

132

Economic Influence of Monasteries

—reverted strenuously to this ideal, from which the Benedictines had fallen away.[1]

The most striking picture of this side of monastic life
is to be found in the description of the monastery at
Solignac, which was founded in A.D. 631 by S. Eligius,
the celebrated goldsmith, with the aid of his royal master, Dagobert. It contained at one time as many as five
hundred brethren; it was so well organised that the
Archbishop of Rouen held it up as a model for all other
establishments. Among the residents were great numbers of artisans, who were skilled in different trades, and
trained as Christians to render prompt obedience.[2] When
we remember how easily the secret of a manual art may
be lost, we cannot but feel how much the industry of me-
diaeval Europe owed to the scattered centres where an
unbroken tradition of skilled labour was maintained, in
the seclusion of the monastery and under vows of obedience.[3]

In so far as the monasteries developed special industrial activity, they would have surplus commodities which
it was advantageous to sell; in some cases they might

[1] As the Benedictine monks confined themselves to artistic or
literary labour, they were dependent on outside help for the
necessaries of life, and their houses came to be the nuclei
round which towns grew up. Levasseur, I, 141.

[2] Vita S. Eligii, c. XVI.

[3] See below, Appendix [to Cunningham]. Household arts
would also be perpetuated by the nuns, who devoted themselves
to ordinary domestic duties in the kitchen and laundry, and also
to the textile arts, including spinning and dyeing, and to such fine
arts as embroidery. Levasseur, I, 139. Eckenstein, Woman
under Monasticism, p. 222 and fol. There would be much economic convenience in the double monasteries like that of Hilda
at Whitby or the houses of Gilbert of Sempringham.

Medieval Civilization

require to purchase materials for their industry; at any rate, it was only natural that they should develop a commercial side, and thus be brought as communities into constant economic relation with the outside world. This important business was assigned to an official specially selected for the purpose—the *negociator ecclesiæ;* [1] and the principles of fair dealing, by which he should be guided, were carefully laid down. The " immunities " granted to abbeys by the Merovingian kings enabled the inmates to purchase the goods they required and to transmit them free of toll; the religious houses gradually increased their commercial connections, and not only bought for themselves, but traded on a considerable scale. The wine of Burgundy was transported in large quantities down the Seine by the negotiators of S. Wandrille, Jumièges and Fécamp; and Rouen [2] served as a port from which it could be shipped across the sea. Our best evidence of the early development of the clothing trades in Flanders comes from the fact that, in the eighth century, the agents of the monks of S. Wandrille went thither to purchase woollen stuffs; while the merchants of Prüm are mentioned as travelling to Aix, Cologne, Coblenz, and other towns along the Rhine. [3] After the establishment of the Carolingian Empire there was an extension of this monastic trading, and Louis the Debon-

[1] Negociator ergo Ecclesiæ talis sit, ut nunquam, vel raro decipi valeat et studiose neminem ipse decipiat : qui nec, ut charius vendat, nec ut vilius emat, ore suo fallaciam proferat, vel juramentum ab his exigat aut ipse exhibeat. Reg. B. Petri de Honestis, III, c. XXIX.

[2] De Freville, Commerce maritime de Rouen, p. 50.

[3] Imbart de la Tour, Des immunités commerciales in Études du Moyen Age, dédiées à G. Monod, p. 74.

Economic Influence of Monasteries

naire granted to the monks of Tours freedom from toll in Provence and Italy, and throughout his dominions.[1]

The existence of this large trade gave the monasteries a commercial as well as a religious interest in the improvement of internal communications. The repair of bridges and maintenance of roads was, it is true, an obligation on landowners generally,[2] but it was also regarded as a pious labour, and is treated as such in the beautiful legend [3] of S. Christopher. This useful work was undertaken by many of the abbeys, and in the twelfth century some religious houses were specially founded to perform the duty.[4] We can also trace the beginnings of a regular system of transport. The great abbeys on the Loire and the Seine had large numbers of vessels for carrying on their trade; and the peasants on their estates were required either to provide oxen and carriages for land transport, or to pay a commutation which enabled the monks to organise an independent service.[5] The foundations of this traffic were laid before the time of Charles the Great; but under his protecting care it was greatly expanded, so that religious houses became the chief centres of mercantile activity. When we realise the extent to which this commercial side of monastic life was developed, we can the better understand why Danish raids were so frequently directed against these establishments.[6] Perhaps they paid an even heavier penalty for

---

[1] Levasseur, I, 141.
[2] Capitulare, A.D. 803; Migne, I, col, 254, c. 18.
[3] A. Jameson, Sacred and Legendary Art, II, 433.
[4] Levasseur, I, 143.
[5] Imbart de la Tour, op. cit. 75, 76.
[6] Keary, The Vikings in Western Christendom, 127.

Medieval Civilization

their commercial success: for devout men seem to have
felt, as early as the ninth century, that there was a danger
that the business enterprises of the monasteries would
divert the brethren from sacred occupations.[1]

[1] Levasseur, I, 143. Also Capit. Migne, I, col. 227, c. 17.

Cluny

Adapted from A. Luchaire, in Lavisse: *Histoire de France,*
Vol. II, Part II, 1901, pp. 123–132.

THE great house of Cluny is the typical *exempt* abbey
and the highest manifestation of monastic power.
It wielded an unrivaled authority over peoples and kings,
precisely because it stood, better than any other abbey,
for resistance to feudalism, and contemned the lower
things of life. When the papacy undertook to subordinate the faithful of Europe to itself, and thus regenerate
them, its missionaries and soldiers were recruited from
monastic Cluny, whose aspirations were in accord with
its own. Henceforward, the Cluniac community developed with such prodigious rapidity that the secular
Church was alarmed. The unparalleled prosperity of
Cluny was due to its institutions, but also, in no small
measure, to the remarkable men whom it had the good
fortune or cleverness to place at its head.

The prime characteristic of the new monasticism was
its absolute independence of the lay powers. It was
needful that there should be a reaction against one of the
most typical abuses of the tenth century—the invasion
of the cloister by worldly dukes and counts, who obtained the position of abbot that they might the more ef-
fectually appropriate the possessions of the monastery.

Medieval Civilization

Cluny, the model abbey, was to be an island of autonomy in the midst of an ocean of jurisdictions and feudal servitudes. William of Aquitaine, its founder, recognized this necessity in his deed of gift (910 A.D.) : " It has seemed good to me to determine, by this charter, that from this day the monks shall be withdrawn from all lay dominion, whether of ourselves, our relations, or even the king." Cluny was happily located for independence —in Burgundy, a neutral zone between France and Germany, where the authority of the king and that of the emperor were in such equilibrium that they annulled each other. The duke of Burgundy possessed only nominal authority; his suzerain, the king of France, was involved in unsuccessful conflicts with his great vassals, or with the Normans; no circumstances could be more favorable for Cluny. Charles the Simple, the contemporary of its founder, paid no attention to it, and Louis d'Outremer could only confirm the privilege which made the abbey completely independent of the temporal power (939). From its inception, Cluny held of no secular master.

It was necessary that the monks should be able to elect their abbot freely, untouched by any lay influence or any external pressure whatsoever. This principle was laid down by William of Aquitaine himself. But the unconditional exercise of such electoral freedom might not have been safe. It was to be feared that the monks, invested with this right, might so far yield to the manners of the age as to leave the door open to external intervention. Consequently, the first abbots participated in the choice of their successors. Each of them chose a coadjutor, and, before death, recommended him to the votes of the community. Their authority was so great that such a recommendation was always ratified by the chapter, from the foundation of the monastery until 1049. In that year another plan was followed, which was equally efficacious in preserving the monks from caprice or external interference. This was to regard the grand prior, the dignitary who took the place of the abbot when disabled, as virtually marked out for election as next successor.

The Cluniacs were exempt from the authority of the bishop of Mâcon, in whose diocese they were located; but they were, none the less, a part of the great ecclesiastical organism. Their founder had, at the very beginning, attached them to the center of Christianity, the Roman Church. The gift of 910 placed the monastery under the protection of the apostles Peter and Paul, and transferred to them all the property rights which William of Aquitaine exercised over his villa of Cluny. Every five years the monks were bound to make a payment at Rome of ten golden sous for the maintenance of the light in the apostolic church, and Cluny belonged to the Holy See as an inalienable property which was vested in it, solely for the purpose of protection. And, assuredly, the new abbey could undergo no lighter or less dangerous subjection than that of an authority sufficiently imposing to render efficacious protection, even at a distance; and, on the other hand, so far removed and relatively weak in material resources that it could not excite the fears of its ward. To be sure, this was not the first time that a French monastery was made directly dependent upon the pope, but the example of Cluny rendered the practice contagious. It is in this way that there arose those intimate relations between the papacy and the heads of the abbey—the close community of ideas and interests which united them, the frequent visits of the abbots to Italy and their long sojourns in the capital of the apostles. As counselors and official diplomatists of the Roman power, they lent their aid in times of peril, and served as intermediaries at the courts of kings. When the reform crisis came, the bond uniting the papacy and Cluny grew closer. Popes and abbots, united for war as for peace, then attacked the same abuses, struggled against the same enemies, and repulsed the same assaults. The identification became complete when Urban II, a militant Cluniac, ascended the papal throne.

The papacy is not in Cluny's debt. From the time that John XI, in 931, solemnly confirmed the clauses of the charter of foundation, the popes of the tenth and eleventh centuries vied with one another in legislating in favor of the great monastery. They recognized its right to coin a special money; they freed it from obedience to the diocesan bishop; they forbade any bishop to excommunicate it, and conferred upon the head of the abbey the episcopal insignia and the title of "arch-abbot." They sent legates whose special mission it was to defend the order, and chastise those who attacked it. They encouraged, in every possible way, the faithful who desired to enrich the monastery; for was not a gift to Cluny a gift to the holy apostles, proprietors of the abbey and of the Church universal? Gifts and legacies rained upon the monastery from all parts of France and of the world. A host of new monasteries were dedicated to

Cluny

St. Peter, and incorporated in the Cluniac Church. Flourishing abbeys placed themselves under its yoke, in order to enjoy the benefits attached to the observance of its rule and the protection of the Holy See.

Fifty years after its foundation, the modest religious house in which William of Aquitaine had placed twelve monks—the little abbey hidden among the high, wooded hills of the valley of the Grosne—attracted the attention and the riches of all Europe. At the end of two centuries, it was the capital of the vastest monastic empire Christianity had ever known. Out of its French possessions, Cluny ultimately erected seven provinces; and England, Germany, Poland, Italy, and, in an especial degree, Spain were filled with its priories. The extraordinary influence which Cluny exerted upon the minds of men of all social classes may be measured by the extent of its domination.

The empire of Cluny formed an organism, and this was another novelty in the monastic world. To the end that it might have a powerful and far-extending sway, Cluny made itself a " congregation." In those days of the indefinite subdivision of jurisdiction and sovereignty, the system of isolation was perilous for the clergy of the cloisters, for it left them defenseless before the lay lords. The vital interests of monachism demanded that it should be made into a body capable of moving and acting harmoniously and promptly, under the impulse of one master will. In Cluny, the principle of unity and the mainspring of centralization were to be found in the power entrusted to the chief of the community.

The omnipotence of the abbot was an essential princi-

ple among the monks of the West, and the government
of a Benedictine abbey bore a close resemblance to that
of an absolute monarchy. The organization of the congregation of Cluny demanded only that this direct power
of the abbot should be applied to all the monasteries of
the order. Accordingly, in the dependent monasteries
the title of abbot was suppressed, and their heads took
the significant name of " priors." There was but one
abbot for the whole organism—the head of the mother
monastery; and he was the immediate sovereign of the
great abbey, and of all the smaller ones. The head of
an affiliated establishment was not elected directly by
his own monks, but nominated by the abbot-general.
This right of nomination was a daring novelty, and was
opposed to tradition, to the Benedictine rule, and to the
sacred principle of the freedom of abbatial elections. It
stirred up lively resistance and terrible tempests. But
such a vast and rigorously centralized dominion is not
founded by peace alone.

A certain number of abbeys refused to allow themselves to be swallowed up in the congregation without
protesting. They declined to surrender the rank which
was theirs, by reason of the number of their priories, the
fame of their relics, and the antiquity of their origin.
They refused to accept with a good grace the abbots and
monks sent to them from Burgundy, and clung obsti-
nately to their autonomy. Opposition sprang up, for
example, in northern as well as in southern France; and
it was fanned by jealous bishops who were suspicious of
the growing power of Cluny. Conflicts of an extreme
violence demonstrated to the Cluniacs that they were

assuming too heavy a burden, and that the whole religious world was not disposed to enter into their obedience.

The abbey of St. Martial at Limoges began the struggle in 1063, and would hardly admit that it was beaten in 1240. Many others resisted annexation, and the consequent disorders now and then involved the effusion of blood. The intensity of these quarrels is explained by the desire to escape reform and the rigors of the Cluniac rule, and by the spirit of independence and regional particularism. But Cluny shattered or turned the obstacles, and the victory rested with her. If the work of centralization was not always disinterested, if it was accomplished in several cases with blameworthy harshness, the abbots-general, backed up by opinion and straining their energies under the firm conviction of the utility and grandeur of the enterprise, stubbornly refused to yield, and, in particular, to surrender the direct nomination of the priors. Their goal was to liberate the cloisters from simony, irregularity, and moral and material disorder, and to regenerate the monastic world through the lesson of obedience, so that it might become the instrument of the reform and emancipation of the Church. Despite all difficulties, the congregation won the day.

Contact between the abbot and the affiliated houses was frequent and regular. It was established by the visitation of the supreme chief, a guarantee of unity and order —but a most absorbing and burdensome duty. When the order embraced all France, and the bulk of Western Europe, the abbot had to spend his life upon the highways. He held in his hands the strings which moved men and affairs, and at first he felt obliged to see everything and do everything himself. The earlier abbots seem to have possessed the gift of ubiquity.

The organization of the visitation was completed by that of the "chapter-general," which was an assembly of priors, or dependent abbots, held periodically at Cluny under the presidency of the archabbot. The documents of the eleventh century establish the existence of these imposing synods, and the attendance of bishops and high church dignitaries, in addition to the Cluniacs proper. The chapter-general did not become a regular institution until the beginning of the thirteenth century, when its form became definitive—a complex organism of political, administrative, and judicial bodies, with its personnel of "visitors" and of *definitors,* and its ceaselessly increasing powers. In the fourteenth century the chapter-general even tended to become a sort of representative assembly, exercising its control over the abbot-general and transforming his absolute authority into a limited monarchy. But in the eleventh century, the golden age of the congregation, the synod was still only a consultative body,—resembling the formal curia with which the king of France surrounded himself,—and the autocracy of the abbot was complete and uncontested.

The observance of a common rule was the moral bond which united the members of the order. The rule of Cluny was a revision of the general rule of St. Benedict, accommodating it to the transformations which had taken place in monastic life.

This law of a great monastic people had not the in-

Cluny

flexible character which some have been tempted to attribute to it. It had a certain suppleness of application; the first abbots were intelligent men, whose love of duty did not blind them to the necessity of making provision for the differences between different parts of Europe. They could not be satisfied simply to impose the rule; they saw that it was needful to make it endurable if not attractive, if the mother house was to have a lasting dominion. When the abbot Hugh I (elected 1049) transmitted the text of the rule to the monastery of Spires, he authorized, and even pledged, the German abbot to modify or extend it in points required by the peculiar usages of the country.

The first general modification consisted in the great emphasis which was laid upon labors of the mind. Manual labor was retained by Cluny, but only sufficiently to recall to the monk the precept of humility—one of the foundation principles of monachism. The rule obliged the Cluniacs to shell beans, pull up weeds, make bread— but only for a short time. The hours which were not consecrated to prayer and the offices they employed, above all, in learning singing, copying manuscripts, and reading works of sacred and even profane literature. The Cluniac reform has been falsely charged with laying it down as a principle that the literature of the ancients should be ignored and despised. The abbot Odo (926–948) dreaming that his Vergil was transformed into a magnificent vase, out of which swarmed serpents which encircled him in their folds; the abbot Majolus (948–994) prohibiting the reading of the Æneid, and erasing from the manuscripts all passages which spoke of love—these pious legends did not prevent the Cluniac writers from becoming impregnated with classical literature, from mixing sacred and profane, and from defending the opinions of the Fathers with citations from the Latin authors. The exclusion of classical antiquity was so little a custom and a law for the monks of Cluny that, in the twelfth century, the disciples of St. Bernard bitterly reproached them with having an excessive love for pagan letters and poetry. The labor of the hands, especially in clearing the soil, was indispensable under a system of isolated monasteries, at a time when the bulk of the land was wild; but the necessity had ceased to be imperative in the eleventh century. A congregation like Cluny, proprietor of vast domains with a population of colons and serfs, no longer required the manual labor of the monks for the exploitation of the soil. Besides, it was the design of Cluny to save the Church from absorption in the pursuit of material interests, and to react against the feudal society in which abasement of the mind went hand in hand with brutality and coarseness of manners.

The struggle against ignorance was one of the first articles in the reform program. Cluny must dominate by the mind, and shed abroad intellectual light as well as morality. As a result of this desire to act upon the understanding, the great abbey was a center of teaching —a school where masters of reputation instructed and educated the novices. In these boys' schools, the discipline was harsh. The Cluniac masters, like all those of the Middle Ages, administered corporal punishment for the slightest infraction of the rules. But the monastic idea supported this discipline, and caused it to be accepted by all. The minute educational details into which the legislator of the order enters prove clearly that Cluny was solicitous for the physical health of children, as well as for their moral development.

On the other side, Cluny offered a salutary example to the monastic world: the rule exalted the duties of hospitality and charity. Cluny did not create, of course, but she developed, under the form of regular and permanent obligations, the institutions of public assistance and almsgiving. Two important functionaries were entrusted with the entertainment of guests and the care of the poor—the "guardian of the guest-rooms," who received horsemen, and the "almoner," charged with welcoming pedestrians and mendicants. Every day abundant alms were distributed to the poor of the locality, and to outsiders as well. Udalric (1018–1093), one of the writers of the Cluniac rule, estimates that in the year in which he wrote his *Customs* 17,000 indigents received aid. The affiliated houses followed the example of the metropolis. At Hirschau, one of the German priories, the monks found means in one of the worst years to succor thirty poor each day. The abbot Odilo (990–1049) sold the sacred vases of his treasure, in order to feed the starving in a time of famine. The abbots of Cluny never ceased to repeat and, better still, to practise the maxim of St. Ambrose: "The money of the Church is not made to be heaped up, but to be distributed to those in need." Everywhere that St. Hugh went, throngs of the wretched rushed to meet him and receive money and food at his hands.

Medieval Civilization

Thus spoke and acted the Cluniacs of at least the first centuries. The immense popularity which Cluny enjoyed among the inferior classes contributed still more to the prosperity of an order which enjoyed the protection of the popes and the rich gifts of all Europe.

Cluny had also the special good fortune to be organized and directed, in the eleventh century, by superior men, true monks, apostles devoted to their work, and men of remarkable vigor and longevity. Majolus administered Cluny for forty-six years, Odilo for fifty-nine, and Hugh for sixty. These men rendered their abbey the great service of living long, and were able to give it stability, unity of direction, and permanent traditions. The first four abbots have been placed by the Church in the calendar of saints; but the Middle Ages had deified them, almost, in their lifetime, making of them wonder-workers freed from the limitations of human existence. The divine protection never left them. Odo, praying at the tomb of St. Martin of Tours, was assailed and bitten by foxes; an enormous wolf promptly appeared upon the scene, put them to flight, and remained thereafter the faithful companion of the saint. One night a thief sought to steal Odilo's horse, but just outside the abbey portals man and horse were fixed, unable to move a muscle. At daybreak Odilo went out and discovered the rigid culprit. "My friend," said the abbot, gently, "it is not fair that you have lost a whole night guarding my horse,"—and he threw him some pieces of money. When the streams, swollen by a flood, barred the road of the man of God, he crossed them dry-shod. Odilo repeated the miracles of the fishes at

Cluny

St. Martin of Tours, and that of the marriage of Cana at an Italian monastery. One day when Hugh I was crossing the Alps on the way to Rome, an old woman, hidden in a tree, frightened the mule upon which he rode. Hugh and his mount fell over a frightful precipice. In the midst of the general terror, the abbot was discovered caught in the branches of a small tree; he was rescued, and the tree miraculously disappeared. The life of the first abbots was veritable enchantment!

Underneath this cloud of edifying legend, the physical and moral personality of the leaders does not always stand out sharply. And yet certain figures of the eleventh century can be adequately drawn. Odilo, a thin, lithe, pale-hued, nervous man, devoured by an inner flame which shone through his mobile face and quick eyes, was a mediocre orator, but a clever and prolific writer. In him are to be found the qualities common to all the creators of Cluny: charity, sweetness, robust faith in monastic work, love both for teaching and for the active life, endurance, and marvelous activity. We see him on all the highways of Europe, descending unexpectedly upon the most distant monasteries, correcting their abuses and scandals, aiding kings and popes to reform degenerated cloisters, or to solve the highest questions of religion and of politics, and, notwithstanding his exhausting physical and mental labors, attaining, in full possession of his faculties, an advanced age.

His successor, Hugh I, was a man of good height, an eloquent speaker, a supple and persuasive diplomat, born for politics and affairs, the friend and collaborator of Gregory VII. None contributed more to the greatness

of Cluny, none labored more zealously at the foundation of the Roman theocracy, than he. He was an advocate of the papacy, spoke for it in all the councils, and
never ceased to give it comfort by his presence and advice. His saintly reputation made him the necessary man,
the arbitrator always chosen to settle the most delicate
and most serious quarrels. High barons, bishops, kings,
and popes had recourse to his intelligence and his
justice. Through the ascendancy of his personal authority, quite as much as by virtue of the power of
his order, this monk treated as an equal with the chiefs
of the lay world, as well as of the Church. His independence was absolute. He refused the pontifical dignity, which could not have increased his power over the
Christian world.

Although it was against the express wish of Gregory
VII, he did not hesitate to make Duke Hugh I of Burgundy a monk of Cluny. He desired to attract King
Philip I of France into his cloister. The abbot rightly
held that the kingdom of France would lose nothing if
Philip buried himself in the monastery; for he was an
old king, already practically replaced by his son, and his
continuing reign was only a scandal. But Philip did
not fall in with the abbot's plan. On the other hand,
when Alphonso VI, king of Castile, thought seriously
of abdicating and devoting his remaining years to the
monastic life, the abbot reminded him that he had a task
to perform,—that it was his duty to war against the
Mussulmans and bring religious and political deliverance
to Spain,—and he kept him upon the throne. Hugh rep-
rimanded kings, as did Gregory VII, but he did it tact-

fully. He told them the truth with gentleness and respect. " O King, worthy to be loved," he wrote to
Philip I, " open fully your soul to the fear of the Lord.
Alas! the perils which environ your life are numberless!
Death presents itself under all its forms, and it is a
terrible thing to fall into the hands of the living God!
Change, therefore, your life; correct your habits; draw
near to God, through true penitence and a perfect conversion." William the Conqueror wished to have Cluniac
monks in England, and offered Hugh, if necessary, " to
pay for them with their weight in gold." The words
were imprudent at this time, when the Church was wag-
ing ardent war against simoniacs. The abbot of Cluny
answered without acerbity, but with firmness: " Before
God, gold is valueless, and silver profiteth not. What
doth it profit a man, if he gain the whole world and lose
his own soul? At no price, most dear lord, would I
wish to sell my own soul; and I should assuredly be selling it if I sent a single one of my brothers where I am
convinced that he would be lost. Moreover, I have a
great need of monks for the divers localities which we
must provide for. Far from selling them, I should give
money to get them." William recognized that the last
word had been said. The congregation entered England
by another route.

The eleventh century was the apogee of the order of
Cluny. Later, the prestige of its monks declined, and
the twelfth century saw the first signs of its decadence.
The abbey fell a prey to civil war, through competition
with the new orders. Superabundance of worldly goods
cooled the fervor and slackened the discipline of the

brethren. The powers of the abbot, who was the key-stone of the edifice, were shaken by the increasing authority of the chapters-general. In the thirteenth and fourteenth centuries still further departures were made from the primitive organization. The pope and the king of France finally secured the right to nominate alternately the abbot. Cluny then lost its independence, and with it the whole institution fell with an irremediable fall, for it lived only by liberty.

Monks of the Twelfth Century

Adapted from L. Garreau: *L'État social de la France au temps des croisades,* 1899, pp. 437–445.

IN the second half of the eleventh century, several congregations were formed in France, and in the twelfth century these spread over all Catholic Europe, eclipsing to some extent the renown of the Cluniacs. The most important was the congregation of Citeaux.

The Cistercians were mystics and anchorites. They did not attempt to influence the world as the Cluniacs did. They wanted to flee from the perverse age, to go away where there were no murders, where they would not see the weak oppressed, where life was not passed in managing falcons and weapons, where there were no beautiful temptresses who, on your return to the castle, in taking off your helmet and hauberk with their caressing hands also disarmed your virtue. But they could not escape from this earth. . . . They would at least depart from human society. They would find a deserted spot, and make it their own by cultivation; there would be no feudal obligations, and no serfs. They would free themselves from all the customary conditions of life.

The year in which the first crusaders captured Jerusalem, twenty-one young men, animated by these desires, settled in a wild part of the country of Beaune in Burgundy, and built a wooden retreat in the valley which bore what was then the obscure name of Citeaux (*Cistercium* in the Latin charters).

The kind of life which they desired was to be found in the rule of St. Benedict, of which Cluny practised the spirit, but not the letter. Seven hours of manual labor, seven hours of sleep, seven hours of prayer; two for study; a single meal, consisting of two vegetables and some fruit—this was, according to the rule, the daily program. For clothing they wore that which St. Benedict had seen poor men wearing in the sixth century: a tunic or shirt of undyed wool, covered during work with a long scapulary, and at church with a cowl.

These prescriptions, followed to the letter, made up for the monks of Citeaux a more severe regimen than St. Benedict had wished. The Benedictines, who followed the ancient observance, did not fail to note it. Their holy founder, they said, had written his laws for Italians; the garments which were sufficient in the climate of Campania were not enough for the winters of Gaul; and Gaul did not produce those olives which nourished the monks of Italy during their perpetual fast: a little meat was necessary in Gaul. As for manual labor, Charlemagne and the other benefactors of the monasteries had intended by their gifts to free the monks from the necessity of labor, so that they might be employed more usefully in prayer and study; it was not fitting that knights, " philosophers," and fluent professors could not leave the world without being compelled to work like slaves. Those who spoke thus invoked, in addition, the precept which runs through the whole rule of St. Benedict: "Be moderate in everything, and consider human weakness."

But the men that Citeaux attracted were not moderate. They were fanatical. They felt unable to govern their fury, and to observe moderation in the use of that boundless liberty which the world then allowed nobles; and for this reason they resigned nobility and liberty. Their fiery imagination, reinforced by pitiless logic, conceived of a very lofty type of the Christian knight, of the bishop of Jesus Christ; they were indignant at seeing so few of their contemporaries attain this ideal, and, realizing that they were too often the plaything of momentary instinct and feeling, they despaired of realizing it themselves. Then they thought only of finding, under a terrible rule, a yoke that was heavy enough to overcome their too passionate natures. Fasting and work were needed to master the exuberance of their physical force; complete silence was necessary to give peace to such souls.

Moreover, such rigor alone could satisfy fully one of the aspirations which drove into the cloisters so many members of the ruling class: the desire of joining, by sharing their sufferings, the ranks of those who ate black bread in the sweat of their brow. This was, indeed, the impelling force in very many conversions; and, even before the foundation of Citeaux, knights had been seen disguising themselves in the garb of poor wretches, and living among the peasants by some hard manual occupation. This need of real poverty had not been satisfied in a rich Cluniac monastery; it was satisfied under the rule of Citeaux and other Benedictine congregations founded at the same time and with the same spirit.

Medieval Civilization

In 1047 a member of the family of the counts of Auvergne, named Robert, retired with two knights to the heart of a forest in Velay, so vast, says a contemporary, that a swift horse would have taken four days to cross it. They had scarcely discovered a retreat when other knights wanted to share their hard life; the oratory which they built became the celebrated monastery of Chaise-Dieu, and from it went forth the founders of two hundred and ninety-three priories, in France, Spain, and Italy.

In 1079 the Grande-Sauve, or great forest between the Dordogne and the Garonne, sheltered a few knights who had come from Picardy in search of an unknown spot where, fasting and praying, they might live by the work of their hands. Their director was a monk who has since been known by the name of St. Gerard. Like Chaise-Dieu, the Grande-Sauve became the chief center of a congregation which spread over both slopes of the Pyrenees. The order of Grammont had a similar origin in the same epoch.

In 1070 Bruno, a young clerk at Rheims, who had formerly been enamored of learning and eloquence, left his professional chair in order to flee from the sight of a simoniacal archbishop, " whose pride," says the chronicler, " recalled the pride of kings." Drawn to Grenoble by the holy man who was then bishop, he had gone one day to meditate and pray on the mountains, which rose abrupt and wild to the north of this city, and whose lowest summits are surrounded by the Isère. Several disciples had followed him. They discovered a magnificent place, surrounded by a circle of almost impassable mountains—gigantic ramparts, in which the torrents had hollowed out two narrow gates. They felt themselves in a land apart, more beautiful than the habitable earth, and wholly imprinted with the greatness of God. How could they leave it and return to the petty cares of men? They remained in their mountains, and from the local name, *Mons Cartusianus,*—Chartreuse, in the vulgar tongue,—they were called Carthusians.

About the year 1100, Robert d'Arbrissel, "the great converter," led into the forest of Fontevrault a band of men of all ranks and women of every sort,—a heterogeneous troop,—which was the object of great suspicion to the prudent people who followed the steps of the missionary in order to lead under his guidance a holy life. A shelter and a cloister for the women were built out of the first trees that were felled; then the men sowed wheat in place of the bushes which they had torn up, and when winter came they built a home for themselves. These two wooded shelters became twin monasteries, which had this touching peculiarity that both were under the rule of the abbess of the women's convent. The monks, accepting from their devotion to the Virgin Mary the rule of their sisters, supported them by the fruits of their toil.

The congregations of Vallombrosa and Camaldoli sprang up in Italy at the same time, in the same spontaneous fashion, and without preconceived plan. Like those which were formed in France, they were founded under the rule of St. Benedict.

The congregation of Cîteaux was, therefore, not an isolated phenomenon: it was the most important manifestation of a current directed both by the extreme ardor of the individual characters, and by the sight of irremediable social vices. In the course of the twelfth century, if we may believe the calculations of ancient authors, 22,000 men became Cistercians. From Spain to Poland, and from Scotland to Sicily, wherever there was an abandoned piece of land or a valley that seemed too swampy to be inhabited, a monastery of this order was built. Thus there was throughout Christendom a second flowering of Benedictine laborers, like the first one, which, after the fall of the Roman Empire, brought Europe again under cultivation. But this second monastic colonization was very much more active, and in a few years occupied all the sites that the first had not reclaimed.

The Elements of Feudalism

Adapted from A. Esmein: *Cours élémentaire d'histoire du droit français,* 1901, pp. 175–184.

FEUDALISM is a form of social and political organization which existed in the Middle Ages throughout all Western Europe. It has existed in other parts of the world, and at other epochs—for example, Japan began to abolish her highly developed feudalism as late as 1867; but this discussion deals only with the feudalism of Western Christendom.

There are two constituent elements in feudalism: the *feudal group* and the *lordship* (*seigneurie*).

The basis of the feudal group is the fief. The fief was a piece of land, or a vested right, granted by a man who was called lord of the fief to another man who was called vassal, on condition that he render certain services. The vassal did not promise the lord, in the formal act of homage, that he would pay a sum of money, or a rent equivalent to money; he promised, rather, that he would be absolutely faithful to him, and also that he would perform certain services which resembled the ordinary obligations of a citizen to the State. These can be brought under three heads: the vassal had to fight for his lord when required to do so; he had to submit himself to the justice of his lord, or aid him in his court; he had, on demand, to give him counsel and advice. Finally, if the terms upon which he held his fief did not require a periodical money payment, he was obliged, in a few cases which were fixed by custom, when the lord had pressing need of money, to give him financial assistance by paying a feudal *aid*. The lord, on his side, owed his vassal fidelity, justice, and protection.

This peculiar contract of mutual assistance shows clearly that in feudal times the old notion of the State had undergone profound modifications. These two men, who pledged each other mutual support, supplemented, or took the place of, the weak or absent authority of the State. In the nature of things, the association was not restricted to these two men.

Ordinarily, the lord of the fief granted fiefs to several persons, and thus secured a number of vassals. This was inevitable in an age of force and violence, for a man had to be rich and powerful before he could become a leader and protector. The different vassals of the same lord, who were united to him by the same bonds of duty, constituted the feudal group, and this was the very soul of feudal society. It really formed a species of little State, provided with its own government, and capable of performing all the essential functions of the State. By virtue of the vassals' service in war, the feudal group was an army; through their judicial service, it was a court of justice; through their advisory service, it was a council of government. This, of course, presupposes that the large State, within which these little States developed, could no longer guarantee justice, security, and internal peace.

But the feudal group, thus constituted, was not yet

The Elements of Feudalism

complete. Still others connected themselves with it, although their rôle was a secondary and subordinate one. These were the cultivators—the *villeins* and the *serfs*. They were often villeins of free condition, who received concessions of land from the lord or from his vassals; but these concessions were, in their nature, quite unlike the fief—they were made in consideration of payments in money, or in kind. There were, also, the serfs, who were bound to the soil of the lord or his vassals. But the free villein and the serf were not active members of the feudal group described above. They had direct relations only with the persons whose tenants they were, or with the land to which they were bound, and their condition was one of duties rather than of rights. But they gravitated in the orbit of the feudal group, since they were connected either with the lord or with the vassals who together composed it. They constituted the class whose labors and payments supplied the economic needs of the entire group. They were not strictly members of it, but they found their protection from external violence in the military and social force which the group controlled, since those of whom they held had the right to invoke its aid.

The bond which united all these men into an organic whole—lords, vassals, tenants, and serfs—was the land. Some of them granted it; the others received it on certain conditions. But this of itself transformed landed property. Free and absolute ownership passed away, save here and there; it gave place almost wholly to *tenure*, for nearly every one held his land of some one else, by virtue of a conditional and limited grant.

The feudal group was, as has been shown, organized

Medieval Civilization

to be self-sufficient; that does not mean that it was necessarily isolated in the feudal society; as a rule, it could
not be. For the lord, the head of the group, usually
entered as a vassal into another group of the same sort,
whose lord and head was ordinarily more powerful than
he was. Consequently, his own lands were held directly
of this lord as a fief, and the lands of his vassals were
held indirectly of this lord, as fiefs of the second rank
(*arrière-fiefs*). The first group was thus linked with a
second, and the second might be linked with a third,
and so on until a lord was reached who recognized no
superior, who held his rights of no one, who was, in
France, the king. When these connections were completed, the king would have under him, in radiating
series, all the fiefs and all the feudal tenures of the kingdom. This hierarchical arrangement made possible the
preservation of national unity, at least in theory; and, in
course of time, the monarchy derived great advantages
from it. But it is to be remembered that, according to
feudal principles, each vassal had duties and obligations
only to his own lord. He was not the *man* of the superior suzerain—he owed him nothing; only, now and then,
his own lord might require him, by virtue of his personal authority, to aid the superior suzerain. In the
course of time, it is true, this principle was weakened,
and fixed relations were established between the superior
suzerain and the rear vassals; but even in these cases
their own lord was always the intermediary.

In France, this wise arrangement was not as old as
feudalism; in some respects it was very slow to take root.
French feudalism grew up in a period of profound

The Elements of Feudalism

anarchy, and, as a natural result, there were many lords in the beginning who were absolutely independent and many feudal groups which were absolutely isolated. The feudal hierarchy was established only very gradually. The more powerful lords secured the homage of the more feeble, and the king secured the homage of the superior lords. But the Capetian monarchy had at first much trouble in securing the homage of certain lords, and the feudal obligations of great vassals, who were as powerful as the king himself, very often remained a dead letter.

The second constituent element of feudalism is the *seigneurie,* or lordship.

The right to rule, in feudal times, was not derived solely from the contracts and grants of land, which gave birth to the feudal groups. There was another source for it—the authority of the State itself. This authority, formerly incarnated in the sovereign, never vanished entirely, although the rights springing from the feudal associations seemed to threaten its extinction. It survived, in a distorted and dismembered form, as the *seigneurie.* This was merely sovereignty, or a fragment of sovereignty, which had become private property by passing into the possession of individuals. This acquisition of sovereignty was the result of concessions from the monarch himself, or was the product of pure usurpation consolidated by length of possession and confirmed by custom. Sometimes this fragment of sovereignty, exercised over a definite extent of territory, was attached as an appendix to the lands or vested rights with which it was owned and transmitted; at other times it constituted a distinct piece of property, which had an existence of its own. But whenever the feudal hierarchy was fully developed, this fragment of sovereignty was clothed in feudal forms, and was always held as a fief, either of a lord or of the king. Thus the authority of the State adapted itself to the genius of hierarchical feudalism. All the *seigneuries* were similar in kind, but they differed enormously in the territory they embraced and the attributes which they conferred. There was at first a superior class which represented complete sovereignty over a territory, as far as one may speak of sovereignty in a feudal society. The lord of such a fief had the right to exercise within his territory, however large, all the royal rights which had not been absorbed by the inferior lords. Generally, such fiefs were held directly of the crown, and they gave to feudal France the appearance of a federation of private individuals under the presidency of the king. These *seigneuries* were ordinarily called the great fiefs; their holders are often spoken of by the older writers as the barons of the kingdom of France. All these superior *seigneuries* carried with them special titles of dignity. First of all came the duchies and the counties, and here the origin of the *seigneurie* and of the title is easily seen. The feudal duchies and counties were the large administrative divisions of the Carolingian monarchy, from which they sprang; their birth was due to the appropriation of state functions by the dukes and counts. Next in order of dignity were the baronies—a new creation, a product of the age when feudalism was formed. They do not correspond to any function of the Carolingian monarchy. At first

The Elements of Feudalism

de facto powers, they later became the typical form of the fully developed feudal *seigneurie*. Below them were the viscounties and the castellanies. The viscount was, in the Frankish monarchy, the deputy of the count. The castellan was originally the officer of a baron, and it was his duty to administer for the baron one or more castles with their lands. There were, however, some viscounts who obtained their independence, or became direct vassals of the crown, and who had as much power as the counts or the dukes. Finally, there was a class of *seigneuries* which conferred on their holders no title other than lord, but gave them the exercise of the functions of high or low justice, as the case might be. It is very difficult to state, in general terms, the exact extent of the rights of these lords, and the particular sovereign attributes which each of them exercised within his territory; for it was custom which above all determined these in feudal times, and custom varied from place to place. Two general conclusions, however, can be presented. First, the *seigneurie* which ordinarily represented the plenitude of sovereignty was the barony; secondly, the *lord* who exercised the most precious attributes of sovereign power was the lord high justiciar (the lord who possessed the right of life and death). Throughout his territory he dispensed civil and criminal justice with an unlimited jurisdiction, and, for a long time, his decrees continued to have sovereign authority. He alone had the right to levy imposts upon his subjects. In his exclusive possession, therefore, were the two essential rights of justice and taxation. It was manifestly high justice which most nearly represented the authority of the State

Medieval Civilization

in feudal society. The rights which the superior lords exercised were very slight unless they kept high justice in their own hands; and their power rested, above all, upon their own domains and the number of their vassals. However, the powers of the high justiciar himself must not be exaggerated; they were limited, both as to taxation and justice, by other feudal principles.

Feudal society was divided into three classes—nobles, villeins, and serfs. The full power of the high justiciar was exercised over villeins and serfs alone; nobles escaped it almost completely. In fact, the latter were exempt in principle from the tax, whether direct or indirect, levied by the high justiciar upon his subjects. Moreover, the noble was always a vassal, and as such recognized as his judge the lord to whom he did homage, and before whom he could find a tribunal of his peers. Thus, in principle, he was not subjected to justice founded upon the public authority. Consequently, he was not amenable to the jurisdiction of the lord high justiciar, unless the latter happened to be at the same time the lord of his fief, and *had not yet received his homage;* and then it was the latter circumstance, and not the former, which established the jurisdiction. Even in matters touching the villein, the lord justiciar might see certain cases escaping his justice.

These are the essential elements of fully developed feudalism.

The feudal régime had a very long life. It was gradually established in the ninth and tenth centuries, reached completion in the eleventh, and certain aspects of it endured in France until the French Revolution. The

The Elements of Feudalism

period when the feudal institutions really represented the political organization of French society, when they were its mainspring, extends from the commencement of the eleventh century to the end of the fourteenth. To be sure, the royal power never disappeared from feudal France; from the twelfth century on, it had a great political rôle, and in the thirteenth and fourteenth centuries it made great progress in spite of the feudal powers.

Mutual Obligations of Lords and Vassals

Adapted from A. Luchaire, in Lavisse: *Histoire de France,*
Vol. II, Part II, 1901, pp. 9–11.

THE feudal obligations were naturally heavier for the
vassal than for the lord. The oath of fidelity required not only that the vassal should not say or do anything which might hurt his lord in his person or in the
person of his near relatives, in his honor or in his goods;
it bound him to devote himself to his lord, and even to
sacrifice his liberty for him. By virtue of the obligations
of guarantee and of hostage, he was responsible in person
and property for the engagements contracted by his suzerain. He really only half belonged to himself, and
even less than that if the lord rigorously exercised the
powers which his rights conferred upon him.

In time of war, military service kept him for a fixed
number of days under the banner of his lord. Even his
castle was not fully his own; his suzerain might demand
the keys and put a garrison in it. Furthermore, he must
guard the castle of his lord, and, in any case, do garrison
duty there once a year. In times of peace he was bound
to come, at his lord's requisition, to judge or give counsel
in his court, or even simply to increase his suite at all the

Lords and Vassals

great church festivals and in all the important events of his life and of the life of his family.

To the military assistance we must add the financial aid which might legally be demanded of him in certain cases fixed by custom. It is an error to imagine that financial service was peculiar to the tenure of a villein, and that it did not weigh upon the tenure of the noble. The noble paid his suzerain for the right of inheriting the fief, especially if he were a collateral heir; he paid for the right of transferring the fief, for freeing his serfs, or for giving lands to the Church. Furthermore, he was liable for a contribution, the feudal *aid,* every time his lord made an extraordinary expenditure. Finally, he bore the heavy burden of lodging and purveyance: he must welcome and defray the expenses of the lord and his suite, just as monks and peasants who were subjects of the lord had to do.

When the vassal had performed his duty and had fulfilled the services he was bound to perform, he was not then at liberty to dispose, in full independence, of his person and of his fief. The ever-present authority of his suzerain made itself felt even in the domain of private life. According to the letter of the law, the vassal could not absent himself from his fief, travel, undertake a distant pilgrimage, get married, or give in marriage his son, and especially his daughter, without the permission of his lord. If, at his death, his heir was under age, the suzerain legally assumed the guardianship, that is to say, he became for the time being the absolute master of the fief, until the heir reached his majority or the heiress was married. There were still other circumstances, such as those of disinheritance and confiscation, which allowed the lord to enter into definitive possession of the fief. Vassalage, then, was not merely the limited exploitation of the feudatory by the suzerain; in fact, it looks as if the vassal was only the holder of the fief, while the lord was, in truth, the real owner.

In his turn, the suzerain had duties to perform toward his vassal. He was forbidden to injure him, to take the homage of his men away from him, to construct fortresses upon his fiefs, or to increase, without consultation with him, the dues fixed by custom or contract. He must render exact justice to the vassal, and protect him against his enemies. If the faithlessness of the vassal involved, in law, the confiscation of his fief, the disloyalty of the suzerain was punished with the refusal of homage and the breaking of the feudal bond. But how unequal the situations of the two were, and how superior the advantages enjoyed by the dominant lord under the law of fiefs! The duties of the suzerain were principally negative, and undoubtedly the less onerous of the two. The fact that the suzerain was himself the vassal of another did something to reëstablish the equilibrium, but, on the other hand, the feudal obligations became less heavy and less complex in proportion as the feudatory occupied a more exalted place in the feudal hierarchy.

The Realities of Feudalism

Adapted from A. Luchaire, in Lavisse: *Histoire de France,*
Vol. II, Part II, 1901, pp. 11–14.

IF we look only at the externals of feudalism, where
everything seems so rigorously thought out and regulated by law, we are tempted to see in it a group of institutions capable of taking the place of the State which had
been destroyed. The feudal régime, which was founded
upon the sanctity of an oath and respect for good faith,
possessed a moral basis; on the other hand, it manifestly
favored, more than any other régime, the play of individual forces and individual liberty.

It is a great error to suppose that the feudal relations
rested solely upon the contract. Such a view leaves out
of account the frequency with which they had their origin
in the continued exercise of *de facto* power, in violent
usurpation and brutal conquest. Still, it is not to be denied that in certain cases they originated in an agreement
freely entered into between the protector and the protected. Moreover, homage might be demanded at each
change of suzerain or vassal, and that involves in principle the consent of the parties. The fixity of the feudal
obligations, the necessity the suzerain was under to obtain
the assent of the vassal, even to the slightest modification
of them, and finally, and above all, the principle that the

vassal was tried by his peers, *i. e.,* by his equals, were all precious guarantees of the independence and security of the individual. But any one who wishes to form a just estimate of feudalism must get at the fundamental facts and contrast the reality with the theory and the law.

Closely viewed, the edifice raised by feudalism is seen to have been poorly joined together, and to have been in a condition of imperfect equilibrium. Relations were established by law between suzerains and vassals, from the top to the bottom of the hierarchy. But lateral relations, *between* the peers, were non-existent. The nobles upon the same stage of the feudal hierarchy lived as strangers to one another; there was no bond between them except the accidental association which sprang from the necessity of performing common duties toward a common suzerain. Among them isolation was so habitual as to be almost the rule. But was the bond connecting vassal and lord itself strong? Not only was the vassal able to weaken it to the very point of extinction by the mere force of inertia, by staying at home, or by omitting to appear at the court of his lord, but even the law itself gave him a thousand opportunities or a thousand pretexts for breaking it. The feudal bond was originally established only by his consenting to perform the act of homage. When it weighed upon him, he could withdraw from under it by alleging the disloyalty of his suzerain, or he could, even without giving any reason, by a simple declaration renounce his fief. In certain cases, of course, the suzerain had the right to denounce the feudal contract and dissolve the association.

However suitable the judicial organization of feudal-

The Realities of Feudalism

ism may have been for safeguarding the rights of the individual, it produced, in practice, the most unhappy results. The much-vaunted justice rendered by one's peers had no *sanction;* it settled the difficulties most usually by the judicial combat or, what was much worse, by private war. So that one may say, without transgressing the truth, that the feudal régime isolated the individual more than it liberated him.

The law of the feudal hierarchy was no more real a guarantee of peace and union than the law of vassalage. The uncertainty as to who was really lord of the fief, the custom of doing homage to several suzerains, the introduction of new *seigneuries,* and the multiform attempts of the suzerains to secure the homage of the vassals altered, from the eleventh century on, the existing conditions, and tended to throw the whole system out of joint. The establishment of the feudal hierarchy, which was to introduce harmony and order into the chaos of *seigneuries,* on the contrary produced, all too frequently, an entanglement of dominations and a confusion of powers. War sprang from the hierarchical principle, as it did from vassalage.

The living reality as it stands forth from the chronicles and documents of the time shows that brute force dominated everything. The feudal obligations were performed, the feudal contracts were respected, the feudal customs were observed, only when the suzerain was powerful enough to compel obedience. The bond of vassalage became weaker and weaker as the noble rose in the hierarchy. But at the bottom, as at the top, it was ceaselessly broken, and good faith was constantly violated by vassal and lord alike. The ineradicable habits of a military people, the instinctive hatred of the neighbor, the conflict of rights which were ill-defined and of interests which were poorly adjusted, caused perpetual struggles. There was no feudatory who was not at loggerheads with his different suzerains, with the bishops and abbots of the country round, with his peers, and with his vassals. War raged not only between the possessors of the fiefs, but in the bosom of every family. Quarrels between relatives over inheritance heaped up the measure of strife.

It is, then, no slander upon feudalism to point out the permanent anarchy, the profound disagreement between law and fact, which characterized it. Feudalism had its *raison d'être* and its period of usefulness in the tenth century, when the collapse of governmental power and the Norman invasions constrained the people to accept, as a benefit, the patronage of local magnates. But never did a régime pass more quickly from legitimacy to excess. If it was beneficent at a given moment in the beginning, that moment must have been a very fugitive one, and the historical documents at least bring down to us but slight evidences of its beneficence. Some admirers of the Middle Ages have pretended that France really knew an epoch when the castle of the lord served principally as a refuge for the burgesses and the peasants menaced by a foreign foe; when the lord, in the shadow of his fortress, thought only of obtaining for those under his protection security for their material life and the means of trading and laboring. They depict the lord opening markets for them, providing them with a wine-press, a bakery, and

The Realities of Feudalism

a mill, and fixing the time for the crops and the conditions of the sale of goods in the exclusive interest of the inhabitants of the *seigneurie,* in order to save them from famine. They exhibit the lord levying taxes only to assure public defense and the maintenance of bridges and roads; and even erecting churches and abbeys to give to the group of men placed under his guardianship the means of satisfying their moral and religious needs. This golden age of feudalism, if it ever existed anywhere in its entirety, was already no more than an ideal when feudalism appeared, fully armed, at the fall of the last Carolingian monarch.

The castellans, the viscounts, and the lesser nobles (who were the most numerous and who were in direct contact with the people) were less occupied with organizing than with destroying, less anxious to govern than to fleece, exploit, and pillage. Instead of protecting, they oppressed. Seignorial patronage seems to have had as its immediate consequences the enslavement of the protected and the habitual exaction of intolerable payments. All the services of common interest, even justice itself, became the private patrimony of a noble family, and were henceforth mere instruments of extortion. Those feudal nobles who are held up to us as creators of all the economic institutions of the Middle Ages really found them established and, perhaps, even in operation from time immemorial. They simply confiscated them and monopolized them to their own profit. Not only were order and justice lacking under the feudal régime, but liberty itself; for liberty did not exist for the great majority; it was the privilege of nobles, who used it, above all, to fight

Medieval Civilization

among themselves. We know only too well how much
the men of the Middle Ages suffered from feudalism to
believe that everything which has occurred in the course
of history has been advantageous to the nations merely
because it happened and they survived.

Feudal Wars

Adapted from A. Luchaire: *Manuel des institutions françaises,*
1892, pp. 228–234.

WAR, in all its forms, may be said to have been the
law of the feudal world.   It was the principal
occupation of that stirring aristocracy which kept land
and sovereignty in its grasp.   The deep-rooted habits of
a military race, the hatred of strangers and neighbors,
the clash of ill-defined rights, selfishness and covetousness, perpetually gave rise to bloody struggles, and made
each lord the enemy of all around him.   Every feudatory
made war at least once upon his different suzerains,
upon the bishops and abbots with whom he was in contact, upon his fellow-vassals and peers, and upon his
own vassals.   The feudal ties seem rather to have been
a permanent cause of violent conflicts than a guarantee
of peace and concord.   The sole ambition of the baron
was to round out his domain at the expense of vassals
who were too weak to resist him; the vassal took advantage of the youth or absence of his suzerain, or of the
regency of a woman, to throw himself upon his lord's
territory and injure it as much as possible.   Battles were
fought over the succession to a bit of land, over a frontier lawsuit, and over the exact nature of a feudal tenure.
In law and in theory, the suzerain could compel his vas-

sals of the same grade to settle their quarrels in his court of justice; but he was rarely able to intervene and cause his intervention to prevail. Usually, he was compelled to let the belligerents fight, and interfered only to get the parties to make a truce when hostilities threatened to continue indefinitely. In law, he was the guardian of the peace in his fief, and was in duty bound to see that it was preserved; in fact, his right was generally purely nominal, since he lacked the strength to enforce it.

War raged not only between suzerains and vassals and between the vassals of the same fief, but also in the bosom of all the feudal families. The son fought against his father, because he could not wait until his father's death to enjoy the lands and the rights which would, in due course, descend to him; the younger brothers attacked the elder, for the reason that he received a disproportionate share of the inheritance; nephews waged war on uncles, because these wished to prolong their guardianship unduly, or refused to recognize the custom which excluded collateral heirs from the inheritance; and the son took arms against his widowed mother, to force her to relinquish the absolute possession of her dower lands. Explosions of covetousness, and odious and inveterate struggles over inheritance, tore family ties to pieces.

In the rare intervals of calm, when serious wars were accidentally non-existent, the nobles sought consolation in the artificial quarrels of the tournament. The tournaments of the eleventh century were very different from the well-known affairs described by the chivalric chroniclers of the fourteenth and fifteenth centuries. The latter were mere military fêtes and tilts, in which the knights competed with one another in luxury and elegance, and in strength and the skilful wielding of their arms. The tournaments of the early Capetian period were genuine war on a small scale; all the nobility of two hostile neighboring territories were in attendance; and they were occasionally the scenes of regular battles between marshaled hosts, with bloody and murderous consequences for the men, and especially for the horses. At times knights struggled, two by two, with blunted arms; at other times whole troops crashed together. The sanguinary character of these earlier tournaments explains the severe and constantly repeated prohibitions leveled against them by popes and church councils, and even by the kings of France, who deplored such a waste of the military resources of the kingdom. But the habitual violence and warlike instincts of the nobility were stronger than all the inhibitions of the ecclesiastical and lay authorities. The kings themselves shared the general fondness for these warlike exercises, and made haste to forget their own prohibitions when a favorable opportunity presented itself. The attitude of the bourgeois toward the tournaments was hardly less friendly than was that of the nobility, since the tournaments stimulated trade. St. Louis was the only French monarch who made a serious effort to put down the tournament, and his success was not marked.

The regulations with regard to the *judicial duel* had a similar history. This was only a modified species of private war, regulated by the presence of judges, and lim-

ited by customary forms. It was war in the service of
justice. The bloody spectacles to which it frequently
gave rise were not calculated to calm, in the men of
medieval times, the warlike passions which were the very
foundation of their character.

Feudal war was more than a habit and a fact. Even
at the close of the thirteenth century, when the French
monarchy strove in every way to prevent, or at least to
restrict, the consequences of the general savagery of
manners, the men who drew up the *customs* of feudal
jurisprudence, and who were more or less saturated with
monarchical ideas, were obliged to recognize that the
nobles still had the right to take the law into their own
hands. It was admitted that they had *the right of private war*. It would seem, however, that this right was
not so absolute and so complete under St. Louis as it
had been in the eleventh century. The minute care with
which the scribes of local *customs,* from the beginning
of the twelfth century, laid down the rules governing the
judicial duel, the gages of battle, and even the practice
of private war, was in itself a limitation of the right of
war. The very regulation of disorder and violence was
a step in advance. To state by law how far feudal brutality might go was equivalent to restraining it. The
restriction, however, was slight.

The rules of the customary law of Anjou, which are
embodied in the *Establishments of St. Louis,* show that
if certain legal formalities were observed private war between vassals of the same rank was still absolutely free,
and, generally speaking, against any other person save
the suzerain. Even in this latter case it was tacitly con-

ceded that the vassal might wage war upon his suzerain,
if he secured the assistance of none but members of his
own family. The vassal, then, was not absolutely forbidden to wage war on his suzerain. That tells the whole
story. There were other *customs* which were less favorable to private war than those of Anjou—*customs* which
even seem to condemn it; but it is perfectly plain that
this condemnation was Platonic, and that it corresponded
neither to habits nor to facts. Public opinion undoubtedly considered feudal war legitimate, and all it strove
to do was to lay down certain rules for its exercise.

The right to wage war was a privilege which belonged
to nobles; commoners settled their differences before the
courts of justice. If a war was to be waged according
to legal formalities, hostilities had to be preceded by a
challenge, which was made in writing or through the
medium of a herald. In a war between suzerain and
vassal, a challenge was permissible only after the suzerain
had summoned the vassal to appear before his court, and
had had him condemned either in person or by default.
Custom ordinarily prescribed that an interval of one or
two weeks should elapse between the issue of the challenge and the opening of hostilities, to allow for preparations. The relatives of the belligerents, to at least the
fourth degree, were included in the war, but they could
not lawfully be attacked until forty days after the opening of hostilities. Any one violating this forty days'
exemption was guilty of the crime of treason. The relatives of a principal could secure neutrality for themselves
by disowning him, and by having it assured by his adversary. Certain classes of persons had a right to pro-

Medieval Civilization

tection, and could not be included in the hostilities; these were ecclesiastics, women, minors, and pilgrims. War was terminated temporarily by a truce, which was a suspension of arms for a period determined upon by the two parties. The truce was concluded either by a simple agreement before common friends, by a court decision, or by the direction of the suzerain. Infraction of the truce was a very grave crime, cognizable only by high justiciars. War was definitively terminated by the peace. All the relatives were included, *ipso facto,* in the treaty of peace; but they had the right to reject it, so far as they themselves were concerned, by a suitable notification to the principals. Once peace was concluded and accepted by an oath, it was regarded as solemnly binding, and any one guilty of *infractio pacis* was liable to severe punishment.

The history of feudal society is largely a chronicle of all kinds of wars, to which it never ceased to be a prey. At the same time, it must not be forgotten that serious efforts were made, throughout the whole period, to stamp out the scourge. The enlightened opinion of Europe finally recognized, after the chaos of the tenth century, that society could not be based upon war, isolation, and anarchy. The necessity for peace appeared the more urgent inasmuch as the common people were at this time beginning to secure emancipation, and commerce and industry were springing up in the large towns. In the eleventh century, the only power sufficiently intelligent and respected to conceive the necessity for peace, and to take measures to secure it, was the Church, represented by its supreme head, the pope, its councils, and its

Feudal Wars

bishops. The Church took the initiative in the first measures to secure peace—the *Truce of God* and the *Peace of God*. It is to the eternal honor of the ecclesiastical society of the Middle Ages that it attempted the work of pacification, and strove to make it successful. The measures first taken were local, and the principle was not definitively asserted and made generally applicable until the Council of Clermont in 1095.

The Truce of God, which rescued certain days of the week from the brutality of the nobles, originated in southern France in the last years of the tenth century, and quickly spread into the neighboring French dioceses at the beginning of the next century. Councils and bishops constrained the barons to swear to observe the Truce; but they never succeeded in securing the adhesion of all the barons, and those who did take the oath did not fail to break it. The Truce of God did not bear the fruits which the Church expected of it, because its sanction depended upon excommunication; and though this arm still struck terror and secured respect, its moral strength was not always sufficient to stem the rush of brute force.

The Church recognized the defects of this its first device, and resolved to give it the permanence and regularity which it lacked. The second half of the eleventh century, therefore, saw a new phase of the clerical movement to secure release from feudal disorder, in the Peace of God. Each diocese became the center of a veritable peace association or league. It was directed by the bishop; it had its regular statutes, its treasury, its magistrates; and, what was vitally important, it had its armed force, capable of reëstablishing order where it was disturbed, and of punishing, by weapons more swift than spiritual menaces, the nobles who had violated their oaths to keep the peace. Violations of the peace were brought before the so-called *judges of the Peace,* a tribunal which depended upon and was presided over by the bishop of the diocese. The barons who did not submit to the decrees of this court, and did not bow to excommunication, were pursued and punished by the *army of the Peace,* which was largely made up of parish militia enrolled under the episcopal banner. Such was, in brief, the Peace of God—the first regular and consistently followed manifestation of order in the midst of an incoherent and disordered society. It worked fairly well, and produced good results in certain provinces. But in the great majority of cases it was no more successful in preventing private wars than the Truce of God had been. The bishops had not sufficient authority to compel the noble members of the peace association to undertake a conflict with their peers, in order to punish them for acts which were not repugnant to feudal ideas. It was very difficult to get the army of the association under way. The abstention of the nobility often reduced it to the men of the bishop and some rural militia, led by their parish priests.

The efforts of these peace associations were only partially successful. Their indirect services, however, were very considerable. At the beginning of the twelfth century, they were utilized by the French monarchy when, under Louis the Fat, it began its serious and more effective struggle against the disturbers of the public peace.

Feudal Wars

The Church was not the only institution that in the twelfth century strove to pacify the land. Excommunication was beginning to lose its power, and in the thirteenth century it became a very rusty weapon. The bishops ceased to possess adequate authority to maintain public tranquillity. To be sure, the papacy, whose power was now augmented by reason of the ecclesiastical reforms, had undertaken the beneficent rôle of universal peacemaker. Papal legates began to interfere, with success, in the wars of the nobles, and began to impose armistices and truces. But the real source of the order and peace which appeared during and after the reign of Louis the Fat was not the papacy, but the monarchy. The monarchy was not only armed with real military force, but it possessed a moral and political superiority over the mass of feudal lords which did much to further its program. The king succeeded the Church as public pacificator. His policy was naturally directed toward replacing private war with judicial trials, conducted before his tribunal, the *parlement,* which was an emanation from his royal power. He aspired to the position of universal judge, and in the thirteenth century felt himself strong enough to issue ordinances of a general application prohibiting tournaments, judicial duels, and private wars. St. Louis made the greatest efforts in this direction, although he was only partially successful. Despite the efforts of Church and king, feudalism clung to its former customs and passions, especially in those portions of the kingdom which were not directly governed by the king, and sometimes even in the *Île de France* itself. The diminution of private wars, and the

185

lessening of the atrocity which marked their progress, came not so much from royal enactments as from the slow but progressive improvement of public morals, and the imperious need of security and well-being which all classes of society began to feel.

There can be no doubt that the thirteenth century exhibited a marked advance in these particulars over the twelfth. The documents of the period show that the practice of *assecuratio* was by this time customary throughout France. If one of the belligerent parties, either before or after the opening of hostilities, felt that he was too feeble to resist the attack of his enemy and desired to protect himself against the threatening danger, or to secure the termination of the conflict, he addressed himself to the judge who personified the authority of the king, the suzerain, or the commune, and prayed for security. Thereupon, his enemy was legally bound to come before the judge and solemnly promise, on oath, that he would respect the person and property of the adverse party, that he would *give peace* to him and his. Whether he refused or consented to give this *assecuratio,* the result was the same. From the time that the judge extended the *assecuratio,* the guarantee of security, to the petitioner, the law made his enemy responsible for all loss that he suffered, and declared him, if faithless, guilty of the crime of breach of security (*assecurationis fractio*), a crime severely punished in feudal law. The *assecuratio pacis* must not be confounded with a truce. A truce was a suspension of hostilities agreed upon by the two belligerents, while the *assecuratio* was a forced peace, which was extorted judicially from one party by

Feudal Wars

the judge to whom the other party appealed. It is hardly necessary to remark that this institution became a real guarantee of peace and social order only when the feudal nobles had acquired the habit of respecting the judicial authority and submitting to its decisions. The *assecuratio* became especially difficult to refuse or to violate when the judge who imposed it was a royal justice, or the *parlement* itself, for the *Olim* show a number of cases in which the *assecuratio* was pronounced in the full court of the king. The use of this institution presupposes a marked softening of manners, and a considerable advance in the principle of order. In any case, it was a genuine limitation upon the right of private war, since it permitted one of the parties to stop the war. But neither this institution nor any of the other peace institutions which we have discussed completely modified social conditions, or rendered private war impossible. The evil was too profound, too firmly fixed in the very constitution of society, to make any one remedy more than a palliative. Private war ceased when feudalism ceased, and not sooner.

The Church and Feudalism

Adapted from P. Viollet: *Histoire des institutions politiques et administratives de la France,* 1898, Vol. II, pp. 398–414; and L. Garreau: *L'État social de la France au temps des croisades,* 1899, pp. 374–377.

THE generosity of the faithful in giving their property to the Church, and thus heaping up treasure in heaven, was inexhaustible. They gave throughout their lifetime; they gave especially when death drew near. There were few who were willing to die unconfessed and intestate. The Church, which ceaselessly received, never alienated; both civil and ecclesiastical laws forbade. From time to time it suffered terrible spoliations, but it was the beneficiary of such great repentances that its wealth constantly increased from age to age.

The strength and tenacity of the Church have been the marvel of the ages. The invasions poured their flood of barbarism over Europe, but the Church stood, unsubmerged, above the waters; feudalism, that aftermath of barbarism, transformed all the other institutions of medieval Europe, but was powerless to alter fundamentally the constitution of the Church. And yet, because of its wealth, it seemed, for a time, as if the Church must be feudalized.

The possessions which the Church had obtained in the

The Church and Feudalism

age preceding feudalism, the episcopal and monastic domains, were then *allodial:* they were its property in full possession. The gifts which it received during the feudal era quite naturally possessed a feudal character. Not only so, but various influences were at work tending to feudalize all the possessions of the Church, and even the Church itself. In the feudal epoch the ecclesiastical authorities bestowed Church lands upon others, who thereby became the vassals of the abbey or bishopric or church, as the case might be, and with respect to these lands, whatever their origin, the church authorities were feudal suzerains. Furthermore, the bishops and abbots who, in this country and that, remained subject to certain obligations to the civil power, were frequently regarded *ipso facto* as feudally obligated to the civil power, and the lands they administered were consequently held to be fiefs.

Thus, while the clergy, as members of the Church, formed a hierarchy which was independent of the civil society of the time, they were, by virtue of their landed possessions, members, in a sense, of the feudal hierarchy. Grave inconveniences, both spiritual and temporal, resulted from their quasi-incorporation into the feudal structure. The clergy were obliged to perform many feudal functions incompatible with their ecclesiastical character. The freedom of church elections was materially diminished. It was practically inevitable, in cases where the holder of the church office would have to administer lands held feudally of a lay lord, that the latter should interfere in the election. In the third place, the financial situation of the Church was modified by feudalism. It is this particular phase of the relations between the Church and feudalism that will now be surveyed.

From the feudal point of view, the Church never enjoyed any general immunity for all its property. The feudal burdens which weighed upon the property of laymen weighed also upon the property of the Church, with the exception of what had been entrusted to it for purposes of almsgiving; the property which it possessed feudally was liable, in principle, to feudal burdens. But in fact, and by the very force of circumstances, the suzerain lost a considerable part of his income when the holder was a church. Reliefs, escheats, and similar sources of feudal wealth were cut off, since the Church never died; payments on alienation failed him, for the Church never alienated; there was no opportunity for forfeiture or confiscation; for the rule held that the Church should not suffer loss by reason of the wrong-doing of an individual cleric (*delictum personæ in damnum Ecclesiæ non est convertendum*). Moreover, the Church was rather awkwardly situated for fulfilling the military duties attached to a noble fief, since it was an accepted principle, although the practice was not always consistent, that he who became a soldier of Christ ceased to be a secular soldier. Manifestly, the suzerain of a church suffered real loss.

The advantages which the Church enjoyed, from the feudal point of view, were, however, counterbalanced by special burdens. For the feudal lords soon realized that the increase of the possessions of the Church was drying up their revenues, and they cleverly adjusted the feudal law to suit the needs of the situation.

The first royal attacks upon the immunity of the

The Church and Feudalism

clergy in France date back, perhaps, as far as Louis VII. This king, in order to raise funds for the second crusade, imposed such a heavy contribution upon the entire kingdom in 1146 that several abbeys had to sell or pledge their most precious possessions. Measures of this sort were repeated. We find the Council of Tours protesting against these exactions in 1163, and the general Lateran Council of 1179 prohibited the taxation of the churches without the previous consent of the bishops and the clergy.

Philip Augustus not only continued, but increased the taxation of the clergy. In 1188 he raised, *with the consent of clergy and people,* the famous Saladin tithe, which was so heavy that he solemnly promised the clergy and the barons, in 1189, never to renew it. Nevertheless, he did not cease to extort large sums of money from the churches and monasteries for the maintenance of his soldiers. The clergy, the whole people, in fact, complained of the exactions of Philip Augustus. His contemporary, Richard the Lion-Hearted, treated Normandy in the same way, notwithstanding the fact that the principle of the exemption of the Norman clergy from taxation was admitted.

The Lateran Council of 1215 renewed and strengthened the declarations of the Council of 1179. It laid down the important restriction that the bishops must henceforth consult the sovereign pontiff before consenting to a tax. The same Council exhibited its interest in the affairs of the Holy Land by decreeing a general tax, to last for three years, upon all ecclesiastical revenues. These two decisions opened a new era.

Medieval Civilization

From the year 1215 the place of the pope, in ecclesiastical taxation, became more and more important. At one time he defended the French churches against the demands of the king; at another, he granted the king the right to levy taxes upon them; and again, he himself taxed them for the purposes of a crusade, a quasi-crusade, or for any motive he chose to honor. Boniface VIII formulated in absolute terms the theory of the right of the pope to control absolutely the taxation of the clergy everywhere; and the French churches, from the thirteenth century on, made bitter lamentation over the burdens they had to bear.

Mention has just been made of the vacillating protection the pope gave the Church in France against royal taxation. Every one knows that the celebrated bull, *Clericis laicos,* issued by Boniface VIII in 1296, was called forth by the royal levy of two-tenths upon the ecclesiastical wealth of that kingdom. It is true that the bishops, convoked at Paris, had consented to the levy. But the powerful Cistercian monks refused to submit. They addressed a vehement protest to the pope: "These docile bishops," they said, "are mute dogs who cannot bark," and they added that Philip was a new Pharaoh. Boniface VIII entertained the appeal, and issued his bull, *Clericis laicos,* threatening with excommunication and anathema both the laymen who collected and the clerics who paid taxes on church property without papal authorization. At the same time, Boniface declared that if ever the kingdom of France was in danger, he would hasten to command the Church to strip herself of her property for the common welfare.

The Church and Feudalism

In 1297 Philip and Boniface were reconciled and the pope accorded to the king a double tenth, and also recognized his and his successor's right to ask and receive contributions from the clergy, *for the defense of the kingdom,* without the further authorization of the Holy See.

After the celebrated incident of 1296–7, as before, the levy of ecclesiastical tenths by the king of France was incessant, and many were the dolorous lamentations of the clergy. At times the kings availed themselves of their right, conceded in 1297, to tax the clergy for the defense of the kingdom, and again they sought, and obtained, special authorizations from the pope.

Probably the property of the Church, whatever its source or special purpose, was usually subject to these tenths; they were taxes on the church revenues, whatever the source of the revenues.

From Carolingian times down to the beginning of the fourteenth century, the churches, in their search for protectors and guarantees, frequently had their territorial possessions confirmed by the king or the sovereign pontiff. Such confirmations were less frequent at the end of the thirteenth century, were very rare at the beginning of the fourteenth, and thereafter ceased entirely. The fact is that the two great protectors of the churches, the pope and the king, were thenceforward too frequent and insistent in their demands for pecuniary aid. The churches ceased to beg them to defend their property; they strove to defend it *against* them.

It was a feudal principle, firmly established from the beginning, that a fief could not be alienated or curtailed without the authorization of the suzerain. This principle was utilized to hedge about with obstacles the acquisition of property by the Church, or at least to secure compensation. In a considerable number of countries the acquisition of landed possessions by the Church was absolutely forbidden. Such a prohibition was merely an extension, a working out, of the feudal principle which required that the suzerain must authorize every curtailment or alienation of the fief. When the king, for example, forbade the Church to acquire fresh lands, we have merely a case in which the supreme suzerain refused this authorization once for all. The methods adopted in other countries were not always so harsh. In some cases the Church was conceded a year and a day in which to dispose of its newly acquired property. The Church, in other words, had to alienate its new *immovable,* retaining in its own hands, of course, the proceeds of the sale, or else it had to devise some combination which might be considered equivalent to alienation. In several of the provinces of France, the Church was permitted to furnish the suzerain with a *living and dying man,* a sort of vicar whose death should place the suzerain in the same position, as to the exercise of feudal rights, as if the vicar were the vassal.

The churches themselves were very commonly feudal suzerains. In such cases it was as much to their interest as it was to the interest of any lay suzerain that their vassals should live and die, especially die. And as a church did not die, it was as unsatisfactory a vassal for a clerical suzerain as for a lay suzerain. Accordingly, we find that ecclesiastical suzerains took the same precautions toward ecclesiastical vassals as lay suzerains did. We have repeated proofs of this from the charters.

The Church and Feudalism

Both lay and ecclesiastical suzerains, however, devised at an early time a scheme for safeguarding their rights which was much simpler than either of the two just discussed. They authorized ecclesiastical bodies, in return for an adequate indemnity, to acquire lands in vassalage. This is the right of *amortissement,* which appeared in the eleventh century and was commonly employed in the twelfth and in the thirteenth. A fifteenth-century author, in a little book on feudalism, explains the right as follows:

Question: " What is *amortissement?* "

Answer: "*Amortissement* is a grant or concession which a lord of high justice makes to persons or people of the Church, communities, or other artificial persons, to hold a certain piece of property in their hands in perpetuity, and by it the suzerain renounces, for himself and his heirs, all right to compel them to put the said property out of their hands."

Question: " Why was *amortissement* devised? "

Answer: "*Amortissement* was devised because churchmen willingly bought property but never sold any. If they continued at liberty to buy freely and without the consent of the aforesaid lord high justiciar, like ordinary individuals, nothing would escape purchase at their hands."

This citation shows that the system of amortissement, originally devised against acquisitions by the Church, was extended to acquisitions by lay communities and colleges, which, like the churches, never died, and also, like them, never sold.

The right of amortissement was seen to offer a convenient method for extracting money from the Church.

Accordingly, the suzerain (of the lord who had granted the concession) took the ground that *his* rights could not be affected by such a grant; he seized the property which a church, for example, had just acquired under a deed of amortissement, and refusing to allow this church to hold it, demanded that the church should put it out of its hands within a year and a day (the old limitation), or come to terms with *him*. In this way the church had to buy exemption a second time. Nor did its troubles end here, for the suzerain of the suzerain of the lord from whom the church had acquired the property insisted that *his* rights be compounded for, and so on, until the king, the supreme suzerain, was reached. The burden became so crushing that in 1275 King Philip the Rash decided that all ecclesiastics who could produce letters of amortissement from three suzerains, in addition to the lord from whom they had first acquired the land, should not be disturbed in their possession. But this amelioration of the lot of the churches was soon counterbalanced by an increase in the cost of the right, and by its extension from feudal to allodial lands.

Philip the Rash, in his ordinance of 1275, held that a piece of property was effectively transferred to an artificial person if the right had been purchased from three successive suzerains, even if the king was not one of the three. Charles V laid down a rule which was more favorable to the monarchy: he declared that the king (for himself and for the whole kingdom) had the sole final right to liberate from the obligations of mortmain. The lords, who were subjects of the king, might liberate from these obligations all the property held by them, as far as concerned their rights; but no property whatever was to be regarded as fully liberated until the king had made the final grant. So long as he had not received the money to which he had a right, he might require the possessors to put the property out of their hands within a year and a day, under penalty of confiscation.

The Church protested against all these financial interferences—against the tenths and the *tailles,* against the customary obligation to empty its hands within a fixed period, and sometimes even against the requirement to purchase liberation from this obligation. Many church councils demanded exemption not only from all taxation on the lands of the Church, but even on the hereditary property of the clerks. The protestations and complaints of the Church never produced any permanent result.

If the laymen were frightened at the prodigious growth of property in mortmain,—a not unreasonable fear at a time when land was almost the sole wealth,—the churches, for their part, had their fears, although they were of quite another order. It is curious, but true, that these fears gave rise, now and then, to precautions analogous to those taken by the lay portion of society. We see powerful churches disturbed by the possible entry into their territories of personages who might become for them troublesome or redoubtable vassals; we see them bar the way to lords and to knights who, turbulent, grasping, or thievish, would have quickly crushed a pacific abbey. Hence those regulations or conventions which prohibited a knight acquiring any ecclesiastical territories; for the caprice of an enterprising knight might, at any moment, overturn the whole equilibrium of the country-side. Certain churches went to the length of forbidding such laymen even to enter their territories. Some Italian abbeys prudently inserted in their emphyteutic leases a clause which permitted subletting except to two classes of persons: knights and churches. Both of these were importunate guests, although for different reasons. The powerful commune of Strasburg was especially afraid of churches; it inserted in a certain contract of enfeoffment a provision which forbade any sort of alienation that should redound to the benefit of any church whatsoever. The republic of Strasburg finally forbade any legacy for pious purposes.

Lay society, however, was not always perfectly contented with such measures of defense against the excessive wealth of the Church. There were ardent spirits who could not be satisfied with what they considered mere palliatives. These radicals lifted up their voices for confiscation. In the twelfth century, Arnold of Brescia maintained that neither the secular nor the regular clergy ought to possess landed property. In the fourteenth, Wyclif taught that temporal princes had a right to confiscate the property of the Church if it were abused or misused. In the fifteenth, John Huss went even further than this, and asserted that any one who should maintain that the priests and Levites might have temporal possessions was the greatest of heretics. Such demands were not novel; they were nothing but a translation into revolutionary language of the aspirations of a Joachim de Flore and a John of Parma. Nay, more: the whole Franciscan order was a permanent protest against a wealthy clergy, and it itself issued from a still earlier movement.

The Church and Feudalism

Adapted from C. Seignobos, in Lavisse et Rambaud:
Histoire Générale, Vol. II, 1893, pp. 43-45.

FEUDALISM did not involve the abandonment by the clergy of their ancient organization, whose foundation principles were the hierarchy of offices and the absolute obedience of inferiors to superiors. Even in the most confused epochs, when the " spirit of the times " affected the clergy most deeply, the Church never incorporated a feudal principle into its organization, and the inferior churchman never did homage to a superior churchman nor accepted from him his office as a fief.

Clerks, like women, were in theory strangers to feudalism, since they were forbidden by the law of the Church to bear arms. Nevertheless, the clergy, at least the higher clergy, had, like the women, their part in the feudal régime, for the parish priests who served their bishop or the patron of their church, and the monks who rendered obedience to their abbot, were in a state of subjection not unlike that of the tenant to his lord.

The higher clergy possessed great domains, the accumulated gifts of centuries, presented to the Church in every Christian land by lay proprietors seeking their favor, in order that the patron saint of church or abbey might make intercession in heaven on their behalf.

Hence the landowners frequently gave, especially by way of bequest, to a saint or his church, " for the redemption of their sins " or " for the safety of their soul," a part of their "terrestrial property," often some pieces of land, sometimes whole villages. There was no bishopric, abbey, chapter of canons, or collegiate church which had not in this way become a great landowner. Because of their riches, they required, like lay lords, an escort of soldiers to defend them or enhance their dignity, and they accordingly divided up a portion of the church lands into fiefs and secured vassals who owed them homage and service.

The bishops and abbots were assimilated, since the time of Charlemagne, with the high officials of the State. They owed homage to the king, and were bound to lead their men to his army. This usage held its ground in the north of the kingdom of France, and took such root in the kingdom of Germany that the bishops and abbots came, at length, to consider their ecclesiastical offices as fiefs held of the king, and received investiture from him by receiving a banner in the same fashion as lay recipients of fiefs.

The prelates thus formed a superior class of the clergy, which fused with the higher feudal nobility. In all Christian lands, these prelates, as celibates, could not recruit their ranks by heredity, and their successors were almost always chosen from clerks of noble birth. Ecclesiastical dignities served thus as a provision for younger sons of great families. Many of these retained in their high ecclesiastical offices the habits of their youth; they continued to be hunters, topers, and warriors, after the fashion of the well-known archbishop of Mainz who, to avoid

The Church and Feudalism

the shedding of blood, which was forbidden to a church-man, fought with a club.

The monasteries required defense against the knights who lived near them, and who were not always to be intimidated by excommunication. Many of them came to an understanding with a lord, who undertook to defend them in return for dues to be collected from the monastery's tenants. Such a lord was known as the monastery's guardian or advocate. As a rule, the advocate was an oppressor rather than a defender, and the monastic documents teem with complaints against the advocates. The bishops also had, occasionally, lay defenders of this sort.

The Exercise of Feudal Rights over the Church in Languedoc, 900 - 1250

Adapted from A. Molinier, in Dom. Cl. Devic et Dom. J. Vaissete: *Histoire Générale de Languedoc,* Édition Privat, Vol. VII, 1879, pp. 167–171.

IN the Middle Ages the Church had possession of the greater part of the arable land, and the feudal era, when brute force only too often triumphed over right, exposed it to a variety of dangers.

The churches of Languedoc had received rich gifts and most extensive privileges from the Carolingian princes, and when feudalism became prevalent they sought to keep intact the heritage of the past. As long as a king of the legitimate line reigned at Paris or Laon, the bishops and abbots sought from him the confirmation of their privileges, and many of the prelates secured further confirmations from the Capetians. By such measures, the majority of the cathedral churches of Languedoc obtained possession of a number of sovereign rights within their dioceses, and when the time of feudal usurpations came, some of them were able to offer a successful resistance. In general the feudal powers made serious inroads upon them, and it was only after the reforms of

The Church in Languedoc

Gregory VII, and the journeys of Urban II and Calixtus II into Languedoc, that they regained the tithes and secured the restoration of the members of the clergy to the enjoyment of all their privileges.

The lands of the Church were spoken of as *allodial;* they were considered free. As such, they were exempt from all the imposts which bore so heavily upon the rest of the country. The Church had no tax to pay for the houses which it owned in the cities. Its buildings enjoyed the right of asylum, and this right, though often violated, was always formally recognized.

The Carolingian epoch witnessed the imposition of burdens upon the Church. The majority of the cathedral churches and abbeys of the Frankish kingdom had secured the royal protection (*mundium*). This naturally placed them, the protected, under obligations to their protector, and in virtue of their position the abbot and the bishop were regarded as the vassals of the prince, and their lands were said to be held of him as benefices. The count, who was the local representative of the royal power, quite as naturally exercised a certain jurisdiction over the lands in question, and this increased as the monarchy declined. When, about the middle of the tenth century, the royal power ceased to be felt in Languedoc, the prelates became the vassals of the count, who, so far as authority over the Church was concerned, now stepped into the royal shoes. The Church remained in about the same condition as in the first period of the feudal era; it had to submit to the same yoke, although the weight was probably heavier by reason of the nearness of the suzerain.

The peculiar situation in which the cathedral and abbey

churches thus found themselves exposed the election of
the bishops and abbots to lay influences, *i. e.,* to simony.
This trafficking in ecclesiastical offices had existed from
an early period, and had been a common practice of the
Merovingian kings. Charlemagne repressed it, but it
reappeared under his successors, and in the tenth century
was still common. For example, Guigo, although canonically elected, could not become bishop of Gérone until he
had received formal consent from Charles the Simple.
In the succeeding age, when the bishoprics had become
veritable fiefs, the offices were sold. In a list of possessions which he divided among his children in 1002, Roger
the Old, count of Carcassonne, includes bishoprics and
abbeys. Several extant charters prove that the bishop-
elect, before entering into possession of his see, had to
pay to the prince of the land a sum of money varying according to time and place. The right to receive the gift
made by the bishop on his election, the *donum de episcopo
Albiensi,* was presented by Count Pons to his wife, in
1037, as a dowry. A certain family partition of 1035 involved the greatest abbeys of lower Languedoc, just as if
they were so many fiefs, and the suzerain of these " fiefs "
had the right to choose the abbot (*electio*) and to receive
the customary gift (*donum*). In 1038 the bishopric of
Albi was a true fief; the reversion was sold to a certain
individual who was not even called a clerk, and the payment he made for the ultimate right of succession was
divided between the count of Toulouse, who was the overlord, and the immediate suzerain. In 1132 the overlord
sold out his right of *electio* to the immediate suzerain.
The history of the sale of the archbishopric of Narbonne

gives the clearest possible evidence of the state of affairs. It was sold to the ten-year-old son of the count of Cerdagne. The count himself was a man of exemplary piety, the founder of a monastery, and the viscount of Narbonne gave a fully detailed account of the whole commercial transaction before an assembly of prelates.

By reason of this vassalage, the bishop had to take the oath of fidelity to his suzerain. In 1069 the bishop of Urgel swore fidelity to the count of Cerdagne and formally admitted that he and his successors were bound in perpetuity, and that the bishop must take the oath before he could exercise his functions.

The right to take possession of the property of a deceased bishop, abbot, or parish priest (*droit de dépouilles*) and to pillage it was another right which was exercised by the feudal lord over the Church. Prelates and priests were thus regarded as subject to the rules of mortmain, and were held incapable of making a will. There is no doubt that from the eleventh century many a bishop was freed from this barbarous right. We know that in 974 the bishop of Toulouse, and in 1006 the archbishop of Narbonne, freely disposed of their movable and immovable property by will; but perhaps they enjoyed this privilege because of their noble birth, and their relationship to the princes of the land. Whether this be so or not, our knowledge of this feudal right is derived only from the charters of exemption granted by feudal lords to churches. The first bears the date of 1084, coming thus from the epoch when Gregory VII fought his great battle against simony. In it the count of Toulouse renounced the exercise of the right at Béziers, and authorized the bishops to leave their property to the cathedral clergy. We have several similar charters from the first half of the twelfth century. In 1163 exemption from this right is mentioned in a diploma of Louis VII in favor of the church of Lodève. Already in 1137 Louis had granted this exemption to all the episcopal churches in the province of Bordeaux. Many other cases might be adduced.

Notwithstanding the exemptions from the *droit de dépouilles* accorded to the various churches of Provence, fragmentary survivals of the right always remained. In 1213, Bernard of Béziers renounced his rights over the sacerdotal vestments and the equipage used by the bishop on his first entrance into his episcopal city. An analogous right was enforced against the property of the parish priests. This right, which several feudal lords of Rouergue renounced, appears to have been called the *right of testament.*

The Church was both rich and feeble, and, isolated in the midst of a divided and warring society, awakened the cupidity of all the unscrupulous barons. From the days of the Merovingians, the rich domains which it owed to the liberality of emperors, kings, and the faithful were a prey to the powerful men who were partitioning the land. Charlemagne found it impossible to restore the lost property of the Church, and by way of compensation established and enforced throughout the whole extent of his empire the obligation to pay the Jewish tithe upon all the fruits of the soil. But these tithes became an additional source of temptation to the laymen, who coveted even the country churches themselves. From the middle of the tenth century we find country churches trans-

The Church in Languedoc

formed into fiefs, and the priests who celebrated the offices therein were treated as vassals, administering the property of the lord. There is ample evidence that most of the country churches of Languedoc suffered this fate. The churches became a part of the patrimony of this or that lord; they were divided up, by halves, quarters, and eighths, etc., and underwent the usual vicissitudes of ordinary property.

The same fate overtook the tithes and first-fruits; they were usurped by the lords and either granted as fiefs to third persons or collected directly. In the majority of the cases of the sale of churches in the seventh century, with which we are familiar, the revenues which the priest was entitled to collect went along with the church, and these revenues must have been of considerable value, since the parishes were generally large, especially in southern Toulousain.

The prelates of Languedoc, backed up energetically by the Holy See, made great efforts to recover their property. In 990 a provincial council held at Narbonne decreed excommunication against those who kept ecclesiastical possessions. The most successful assembly in this particular, however, was held at Toulouse in 1054, under the presidency of a legate of Pope Nicholas II; several charters of restitution make references to it. To this council, no less than to the efforts of Gregory VII, Urban II, and Calixtus II, must be attributed, it would seem, the very marked movement toward the restoration of monasteries and the restitution of ecclesiastical property which signalized the beginning of the twelfth century.

It was the tithes, especially, which the prelates of the

twelfth century sought to have restored. The bishops of
Albi and Béziers, and the abbot of Lézat, in the diocese
of Toulouse, strove in this way to reconstitute the patrimony of the Church. One result was the appearance of
the large tithe-owners (*gros décimateurs*) ; the bishop of
Albi owned the greater part of the tithes in his diocese,
and in the eighteenth century the bulk of his income was
still derived from this source. The bishop of Béziers
secured the assistance of the count of Montfort, and
through his agency obtained, in 1211, the restitution of a
large number of tithes which had been conferred as fiefs.
Now and then the Church legalized the enfeoffment of
the tithes in return for an annual payment in wheat; at
other times the restorer of usurped tithes reserved the
right to act as collector and retain a percentage of the
product for his trouble. In 1215, the half of the tithes in
the diocese of Viviers was granted in fief to Simon de
Montfort for five years; at the end of that time he was
to return it, and he also agreed that he would compel the
laymen to pay their tithes.

This custom of securing the aid of powerful laymen by
the gift of a portion of its income was not a new one in
the Church. Abandoned by the kings, whose charters
were powerless to protect them, the abbeys at first secured the protection of the princes of the country, of the
new dynasties. For example, in 977 a sort of provincial
council, made up of the principal lay and ecclesiastical
lords of the Spanish March, confirmed the immunity enjoyed by the abbeys of Provence, including the right of
high justice. Frequently the churches made use of an
institution analogous to that of the *vidame* in the North,

The Church in Languedoc

and created officers whose duty it was to protect them, in return for certain revenues. About 960 Raoul, abbot of Figeac, transferred sixty churches to a lord of Rouergue, to be held by him in fief, on condition that he raised three hundred men for the defense of the monastery. In 1076 Artaud, count of Pailhas, acknowledged himself to be the *cavallarius* of the abbey of Cuxa, and promised faithfully to protect it against all enemies.

The Non-Universality of Feudalism

Adapted from G. Saige: *Une alliance défensive entre proprié-taires allodiaux au XIIième siècle. Bibliothèque de l'École des Chartes,* 1861, pp. 374, 375.

THE fief was by no means universal on the continent of Europe, even when feudalism was at its height. There were always territories where land continued to be held allodially. Such was the county of Toulouse, now a part of southern France, where, in the twelfth century, the allod was the general rule and the fief the exception. The land-holders were consequently free from all feudal services, but, on the other hand, they were left to their own resources for the defense of their lands in case of war or violent usurpation. It necessarily followed that, lacking a suzerain whose feudal duty it was to protect them, they were compelled to resort to other means to safeguard their property.

To be sure, they might beg the protection of a neighboring lord, but such protection was often illusory, and had this grave inconvenience, that it gave the lord an opportunity to assert rights over the property entrusted to his protection, and thus to absorb, to his own advantage, the independence of the allodial lands.

The allodial proprietors of Languedoc fully appreciated the peril, and they devised another method of defense, which gave them the same security and at the same time permitted them to escape the ruinous protection of a feudal lord. The method was, in brief, for several neighboring proprietors to join together and form a sort of league or confederation, in which all guaranteed reciprocal assistance to each. As long as the alliance held, each member was bound, in the interests of the common defense, to occupy those positions in the domains of his allies which were most menaced. The obligations of each member varied according to the importance of his property and according to the needs of adequate defense.

Byzantine Civilization

Adapted from C. Bayet, in Lavisse et Rambaud: *Histoire
Générale,* Vol. I, 1893, pp. 672–682.

FROM the middle of the ninth to the middle of the
eleventh century the Byzantine Empire enjoyed its
highest degree of prosperity. Constantinople was then,
in every one's estimation, the first city in the world. Since
then, unfortunately, the Byzantine city has almost entirely
disappeared. A part of the walls, and some churches
transformed into mosques, like St. Sophia, are the only
remains. In order to form an idea of its extent, and of
the number of buildings in the fourteen regions of which
it was composed, the texts must be consulted. Du Cange,
in his *Constantinopolis christiana* of the seventeenth
century, attempted to reconstruct the topography of the
city, and new researches have completed his work in some
respects. It is not possible to enter into these details here,
but it is important to notice that some institutions which
are considered peculiar to our modern cities were already
in existence at Constantinople. Such was, for example,
the department of public charities, which included a large
number of hospitals, orphan-asylums, and schools.

When strangers arrived at Constantinople they were
filled with naïve admiration for the imperial palaces,
which extended over entire quarters, the churches spark-

ling with the glory of mosaics, gold, and silver, and the squares and streets decorated with the masterpieces of ancient sculpture. No secondary account is as valuable as their direct testimony. The Jew, Benjamin of Tudela, who traveled over the world in the twelfth century, wrote:[1] " Great stir and bustle prevail at Constantinople in consequence of the conflux of many merchants, who resort thither, both by land and by sea, from all parts of the world for purposes of trade, including merchants from Babylon and from Mesopotamia, from Media and Persia, from Egypt and Palestine, as well as from Russia, Hungary, Patzinakia, Budia, Lombardy, and Spain. In this respect the city is equaled only by Bagdad, the metropolis of the Mohammedans. At Constantinople is the place of worship called St. Sophia, and the metropolitan seat of the pope of the Greeks, who are at variance with the pope of Rome. It contains as many altars as there are days of the year, and possesses innumerable riches, which are augmented every year by the contributions of the two islands and of the adjacent towns and villages. All the other places of worship in the whole world do not equal St. Sophia in riches. It is ornamented with pillars of gold and silver, and with innumerable lamps of the same precious materials. The Hippodrome is a public place near the wall of the palace, set aside for the king's sports. Every year the birthday of Jesus the Nazarene is celebrated there with public rejoicings. On these occasions you may see there representations of all the nations who inhabit the different parts of the world, with surprising feats of jugglery. Lions, bears, leopards, and

[1] Translation from Wright's Early Travels in Palestine.

wild asses, as well as birds, which have been trained to fight each other, are also exhibited."

He who is usually deplorably dry breaks into a veritable dithyramb when he remembers the riches of Constantinople: " The tribute which is brought to Constantinople every year from all parts of Greece, consisting of silks, and purple cloths, and gold, fills many towers. These riches and buildings are equaled nowhere in the world. They say that the tribute of the city alone amounts every day to twenty thousand florins, arising from rents of hostelries and bazaars, and from the duties paid by merchants who arrive by sea and by land. The Greeks who inhabit the country are extremely rich, and possess great wealth in gold and precious stones. They dress in garments of silk, ornamented with gold and other valuable materials. They ride upon horses, and in their appearance they are like princes. The country is rich, producing all sorts of delicacies, as well as abundance of bread, meat, and wine."

The Byzantine Empire had commercial relations with all the peoples who surrounded it. From Damascus and Aleppo it received the wares of the far East. When the Greeks reconquered Antioch, a treaty was made with the prince of Aleppo (969–970) ; freedom of trade for the caravans and the Greek merchants was stipulated, and we see that, if Antioch received Oriental goods which passed through it to the West, on the other hand articles of Byzantine manufacture, especially cloth stuffs, were exported to the Arabic lands.

On the north, Trebizond was very important as the warehouse for the trade of the Levant. The Arabic geographer Istakhri wrote in the tenth century: "Trebizond is the frontier city of the Greeks. All our merchants go there, all the cloths of Byzantine manufacture come there, all the brocades which are imported into our country come by way of Trebizond." In another direction the Greek merchants were in constant intercourse with Alexandria. At the beginning of the ninth century Leo V had forbidden the Greeks to go to Egypt and Syria, but such a prohibition could not be enforced. Eastern wares, spices from the Indies, drugs, precious stones, fabrics of Arabian silk, were carried then, in great quantities, to Constantinople, to Salonica, and to Cherson, and thence spread throughout the empire and among the neighboring countries.

Still farther north, the most ancient Russian chroniclers speak of a route from Constantinople to the Baltic, which started at the mouth of the Dnieper, on the Black Sea, and ended at the mouth of the Neva, after having passed the great cities of Kiev and Novgorod. It was less used by the Greek merchants than by the Scandinavians and the Russians. Many Russian merchants went to Constantinople, but they were very closely watched there; they had to live in a quarter outside the city, and were never allowed to remain during the winter. They carried with them furs, honey, wax, and slaves, and they took back silks, gold and silver brocades, and wine. It seems that the Byzantine wares reached Germany only through the agency of Venetians, Slavs, or Bulgarians. Bulgarian merchants had settled at Constantinople. To allay the jealousy of the Greek merchants an attempt was made to force them to move their shops to Salonica. This was the cause of the war between Leo VI and Czar Simeon.

Medieval Civilization

In France the Byzantine wares, which were very much sought after, came by way of Italy. Several Italian cities, especially Bari, Amalfi, and Venice, carried on an active commerce with the East. The Genoese and the Pisans did not have any commercial relations with Greece before the crusades.

The emperors have been blamed for not understanding " the advantages of a broad, commercial policy; " in fact, they adopted certain restrictive measures. The Byzantine custom-house officers allowed foreign wares to enter the empire only after having inspected and examined them minutely. The lead seal which they attached to the packages indicated that the import duties had been paid. The export of Greek products was watched with equal care. The luxurious fabrics were the principal objects of exportation to the West, but the emperors refused to let the most beautiful cloths, made in the imperial manufactories, go out of the country. They were reserved for the palace, for St. Sophia, and for the magnificent gifts made to foreign kings. They have also been blamed for giving up their commerce to foreigners, especially to Italians, and for burdening the exports with excessive duties, which are reckoned at ten per cent. It should not be forgotten that these duties, which did not prevent commerce, furnished to the empire a great part of the resources which it needed. There are no definite details for the total revenue of the Byzantine State, but from the partial records it is supposed that, at the time of the fourth crusade, they must have reached a sum which would be worth about $600,000,000 to-day. This figure is high; but, according to Benjamin of Tudela, Constantinople alone paid to the treasury nearly one sixth of this sum. In addition, it is certain that some emperors, thanks to their wise management, left considerable amounts in the treasury. Thus, after the death of Basil II, the reserve amounted to about $200,000,000 in our money. If this emperor, while paying ordinary expenses, effected such a saving, it must be admitted that the revenues of the empire were immense.

In addition to military strength and wealth, the empire can glory to a certain extent in its literature. At Byzantium, from the ninth to the twelfth century, there was a renaissance movement which produced neither genius nor talent of great originality, but shows at least a taste for intellectual pursuits and learned researches. Most of the manuscripts by which the works of Greek literature have been preserved date from this epoch.

The studies languished in the Orient after Justinian closed the schools of Athens and suppressed the teaching of law except at Constantinople and Beyrout. The great university of Constantinople, founded by Theodosius II in 425, became the only important center for study, and even there instruction was often neglected. Literature had taken on, since Justinian's time, an almost exclusively monastic character. An important reform was accomplished immediately after the iconoclastic controversy. Bardas, brother of the empress Theodora, very carefully reorganized the school in the palace of Magnaurus. Although he was opposed to the iconoclasts, he did not hesitate to place at the head of the school Leo, who had been archbishop of Salonica during the preceding reign, and had resigned when the images were reinstated. Philosophy, grammar, geometry, and astronomy were taught there. The professors were chosen from the wisest men of the day; students were admitted without charge to the courses. Those who worked were sure of the imperial favor, and the protection was not merely temporary. Under Constantine VII the schools at Constantinople were very prosperous. The masters figured among the great personages of the empire; official documents mention the " prince of the rhetoricians " and the " consul of the philosophers." Students could expect their knowledge to raise them to the highest offices. A historian of Constantine VII described him as admitting students to his table, chatting with them and encouraging them; from among them he chose his officials and bishops. If the university of Constantinople lost its prestige later, it rose again, in the eleventh century, under Constantine *Monomachos*, thanks to one of the most celebrated Byzantine scholars of the Middle Ages, Michael Psellus. After rising to the highest offices through his reputation as a scholar, Psellus reorganized the university and taught philosophy, and his friend Xiphilin taught law. Psellus lectured on the philosophers and the ancient poets. Even Arabs came to listen to him. His success alarmed the Church and the emperor; the university was closed, and Psellus retired into a monastery.

The emperors themselves set the example, and several of them are known as authors. Basil I, although a soldier of fortune, attempted to bring the law of Justinian into favor again by two manuals, the *Prochiron,* which was published between 870 and 879, and the *Epanagogos,* between 879 and 886; but the latter was not officially pro-

Byzantine Civilization

mulgated. His eldest son, Constantine, wrote a treatise on tactics. His second son, Leo VI, was a poet, theologian, and writer on military matters; he continued the juridical work of his father, and published the vast collection of the *Basilica* in sixty books. Constantine VII *Porphyrogenetos* directed the literary movement of his age, and wrote the life of Basil, the founder of the dynasty. In the book of *Themes* he traced—in a very defective manner, it is true—the political geography of the empire. His treatise upon *The Administration of the Empire* is a manual of diplomacy composed for his son. In it he reviews the peoples with which Byzantium had dealings; he describes their institutions and indicates the policy which ought to be followed toward them. The last chapters give some details upon the internal organization. In his work upon *Ceremonies of the Court of Byzantium*, along with a manual of imperial etiquette, there are documents of all kinds and schedules of expenses for some expeditions. These traditions were not lost in the eleventh century; for Cæsar Nicephorus Briennius wrote a history of his own times, and his wife, the learned and ambitious Anna Comnena, celebrated, in her *Alexiad*, the reign of her father Alexius I.

This literature is especially distinguished for its erudition. In the presence of the treasure of learning and the works which antiquity had bequeathed to them, the Greeks of Byzantium were dazzled, and often lost the feeling for their own individuality. They thought of little else than placing themselves in the midst of all these riches and making an inventory of them; they formed immense collections of extracts, notes, and summaries.

Medieval Civilization

Photius, the most illustrious of the Byzantine scholars, was a compiler. He seems to have read everything, pagan or Christian, which the Hellenic literature had produced, in order to compose his *Library* or *Myriobiblos,* a vast collection of analyses and selections. Constantine *Porphyrogenetos* and the group of writers who worked under his orders were inveterate compilers. Constantine found that the historical works were so numerous that no one dared to venture into this confused medley, which frightened people even when they heard it spoken of. " In order to aid the drowning science " he got together all these works and had extracts and summaries made in fifty-three books; two were to be devoted to *Embassies,* one to *Conspiracies,* one to the *Capture of Cities,* one to *Sentences,* etc. Only a small part of this immense collection is extant. Another collection, the *Geoponics,* contains extracts upon agriculture, in twenty books. Others relate to morals, military science, medicine, or veterinary science. Symeon Metaphrastus, one of the chief officials of Constantine VII, compiled a celebrated collection of *Lives of the Saints.* He preceded the Bollandists, but he was an uncritical Bollandist. In the last half of the tenth century and at the beginning of the eleventh, Suidas, author of the lexicon so well known under this name, was merely a compiler. Many ancient works were lost because of these curious encyclopedias; when the latter were at hand, people too often ceased to read and copy the originals.

Although this spirit dominates the literature, it would be wrong to limit our attention to this side alone. Minds were not always bound slavishly to tradition. Sometimes in his sermons Photius applied the doctrine of Plato to

Byzantine Civilization

Christianity; he even recognized that it was right to examine critically the text of the Holy Bible. He refused to see in earthquakes or hurricanes signs of the divine anger chastising men or showing disapprobation of contemporary events. In a dialogue, *Philopatris,* or *The Friend of his Country,* which was long attributed to Lucian, and dates from the second half of the tenth century, the interlocutors discuss religion and politics freely, and one defends the pagan beliefs. Apparently, this work was intended as a defense of the measures of Nicephorus Phocas against the monks. There were many historians and chroniclers during this period, and in general they were more exact and intelligent than those of the preceding epoch. Some works of Psellus give a vivid idea of the society in the eleventh century, and at times they are written in a lively manner. Finally, poetry produced epopees inspired by contemporary events, which may be called the *chansons de gestes* of the Orient. In Asia, the struggles against the Arabs gave birth to heroic and marvelous tales,—*tragoudia,* or melodies,—which occasionally a more learned author brought together in a poem. Such is the recently discovered epopee of Digenis Akritas, defender of the empire in the tenth century and the terror of the Saracens, but weak in love. The hero of this poem, in which warlike and fanciful themes are mingled, really lived under the name of Pantherius. Many of the Greek popular songs of the Middle Ages have been handed down from one generation to another until our own day.

It was also a beautiful period for Byzantine art. The emperors were great builders. Constantine VII was an artist as well as an author. He painted, he directed sculptors and goldsmiths. The great imperial palace at Constantinople was added to until it covered an entire quarter. The texts by which modern scholars have been able to reconstruct its plan and appearance overwhelm our imagination with the unheard-of luxury which they depict. Religious architecture, which always followed the cupola style, attempted a revival by giving more elegant proportions to the churches, as in the church of the Mother of God at Constantinople, and others. In painting, most of the beautiful mosaics and mural decorations of that age have disappeared; but some manuscripts with miniatures, like the *Psalter* of the ninth or tenth century which is preserved in the *Bibliothèque Nationale,* show a curious attempt on the part of the artists to free themselves from the monastic influence and to draw inspiration, even for Christian subjects, from the compositions and style of ancient art. If this tendency seems to have waned very soon, nevertheless sacred iconography, as it then took shape, is distinguished by certain qualities of workmanship and by remarkably well arranged compositions. The sculptors had practically ceased to make large statues, but the Byzantine artists made a great many ivory caskets and diptychs. Specimens of these are to be found in all the great museums of Europe, and they delight us by the delicacy of the workmanship, and at times by the beauty and elegance of the figures. The goldsmiths produced superb objects in gold and silver, decorated with enamel. Very many of these were carried off at the time of the capture of Constantinople, and first enriched the churches and, later, the museums of the West. For instance, St. Marks at Venice possesses a treasury made up largely of Byzantine objects; the most beautiful of

Byzantine Civilization

all is the great reredos known as the *Pala d'Oro,* which is adorned with twenty-four enameled pictures or figures. The popularity of the fabrics which were made in Greece has been mentioned already. Very many of them depicted scenes and were covered with ornaments, fantastic animals, or designs, so that they were really works of art; the imperial dalmatica kept in St. Peter's at Rome shows several religious scenes, in particular a " Triumph of Christ " in which there are fifty-four figures.

Until the eleventh century it may be said that Byzantine art was the only Christian art which actually possessed originality. Its influence spread widely. Russian art was formed in this school, and after the conversion of Vladimir his successors endeavored at Kiev to copy Constantinople when they constructed or decorated churches. Georgian and Armenian art bear a family resemblance to Greek art. Even the Arabs, hostile to the Christian name and the empire, were in this respect tributary to Byzantium; the califs of Damascus and Cordova borrowed its artists. In the West, if we visit to-day Sicily, southern Italy, Rome, or Venice, we constantly find persistent traces of the Byzantine influence. These are also to be found in France, whose Roman architecture is connected with Byzantine architecture; and a whole group of churches in Périgord, Angoumois, and Saintonge are in the style of the Oriental cupola.

In short, in the history of medieval civilization, before the eleventh century, Byzantium played a rôle analogous to that of Athens and Rome in antiquity or Paris in modern times. Its influence extended over the whole world; it was preëminently *the city.*

Moslem Civilization in Spain

Adapted from A. Dozy: *Recherches sur l'histoire et la littérature de l'Espagne pendant le moyen âge,* 1881, Vol. II, pp. 103, 104, and Vol. I, pp. 241–265.

IN certain respects, the two peoples who, in the eleventh century, were disputing over the remnants of the califate of Cordova were as unlike as possible. Vivacious, ingenious, and civilized, but enervated and skeptical, the Moors lived only for pleasure; while the Spaniards of the North, still semi-barbaric, but brave and animated by the most ardent fanaticism, cared only for war, and wanted it gory. However, these two nations, so different in appearance, really had several traits in common: both were corrupt, perfidious, and cruel; and if the Moors were generally indifferent enough about matters of faith, if they consulted astrologers in preference to doctors of religion, if they were not ashamed to serve under a Christian prince, there were a great many Castilian knights who did not scruple " to live by fortune," as they said then, to take Mussulmans into their pay, to wage war against their religion and country under the standard of an Arab knight, or to pillage and burn cloisters and churches.

At this time the principality of Almeria, although it was not as important as it had been, was still of considerable

size. But after the death of Man, in consequence of revolts on the part of governors and the encroachments of
neighboring princes, it became smaller and smaller.
After 1054, when Motacim reigned alone, everything went
from bad to worse. Seeing the throne of Almeria occupied by a young man without experience or military talent, the other princes thought they had a right to take
from this feeble neighbor the cities and districts which
were conveniently located, so that Motacim was soon deprived of all his States, with the exception of his capital
and its environs.

It was a very little kingdom—so small, in fact, that contemporaries spoke of it only jokingly, and the more so
because, as a whole, it had few natural advantages. For
example, this is the way that an Arab author speaks of it:
" This province is very small, it produces little, and the
whole can be seen in a single glance; the clouds rain upon
it their beneficent drops to no advantage, for it produces
neither fruit nor grain; almost all the fields are barren,
nothing but wormwood grows there. But, may Allah
forgive me! I am forgetting to speak of the river
Péchina, this great river which sometimes becomes as big
as a rope! Its source often dries up, but it is consoled
when the drops of dew or rain come to swell it." In
these malicious words there is a great deal of truth. The
country between Almanzora and Almeria is sandy and
barren, and the plain which extends from Almeria to the
Cape of Gata is a veritable desert. On the other hand,
the country is more fertile toward the southwest. The
plain of Daleya is not cultivated now, but at that time
some reservoirs built by the Moors were still to be seen,

and, if we can believe a modern traveler, a few springs would be enough to change it into a delightful garden. This it was under the Moors.

On the whole, in spite of the narrow limits of his kingdom, Motacim was not so badly off; especially as his capital, thanks to commerce and industry, was flourishing and prosperous. In only a few points did it resemble the present Almeria; for if the Moorish aspect of the city, with its low and flat-roofed houses, if the pleasing manners and exquisite politeness of its inhabitants, if the melodious voices and somewhat swarthy complexions of its women, still recall to memory this noble nation which was once the most civilized and enterprising in the world, nothing, on the contrary, except its ruins, leads us to suspect that in the Middle Ages Almeria was the most important port in Spain, that it was frequented by Syrian and Egyptian vessels, as well as Pisan and Genoese; that it contained a thousand inns and four thousand weaving-looms; and that it made all kinds of utensils of iron, copper, and glass.

The sovereign who dwelt there was the finished model of the most pleasing virtues. Peaceful above all else, and not desiring to trouble the quiet of his subjects for questions of personal interest, he was content in his little State and did not seek to enlarge it. He treated his kinsmen, people, and soldiers with fatherly kindness, and strangers who came to his court were welcomed with generous hospitality. An enlightened patron of art and learning, he encouraged and recompensed talents of every nature. Full of respect for religion and its ministers, he loved to hear fakirs discourse upon the sacred texts, and for this

Moslem Civilization in Spain

purpose assembled them regularly, once a week, in a room in his palace. He governed justly. When he built the magnificent palace since known as the Çomâdihîa, the workmen took possession of a garden which belonged to some orphans. Their guardian protested in vain against this arbitrary action. Then he resolved to appeal to the prince. So one day when Motacim was in his park he saw in the canal which traversed it a floating reed closed with wax at both ends. He had it brought to him, and, breaking the wax, he found a note in which the guardian accused him of being responsible in God's sight for the injustice committed by his workmen. The prince summoned the latter immediately, scolded them severely, and, although the land in question was necessary for the symmetry of the buildings, he restored it to the orphans. When the palace was completed every one saw that there was something lacking. When some one called the prince's attention to this he responded: "You are perfectly right; but as I had to choose between being blamed by men of taste, and by Allah, my choice could not be doubtful. I assure you that to me the most pleasing part of my palace is precisely the missing portion."

Besides being just, Motacim loved to pardon offenses. He had heaped a poet with his favors; but when the latter went to Seville to the court of Motadhia ibn-Abbâd he was so ungrateful that he dared to insert this verse in a dithyramb composed in honor of this prince:

"Ibn-Abbâd exterminated the Berbers, Ibn-Man the chickens in his villages."

Motacim was informed of the poet's joke; but the careless child of the muses had forgotten it and returned to

Medieval Civilization

Almeria some time later. When he was invited to supper at the palace he was very much astonished to see on the table nothing but chickens. " But, my lord," he said, " have you nothing else to eat in Almeria except chickens?" "We have other things," replied Motacim, " but I wanted to show you that you were mistaken when you said that Ibn-Man had exterminated the chickens in his villages." The poet then recalled his unfortunate verses and attempted to make an excuse; but the prince said: " Don't be uneasy; a man of your profession makes his living only when he acts as you have done; I am angry only with the prince who heard you recite this verse and did not protest when you insulted one of his equals." Then wishing to show the poet that he did not harbor malice, he gave him some presents.

Certainly, if such a noble, generous, just, and peaceful prince had ruled at another time and over a more extensive land, his name would be illustrious among those truly great rulers who do not owe their renown to the torrents of blood shed in order to extend the limits of their states by a few leagues, but to the good that they did, and to the measures that they took for improving the condition of their subjects. At that time such kings were rare, as in all times, and, compared with the other princes who were then ruling in Spain, Motacim was an extraordinary man in every respect. He had nothing in common with the other princes except one characteristic: he was passionately fond of literature, and we shall attempt to give a sketch, however weak and imperfect it may be, of the literary movement at the little court of Almeria.

Moslem Civilization in Spain

The munificence of Motacim had already drawn to his capital a large number of wits when one day a poor young man appeared; he was badly dressed, and no one knew him. He came from the village of Berja, where he had been brought up by his father, a man of great wit and learning, and his name was Abou-'l Fadhl Djafar ibn-Charaf. He had been seized by the idea of going to Almeria to seek his fortune, and, in spite of his more than modest costume, he dared to present himself at the palace, hoping that his title of poet (for he was one) would suffice to open its doors to him. His hopes were realized, and when he stood in the presence of the prince he recited a poem which began thus:

"For a long time Night, very slow in departing, had been promising that the Dawn would appear; and the stars were already complaining of their long watch, when suddenly a fresh breeze came out of the East to scatter the darkness. Then the flowers breathed forth their perfume, and Aurora rose, blushing with modesty, but cheeks bathed with dew, while Night passed from one star to another, giving them permission to seek repose; then they sank slowly, one after another, as the leaves fall from the trees."

Continuing in this style, Ibn-Charaf ended his poem with a pompous eulogy of Motacim.

The prince was charmed with what he had just heard, and loudly expressed his admiration for the young poet who knew how to clothe his thoughts in such fresh and gracious colors. From that moment the fortune of Ibn-Charaf was made. He himself might perchance still be ignorant of it, but the poets of the court had no doubt about it, and some of them were extremely jealous of him. One of these was Ibn-okht-Ghânim of Malaga. His real name was Abou-Abdallâh Mohammed ibn-Mamar; but as he was not of distinguished rank by birth, and as his father had no other merit than being the husband of the sister of the celebrated philologist Ghânim, he was never called anything but Ibn-okht-Ghânim, *the son of the sister of Ghânim,* a very disagreeable and humiliating nickname for a man who lived in such a rich and aristocratic society as the Andalusian then was. Moreover, he was a very good poet and a veritable well of science. He had read an immense number of books on grammar, jurisprudence, theology, and medicine; and, more than that, he knew them by heart, for he had a prodigious memory. But he was envious, and he saw in the newcomer a rival who might well supplant him, some day, in the favor of the sovereign. Wishing, accordingly, to confuse him, he began to look at his rustic costume with very impertinent curiosity, and asked him from what desert he came. He paid dearly for his insolence. Without being disconcerted, Ibn-Charaf, whose name taken in the sense of an appellation signifies *son of the nobility,* replied proudly: " Although my costume is that of an inhabitant of the desert, I am, however, of a noble family. I have no reason to blush for my rank, and I am not known by the name of a maternal uncle." He had the laugh on his side, and for the moment his adversary, ashamed of his discomfiture, kept silent; but later he took revenge in composing the following satire against Ibn-Charaf:

" Ask the poet of Berja if he thinks that he comes

from Irac and has the genius of Bohtorî. This plagiarist brings poems which cry out when he holds them in his hand, ' What, then! ought we to be attributed to this insipid rhymster?' Really, Djafar, leave poetry to the true poets, cease to imitate unsuccessfully the great masters, and make haste to renounce your ridiculous pretensions, for the delicate lips of Poesy repudiate your unclean kisses."

Fortunately, Ibn-Charaf could do without the esteem of the nephew of Ghânim. He had been successful in pleasing the sovereign, who heaped favors upon him. Once, when he had trouble with a steward who wished to make him pay too heavy taxes for a field which he cultivated near a village, he complained to the monarch; afterward he recited to him a poem containing this verse:

" Under the reign of this prince all tyranny has disappeared, except that exercised by the maidens with bright eyes and slender forms."

" How many houses [bait] are there in the village of which you were speaking to me?" Motacim asked. "About fifty," replied Ibn-Charaf. "Well," the prince replied, "I will give them to you for this single verse [bait]." And he at once gave him the whole village, with exemption from all taxes.

Ibn-Charaf was not merely a poet: he was also distinguished in medicine; and he published two collections of moral maxims, one in prose, the other in verse. Some of these sayings have been preserved, and the following may be given as an example:

" It is better to confide in your own strength, however small it may be, than in that of your friends, how-

ever great the latter may seem; for a living man supported by his own legs, which are only two, is stronger
than a dead man borne by the legs of those who carry him
to the cemetery, although they are eight in number."

Among the poets at the court of Motacim, Abou-Abdallâh ibn-al-Haddâd of Guadix was especially distinguished. In his youth he had been madly in love with a
Christian girl named Djamîla, whom he celebrated in
verse under the name of Nowaïra; for the Arab poets,
like those of Rome, were accustomed to address their
mistresses by assumed names. However, he appears not
to have been always a faithful lover, if we may judge by
the advice which he gave in this piece:

" Deceive your mistress as she deceives you, and you
will be just; learn to overcome by forgetfulness and carelessness the love which she has inspired in you! For
young girls are as beautiful and as prodigal of their gifts
as rose-bushes; a passer-by has plucked one rose, the next
one plucks another."

This prolific poet—his collected verses formed three
large volumes—enjoyed great favor from Motacim, and
he deserved it by his ability and varied knowledge, for he
was eminent also as a mathematician and philosopher.
He wrote upon versification, and he solved riddles with
rare ease, a talent which the Arabs appreciate especially.
But he lost the good will of the prince by his ingratitude,
his irascible temper, and his caustic wit. Motacim was
not easily angered. When one of the men of letters at his
court recited to him these two verses, " Pardon your
brother if he commits a fault against you, for perfection is a very rare thing; everything has its bad side,

and, in spite of its splendor, the torch smokes," the prince was astonished, and asked what poet had composed them. Informed that it was Ibn-al-Haddâd, he replied smilingly: "Do you know whom he meant?" "No," replied the other; "I only know that it is an ingenious idea." "When I was young and he was with me," Motacim said, "I was called the Torch of the Empire. May Allah curse the impertinent rascal, but what admirable verses he makes!"

Sometimes, however, the insults of the poets were so cutting that they forced even Motacim, good-natured as he was, to be less clement than usual. The poets were very hard to please at that time; they became angry as soon as they were not given everything that they demanded, and, like wholly spoiled children as they were, they then abused their freedom to say everything they chose. This happened in the case of Ibn-al-Haddâd. Mortified because Motacim had refused one of his exorbitant demands, he composed this virulent satire against him:

"O seeker after gifts, leave the court of Ibn-Çomâdih, this man who, when he has given you a grain of mustard, retains you in chains like a captive condemned to death. If you were to pass at his court as long a life as Noah's, you would be just as poor as if you had never seen him."

This insult was too cutting to be pardoned. Motacim had been able to bear Nahli's jokes about his love of peace, but he could not stand an accusation of avarice. So Ibn-al-Haddâd's disgrace was complete, and as misfortunes never come singly, his brother happened to commit a murder, and the order was given to arrest both.

Medieval Civilization

They succeeded for some time in hiding, but at last the murderer was discovered and put in prison. Then Ibn-al-Haddâd left Almeria hastily, and took refuge in Murcia. Deprived of his brother, whom he loved tenderly, he was profoundly unhappy, as is seen in these verses:

" A hostile destiny ever pursues us; we ought to submit to its decrees, whatever they may be. Ah! I know it now; unless fortune follows our steps, all that we attempt is useless. Of what advantage is our struggling, if fortune refuses to be propitious? Alas! what shall I do now that I am like a lance which has lost its point? "

When Motacim heard this piece recited he said: " There is more common sense in his verses than in his actions. He speaks the truth; there is no happiness at all for him without his brother. Well, let his brother be released and go to him."

In accusing Motacim of stinginess Ibn-al-Haddâd had wounded him where he felt it the most keenly. Motacim clung with an almost morbid sensibility to his reputation as a generous prince and liberal protector of men of letters. If any one denied to him this rôle, which was in his eyes the highest of all, he was mortally offended; recognizing it was, on the other hand, the surest way of gaining his good will. Moreover, it was necessary to do so, if not tactfully (the prince was too much accustomed to flattery to be very particular in this respect), at least in a graceful manner and especially through poetry.

The number of poets at the court of Motacim was very large, and many of them were Almerians. There were, however, others, and notably a whole colony of refugees from Granada. Its inhabitants were very unfortunate at that time. They were delivered, bound hand and foot, to the strange and bloody caprices of their African princes, whom they despised for their lack of civilization as much as they feared them for their cruelty. Men of letters had still more reason to complain than the rest of the people; for, in the eyes of the ferocious tyrants of Granada, human intelligence was a dangerous enemy which must be crushed at any price. Accordingly, seeing a sword always suspended above their heads, representatives of knowledge emigrated in great numbers, but at different times, and most of them went to Almeria. They knew that they would be well received by the generous sovereign who ruled there and, like the true Arab that he was, hated the Berbers as much as they themselves did. The nephew of Ghânim, of whom we have already spoken, was one of these refugees. His uncle, the great philologist, with whom he lived, had urged him to leave the States of Bâdîs. " This tyrant," he had said to him, " begrudges life to all men of letters. For my own part, I do not cling to life; I am old, and I shall die to-day or to-morrow: but I cling to my works, and I do not wish them to perish. Here they are—take them; you are young. Go and live in Almeria. The tyrant will be able then to kill me, but I shall at least carry to the tomb the consoling thought that my works will survive me."

Another of these refugees was Somaisir of Elvira, one of the most ingenious poets of the period. Proscribed for satires which he had composed against the Berbers in general and their king in particular, he was already in the territory of Almeria, where he thought himself safe, when he was arrested by the order of Motacim, who had been led to believe that the poet had also composed satires against him. Led before the prince and ordered to recite these satires, he cried:

"I swear by Him who has delivered me into your hands I have said nothing spiteful about you, but here is what I said:

"'Adam appeared to me in a dream. "O father of men," I said to him, "can what they say be true? Can it be that the Berbers are your children?" "Ah!" he cried indignantly, "if that is so, I'll divorce Eve."' Prince Abdallâh has proscribed me for these verses. Fortunately, I succeeded in escaping by putting the boundary between him and me. Then he plotted to bribe some one to report to you verses that I had never made. He hoped that you would kill me, and the plan was a clever one; for if it had succeeded he would have been revenged and at the same time he would have thrown upon you the odium of this unjust act."

"What you say appears to me very plausible. But since you have recited to me the verses which you composed against his nation in general, I should like also to hear those which relate more especially to him."

"When I saw him busy in fortifying his castle at Granada, I said: 'Like the madman that he is, he is building his prison; ah, it is a silkworm spinning its cocoon.'"

"You abused him finely, and you did well. I want to do something for you. Do you wish me to give you a present and let you go, or shall I protect you against him?"

The poet having replied in two very well turned verses that in his opinion these two propositions could be reconciled remarkably well, Motacim said: "You are a clever devil, but so be it: I grant you my protection and a present."

Somaisir remained at the court of Motacim until the death of this prince. He published a volume of satires with this title: *Remedy against Diseases; Usurped Reputations Reduced to their Proper Value.* He never had any reason to complain of Motacim; but once he had a dispute with an Almerian noble who, after ordering a poem in his own praise, refused to pay for it. The poet knew how to avenge himself for this slight. When the noble had gone to enormous expense for an entertainment to which he had invited the king, Somaisir posted himself on the road the prince had to take to go to his host's house; as soon as the prince appeared he addressed to him these two verses calculated to arouse his suspicions: "O King, whose appearance brings good fortune and whose countenance fills with joy those who are plunged in grief, do not go to eat at the house of others! Lions are surprised at the moment when they are eating."

"By Allah!" said Motacim, "he is right," and he returned to his own palace. The noble lost his expenses, and the poet was avenged.

The court of Almeria gloried not only in its poets, but also in its learned men, among whom there were some of the first rank, such as Abou-Obaid Becrî, the greatest geographer that Arab Spain produced. He was the son of a sovereign in miniature (a lord of Huelva, who had sold his principality to the king of Seville), and had been educated at Cordova, where he won the hearts of all by his graceful figure, vivacious wit, and extensive literary knowledge. He was the intimate friend of Motacim, who heaped honors and riches upon him. Viewing life as society then viewed it, he joyously divided his time between study and pleasure. Nothing was more varied than his occupations: sometimes he went to negotiate, in the name of his master, a treaty of alliance or peace; sometimes he labored upon his great work on *The Roads and the Kingdoms* (a capital book of which we still possess some parts, such as the description of Africa), or else upon his geographical dictionary, his *Modjam,* which has come down to us complete and contains the analytical nomenclature of a host of names of places, mountains, and rivers mentioned in the history and poems of the ancient Arabs; sometimes he relaxed from his serious affairs and took part in a festival where wanton gaiety reigned. " Ah, my friends," he then sang, " I am burning to hold the cup in my hands and to breathe the perfume of violets and myrtle. Come, then, let us abandon ourselves to pleasure; let us listen to the songs; let us enjoy this day far from the eyes of the indiscreet ! " The next day, either from remorse of conscience or because he wished to silence his enemies who harshly accused him of drunkenness, he zealously went to work again, but this time to write a serious and edifying book, a treatise in which he proposed to demonstrate that, in spite of the objections of the incredulous, Mohammed had really been the prophet of God.

Nothing, indeed, could give a sufficiently vivid idea of this passion for intellectual pursuits which formed one of the most distinctive characteristics of the court of Al-

Moslem Civilization in Spain

meria. Every one there made verses; Motacim himself did it, as well as his sons and even his daughters.

These little courts in Andalusia, like Almeria, where the people gave themselves up to pleasure thoughtless of the morrow, where at every opportunity they voyaged to the joyous country of fancy, presented a charming spectacle. But, alas! all that was too beautiful to endure. Side by side with the poetry there was the sad and stern reality personified in the two neighboring kings, Alphonso VI of Castile and Yusuf the Berber, who despised intellectual pursuits, of which they understood nothing, but who both possessed, on the other hand, an immovable determination and a courage which was proof against every danger—qualities which the Andalusians had lost.

Chivalry

Adapted from J. Flach: *Les origines de l'ancienne France,*
Vol. II, 1893, pp. 562–576.

A MILES, or knight, had to possess ability in various
directions. {He had to be strong, robust, and ath-
letic, in order to support the weight of his armor; he had
to be trained in riding and in wielding lance and sword.
He had to be a member of a wealthy family, or, if he were
merely in the lower ranks of the army, he had to win his
horse and armor on the field of battle, or else by some
striking service to obtain his outfit from some lord.}

The knight was, therefore, a chosen warrior and consequently a man of superior rank. He took precedence
of the other members of his family and of the other vassals; he was invested with a kind of social supremacy.
In all countries where militarism occupies a preponderant
position, army chiefs hold the highest rank. The difference in rank between a non-military vassal and a knight
was as great as the difference which exists in some countries at the present day between an officer who is a noble
and a peasant or citizen. Chivalry tended thus to become
a military caste, as among the Romans and the Gauls. It
is in this sense that Richer speaks of the *ordo militaris,
equestris.*

Just as the different categories of persons composing

240

Chivalry

the feudal clan were distinguished from the point of view
of military service, so also they were differentiated by the
more or less close relationship in which they stood to the
chief.   Naturally, the most esteemed and also the most
faithful were the direct descendants and the adopted kinsmen who were assimilated to them.   Now, true adoption
" in the place of a son " took place, exactly in accordance
with the Germanic custom, by the gift of a complete outfit of arms.   This gift was made regularly by the father
when the son was old enough to bear arms ; consequently,
if a stranger made the gift he took the place of the father.
The man thus armed by the hand of a lord was assimilated
to his son by blood and was placed in a closer relationship,
both in fact and in law, than that which was created by
the mere gift of some symbol to the ordinary vassal.

{For this reason the knight held a double position : he
was both the best soldier and the best vassal.   The
knightly order formed the élite of the army and the élite
of feudalism.}

This double position is shown in all the old French
poems.   They represent chivalry as synonymous with the
art of war, with its training, its stratagems, its discipline,
and its perfected equipment ; and they represent chivalry
as also synonymous with bravery, resistance to fatigue,
and the necessary physical force.   The true knight was
the model warrior.   Bravery consisted in defending one's
arms.

At the same time chivalry meant perfect fidelity and
devotion to death to the chief who had formed the knight
for the profession of arms, had clothed him in armor, had
girded him with his sword, and had mounted him on a

war-horse. The chief had a right to expect eternal gratitude for the arms which he had given, for the presents which he had added, and for the income which he often gave to the newly dubbed knight.

The ceremony of bestowing knighthood shows equally clearly the twofold character of primitive chivalry. The youth who was armed as a knight had to be strong, skilful in the use of his weapons, and an excellent horseman; he had to exhibit his ability in public by putting his horse to a gallop and striking the quintain. That is one side of his character. The second side is that he became the godson, the adopted son, of the lord who made him a knight. That lord presided in person, like a father, when the knight was armed, and attached to his side the principal weapon, the sword. The lord had him furnished with clothing befitting his new station, a mantle of silk and rich furs. By the arms which he received the new knight was associated with the military fortunes of his adopted father; through the precious stuffs and furs with which he was clothed he took his position in the feudal court.

The exhortations addressed to the knight also had a double object. Be brave, was one; be faithful, was the other. Be *preux* summed up the whole.

The *colée,* or blow on the nape of the neck with the palm of the hand, also had a double significance, which was a survival of an old German custom. It was intended to fix in the memory, in such a manner that they could not be forgotten, both the ceremony and the knight who performed it. It had to be energetic to accomplish its purpose, and its energy bore witness both to the moral

endurance of the new knight and to the strength of his
body.

Such was the chivalry of the tenth and eleventh centuries. As yet it was not a distinct institution, and it had
none of the generous sentiments which have been attributed to it or practised by it later. The duties of the
knight were entirely relative. They were the duties of
a soldier and a vassal, and reciprocally those of a suzerain also. Aid to the *poor* extended only to knights without fortune or vassals who were in distress.

In fact, according to the testimony of both the legal
documents and the poems, the knights were far from
being defenders of women and the helpless; they were,
on the contrary, their oppressors, despots, or executioners.
The primitive types of Raoul de Cambrai and Ogier
depict knights and redskins, lions and tigers. In their
savage outbursts of anger or their cold ferocity nothing
restrained them; regard for weakness and religious fear
had no influence. They killed unarmed men without
mercy; they burned nuns in their convent. The only sentiments praised in the great epopee of the eleventh century, the sublime *Song of Roland,* are bravery, family
honor, and fidelity to God, to the feudal lord, to the associate, and to the native land.

The feeble had no rights in the presence of the strong.
Women were fought over, and carried off as the legitimate prey of the stronger. A knight defended them only
to possess them. They knew it and were resigned. A
young girl delivered by Ogier from the hands of the
Saracens immediately said to him: "You have rescued
me: I am at your command. Do with me whatever you

please." A knight protected a merchant, pilgrim, peasant, or citizen only when he was paid for the protection.

Chivalry at that time was not, properly speaking, an order of which the knights were members, and with rules and statutes which they followed. No one was a knight unless he was the knight of some lord who had given him the *colée,* or to whom he had afterward pledged his services.

From what source did the chivalry of the later centuries spring? Was it a foreign importation from the Saracens or Scandinavians? Was it due to the infiltration of Celtic or Breton customs? I do not think so. Thanks to the social transformations which were going on, it developed gradually under the double aspect which has been attributed to it.

The brutal and violent warrior, who always went armed, valued bravery in others as he gloried in his own. Thence sprang some laws of war, such as generosity and loyalty among opponents. When a knight was also a feudal lord and had associates of all ranks under his command, he had to protect and defend them, under penalty of being abandoned by them and scorned by his peers as a coward. This duty was a point of honor. In time this point of honor grew by reason of their great boastfulness, which the heroes of the old chansons exhibited in rodomontades, and in bold and rash undertakings. Any wrong done to a protégé was an outrage to the protector. When a knight made himself the champion of all the feeble, he gave the most striking proof that he feared no rival, because he was under the necessity of fighting at any moment against all comers.

Chivalry

Magnanimity might thus arise from the intoxication of pride, and from the exuberance of strength and individuality.

The fidelity owed to the lord and the duties to be performed about his person aided especially in the birth of a chivalric ideal. Devotion, self-abnegation, and loyalty rose from vassalage by a gradual broadening of ideas. A certain sociability and a certain delicacy in sentiment, in short *courtesy,* rose from the periodical residence at the court of the lord. It became the ambition of even the roughest warrior to merit the approbation of the women who formed the charm of this court. He was also ambitious to merit the praises of the trouvères who were familiar guests at banquets, or at least to escape from their biting satire.

Warlike songs and verses have been recited at banquets from time immemorial; the *chansons de gestes* date from the ninth century at the latest, and their success increased constantly during the next three centuries. The trouvères were the real dispensers of glory. The name which they celebrated lived in the memory of men, the name which they branded was consigned to eternal opprobrium. A poetic ideal was created, and from poetry it descended into every-day life. Undoubtedly, it was ideal in comparison with the ferocious manners; but it was also in advance of them, assigning to combat more noble motives than self-interest, booty, or the satisfaction of sensual and bloody passions. The cult of honor and inviolable fidelity to family, companion, lord, king, country, and God, protection for women, the weak, and the humble, liberality, and exact justice were the qualities celebrated by trouvères and became the goal of all who were ambitious for public praise.

The profound influence of German and Norman traditions must have been exercised in this way; perchance even the Celtic traditions, embodied in ancient songs that each generation adapted to its own environment, had some influence; the Arabs, too, may have had some effect upon the development of chivalry, even before the time of the crusades. The relations between the Franks and the Saracens were constant. Saracen invasions in the South were extended and prolonged, and a great number of Franks were held as prisoners in Spain for interminable years. Consequently the old Arabic songs contributed their influence, for they corresponded closely to the most striking features of the feudal society; they glorified independence and personal courage, respect for the sworn faith, the knight and his horse, the lance and the sword. A breath of the generosity of the free children of the Arab desert must have been infused into the poetic ideal of the French trouvères.

 The elevation and purification of manners and sentiments by heroic poetry were, however, not at all perfect. They could not transform chivalry into an institution. More was needed, especially the great religious impulse which made warriors into "knights of God," which brought about, in the happy phrase of a brilliant scholar, the formation of the "Christian mode" of chivalry. Above all, it was essential that chivalry should be detached from feudalism. This separation was accomplished when the clan organization passed into the organization based upon land. Then the dubbing was no longer

Chivalry

adoption and entrance into the closest bonds of vassalage. It became merely an honorary adoption by a godfather. It continued to produce an *esprit de corps,* a spirit of fraternity. The military orders did not create the *esprit de corps* and feeling of solidarity; they merely strengthened it. A man was a knight before entering an order. They solidified one of the historical foundations of chivalry and infused new blood into an ancient institution.

Character and Results of the Crusades

Adapted from C. Seignobos, in Lavisse et Rambaud: *Histoire Générale*, Vol. II, 1893, pp. 342-348.

THE crusades were expeditions of Christians organized by the pope, the common chief of the Catholics. Every crusader was an armed pilgrim to whom the Church, in consideration of his pilgrimage, remitted the penance which he owed. The pilgrims came together in great crowds, gathering around a king, a powerful lord, or a papal legate—but they were under no discipline; they were free to go to another troop, or even to abandon the expedition when they believed that their vow had been accomplished. An army of crusaders was nothing more than a union of bands following the same road. They marched slowly and without any order, mounted upon great horses, and encumbered with baggage, servants, and camp-followers. They were obliged to put on heavy coats of mail when they fought.

They lost months in crossing the Byzantine Empire and in fighting Turkish horsemen in Asia Minor. In the deserts, where there was no water and where no provisions could be found, men and horses died of hunger, thirst, and fatigue. In the camps where the crusaders stopped, lack of care, privations, and starvation alternated with excessive eating and drinking, caused epidemics which carried them off by thousands. Very few of those who set out got as far as Syria. Especially in the twelfth century, there was a frightful waste of men on the road to the Holy Land. At last the crusaders gave up this dangerous land pilgrimage. In the thirteenth century they went by sea. Italian vessels carried them and their horses in a few months to the Holy Land, where the real war was fought. This change in route modified profoundly the character of the crusades.

In the combats against the Mussulmans, when the numbers were equal, the knights were ordinarily successful. With their great horses and impenetrable armor, they formed compact battalions that the Saracens, mounted upon small horses, could not break with their arrows and sabers. It is true that their victories had scarcely any lasting results. The crusaders returned to Europe, leaving the field free to the Mussulmans.

These intermittent armies might have conquered the Holy Land, but they would not have been sufficient to hold it. But, in addition to the crusaders who came for their souls' salvation, there were knights who came to conquer the land, and merchants who came to make their fortunes—and these held the country. They won all the victories for the crusaders by utilizing the sporadic forces which the masses of pilgrims furnished. They directed the operations, they constructed the siege machines, they took the cities and fortified them against the enemy's return. The crusaders were unable to carry on war in distant countries when compelled to depend upon their own strength. All the pompous expeditions led by sovereigns failed wretchedly. The only crusades which were at all successful were the first, which conquered Syria, and the fourth, which conquered the Greek Empire; and these were directed by the Normans of Italy, and by the Venetians. The enthusiasm and bravery of the crusaders were a blind force, which needed to be directed by men of experience. The crusaders proper were only the tools. The true founders of the Christian kingdoms were the adventurers and the merchants, who, like modern emigrants, set out to establish themselves in the Orient.

These emigrants were never numerous enough to people the country; they only camped in the midst of the native populations. The Frankish principalities always consisted of an aristocracy made up of a few thousand French knights and Italian merchants. It was impossible that they should have the solidity of the European States of the Occident, which rested upon nations. They resembled those States founded by the chiefs of Arabic or Turkish warriors, where the subject population was indifferent as to its ruler, and where the State was the army and perished with it. These principalities lasted nearly two centuries—a long time for Oriental States. Only an extensive emigration would have sufficed to maintain them in the face of the Mussulmans and Byzantines of Asia. Europe in the Middle Ages could not furnish such an emigration.

For half a century the Christian States had only to contend against the little princes of Syria and the *atâbek* of Mosul. The Mussulmans of Egypt were at peace with them. This half-century was their period of prosperity. But when the califate of Cairo, destroyed by Saladin, had been replaced by the military State of the Mamelukes, the Christians were attacked from Egypt and could not resist any longer; the victories of Saladin are a sufficient proof of this. For another century they kept the remnants of their States, but it was because the sultans were not anxious to destroy them. Undoubtedly, the war was, for the Mussulmans as for the Christians, a holy war, but it was not continuous; it was interrupted by frequent truces, some of which lasted several years. We must not think that all the Christian princes were united against all the Mussulman princes. Political interests were ordinarily stronger than religious hatred. Christians constantly fought against Christians, and Mussulmans against Mussulmans. Often a Christian prince made an alliance with a Mussulman prince against another Christian prince.

There never was complete harmony in the camp of the Christians. The religious enthusiasm which united them did not destroy their commercial rivalry or their race hatred. There were continual disputes among the princes of France, Germany, and England, between the merchants of Genoa and Venice, and between the Templars and the Hospitalers. More than once they came to blows. In 1256 the Venetians fought the Genoese over a convent built upon the hill which separated their two quarters in Acre. The Hospitalers, the Catalans, and the men of Ancona and Pisa sided with Genoa; the Templars, the Teutonic knights, the Provençals, the patriarch of Jerusalem, and the king of Cyprus sided with Venice. The Genoese destroyed the Pisans' tower; the Venetians burned the Genoese ships, and took their quarter by storm. This war lasted for two years.

There was the same lack of unity between the crusaders who came from Europe and the Franks who were settled in Syria. Living in the midst of the Orientals, the Franks had adopted many of their customs, such as the use of the bath and flowing garments. They had organized a light cavalry, armed in Turkish fashion. They had taken Mussulman soldiers (*Turcopoles*) into their service. They were inclined to treat the Mussulman princes as neighbors, and not to make war on them without cause. The knights from the West, who arrived in the East full of hatred for the infidels, wanted to exterminate them all, and were indignant at this tolerance. As soon as they landed, they rushed upon the Mussulman territory, in haste to fight and to pillage,—often without listening to the advice of the Christians who lived in the country, and who were more experienced in Eastern warfare. Western writers of the Middle Ages consider the Christians of the Holy Land treacherous and corrupt, and blame them for the ruin of the States in Syria. How much truth is there in these accusations? Undoubtedly, those Frankish adventurers who had quickly grown wealthy and lived in luxury in contact with vicious populations must have adopted many of their vices, especially those who were born in Syria (these were called *Pullani*). But the European crusaders were not in the right position to judge them. They caused more disasters by their imprudence and their lack of discipline than the Christians in Syria by their weakness.

The direct result of the crusades, without speaking of the millions of men who perished in them, was the creation in the Orient of new Catholic States, occupied by Frankish knights and Italian merchants. These were founded at the expense of the Mussulmans and of the Byzantines. After a time, the European settlers, who were always few in number, were expelled without leaving behind them any other traces than the ruins of their castles, built in the seaports and upon the rocks of Greece and Syria; but, during the two centuries of their rule, they maintained regular relations between the Christians in Europe and the Oriental peoples.

In order to carry pilgrims to the Holy Land, the Mediterranean cities organized a transport service. The horses, which the knights always carried with them, were loaded upon transports whose hulls opened by doors upon the side. For protection against pirates, they used armed ships, and the vessels voyaged in fleets. There were two regular times for the journey: one in the spring (the great passage) for pilgrims who went to the Easter festival, the other in summer. The transportation of pilgrims was a profitable business, and the powerful States, accordingly, kept it for themselves. Travelers could set out from only a few ports—Venice, Pisa, and Genoa in Italy, and Marseilles in France. The Templars obtained the privilege of sending a vessel in each fleet.

By land or sea, the European Christians went by millions to the Orient. The crusades were a sort of educational trip for them. They set out from their castles or villages without having seen anything; they were more ignorant than the peasants of to-day. They suddenly found themselves in great cities, in the midst of new countries, and in the presence of unknown customs. All that set them to thinking and gave them new ideas. They got acquainted with the Oriental peoples; they carried back some of their industries and some of their customs.

Thus they obtained a more correct idea of the Mussulmans. The first crusaders believed that the latter were savages and idolaters; they took Mohammed for an idol —later they regarded him as a heretic. In the thirteenth century, the Christians knew at last what Islam really was, and recognized that the Mussulmans were more civilized than they were themselves.

It is very difficult, however, to know exactly what Europe owes to the crusades. The Christians of the West, during the Middle Ages, borrowed from the Arabs and the Byzantines very many inventions and customs. It is natural to think, as soon as an Oriental usage is found in Europe, that it was brought in by the crusaders; but the crusades were not the only means that the Christians had of knowing the other civilizations. The Oriental civilization was established on the whole northern coast of Africa and in the south of Spain. The Christians entered into regular commerce with the Mussulmans of Egypt, Tunis, and Spain, and with the orthodox Christians at Constantinople. It is easy to tell in general what the Christians borrowed from the East; but it is difficult to say in the case of any object or custom whether it came by way of Spain, Sicily, or the Byzan-

Results of the Crusades

tine Empire, or through the crusades. If we attribute to the crusades all the Oriental customs introduced into Europe during the Middle Ages, we exaggerate their influence, and confuse under one name all the relations between the Christians and the Mussulmans.

It is undoubtedly true that Europe, in the Middle Ages, learned a great deal from the Orientals; but it is impossible to determine the exact share of the crusades in this educational work. All that one may rightly attribute to them with exactitude is the customs which came directly from Syria: some military implements, as the crossbow, the drum, the trumpet, and the lance adorned the streamers; some plants, as sesame, apricot (in Italian, *damasco*), garlic (*échalote,* from Ascalon), and watermelon. In the Orient the Christians, who up to that time had shaved, commenced to wear beards. It is also probable that the use of windmills came from Syria.

In order to distinguish one warrior from another in the enormous crowd, the knights needed distinctive marks. They already had a habit of painting some ornament upon their shields. During the crusades, the ornament became the badge of a family, and from that time remained unchanged. Thus the system of coats of arms grew up—which was later called blazonry. It arose in the East, as is proved by the Oriental names used in it: *gules* (red) is an Arabian word from *gûl* (rose); *azure* (blue), a Persian word; *sinople* (green), a Greek word; the gold pieces are called *bezants* (pieces of Byzantine gold); the cross in blazonry is a Greek cross.

Many other results have been attributed to the cru-

Medieval Civilization

sades: the enfranchisement of the serfs, the increase of royal power, the transformation of the feudal régime, the development of epic poetry, the wealth of Italy— even the enfeeblement of the spirit of devotion and the decline in the power of the pope; in short, almost all the changes which took place in the nations of the West from the eleventh to the thirteenth century. The crusades undoubtedly had a general effect upon the Christian societies; but for all these effects there were more active and more positive causes in the people of the West.

Ibn Jubair's Account of his Journey through Syria

Adapted from the text in the *Recueil des historiens des croisades: historiens orientaux,* Vol. III, 1884, pp. 443–456.

IBN JUBAIR was born at Valencia, in Spain, in the year 540 of the Hegira (1145–1146 A.D.). He received an excellent education, and was, for a time, in the service of one of the Almohade princes of Granada. In 1183 he set out on a pilgrimage to Mecca. The description printed below is taken from his account of a portion of this pilgrimage. As he was in Syria in 1184, only three years before the capture of Jerusalem by Saladin, his statements possess a peculiar value. He observed the country and the people very carefully, and recorded his opinions impartially. The facts which he recounts throw a flood of light upon the conditions in Syria under the Frankish rule. It is wisest to allow him to tell his own story in his own words, and not to divert the reader's attention by any comments.

" We were at Damascus, and ready to set out for Acre. May Allah deliver this city into our hands! It was the time of the new moon and the beginning of the month of *Djomada* second, or Sunday, the ninth day of the month which the Christians call September. We were planning to embark, with some Christian merchants, on vessels built for sailing in autumn, and named by them *salîbiya*.[1] We did set out on Thursday evening, the fifth of this month (*Djomada* second), with a crowd of merchants who were going to Acre with their merchandise. We passed the night at Dariya, a village which was a parasang and a half from Damascus, and we set out again on Friday morning at daybreak for another place surrounded by hills and named Beit Djann. Saturday morning we set out for Paneas. When we had gone half the way, we came to an oak with an enormous trunk and large branches, which they told us was called "the tree of the balance." In response to our questions, they said that the name was given because the tree marked on this road the boundary between security and the danger of attack by Frankish brigands, *i. e.*, either scouts or highwaymen. They seize as prisoners all whom they find beyond this tree on the Mussulman side, even if it is only by a span's distance; on the contrary, whosoever is beyond the tree on the Frankish side by the same distance can continue his journey in freedom. This regulation, which had been agreed upon, was observed strictly. At that point is situated one of the most remarkable watch-towers that the Franks have set upon their frontiers.

"This city of Paneas—may Allah protect it!—is the frontier town of the Mussulman territory. It is small, but has a castle surrounded by a stream which flows under the walls and runs toward one of the gates of the city. It is used to turn several mills. Noureddin reconquered

---

[1] That is, vessels with square sails.

this place from the Franks. In the neighboring plain there is a vast extent of cultivated land, dominated by a fort belonging to the Franks and named Honein. This is three parasangs from Paneas. The district formed by this plain is shared equally by the Franks and the Mussulmans,—*i. e.*, the two peoples divide into equal shares the crops which grow in it, and the herds of the two peoples pasture together without any wrong being done by either party.

" The same Saturday evening we set out for the village of Meciya, near the Frankish fort of which we have just spoken, and we passed the night there. Sunday, at dawn, we again proceeded on the road from Honein to Tibnîn [Toron], through a valley full of trees which were mostly laurels. This valley is of great depth, and resembles a vast trench or fissure in the mountains, above which the summits meet. The highest portion reaches to the sky. It is called Al-Astil. It contains retreats, where armed men can enter and conceal themselves. Any one who goes in has no chance of escape from an enemy who is seeking him.[1] At the entrance and the exit there are rapid descents, and we were astounded when we saw these places. Soon after we had passed them, we reached Tibnîn, a large and strong castle belonging to the Franks, where they collect the tolls from the caravans. It belongs to a sow [princess] known as the *queen,* and mother of this hog [king] of Acre—may Allah destroy him! We passed the night at the foot of this castle, and our company had to pay an impost which is not exces-

---

[1] Probably this is a mistake in the manuscript and the author meant to say just the opposite.

sive, *viz.*, a *dînar* and a *kîrat* in Syrian [Tyrian] *dînars* per head. Merchants do not have to pay it when they go to the city which the Christian prince inhabits, where a tax is exacted on the merchandise. This tax amounts to a *kîrat* per *dînar,* and twenty-four *kîrats* make a *dînar.* It is mainly Western Mussulmans who pay it; the other inhabitants of the Mussulman countries are usually exempt. It originated in a circumstance which brought down the anger of the Franks upon the former. In the time of the late Noureddin, a band of brave Maghrebins participated with this prince in an expedition which resulted in the capture of a strong castle held by the enemy, and in which the Maghrebins rendered great service. In retaliation for this act of hostility, the tax of a *dînar,* of which we have just spoken, was placed upon the Mussulmans from the West who travel in the country; for, said the Franks, these Westerners ' were frequenting our land, and we respected their persons and their property; but then, when they turned against us and made an alliance with their Mussulman brothers (of this country), it was certainly necessary to punish them by this tax.' For the Maghrebins it is only a glorious souvenir of the loss which they caused the enemy —a souvenir which ought to make the payment easy, and to solace their regret for being subject to it.

" We left Tibnîn early Monday morning by a road which passed a continuous row of farms, wholly inhabited by Mussulmans, who live in great comfort under the Franks; may Allah preserve us from such a temptation! The terms which are imposed upon them are the surrender of half the crop at the time of harvest, and the

payment of a poll-tax of one *dinar* and five *kirats*. The
Franks demand nothing more, except a light tax upon
the fruits; but the Mussulmans are masters of their dwellings, and govern themselves as they wish. This is the
case in all the territory occupied by the Franks upon the
littoral of Syria, that is, of all the villages inhabited by
the Mussulmans. The hearts of most Mussulmans are
filled with the temptation of settling there, when they
see the condition of their brethren in the districts governed by the Mussulmans, because the state of the latter
is the reverse of comfortable.

" One of the misfortunes which afflict Mussulmans is
that they have always reason for complaint, under their
own government, of the injustice of their chiefs, and
that they have cause only to praise the conduct of the
Franks—and the justice on which one can always depend;
but Allah is the only refuge for any one who complains
of this state of affairs.

" That same Monday we stopped at a farmstead about
a parasang from Acre. The head man who was in charge
was a Mussulman. He had been appointed by the Franks
to have charge of the cultivators. He invited every one
in our caravan to a great banquet in a large room in his
own house. He had all kinds of dishes served, and did
honor to each one.

" After having passed the night there, we set out on
Tuesday morning and soon reached Acre. We were
taken to the custom-house, a caravansary prepared to receive caravans. Before the gate is a carpeted platform,
on which the Christian clerks sit. They have inkstands
of ebony ornamented with gold-work. They keep their

Medieval Civilization

accounts in Arabic, and also speak this language. Their head, who is chief of the customs, is called simply *sahib* —a title derived from the importance of his work; for the Christians employ this name for all their important men who are not in the army. All the receipts belong to the chief of the custom-house, who pays a very large sum to the government. The merchants in our company carried their merchandise thither, and installed themselves in the upper story. The baggage of those who had no merchandise was examined, to make sure that it contained nothing dutiable, and then they were allowed to go where they pleased. The examination was made in a quiet and courteous manner, without any violence or overcharge. We rented from a Christian woman a house which faced upon the sea, and there we stayed.

" Acre is the most important of the Frankish cities in Syria. It is the port ' for the ships, carrying their sails aloft in the sea, like mountains ' (Koran, sura lv, verse 24). All the vessels anchor there, and by its greatness Acre resembles Constantinople. The ships and the caravans resort thither, and it is the meeting-place for Christian and Mussulman merchants of all lands; its streets and lanes are full of people, and there is a continual coming and going. But infidelity and arrogance are present everywhere, and the place swarms with pigs and crosses; it is dirty and smells vilely, for it is full of filth and garbage. The Christians took it from the Mussulmans in the first decade of the sixth century (of the Hegira), and the eyes of Islam were filled with tears, for this was a deep sorrow. The mosques were then turned into churches, and the minaret became a clock-tower. Allah permitted only one corner of the principal mosque to escape profanation; and this became, in the hands of the Mussulmans, a little mosque where strangers gathered to obey the obligatory prescription of prayer. Near the sanctuary is the tomb of the prophet Saleh, a holy spot, by virtue of which the divine favor has permitted this position to escape from the unclean touch of the infidel. In the eastern part of the city is the Spring of the Ox. From this Allah caused the ox to come forth for Adam. The descent to the spring is by polished steps. Near this spring there was formerly a mosque, of which the oratory has remained uninjured. To the east of it the Franks have constructed an oratory; thus, Mussulmans and infidels meet there—although it belongs to the Christians—and each one says his prayers, facing in the direction that his faith prescribes. It is in this venerable and sacred edifice that Allah has reserved for the Mussulmans a place where they can pray.

"After remaining two days at Acre, we set out for Tyre, on Thursday, the twelfth of *Djomada* second [September 20]. We went by land, and passed by a great castle named Az-Zib, which dominates the continuous villages and residences, and by a walled town called Iskandarûnah. We desired to obtain information about a vessel which ought to be at Tyre and was, as we had been told, about to set out for Bugia; our plan was to embark upon it. We reached there on Thursday evening—the distance between the two cities was about thirty miles—and we stopped in a caravansary planned to accommodate Mussulmans.

Medieval Civilization

"Tyre is a city so strongly fortified that it is spoken of proverbially as a city which refuses obedience or submission to every conqueror. The Franks have planned to make it an asylum in case of ill fortune, and they regard it as their chief safety. Its streets and lanes are cleaner than those in Acre; the infidel belief of its inhabitants is of a more courteous character, and their habits and feelings more generous toward foreign Mussulmans; their manners are more refined, their dwellings larger and more comfortable, and the lot of the true believers is more quiet and peaceful. But Acre is larger, and the infidels are more boastful and more numerous. The strength and impregnability of Tyre are of the most marvelous character, and depend mainly upon the fact that there are only two gates. One opens upon the mainland; the other upon the sea, by which the city is entirely surrounded except on one side. The first of these gates is reached only after passing three or four others, all of them surrounded by strong ramparts; the second, which gives access to the harbor, is between two fortified towers. The situation of the harbor itself is different from that of any other maritime city; the walls of the city surround it on three sides, and arches of strong masonry form the fourth side, so that it is under the very ramparts that vessels enter and go to their anchorage-ground. A strong chain is stretched between the two towers of which we have just spoken, and then all entrance and exit become impossible as long as the chain is there. The gate itself is intrusted to guards and watchmen, under whose eyes all who enter or depart from the port must necessarily pass. All this makes a marvelous position. The harbor at Acre, undoubtedly, resembles it; it is equally well arranged and protected, but only vessels of a small tonnage can enter it; large ships anchor in the open sea. The situation of the harbor at Tyre is, therefore, better, more inclusive, and better arranged.

" Our stay in this city lasted eleven days; we entered it on Thursday, and we left on Sunday the twenty-second of *Djomada* second [September 30]. The reason for our delay was that the vessel upon which we hoped to embark seemed too small, and we did not think it prudent to risk ourselves upon it.

" One day, while we were at Tyre, we had an opportunity to see, near the harbor, one of the most pompous spectacles imaginable—a wedding procession. All the Christian men and women present at the fête were drawn up in two lines before the bride's door. Trumpets, flutes, and all kinds of musical instruments resounded. They awaited thus the bride's departure. She appeared, at length, conducted by two men, who supported her on either side and appeared to be her kinsmen. She was splendidly attired, according to their usual mode of dressing, and wore a magnificent silk robe embroidered with golden thread, whose long train swept the ground. Upon her forehead rested a diadem of gold, covered with a fillet of cloth of gold, and her bosom was adorned in the same manner. Thus clad, she advanced trippingly, with measured steps, like a turtle-dove, or like the dust moved by a gentle breeze. May Allah preserve us from the temptations which such spectacles excite! She was preceded by Christian magnates, and followed by Christian women, who advanced mincingly, with their most beautiful or-

naments trailing behind them. The procession started,
the orchestra at the head, while the simple spectators,
Mussulmans and Christians, ranged themselves in two
rows, to be present at the march. The cortège proceeded
to the house of the bridegroom, which the bride entered,
and the whole company spent the day in feasting. Such
was the magnificent spectacle at which chance permitted
me to be present. May Allah preserve us from its seductive influence!

"Having at length returned by sea to Acre, where we
arrived on Monday morning the twenty-third of *Djomada*
second [October 1], we hired places on board a large
vessel which was setting sail for Messina, in the island
of Sicily, and we were heartily desirous that the divine
power and grace might favor our voyage and make it
easy. Mussulmans, in fact, have, in the eyes of Allah,
no excuse for going to a city in the land of the infidels
when they have an opportunity to go through a Mussulman country. In the latter case, they are free from the
insults and dangers to which they are exposed in the
former, such as slavery, the misfortune of paying a
poll-tax, and the grief that troubles the heart of the
faithful when he hears the curses, especially of the people of the lower classes, which are heaped upon him
[Mohammed] whom Allah has exalted. Infidel cities
are filthy, and the faithful have to go and come in the
midst of pigs, and a whole host of other forbidden things
which I could never finish enumerating. May we be
preserved from entering the country of the infidels, and
from being exposed to seeing Mussulman prisoners
marching in fetters and employed in the most arduous

labor, like slaves! Mussulman prisoners are even compelled to wear iron rings on their legs. As I think of their lot, my heart breaks; but my pity is of no advantage to them.

"During our whole stay at Tyre, we found repose only in the mosque which has remained in the hands of our brethren, although there are other mosques.

"Among the principal citizens of Damascus, there were two extremely wealthy merchants. All their trade was carried on along the Frankish coast, where their names were held in high esteem and they had agents under their orders. Caravans which bore their merchandise were constantly going and coming; they had colossal fortunes, as well as great influence both with the Mussulman and Frankish princes. The lord of Acre, whom his subjects call king, was invisible, concealed from every one, for Allah had inflicted him with leprosy. His treasurer had charge of the administration in his place; he was called the count, and he had the oversight of the taxation. All the revenues are paid to him, and, by his rank and authority, he has power over everything. It is this accursed count, lord of Tripoli and Tiberias, who is the most important person among the Franks, with whom he enjoys great power and high rank; he is worthy of the throne for which he seems born, and his intelligence and cunning are remarkable. For about a dozen years, perhaps even longer, he was a prisoner of Noureddin; finally, at the beginning of the reign of Saladin, he bought his liberty for a large ransom. He acknowledged Saladin as his lord and liberator.

"In the plain of Tiberias, because of the convenience

of the road, there is a great passing of caravans from Damascus, for mules have to be used only in going by the Tibnin road, because of its difficulties.

" The two cities of Acre and Tyre are not surrounded by gardens; they are situated in a vast plain, which reaches to the sea, and the fruits which they need are obtained from the orchards in the neighborhood. Each city has extensive lands, and the neighboring hills are covered with villages, which send their fruits to these two cities because they are the most important. To the east of Acre, on the side of the mainland, there is a valley in which a river flows, and between the river and the sea there is the most beautiful plain of fine sand that can be seen anywhere. There is no race-course that can be compared with it. The master of the city goes there every morning and evening, to ride horseback, and it is also the parade-ground for the troops.

" At Tyre, near the gate which opens upon the mainland, there is a spring with steps leading to it, and, in addition, there are many wells and cisterns in the city— every house has its own.

" On Saturday the twenty-eighth of *Djomada* second [October 6], after having laid in a stock of food and water, we embarked upon our vessel, which was very large. The Mussulmans found a place where they would not be in contact with the Franks. Among the passengers there was an innumerable throng of Christian pilgrims, *viz.,* pilgrims to Jerusalem; there must have been more than two thousand of them. Once embarked, trusting in the will of Allah, we waited for a favorable wind and for the vessel to complete its cargo."

Material for Literature from the Crusades

Adapted from Vaublanc: *La France au temps des croisades,* 1844, Vol. II, pp. 182–190.

THE stories of pilgrimages and distant wars, carried from castle to castle, filled the imagination of the people in the West with thoughts of adventurous and inspiring deeds. The epoch of the crusades was marked by the long absence and unexpected return of warriors, and by the impostures of would-be nobles. Fortunate was the true master when, after having told his adventures at the gate of the castle, he did not remain ignored in his beggar's clothes—when his features, altered by sickness, wounds, the heat of the desert, and the damp of prisons, were recognized by a faithful servant, and the best place by the fire was at length restored to its legitimate lord.

Some tales, borrowed from the contemporary chronicles, may enable us to picture in our minds all the curious and marvelous incidents that the wars in the East brought into the every-day life of the people.

In 1176 a pilgrim was seen at Planques, near Douai. He wore a monk's frock and a coat of lambskin; his snow-white beard hung down to his waist, and his white

269

hairs covered his shoulders. He was overheard saying that he had formerly possessed the city of Ardres. Immediately the nobles of that country repaired the road which leads from Douai to Planques, and built for him a little house. He mounted an ass to beg for aid. Meanwhile, a prior informed the count of Ardres that his uncle had returned. The count treated the information as visionary, affirmed that his uncle Baldwin of Ardres had been drowned on his way to the East, and said that this man who pretended to be Baldwin was imposing upon the people. There were, however, some conferences between the count and the pilgrim; the latter received some presents, and went away immediately. Shortly after, reliable information was received of the death of the true lord of Ardres.

Three knights from the district of Laon, who were believed to have died in Palestine, reappeared one day near the city of their birth. They brought with them a beautiful maiden from the Orient, and an image of the Virgin. These knights, long held as captives in Syria, had refused during their imprisonment to abjure the faith. The infidel prince who was persecuting them sent his daughter into their prison to seduce them, but they converted her by showing her an image of the Virgin, which they had preserved. Thanks to the cleverness of their beautiful proselyte, and the especial protection of the Mother of our Lord, they were able to escape from prison, and to bear with them the precious image. When, after a long voyage, they had reached the town of Notre Dame de Liesse, the image suddenly became so heavy that they had to stop. They understood this manifestation of a superior will; a church was soon erected on the very spot where their steps had been miraculously checked.

The sister of Thomas of Beverley, who lived and wrote in France in the thirteenth century, put on men's clothes in order to take part in the holy war, passed through the camp of Saladin, entered Jerusalem, and fought there in defense of the Christians. Wounded by a stone from a siege-machine, she was captured, fell ill, and was at length ransomed and enabled to return to France. Her brother was weeping for her loss when she suddenly stood before him. Both, filled with admiration for the ways of Providence which had brought them together again after such a long separation, abandoned the world and devoted their lives to God.

An event which happened in Burgundy about the same time perpetuated, in the family of Anglure, a most curious tradition. The Saladins of Anglure are said to have been called Saint-Cheron before a brave knight of this name, Jean d'Anglure, had gone to Palestine to fight the sultan Saladin. This Jean d'Anglure was taken prisoner, but obtained permission to return to France to seek his ransom. As a pledge of his return, he left with Saladin only his knightly faith; the latter was content. No one knew him on his return to his native land. Worn out by fatigue, and changed by suffering, his long beard and his poor pilgrim's habit made him unrecognizable. His wife, who believed him dead, was that very day celebrating her marriage with a second husband. Jean had fortunately kept the half of a broken ring of which his wife possessed the other fragment. Upon the faith of this irrefutable testimony, his wife and his manor were restored to him. The day for paying his ransom drew near. He set out to return to his chains, for he had not been able to find the promised sum. If we may believe this romantic chronicle, Saladin, as generous as his prisoner was loyal, made him a present of his freedom, on condition that the eldest son in his family should be called Saladin, and that the coat of arms should be bells supported by crescents.

Other crusaders, who were not expected to return at all, aroused general enthusiasm when they came back. "When the noble lord Humbert de Beaujeu returned from *outre-mer,* he was received by the people of his whole land with a great outburst of joy. If I had not seen with my own eyes the joy that his return caused, I should scarcely have believed it. The clerks rejoiced, the monks were happy, the peasants applauded, the choirs of the neighboring churches resounded with a new song. On the other hand, the robbers were in despair, and the oppressors groaned. The count of Mâcon, that wolf of darkness and night, was already trembling." Unfortunately, the noble had entered the Order of the Temple. He asked to be released from his vows, and did not know whether he ought to take his wife again or abandon her.

Others, less fortunate, never returned to their native land. Thus, the mystery about the death of Baldwin I, count of Flanders and emperor of Constantinople, was never cleared up. The trouvères told how Baldwin, conquered by Johanitsa, king of the Bulgarians (1205), languished at first in close confinement at Terra Nova. According to their story, the wife of the king of the Bul-

garians fell in love with him, but her love was scorned;
she, therefore, accused him to her husband. By the
latter's order, the emperor was murdered at a festival,
and his body was given to the wild beasts for food.
Others add that the mutilated body, while still living,
was abandoned in a deep valley to birds of prey; his
torture was prolonged for three entire days, and nothing
was left but his skull—of which the Bulgarians made a
banqueting-cup.

His daughter Jeanne had inherited the county of
Flanders. She was disturbed (1204) in the enjoyment
of her suzerainty by an event of which the chronicle of
Rheims gives a curious account:

" The great nobles, plotting treason against the countess Jeanne of Flanders, sought out an old man and
placed him, in prisoner's garb, in the forest of Vicoigne,
assuring him that they would make him count of Flanders. They taught him how to answer the questions
which might be put to him. When this unexpected return
was reported, a crowd went to the forest, took the old
man from the hermitage in which he was living, clothed
him in a robe of scarlet lined with vair, and conducted
him on a great war-horse through all the good cities of
Flanders, which paid all his expenses; and all the Flemish held him for their lord.

" He attempted to have the countess seized, when she
was dining at Haisnes in Caisnois. She had barely time
to mount a pack-horse and escape to Mons. She appealed
to the king, who summoned the pretender before the
Parliament of Péronne under a safe-conduct.

" He came on the appointed day, riding an ambling

morel, wearing a great scarlet cape lined with green sendal, and a cap of *bourret.* He held a white rod in his hand, and looked wonderfully like a great nobleman. A large crowd of people followed him. He dismounted at the foot of the stairs leading to the hall, and went up, preceded by his ushers, like a great lord. His arrival was announced to the king, who came out of his room to meet him.

" 'Sire, you are very welcome if you are my uncle, Count Baldwin, who ought to be emperor of Constantinople, king of Salonica, and count of Flanders and Hainault.'

" 'Fair nephew, may God and His sweet Mother favor you! Truly, I am Baldwin; and I should be all that you say if I had my rights. But my daughter wishes to disinherit me, and will not recognize her own father.'

" He besought the king to aid him. The king promised, and, to test him, asked him in what city he had been married.[1] Not knowing what to answer, for no one had coached him on this point, he said that he wished to go to bed—thinking to himself that he would find out the answer from those who were instructing him.

" He was put to bed alone in a room, and the doors were well guarded. When he got up—the same question. He became angry, and said that he wanted to depart. The rascal left the king at once and went to Valenciennes, and at night fled to Rays in Burgundy, where he had been born.

" For six months there was no news of him. One market-day a squire of the lord of Courtenay saw him

---

[1] The king's wife was Iolande, sister of Jeanne.

at Courtenay, and pointed him out to his lord: 'Sire, there is the man who pretended to be Count Baldwin!' 'Hold your tongue—you are lying; that cannot be!' 'Sire,' said the squire, 'hang me by the neck if it is not true!' 'Well,' said the lord, 'take him, then; by St. James, he shall pay me well!' The squire seized him, put him in prison, and found out that it was all true. The countess was informed, and promised a thousand marks of silver, and all the property of the impostor, if he were delivered to her.

"As soon as she saw him, the countess questioned him; and he confessed that his name was Bertrand de Rays, and that he had done as he did at the advice of knights, ladies, and clerks, who had taken him out of the hermitage where he wanted to save his soul.

"'By my faith!' said the countess, 'you were a fool; you wanted to be the sovereign count, to be sure!' Then she had him stripped and clothed in a coarse garment. When they took off his shoes, they found that he had no nails on his feet. He was placed on a stallion and led past the mansions during the fête at Lille, which was just being celebrated.

"In front of each mansion they cried, 'Hear this rascal; listen to him!' 'I am,' he said, 'Bertrand from Rays in Burgundy—a poor man, who ought not to be count, or king, or duke, or emperor; what I did, I did by the advice of knights, ladies, and citizens of this country.'

"Then they silenced him. He was put in a perfectly new pillory, which they set up on the chief street of Lille, with two great rascals beside him, one on his left and the other on his right; then he was hung on a gibbet, with a brand-new chain, so that it should not break.   He hung there more than a year.

" People said: ' A man must be greatly in need of a fool, to make one of himself.' But there were also some who said, under their breath, that the countess of Flanders had put her father to death."

Classical Learning in the Middle Ages

Adapted from G. Voigt: *Die Wiederbelebung des class-ischen Alterthums,* 1893, pp. 4–10.

THE decline of the Roman Empire was accompanied by a gradual decline of taste for Roman literature, until in the seventh century it was as good as extinguished. And yet, not quite extinguished. In addition to the Roman law-books, the Roman historical, philosophical, and poetical literature never lay in entire neglect. Sallust, Livy, some of Cicero's and of Seneca's writings, Vergil and Lucan, Horace and Ovid, Terence and Pliny, were still read, now and then, in the quiet of monastic cells and woven into the ecclesiastical, scholastic, and historical writings of the time. The Church Fathers made many references to the profane authors, and derived from them a good portion of their erudition. Through the writings of the Fathers and the later ecclesiastical compilations such as Bishop Isidore of Seville made, some classical ideas and some extracts from ancient authors remained in steady circulation. Others were handed on, in an equally mangled form, through fables, legends, and poems, like the confused fables of the Trojan war, of Alexander the Great, and of various Roman emperors. Boethius, whose Christo-philosophic *Consolations* was always held in high esteem, gave in his *Commentaries* another impulse to-

Medieval Civilization

ward the study, or at least the consideration, of the Aristotelian philosophy. Hundreds of similar suggestive classical touches are to be found in the other writers. Finally, we possess, from every period of the Middle Ages, written copies of classical authors, which bear witness to an active interest in this literature. If a list were made of those medieval writers who were more or less conversant with this literature, they would form an impressive array, and among them many prominent names would find a place. One would be almost led to conclude that a renaissance of antiquity was quite unnecessary. At the court of Charles the Great the Latin poets were lovingly read and their verses imitated, and never again did they sink into complete oblivion. In many an episcopal court and in the justly famed houses of the Benedictines, the poetic art of the Romans and a knowledge of things Roman found a new abiding-place, and were handed down in library collections and the exercises of the schools. Childish and clumsy the product was, to be sure, but the models followed were good, classical models. Einhard, the biographer of Charles, took Suetonius for his model, and Widukind followed Sallust. Ekkehard of Aura adorned his writings with sayings from Cicero, and in many other ways exhibits no mean familiarity with the ancients. The zeal with which Ratherius of Verona and Gerbert collected and read ancient classical works is known. What a wealth of erudition did John of Salisbury glean from classical literature! He strove to imitate Ovid's verse and Cicero's prose, and to wrest from Quintilian the rules of eloquence. The epic poets of the Middle Ages could find their models in the honored Vergil, in

Classical Learning

Lucan and Claudian. They accustomed themselves to a complete surrender to antiquity.

Some there have been who, on reading the songs of the wandering scholars and Goliards, have regarded them as forerunners of the Humanists, because they boldly praise the world and the lusts of the flesh, now and then introduce the old heathen gods into their songs, and ridicule the institutions of school and Church. But it is only the lust of life and the thoughtlessness of youth which pulsate in these variable and emancipated natures, and their scanty school-day reminiscences show no real intimacy with antiquity. Such work could furnish no enduring impulse for the future.

Let it be conceded that the Middle Ages possessed a mass of antiquarian knowledge; they lacked the classical attitude toward life, they lacked that surrender to the ancient world, that yearning effort to re-live the ancient past and to embrace it with all the strength of their being, which marked the Humanists. None of the great ones of the Middle Ages, neither Ratherius nor Gerbert, Abélard nor John of Salisbury, knew Greek; and, what is more significant, none of them ever expressed a longing to be able to possess the treasures of Hellenic literature, although the Latin writers they read gave utterance to their love and honor for the Greeks. Wherever a spark of the Humanistic spirit slumbered, the name of Homer fanned it into a flame!

The influences which were hostile to antiquity were still far in the ascendant. Christianity and the Church would as yet hear of no reconciliation with the pagan past. They had grown to strength through conflict with the heathen world, and the spark of heathenism, though miserable, still glowed beneath the ruins of its temple, and, though conquered, still remained with its free, art-loving attitude toward life, an enemy ever to be feared. Even in the days of its overthrow, it still seemed to many worthy teachers of the Church, who had formerly been sophists or rhetoricians, a sort of seductive siren. Others there were who had not entirely disowned the heathen mother who had given them spiritual sustenance in their youth. Basil even wrote a little work in her defense, and Gregory Nazianzen, Jerome, and Augustine retained kindly feelings toward her. The rigorism of Gregory the Great has been cited to prove how thoroughly and disdainfully the heathen poets had been trodden under foot in his day; but the very circumstance that Gregory felt it necessary to wage vigorous warfare against them only proves once again that the taste for and seductive power of the " dead " were by no means gone. Alcuin reproved the archbishop of Trèves for his fondness for Vergil, the poet of lies, who estranged men from the Gospel, although he himself had gained much of his culture from Vergil, Cicero, and other of the ancients. Abbott Wibald of Corvey, captivated by Cicero's diction, made a collection of his works, but was none the less timorously on his guard less he should appear more a Ciceronian than a Christian ; he assures us that in such studies he regarded himself as a spy in the camp of the enemy. Even when the war with the surviving vestiges of heathenism sank into the background, when the struggle of popes and emperors engrossed men's minds, when, in the midst of the schism, the learned men of the Church were especially concerned with forging theological and canonical weapons, even then men could not avoid a fearsome shudder at the thought of the vanquished powers of heathenism, which, though as it were chained in hell, still lived and threatened revenge. To these men the age of the Greeks and Romans appeared as a night in which men worshiped impure demons, and these demons, although they were abandoned by the Christian faith, still kept up their homeless existence in the superstitions of the age. No ; so long as the Church strove to oppose the kingdom of God upon earth to the tendencies of the world, she could never reach out the hand of reconciliation to antiquity. She could not suffer that the human spirit should be ravished and absorbed by a past which was not her own, or that the intellect of man should be diverted from the contemplation of the everlasting kingdom promised by Christ, of which she, the Church, alone held the keys.

And so the Church, while the spirit of purification was still alive in her and a holy domination was her ideal, monopolized for her own purposes the mighty lever of men's deeds and emotions and imagination. Through her handmaiden, scholasticism, she kept thought under discipline. She preferred to repress the taste for the beautiful, rather than let it feed upon the materials which were to be found among the classical peoples. It is no accident that when the ecclesiastical sun grew pale the moonlight of heathenism emerged from her long eclipse. If this conclusion be not sound, how explain this fact, that all the interest of individuals in classical literature which we not infrequently meet in the Middle Ages was absolutely unproductive? The truth is that antiquity is

Medieval Civilization

a world apart, and that he alone who grasps it as such, and regards it with a single devotion, can hope to secure its cultural material. No part of knowledge can flourish when condemned to be the slave of another.

It is certain that we are indebted for the preservation of classical literature, as far as it has been preserved, to the monks above all others. For hundreds of years they truly sheltered and preserved the treasures heaped up by those gone before, and also multiplied them through copying. But it was never their vocation; they were not devoted heart and soul to the work. Book-copying was usually a mere arid task. At times it was enjoined by the rules of the order, to soften rude manners through peaceful employment, to occupy the leisure of feeble brothers, or to procure gain for the monastery; again, it was merely permitted, and at times it was actually forbidden. If, in the famous houses of the Benedictines at Monte Cassino, Cluny, St. Gall, or Fulda, some classical volumes were copied along with a lot of theological works, mass- and prayer-books, it was done at the command of the abbot, or was, perhaps, the playful hobby of the brother himself. But they rarely got beyond the dead letter. Many a time, while the aristocratic abbot strode through the fields, his falcon on his wrist, or attended tourneys and celebrations, or gazed at the buffooneries enacted at the gluttonous banquets, and the brethren sauntered around or enlivened their idle speech with wine, the books accumulated dust and moldered away in the darkest and dankest cells, excepting the altar- and prayer-books, and perhaps the books on agriculture upon which the revenues and even the necessaries of the monastery depended.

Classical Learning

Hence it is that in the course of the centuries perhaps quite as much classical literature turned to dust and was lost forever as was saved. The classics were treated as guests, and never enjoyed the rights of the home.

The existence which the classical books lived in the monasteries was the same existence which the contents of these books lived in the minds of men. As long as culture in general, and education in particular, were in ecclesiastical hands exclusively, the ancient literature was treated as a stepchild. That is why the apparent advance made in Carolingian times, and its Ottonian echo, were practically fruitless, just as frequent contact with Byzantium, the archives of Hellenism, produced in the West only fugitive fashions. Continuity of effort and coöperation of the strivers were lacking. The common idea was that the Latin tongue was a primer for the clergy. It was learned out of Donatus and his barbarous successors, which were supplemented by some of Cicero's writings or a poet or two, as a storehouse of examples for the rules of grammar. A more poverty-stricken existence than the Roman authors led during these times is scarcely conceivable—serving for the preparatory training of clerics and as a lifeless kill-time. And they were no better off when they came out of the monastery and were planted in the monastic schools, and then in the universities. Here, too, they were servants to the more important faculties of the university, and never attained an independent existence with spirits of the first rank, such as Abélard and John of Salisbury. Scraps from the classics served at best to fill in the gaps in a theological or philosophical system, just as the marble pillars of ancient temples and

Medieval Civilization

palaces were employed, without shame, for common citizens' houses.

We will not repeat the old song of the complete lack of discernment, of critical power, and of taste in medieval times. And yet, however thoughtlessly it has often been sung, it is, nevertheless, undeniable that the intellectual and esthetic acquisitions, of antiquity were for centuries as good as lost.

The Latin Classics in the Middle Ages

Adapted from A. Graf: *Roma nella memoria e nelle immaginazi-oni del medio evo*, 1883, Vol. II, pp. 153–195, 204–210, 216, 296.

THE Roman emperors, good and bad, who had governed the world, opposed or favored the Church, and filled Rome with the monuments of their pomp and power, gave rise in the Middle Ages, which were essentially fanciful, to numerous legends; and the same is equally true of the Latin authors. In their immortal pages the great soul of Rome seemed still to live and speak, and their books, scattered among the barbarians like the floating timbers of a shattered vessel, were almost the only means of salvation for shipwrecked civilization. The sumptuous edifices of the Cæsars either lay in dust or encumbered with their ruins the devastated capital of the world: but the books written by the poets and historians, by the rhetoricians and philosophers, preserved intact its primitive splendor. They alone could now furnish full and certain evidence of that glorious past of which time was always effacing the remains and increasing the renown. They were the living and imperishable voice of Rome, and through them later ages came to know their own origins and to hold converse with their ancient progenitors.

Medieval Civilization

In endeavoring to gain a general idea of the way in which the Roman writers were studied, and of the esteem in which they were held during the Middle Ages, it will be well to begin with a general consideration of actual conditions.

Rome, as a political and intellectual power, either no longer existed or existed in a state of profound transformation: but the books of her writers, if we disregard the more or less serious changes resulting from the carelessness and ignorance of copyists, or the naïve effrontery of interpolators, remained unaltered. They continued to live, but in a world which was no longer theirs; children of a pagan civilization, they found themselves astray in a rebarbarized and, what is more, a Christian world. Manifestly, their fortune could no longer be the same as in the past, and the judgments formed concerning them were necessarily affected by the changed conditions of civilization and religious belief. Between the Latin and pagan writers on the one hand, and barbarism and Christianity on the other, there were opposition and incompatibility. Barbarism, which in the matter of the classics meant more particularly ignorance, gave rise to errors of judgment and extravagant fancies; Christianity, established in the Church, personified in the ecclesiastical writers, and solicitous for the rooting out of false beliefs, gave rise to moral reprobation. The books and their authors were misunderstood, disguised with legends, and condemned. And yet, at the same time, a sentiment of invincible and almost unconscious admiration for them existed, and ignorance failed to deform them, and faith did not succeed in killing them.

Latin Classics

It is not an easy task to judge fairly the policy of the Church toward the pagan culture; the majority, in such matters, allow themselves to be led astray by passion. To maintain that the Church did not injure pagan culture is as absurd as to refuse to recognize that the Church was bound by its very constitution to combat it. The spirit of paganism survived completely in the poets inspired by it; it survived, too, in the arts produced and nourished by it; and the attractiveness of error, in itself almost irresistible to fallen man, conceived in iniquity, was in this case enhanced by the perilous charm of beauty. In strict logic, a man could not be a good Christian and at the same time find delight in the reading of the poetry of the heathen. Logic, however, has never ruled the world, and even in the midst of the struggle between the waxing Church and the waning paganism, and afterward, when the Church was certain of victory, there were always some who were devoted students of the classical literature and commended the study to others. The Christian apologists studied the pagan classics from the imperious necessity of their office; St. Basil, St. Gregory Nazianzen, St. Jerome, and St. Augustine counseled, with various cautions and restrictions, the study of these works. On the other hand, a great number of examples of a contrary nature might be cited. For example, Theophilus, the renowned bishop of Alexandria, destroyed all the classical books he could lay his hands on, and Gregory the Great made war even on grammar.

This perplexed attitude of Christian sentiment toward the ancient culture and its monuments continued throughout the Middle Ages, so that it is very difficult to say how much the Church hurt, and how much it helped, the classical writers. Every one who is competent to pass an impartial judgment on the matter recognizes that the causes of the decline of pagan literature were, in part, anterior to the period when the Church began to operate with some effectiveness upon pagan society. Nor is it well to forget that all, or almost all, the Latin literature which has come down to us was preserved by the diligence of clerics. They admired the immortal charms of which the pages spoke, the renowned ancient artifices of thought and speech, but they feared their sweet allurements. The evil spirit that could lie in wait in the smile of a beautiful woman, in a cup of generous wine, or in the perfume of a flower, knew well how to set, in a hexameter of Vergil or a choriambic of Horace, insidious ambushes that ensnared the soul. Many, in the presence of the authors of antiquity, found themselves in the frame of mind of a timid lover, tossed about between the desire of passion and the horror of sin. Peter Damiani (988–1072), the great restorer of monastic discipline, says in a sermon: "One time Cicero charmed me, the songs of the poets delighted me, the philosophers shone upon me with golden words, and the sweet sirens sang to my intellect." Do not the good Peter's words reveal fear, fond remembrance, and a lament over lost delights? In others, austerity of temperament, a gloomy and morose nature, and the anguished thought of eternal damnation gave birth to graver doubts and more gloomy fears which expressed themselves in words of contumely and execration. In the seventh century, St. Audoenus, for example, called Homer and Vergil rascals. In the tenth century Leo, abbot of St. Boniface and apostolic legate, answered the accusation of ignorance which the bishops of Gaul made at the synod of Rheims against the Roman ecclesiastics by declaring, in a letter to the kings, Hugh and Robert of France, that the vicars and disciples of St. Peter did not wish to have Plato, Vergil, and the other philosophic cattle as their masters. Radulf Glaber relates in his chronicle the story of a grammarian of Ravenna who was a zealous student of the ancient authors. To him appeared, one night, in the guise of Vergil, Horace, and Juvenal, several devils, who thanked him for the diligence he had shown in their works, and promised him that after death he should share in their own glory. Puffed up by this promise, he began to say many things prejudicial to the true faith, and was condemned as a heretic. In the same way the devil assumed the form of this or that ancient divinity. And yet, if we see on the one hand what a feeling of execration the pagan authors inspired in the most faithful Christians, we see on the other those who were enamoured of the pagan authors and esteemed them glorious. St. Odo, abbot of Cluny, was weaned of his love for reading Vergil by a vision in which he saw a vase, most beautiful without but full of serpents within, which came out and sought to strangle him. He concluded that the serpents were the false teachings of the poets, and the vase the book of Vergil. Helinandus tells how Hugh, abbot of Cluny, about the middle of the eleventh century, while sleeping dreamed that his head rested on a great multitude of serpents. He awoke, raised the bolster, and found beneath it an ancient volume of Vergil. He threw it from him and then went peacefully to sleep.

Medieval Civilization

Some more tolerant churchmen considered the study of the classics useless, inasmuch as the sacred Scriptures and the dogmas of the Church furnished certain and unmistakable truth; others deemed it foolishly hurtful to morals and to the faith. In the *Speculum Exemplorum* it is recorded that St. Francis launched a formidable malediction against one of his followers who had, without permission, set up a school at Bologna. " You wish," said he to the culprit, " to destroy my order. I desired and willed that in accordance with the example of my Lord my little brothers should pray more than they should read." The poor accursed one at once fell ill and took to his bed. A fiery, sulphurous drop fell from the sky and miraculously destroyed his life, piercing both his body and his bed. The devil carried away his soul.

The Dominicans, truth to tell, in spite of their rule, had no such attitude toward the classics, and Jacopo Passavanti, for example, was ordered by his superiors to study at Paris. His *Mirror of True Penitence,* especially the Latin version of it, with its examples drawn from ancient history and fables, bears ample testimony to his profane studies.

If the rules of some monastic orders forbade the reading of the pagan authors, the rules of other orders not only permitted it, but made it an express obligation to copy manuscripts. In this way the monks of the tenth, eleventh, and twelfth centuries rendered services to civilization which will never be forgotten. If there had not been great abbeys where schools of grammar were established, and where as many books as possible were jealously preserved, perhaps not one Latin writer would have come down to us. It is foolish to blame the monks, because they did not regard the pagan authors in the same way that we do; we should rather praise them for having known, in some measure, how to reconcile the love of letters with the religious sentiment, contravening sometimes, as they did, not only the spirit but the very letter of the monastic rules; we should see in this a proof of the great attractiveness which the ancient writings preserved throughout the Middle Ages, and of the aptitude of the men of those times for enjoying the beauties of pagan letters. There were always some who openly advised the reading of the classics. Many who publicly condemned it and dissuaded others from it, enjoyed it themselves, and were proud to be able to show in their own writings the erudition and elegance they had acquired from the ancient authors. The ancient poets, historians, and philosophers were continually mentioned, and their sentences and opinions cited and commented upon, not only in works on profane subjects, but also, and to a much greater extent, in writings on religious subjects, in theological and ascetic treatises, in books on education, and in polemical writings. It is not one of the least curious things in such works to find the pagan writers carefully cited side by side with the Fathers, and their books hobnobbing with the Scriptures. Seneca, Cicero, Juvenal, and even Horace are cited under the honored name of ethical writers (*ethici*); their opinions are repeated without any indication as to the special author from which they were derived, and are simply accompanied with the words "the ethical writer says" (*ethicus ait*); in another medieval work containing forty-seven moral reflections, the majority embody the ideas of pagan writers, especially of Cicero, Seneca, Livy, Ovid, Juvenal, Pliny, Solinus, and Valerius Maximus. It is true that many of those who cite a pagan author know nothing of the man himself save his name, and that only at second or third hand; it is also true that the citations are usually from memory. The significant thing, however, is not the extensive or slight, exact or inexact, knowledge of the classical authors, but the great respect and admiration which the medieval writers have and show for them. Their reputation for wisdom and veracity was universal. William of Hirschau, who died in 1091, relates the opinion of some who founded the whole theory of the four elements (earth, air, fire, and water) upon a verse of Juvenal, and even Dante did not dare to contradict Juvenal without excusing himself for it. The reputation of the Latin writers was so great that many, in order to gain repute for their own works, pretended that they had Latin sources; the writers on natural history especially were wont to palm off, under the names of Pliny, Solinus, and Ælianus, the most extravagant fables. Even at a later time, Christian poets, like Brunetto Latini, Dante, and Fazio degli Uberti, take the pagan writers as their guides upon symbolical journeys, and, under their escort, teach, narrate, and describe the profoundest mysteries of the universe. Some of these worthy pagan guides had already been given a place in the kingdom of heaven; others, who never had baptism but were without sin, were withdrawn from hell and abode with honor, and without punishment, in a separate place. Honorius Augustodunensis, a cleric who lived in the first half of the twelfth century, says in his treatise,

Latin Classics

The Exile and Native Land of the Soul, or the Arts, that
the exile of the soul is none other than ignorance, and
that the native land is knowledge. The return home from
exile is, he says, a road along which ten cities are located.
These are Grammar, Rhetoric, Dialectics, Arithmetic,
Music, Geometry, Astronomy, Physics, Mechanics, and
Economics. In the first city Donatus and Priscian teach;
in the second, Cicero; the third, Aristotle; the fourth,
Boethius; the fifth, disciples of Boethius; the sixth, Ara-
tus; the seventh, Hyginus and Julius Cæsar; and in the
eighth, Hippocrates. He gives no particular master for
the ninth or tenth.

Whatever may have been the natural hostility of the
Church toward the pagan authors, the feeling of admiration they inspired filled the souls of medieval writers, and
forbade that condemnation should pass from theory into
practice. St. Bernard says, in one of his works : " They
all were pleasing to God in their lifetime by rectitude, and
not by knowledge. Peter and Andrew and the sons of
Zebedee and their fellow-disciples did not come out of the
school of the rhetoricians and the philosophers." But he
adds : " I may, perhaps, seem to insult knowledge too
greatly, and as it were to condemn the learned and forbid
zealous studies. Far be it from me." " Moreover, it is to
be borne in mind that a certain classical and pagan tradition, too strongly rooted to be completely destroyed, survived in a greater or less degree in the European provinces which had once been under the sway of Rome. This
reappeared, here and there, in popular literature, perpetuated itself in certain beliefs and customs, manifested itself in certain propensities of mind, and, with-

Medieval Civilization

out being perceived by others, succeeded in softening certain contrasts, and caused the ancient world, as represented by its writers, to seem less strange and less distorted than would otherwise have been the case. This was truer of Italy than elsewhere, and Otto of Freising, in the twelfth century, marveled to find, in Lombardy, the language, the urbanity, and the wisdom of the Romans. The rudest popular songs of Italy, in the eleventh and twelfth centuries, abounded in memories of Rome, of her glories and her divinity. This persistence of a more vital and more jealously guarded classical tradition in Italy helps to explain why the Renaissance originated there, and spread thence to the rest of Europe. The schools of grammar and of rhetoric never died out entirely in Italy or outside of Italy, and, in spite of great changes, they could be traced directly back to the ancient schools of the empire. But the strongest and most efficacious of all bonds between the old age and the new, between the pagan world and the Christian world, was the beautiful, vigorous, and triumphant Latin language. In the conquest of lands and peoples it was not less effective than the arms of the legionaries. The Church had blessed it by confiding to its safe-keeping the truths of the faith, and by making it the august instrument of preaching. For a long time it defended its uncertain dominion against the nascent vulgar tongues, and even when the battle was at length lost, it withdrew but reluctantly from the people, bound itself always more closely to all the thought of the times, and, greatest proof of vitality in languages, it was able to change and transform itself, docilely lending itself to every necessity, and advancing,

step by step, with history. Men wrote, prayed, and
preached in Latin, and rough, unpolished Latin songs
circulated among the people. Strange to relate, Latin
did not become a truly dead language until the beginning
of the Renaissance. The Church spoke the very language
of the ancient poets, and the measures which had been
employed to celebrate Jove and Venus still served to
celebrate Christ and Mary. Unity of language is a bond
fitted to hold morally conjoined, through the ages, the
separate parts of a politically divided people. Would
it not, in this case, despite every other contrast, help to
draw the Christian reader and the pagan writer near to
each other, and to facilitate the conciliation of the ancient
spirit and the new? The Latin language and the Latin
writers were together the best surviving part of the scattered heritage of Rome; the medieval man, reading,
speaking, and writing Latin, could feel that he was Christian and Roman at the same time. This explains the
importance attached to grammatical studies in the Middle
Ages. Nor, in this connection, should we direct exclusive attention to the Latin language. Whatever in the
Middle Ages was able to cause men to feel more profoundly their participation in the life of ancient Rome,
and, much more, to tighten the bonds between descendants
and ancestors, was certain to redound to the advantage of
the pagan writers, shorten distances, awaken sympathies,
and lighten suspicions. Roman law, at least in Italy, had
never fallen into oblivion, and it seems certain that there
it was handed down and practised, without any interrup-
tion. In the first half of the eleventh century, Wipo, the
chaplain of the emperors Conrad II and Henry III,

Medieval Civilization

praised the Italian custom of causing young men to study the law. Whoever invoked or practised Roman law must have regarded the writers of Rome as his illustrious fellow-citizens, and have taken pleasure in them. Wipo says in one of his proverbs: " Knowledge of the classics is the light of the soul "—strange words, truly, in the mouth of an ecclesiastic, who should not have admitted that there was any light for the soul outside of the divine word which radiates from the sacred Scriptures. And it is indubitable that these words expressed a sentiment common to many, as is shown by a countless host of other witnesses. Peter of Blois wrote, about 1170, to a professor at the university of Paris: " Priscian and Cicero, Lucan and Persius, *these* are your gods." It is even more strange, however, that an ecclesiastic's knowledge of the pagan writers could serve as the basis for the warmest eulogy after his death. In the Latin epitaph of a certain Italian cleric named Guido, who died probably about 1095, the following appears in verse: " With the death of Guido the sayings of Plato perish, the work of Cicero is destroyed, the deeds of Vergil cease to speak, and the muse of Ovid is silent. Pythagoras, Socrates, Plato, Cicero, and Vergil, whatever they felt, whatever they taught, this man exhausted it all. Therefore, be pleased to grant this wish: Free from hell, may he reign with the supernal King." Not because he was a Christian, not because he was a minister of the Church, not because he was a careful observer of the divine law, but, according to the mind of the writer, because he had a rich, poetic vein, because he was eloquent, because he was learned in classical wisdom, did Guido merit the kingdom of heaven.

Latin Classics

In every period of the Middle Ages ecclesiastics of the highest repute studied the classics. A volume of examples could easily be collected. St. Aldhelm, born about 640, knew his Latin authors very well, as his writings show; Faritius, his biographer, says of him: "He had drunk deeply of the Latin learning."

Passing over the ecclesiastics at the court of Charles the Great as well known, we may cite Ratherius, bishop of Verona, in the tenth century, who read and loved the poets; about 1061, Benzo, bishop of Alba, in a work dedicated to the emperor Henry III, names Vergil, Lucan, Statius, Pindar, Homer, Horace, Quintilian, and Terence with much complacent exhibition of his classical knowledge. In the tenth century, Gonzo of Novara, being accused and ridiculed by the monks of St. Gall because he had used the accusative where he ought to have employed the ablative, wrote a long letter in defense to the monks of Reichenau, making much display of erudition. In the cloister school of Paderborn they read Vergil, Lucan, Statius, and the *Iliad* abridged by Pindar the Theban. Gerbert (Pope Sylvester II) taught his students Vergil, Lucan, Terence, Juvenal, Statius, and Persius. To all these churchmen, and to many others who could be named, the classical poetry must have seemed as it did to Alcuin—as an intoxicating wine, of another flavor, to be sure, but no less grateful to the palate, than the honey of the sacred Scriptures. Generally speaking, in the ninth and tenth centuries, which are justly considered the darkest of all the Middle Ages, antiquity was loved and studied, and known much more than is commonly believed. Ratherius of Verona declared that he would not ordain any one to holy orders who had not some acquaintance with the classics. In the following century, and in all the subsequent centuries which preceded the Renaissance, the study of classical literature widened and deepened.

But the classics were more than studied; they were imitated. The ancient epics and lyrics served as models for the new epics and lyrics, sometimes with grave loss of Christian sentiment, which seems disguised by the pagan clothing. Without lingering over the court of Charles the Great, we may cite from the second half of the ninth century the Franconian Otfried, who is believed to have been educated in the celebrated school of Fulda, and to have been a disciple of Rabanus Maurus. He was moved to write his poem on Christ not only by the example of Juvencus, Arator, and Prudentius, but also by that of Ovid, Lucan, and Vergil. The nun Roswitha imitated Terence. At a later time, Bernard of Chartres imitated Lucretius, who was almost unknown in the Middle Ages. Many other examples could be given. Not infrequently the imitations overshot the mark, persevering where they should have ceased, and introducing into sacred themes unsuitable names, epithets, and figures. This usage was quite old. About the middle of the fourth century, Aquilinus Juvencus calls Christ the " revered offspring of Jupiter the Thunderer." Alcuin calls the saints " citizens of Olympus, royal race of Jupiter " (*cives Olympi, gens diva Tonantis*).

Figures of speech, verses, and entire sentences were taken in rich profusion from the Latin poets and introduced into medieval writings, both sacred and profane.

Latin Classics

Classical myths and fables were well known, and the writers never lose an opportunity to repeat them, and to use them as examples to enforce some moral lesson. Some of the most famous medieval writers, such as Alain de Lille, Jean d'Hauteville, Alexander Neckham, and John of Salisbury, have a perfectly marvelous knowledge of classical fables. In a Latin poem of the tenth century the author names Venus, the Fates, and Neptune; a twelfth-century poet describes a contest between Ganymede and Helen on the subject of their beauty. In the Middle Ages, too, the stories of Troy, Alexander the Great, Hercules, Jason, the *Æneid, Pharsalia,* and the *Thebaid* were recast in the vulgar languages. Marie of France and others put into renewed circulation the old fables of Æsop and of Phædrus. At the same time, translations multiplied, and in the thirteenth century a Frenchman even succeeded in translating Justinian's *Institutes* into verse. Of the medieval men who had a truly astounding knowledge of classical antiquity, John of Salisbury was the foremost. Of the many others who might be named, Vincent of Beauvais should be mentioned for his citation, in his *Mirror of Nature,* of three hundred and fifty authors.

The classical knowledge of the medieval writers is, however, what may be called *external;* it is restricted to the letter, and is not penetrated by the spirit of antiquity. There is hardly one of them who does not, in speaking of the classical writers, fall into grievous errors and, at times, into rank absurdities. John of Salisbury makes two distinct persons out of Suetonius and Tranquillus, and Vincent of Beauvais likewise divides Sophocles into two, unites the two Senecas into one, makes Cicero an army captain, and writes Scalpurnus for Calpurnius. Others, less erudite, fall into even more serious mistakes. Alars of Cambrai, author of a treatise on the morals of philosophers, believes Tully and Cicero, Vergil and Maro, to be distinct persons. Ranulf Higden styled Plautus rhetorician and doctor.

When such errors as these were possible, imagination, which in all ages willingly exercises itself upon matters of which men have no certain and direct knowledge, had full play. The great writers of antiquity, present always to the memory of the Middle Ages, were unable to withdraw themselves from its grasp. The Middle Ages had their books, but few details of their lives, and the greater the admiration they evoked, the more irresistible was the temptation to resort to fiction. Frequently, too, a common idea, a moral precept expressed in the form of a parable or otherwise, was attached to the name of a great pagan, without other motive than the desire to procure for it a wider circulation and greater credit. It was in this way that Socrates, Plato, Hippocrates, Aristotle, Vergil, and others entered into legends more or less suitable, according to circumstances, to their characters; and, considering the number of fancies which secured circulation in this way, it is not surprising that some are very extravagant. Homer generally passed for a liar who either did not understand aright or else deliberately misstated the facts of the Trojan war. Socrates, whose name was believed to mean *observer of justice,* had two wives who beat him so severely one day that he nearly died. Elsewhere he is made out to be a Roman, and to him the council of

the Eternal City entrust the duty of making a response
to a Greek embassy requesting liberation from tribute.
In the *Gesta Romanorum* it is related that the emperor
Claudius gave his own daughter in marriage to Socrates
on condition that if she should die her husband should
suffer death, and Socrates almost had to pay the penalty.
Plato's name meant *task* or *account*. He was fond of
desert places, and when he lifted up his voice he could
be heard two miles off. He was one of the greatest physicians of antiquity and was very rich. One day Diogenes
went to Plato's house, and seeing the magnificent beds
which it contained, forthwith proceeded to soil the purple
covers with his muddy feet. On leaving the house he
said to Plato: "Thus is your pride brought low by the
pride of another." Plato then retired with his followers
to a pestilential desert spot, "in order that the roughness
of the place might destroy the desire for fleshly luxury."
According to some, he died because he could not solve a
riddle which had been propounded to him. Aristotle
means *perfect in goodness*. Some believed him to be the
son of the devil, but he "did not act contrary to theology,"
and when about to die he asked that his books might be
buried with him, lest Antichrist should use them. Some
say that he died because he could not understand the ebb
and flow of the sea. "Since I cannot comprehend you,"
he is reported to have said, "you shall comprehend me,"
and he cast himself into the water. The Latin writers had
equally strange things told concerning them. In fact, the
pagan philosophers and poets were generally held, because
of their wisdom, to be astrologers, and not a few of them
passed for magicians. Marvelous virtues were ascribed

to some of their books. Even in the classical period Vergil's books were consulted as oracles, and the first passage lighted upon in one of his books was accepted as an oracular response. The use of these " Vergilian lots " continued throughout the Middle Ages, although the *Bible* and the *Lives of the Saints* were consulted in the same way. Æneas Syivius Piccolomini (Pope Pius II) relates in the fifteenth century that Alphonso of Aragon, king of Naples, was cured of a grave malady by reading Quintus Curtius.

Another medieval fancy well worth mentioning consisted in the attribution of Christian qualities to ancient writers. This not only satisfied a sentiment sufficiently natural in those who could not but admire illustrious pagans, but it had practical uses, for it turned aside the aversion of the Church, and eased the scruples of timid consciences. The Church could no longer reasonably prohibit, nor should believers any longer fear, the reading of an ancient writer, when this writer passed for a Christian. The legends in which such fancies appeared were readily believed, and the Church had no great interest in giving the lie to them, since she could not but be pleased at the multiplication of testimonies to the truth from the most celebrated pagans. In every age notable ecclesiastical writers admitted that even before the birth of Christ some of the pagan elect had been able, through divine grace, to have, as it were, a presentiment of the redemption and an anticipatory knowledge of the greater truths of the faith. Justin Martyr, in the first *Apology,* represents Socrates, Plato, and other philosophers of antiquity as propagators and followers of the one true faith.

Latin Classics

St. Ambrose, St. Augustine, and St. John Chrysostom thought that Socrates was saved. St. Thomas admitted that some of the pagan philosophers had held the faith *implicitly*. Plato gained most from this sentiment, for many of the Fathers were instinctively attracted by his doctrines. St. Augustine, in one place in the *City of God,* confutes the opinion that Plato had known Jeremiah, or read the prophetic Scriptures, although he himself had previously held this view. He admits that Plato divined the Trinity. The same concession was made to Aristotle. Abélard admitted that many of the truths of Christianity had been known, in anticipation, to ancient philosophers. In a twelfth-century poem the philosopher Aristotle is said to have trained up Alexander the Great in the Christian faith. Socrates is not said, directly, to have been a Christian, but it is stated that he died because he would not adore idols.

Vergil's wisdom was so great—he was regarded as the most authoritative and legitimate representative of the ancient culture—that it was not difficult to persuade medieval lovers of his works that he had foreknowledge of the coming of Christ. It could not be admitted that such a man as he, versed in all knowledge, even the most hidden, could remain entirely ignorant of the event which was to renew the world. Add to this the common tendency which led men to admit that not a few of the ancients, either through special grace of heaven or through the peerless qualities of their own intellects, had divined some part of the truths of Christianity, and it will not be difficult to understand how the sibylline verses of the fourth *Eclogue,* where Vergil speaks of the birth of a divine youth and of the purification of the world, could be considered as a prophecy of the birth of Christ and of the diffusion of the new faith. Lactantius admitted that Vergil announced the coming of Christ, and this opinion, contradicted by St. Jerome and, later, by St. Isidore, is held by St. Augustine, and commonly accepted throughout the Middle Ages.

According to another opinion Vergil was actually a Christian. Jean d'Outremeuse, who also makes Vergil a Roman lawgiver, says that he announced to the Roman senate the advent and the passion of Christ, taught the doctrine of the Trinity to certain Egyptians, declared the true faith, and was baptized in the hour of death. Long before Jean wrote, however, there were loving souls who could not believe that the good and gentle Vergil was lost. In the life of St. Cadoc of Wales, who flourished in the sixth century, it is recorded that he was once walking in company with St. Gildas upon the sea-shore. He carried a volume of Vergil under his arm, in which he was accustomed to instruct his pupils, and wept in silence. "Why weepest thou?" said St. Gildas. "I weep," he replied, "because the author of this book, which I love and which gives me such lively pleasure, is perchance damned forever." "Without a doubt," answered St. Gildas; "God does not judge these story-tellers differently from other men." At this moment a gust of wind caught the book and bore it into the sea. Great was the consternation of St. Cadoc, and he took a vow never more to eat or drink until it was revealed to him what fate God vouchsafes to those who sing in this world as the angels sing in heaven. Immediately on going to sleep he heard a sweet voice which said: " Pray, pray for me; do not cease to make intercession that I may be permitted to celebrate in eternal song the compassion of the Lord." The following day the saint found his volume of Vergil in the body of a salmon. The poet was undoubtedly saved. In a similar manner, Josephus, Terence, Seneca, Lucan, Statius, and Pliny the Younger were asserted to be Christians, and many of the ancients were regarded as having announced the incarnation of the Word and the birth of the Redeemer.

Some of those who did not believe in the orthodoxy of the pagan writers had a way of excusing them and of rendering the perusal of their books plausible by asserting that in them were to be found, under the veil of fables and poetic ornaments, the profoundest moral truths. Not a few of them allegorized even the obscene stories of Ovid in such a way as to vindicate the morality of the writer. Allegory was at least a veil which, if it did not conceal the nakedness of the written word, disguised it somewhat, and permitted thoughtful men to gaze upon it without being scandalized. Christian thinking and opinion leaned naturally toward allegory and symbolism. At the very beginnings of Christianity we find the art of the catacombs wholly symbolical; the liturgy of the Church is a complicated system of allegories and symbols. It was not long before two senses were distinguished in the Scriptures, the literal and the mystic, and the mystic was subdivided into anagogical, allegorical, and moral. According to William of Occam, the Gospels have four senses, historical, allegorical, tropological, and anagogical. Exaggerating this tendency, the medieval men finally interpreted all history allegorically, and conceived nature as nothing but an immense system of signs and symbols of the supernatural.   Poetry, too, was ultimately regarded as a nobler and more subtle language, whose principal office was to veil, in seemly forms, the august truths of theology and morals.   To Alain de Lille poetry is recondite truth hidden under an exterior of falsehood.   At the threshold of the Renaissance, Dante and Petrarch still believed that the spirit of poetry was essentially to be found in the allegory.   The high opinion of the wisdom of the pagans, which was universal in the Middle Ages, caused men to believe that the most sublime truths were secreted in their verses.

Such wisdom being attributed to the poets, it is not surprising that they were frequently ranked with the philosophers.   Alars of Cambrai, in his *Romance of All the Philosophers,* places Terence, Lucan, Perseus, Horace, Juvenal, Ovid, Sallust, Vergil, and Macrobius among the philosophers, and such confusion of poets and historians with philosophers was especially common in those medieval treatises which purported to give the flowers of ancient wisdom.   He who was not too prone to discover an allegorical meaning in the verses of the poets could not, especially if he were rather austere in his religious sentiments, avoid making a certain difference between poets and philosophers and esteeming the latter the higher in dignity.   The attitude of the Church toward the pagan philosophers was not always consistent, but, generally speaking, philosophic proof was regarded as repugnant to the genius of Christianity, which is founded entirely upon faith.   St. Augustine, at first enthusiastic over the

Greek philosophers, ended by renouncing them. He declared that the Greek philosophers were much more worthy of laughter than of confutation, and said that the only true philosophy was the true faith. Athanasius the Great confessed that the more he speculated upon the divinity of Christ the less he believed it, and he admonished men to believe without seeking to prove. In 1228 Pope Gregory IX exhorted the doctors of the university of Paris to cease adulterating the divine word with the fictions of the philosophers. St. Bernard called the philosophers vain and curious, and a hundred others held the same, or an even worse, opinion of them. The desire to use logic overmuch imperiled the soul. This idea is illustrated by the story of the scholar who appeared after death to his former master, bearing upon his back a hood filled to the top with sophisms. On the other hand, it had already been recognized, even by the early apologists, that pagan philosophy contained some germs of truth, and it is certain that Pythagorism, Platonism, and Stoicism have some marked affiliations with Christianity. Abélard asserted that Christianity was nothing but a popularization of the esoteric doctrines of the ancient philosophers. The pagans Plato and Aristotle governed Christian thinking, and they and other ancient worthies were spoken of with profound admiration in the Middle Ages. In the twelfth and thirteenth centuries the reputation of the philosophers—especially of Aristotle—increased beyond measure and obscured that of the poets.

It is most important to grasp the distinction made between the philosophers who had divined some part of revealed truth and the poets who had decked out the errors of heathenism with all the seductions of art. Abélard, so generous toward the philosophers, was particularly hard on the poets. One of the miniatures which accompanied the original manuscript of Herrad of Landsperg's twelfth-century *Garden of Delights* throws an instructive light on this distinction. In this miniature the seven arts were represented by seven women, within two concentric circles. In the smaller circle a crowned figure, seated upon a throne, represented the Holy Spirit. In his hands he bore a Latin scroll with the motto: "All wisdom is of God. The wise alone are able to accomplish their desires." The crown, upon which three heads, entitled Ethics, Logic, and Physics, appeared, bore the inscription, "Philosophy." To the right of the Holy Spirit appeared the legend: "Seven fountains of wisdom flow from philosophy, and are known as the liberal arts"; on the left: "The Holy Spirit is the author of the seven liberal arts, which are Grammar, Rhetoric, Dialectics, Music, Arithmetic, Geometry, and Astronomy." Beneath the Holy Spirit were the figures of Socrates and Plato, accompanied by the saying: "Philosophy teaches the knowledge of the universal nature of things; philosophers teach first ethics, then physics, and lastly rhetoric; philosophers were the wise men of the world and the clergy of the Gentiles." Outside of the two circles devoted to the realm of the seven arts were four figures which represented "poets or magicians full of the unclean spirit." At the ear of each whispered a crow, emblem of the devil, the inspirer of perverse doctrines. Associated with the four was this saying:

Latin Classics

" These, inspired by unclean spirits, write magic art and poetry, that is, fabulous commentaries."

This, like similar opinions held throughout the Middle Ages, called forth by a faith too narrow and too distrustful, could not prevail against the sentiment of the majority, and against common practice and tradition. The fables of the poets were so attractive that alone they would have been able to conquer every religious and moral repugnance; but ingenious legend lent her aid and with pious deception sought the reconciliation of the poets with the Church, and opened to the pagans the portals of heaven.

The Development of the Romance Languages, Especially Those of France

Adapted from A. Darmesteter: *Cours de grammaire historique de la langue française,* fourth edition, pp. 10–42.

THE French language, like Portuguese, Spanish, Provençal, Italian, Ladin (spoken in the western Tyrol), and Rumanian, has been derived, through a long series of transformations, from Latin, the language of the Romans.

The Latin language underwent tremendous changes before it attained the perfection it enjoyed under Cicero, Livy, Tacitus, Lucretius, Vergil, and Horace. At all times there was a more or less marked divergence between the spoken and the written language, but the variation was, on the whole, slight during the republic and the empire.

The fifth century, however, witnessed a distinct decline in Latin literature and Roman greatness, and accompanying this decline a rapid and independent development of spoken Latin took place. Many constructions, many forms and words, which literary Latin, in the days of Rome's greatness, had been too haughty or too conservative to adopt, now triumphed completely; and as numbers

The Romance Languages

lay down the law in matters of language, and as the plebs formed the great majority of the nation, the ways of speaking which were current with the multitude now dominated. It is from this changing popular, or vulgar, Latin that the Romance tongues sprang; it would, perhaps, be more accurate to say that they *are* vulgar Latin, in its modern stages of development.

There was a remarkable uniformity in the vulgar Latin spoken from the Black Sea to the Atlantic, and from the banks of the Rhine to Mount Atlas; the grammar, syntax, and vocabulary were essentially the same. The pronunciation, of course, varied from place to place. The peoples of different races who had adopted Latin had forgotten their original tongues, but they could not discard their peculiarities of pronunciation.

Gradually, and under the action of complex causes, linguistic varieties assumed form. The most rapid and most characteristic modifications, those which gave to each country its own peculiar language, took place in the seventh, or at latest in the eighth, century. Certain words were in much more common use in one region than in another; words fully alive here were quite unknown or forgotten there; pronunciation took on a more marked character according to time and place, and syntax adopted slightly diverging constructions.

If, however, we consider their common characteristics rather than their differences, if we notice that they have practically the same vocabulary, declensions, and conjugations, the same usages in composition and derivation, and the same syntax, then the Romance languages are seen to be different aspects of one and the same language, varying from one another only as the blossoms of flowers planted in different soils on the same estate.

Each of the Romance languages retained, as its own property, independently of the others, the name *Roman,* which the people of Rome gave to their language. Even to-day the name is borne by the Rumanian and the Ladin, or *Romanche:* Provençal is called the *Roman* tongue, and the Provençal people think that their language has a special right to the name.

In the Middle Ages, Italian, Spanish, Portuguese, and French were often designated by the name *Roman.* In Old French to translate from Latin into *Roman* meant to translate into French. The word *Roman* also meant a literary composition in the vulgar tongue, and the *Roman de la Rose* was the French poem of the rose, and the *Roman de Renard,* the French poem of the fox. Thus the word *Roman,* or Romance, which was everywhere retained by the various idioms sprung from the Latin, bears irrefutable testimony to the original unity of these languages.

Each of them is *a* Romance tongue but not *the* Romance tongue. Romance, or Roman, strictly speaking, is the vulgar Latin which was spoken in the empire from the third to the seventh or eighth century. According to the region in which it was spoken, it bears the names *Gallo-Roman, Hispano-Roman, Italo-Roman*—the vulgar Latin spoken during this period in Gaul, Spain, and Italy respectively. This vulgar Latin was a spoken language, and it must be distinguished from the written Latin of the same period, which is known as *Low Latin.*

Low Latin is the literary Latin which was written by more or less ignorant people, and it is marred by faults

The Romance Languages

springing from their spoken language, much as the Latin of a school-boy to-day is marred by solecisms and barbarisms from his native tongue. In Merovingian times Low Latin was modeled almost wholly upon the spoken language of the time, except by the Church Fathers, and it offers a picture of the most complete barbarism, which, however, makes it peculiarly interesting to the linguistic student, since it enables him to discover, behind its barbaric forms, what the spoken language of the time was.[1] The Carolingian Renaissance did something to purify this corrupted Latin. All the lettered people of the Middle Ages wrote Low Latin. There are, of course, marked differences between Low Latin and Classical Latin. The vocabulary of the former is modified, for it had to express ideas unknown to ancient Rome; it is, in fact, the expression, by an intelligent minority, of a new and very complex civilization. Its grammar and particularly its syntax were influenced by the spoken language, but it had fixed rules of its own. It finally disappeared in the sixteenth century, before the efforts of the Humanists, who, taking Cicero as their model, restored to honor the language of the great classics of Rome.

Let us now consider the history of the Gallo-Roman group of Romance tongues. It will serve as a type.

The vulgar Latin of the Gauls destroyed their Celtic tongue, for the Gauls, once conquered, were sufficiently intelligent and sufficiently advanced in çivilization to recognize the intellectual and moral superiority of Rome,

---

[1] Compare the Low Latin *Vindedi ad illo campello ferente modius tantus* with the classical form, *Vendidi ad illum campellum ferentem modios tantos.*

and to take advantage of it. They threw themselves ardently into the process of Romanization, and the methods of Roman government really facilitated the work. Gaul was the most thoroughly Romanized part of the empire, outside of Italy. Under Augustus 1200 men sufficed for the defense of Gaul, while 15,000 were required in Britain, and 45,000 on the German border. Gallic civilization disappeared as by enchantment before the Roman, and with the civilization went the language, which, after all, was close kin to the Latin. A critical examination of the Celtic element in French shows that French possesses only a few words of Gallic origin, and these entered, moreover, not directly, but through the vulgar Latin. Gallic pronunciation left traces in the Gallo-Roman pronunciation, but the grammar—and grammar is the fundamental element of all languages—was without influence. The grammar which we find in early French, Italian, Spanish, etc., is the same grammar; in each case it is derived from the vulgar Latin.

The existence of the Gallic tongues up to the fourth century is established. Latin conquered the cities first, then gradually subdued the country, leaving to the indigenous tongue vast islets of territory which gradually succumbed. At the moment when the barbarian invasions began, the Gallic speech was no longer to be heard in any part of Gaul; from the Mediterranean to the mouths of the Rhine, from Port Vendres to Antwerp, and from the Atlantic to the Alps, vulgar Latin had supplanted it.

The barbarian invasions had the effect of restricting in one direction, and of expanding in another, the territory

The Romance Languages

of Gallo-Roman. The Visigoths in Aquitaine, the Burgundians in Burgundy, the Salian Franks in the northeast, and the Austrasian Franks in the east, brought in their Germanic idioms with them. These idioms disappeared, after a time, but the northern and eastern frontiers were abandoned by the Gallo-Roman provincials, fleeing before the invaders, and were occupied by the Germans, who settled down and spoke a Low German dialect in what is now Flanders, and a High German dialect in modern Alsace-Lorraine. The Anglo-Saxon invasion of Britain drove a portion of the British population to settle in the lower part of Armorica, which at the time was depopulated, and thus caused a Celtic dialect to spring up again on soil which had witnessed the overthrow of the Gallic at the hands of Latin.[1] In the southwest, the invasions of the Gascons, who crossed the Pyrenees in the sixth century, brought into Gaul from Spain the ancient tongue of the Iberians, which Latin had previously expelled. Lastly, in the eighth century the invasions of the Arabs forced the Hispano-Romans to flee toward the north and leave deserted vast regions on the eastern side of the Spanish peninsula; and Gallo-Romans from Roussillon crossed the Pyrenees to occupy the land, settled in Catalonia, the province of Valencia, and the Balearic Isles, and planted there a Gallo-Roman dialect known as *Catalan*. Such were the changes produced in

---

[1] The Celtic languages are divided into three branches: (1) Gallic, which was spoken in Gaul and disappeared completely in the fourth century; (2) the *Breton* idioms, which survive in Lower Brittany and in Wales; and (3) Gaelic, which includes (*a*) Irish, spoken to-day by several hundred thousand Irish peasants, (*b*) Gaelic proper, spoken in several parts of Scotland, and (*c*) the dialect of the Isle of Man.

the territorial limits of Gallo-Roman speech by the barbarian invasions, and, with minor alterations, these limits
remain to this day.

This vast domain of Gallo-Roman used one language
at first. But as century succeeded century the language
underwent successive changes; it became diversified, and
developed into an infinite variety of local speeches, from
south to north, and from east to west. Each region gave
its own color, its own peculiar aspect, to the Latin; and
yet no sharply defined geographical unities of language
resulted, for the various characteristics of a local speech
were not restricted to its own geographical limits, but
radiated in various directions, affecting in a variable and
more or less profound way the different neighboring
regions.

The changes—and this is a fact of capital importance—
were produced without any breach of continuity; and if
a straight line should be drawn from any point in France
to any other, it would be found that the local speech of
the first would be, by almost imperceptible and yet progressive modifications, transformed into the local speech
of the other. Two neighboring speeches understood each
other; if separated by a third, they would still understand
each other, but with difficulty; separated by several
others, they would be mutually unintelligible.

Thanks to this continuity in the linguistic transformations, the various speeches of a provence exhibit general resemblances as well as specific differences, and that
is why we have been able to give them the name of the
province where they have been spoken, as, for example,
Gascon, Languedocian, and Champenois. But it must al-

The Romance Languages

ways be remembered that these geographical terms designate not a linguistic unity, but the group of speeches employed in the province, considered from the standpoint of that which they have in common. Thus vulgar Latin, sowed by the Roman conquest upon the soil of Gaul, covered it with an immense linguistic flora, which, developing with the utmost freedom in the different districts, assumed infinitely divergent forms.

But at the same time that vulgar Latin was abandoned to itself and delivered over to the mysterious activities which direct the spontaneous evolution of language, and thus was enabled to blossom into a multitude of local speeches, other forces, political and social, intervened to reëstablish a certain unity amid this endless division.

In each region, one of the local speeches, that of a city or an aristocracy, raised itself above its neighbors, and, gaining dignity, threw them into the shade. The local speeches which were cast into the shade are *patois;* those which were raised to literary dignity are *dialects.*

Thus written languages were formed in different centers, which, radiating their influence round about, imposed themselves, like nobles, upon the populations of neighboring regions, and created a linguistic province, a dialect, in which the local patois were gradually effaced or smothered. These dialects no longer expanded by oral tradition, but by literary activities; their development was not a fact of the organic, natural life of the idiom; it was a fact of civilization.

In this new linguistic evolution, the dialects differed from one another in proportion as they were separated by more numerous patois or by wider geographical distances. In conflict with one another, they took on a more characteristic physiognomy and became independent languages.

Thus a series of different regional idioms was formed in France, which generally go by the name of the province in which they have flourished, and the same method is followed in naming the group of patois which continue to live their life of obscurity in the same province. For example, *Norman* is applied to the dialect employed by the Norman writers of the Middle Ages, and also to the mass of patois which lived or live in Normandy.

If the dialects and patois which have flourished on French soil are considered as a whole, it will be at once seen that they fall into two large groups, that of the dialects and patois of the *langue d'oc,* and that of the dialects and patois of the *langue d'oïl.*[1]

Two of the dialects belonging to the *langue d'oc* were considered by the Middle Ages to be independent languages : Gascon and Catalan. The region in which Gascon was spoken is sufficiently indicated by Gascony, and the home of Catalan has already been described. Outside the Gascon and Catalan territories are the Provençal dialects and patois, which cover, wholly or in part, twenty-six of the modern departments of France, and which embrace Limousin, Languedocian, Provençal proper, Savoyard, etc.

---

[1] It was the medieval custom to designate languages according to the word employed for *yes. Langue d'oc* means the language which uses *oc* for *yes,* and *langue d'oïl,* the one which uses *oïl.* The phrases also serve as territorial designations. Thus Dante calls Italy the country of *si:*

Il bel paese la dove il s i suona.

The Romance Languages

As early as the tenth century we find a Provençal literature, and there is extant from this epoch a considerable fragment of an imitation in verse of Boethius's *Consolation of Philosophy*. The twelfth century produced a brilliant literature, largely lyrical, whose authors call themselves troubadours. It disappeared in the middle of the thirteenth century, drowned in the blood of the Albigensian crusade. St. Louis tried in vain to repair the evil and pacify the country; the troubadours left the impoverished land and the abandoned seignorial courts; they went to Aragon and Italy to sing their songs, and the decadence of Provençal literature remained unchecked.

It is not possible to determine scientifically the borderline between the dialects of the *langue d'oc* and the dialects of the *langue d'oïl,* for the simple reason that the local patois of the two languages gradually and imperceptibly shade away into each other. But on the basis of a small number of striking traits an approximate line may be drawn.

Let us cross this frontier and study the development of vulgar Latin in the north of France. Here, as early as the seventh century, this vulgar idiom was so sharply marked off from classical Latin and Low Latin that it was recognized as a new language. In 659 St. Mummolin was called to succeed St. Eloi as bishop of Noyon, because " he was proficient not only in the German tongue [spoken by the conquerors], but also in the Roman tongue [spoken by the people]." In the next century, Gerard, abbot of Sauve-Majeure, praises his master, St. Adalhard, abbot of Corbey, for his knowledge of Romance, Latin, and German: "If he spoke Roman, one would have believed that he knew no other tongue; if he spoke German, his language was even more brilliant; but if he spoke Latin, it was perfection." We possess Latin-Romance and Romance-German glossaries from this century in which Latin and German words are translated by Low Latin or Romance words clearly suggesting French words. In the ninth century the councils of Tours and Rheims ordered the bishops to translate the Sunday sermons into Romance or German, so that they might be more easily understood by all.

It is certain that from the early ninth century the practice of writing in the vulgar tongue was common; but the texts, being written on wax tablets or bits of parchment, were too fragile to come down to us. We have, however, the text of the famous Oaths of Strasburg (842), which were so important that they were reproduced by Nithard, a celebrated contemporary historian. They appear in a manuscript copy of Nithard of the late tenth or early eleventh century. They show that the main traits of the *langue d'oïl* were already fixed, although this text, at first glance, presents a Latin physiognomy.

Passing over several interesting writings from the tenth century, we come to the eleventh century, when literary works of the first rank appeared. The *Chanson de Saint Alexis* and, a little later, the *Chanson de Roland* are two poems which form a worthy opening for French literature. At the end of the century came the *Pilgrimage of Charlemagne to Jerusalem,* a most curious heroic-comic poem in which freedom from constraint, laughter,

The Romance Languages

and parody are joined, without effort, to a lofty style and an epic movement.

The twelfth century is the golden age of Old French literature: in the thirteenth and fourteenth centuries it was, although marvelously fertile and incomparably rich, less original.

This literature was not peculiar to any one region; it extended over the whole domain of the *langue d'oïl,* and it exhibits linguistic peculiarities which vary from province to province. Each dialect had its literature. In short, the *langue d'oïl* may be divided, on the principles explained above, into as many dialects as there are localities.

Until the fourteenth century these dialects were almost entirely independent. Roger Bacon, traveling through France about 1260, states that French is divided into four dialects: French, Picard, Norman, and Burgundian. Peire Cardinal, a troubadour of the thirteenth century, says that he can speak neither Norman nor Poitevin. One of the characters in the Provençal romance *Flamenca* knew how to speak " Burgundian and French, German and Breton." A fourteenth-century translator of the Psalms who wrote in Lorraine announces his work thus: " This is a translation of the Psalms from Latin into Romance—into the Lorraine language."

The independence of the various dialects of the north was, however, threatened quite early. In the very bosom of the feudal anarchy of the eleventh century there was arising, in the Capetian dynasty, a central power which was in time to displace the feudal powers. The royal Capetian house took its rise in the duchy of the *Île de*

Medieval Civilization

France, and had its seat at Paris. The royal court increased the dignity of the dialect which it used, and gradually imposed this upon the aristocracy and the writers. From the twelfth century the preëminence of the French of the *Île de France* was assured, and the glory of the monarchy under Philip Augustus and St. Louis definitely guaranteed its ultimate supremacy.

About 1170 the churchman Garnier boasts that he has written his fine poem upon the life and death of Thomas Becket " in good Romance : " " My language is good, for I was born in the *Île de France*." Conon de Béthune, a great lord of the province of Artois, and a poet contemporary with Philip Augustus, complains that he had called forth the jeers of the young king, the queen mother, and the court, by reciting before them one of his chansons with a local accent and embellished with Artoisan words.

Adenet, the author of *Bertha of the Big Feet,* says that it was the custom, in the days of Pepin, for the German nobility to have Frenchmen at their court to teach their children French, and then he goes on to say that the king, the queen, and Bertha " knew French almost as well as if they had been born in the burg of St. Denis " (Paris).

The trouvère Aimon de Varennes, who wrote in 1188 at Châtillon-sur-Rhone, chose French for his *Roman de Florimont,* because the French esteemed his language barbarous.

A translator of Boethius, born at Meung in the thirteenth century, excuses himself for writing in a language which did not possess the supreme correctness of Parisian, because " I am not a Parisian, and I cling to the speech which my mother taught me at Meung when she suckled me."

In the fourteenth century Chaucer, in the *Prologue* to the *Canterbury Tales,* introduces a nun who spoke " Stratford " French because she was ignorant of Parisian French :

> "And Frensh she spak ful faire and fetysly
> After the scole of Stratford atte Bowe,
> For Frensch of Parys was to hir unknowe."

If in the full tide of the fourteenth century writers continued to use dialects which the preceding age had already pronounced inferior, it is nevertheless certain that these dialects had begun to decline and give place to French, the official language of the royal government, the literary language of the *pays de France,* and the language employed by the upper classes in conversation. Hardly anywhere outside of the country districts did the local tongues really continue to live, develop, and change, in full liberty. With the passing of the centuries they came to differ more and more from one another, and assumed characteristic traits—provided they were not crushed, as were the various patois of the *Île de France* and its environs, by the all-embracing influence of the French of Paris. Only one, the Walloon, survives to-day in the territories of the *langue d'oïl,* in part of Belgium.

The slow and uninterrupted progress of the French of Paris penetrated, by the close of the Middle Ages, all the domains of the *langue d'oïl.* The detailed history of its conquests is yet to be written, but the main outlines are clear. French did not displace the various dialects with-

out being affected by them in some respects. The provinces in adopting the official language could not avoid
intermingling with it some of the tricks of expression,
constructions, and phrases of their own declining patois,
and especially their—what for want of a better name may
be called—*accent*. In this way provincial French was
formed, each province having its own distinctly marked
type. In spite of literary education, provincialisms have
remained to the present day, coloring frequently the conversation of the city folk, if they do not appear in the
work of writers. A provincial, however close to Paris his
home may be, can be told among a thousand by his accent.

At the end of the twelfth century, and especially in the
thirteenth, after the Albigensian war, French had crossed
the frontiers of the *langue d'oïl* and had penetrated into
the cities of Southern France, following the royal administration. We have already noted the abandonment by
a Lyonnais writer of his native dialect for French.
French followed the advance of the monarchy in the fourteenth and fifteenth centuries. From the beginning of
the sixteenth century the great cities of southern France,
Bordeaux, Toulouse, Montpellier, Lyons, Grenoble, etc.,
furnished French works to literature. In another way
French triumphed at the close of the Middle Ages, winning the victory over Low Latin, which up to that time
had been the official language of justice and teaching.
The ordinance of Villers-Cotterets, issued by Francis I
in 1539, declared that "all decrees and proceedings, all
judicial acts and writs and matters whatsoever, shall be
pronounced, registered, and delivered to the parties in the
French mother-tongue, and not otherwise," and the six-

The Romance Languages

teenth century saw also the appearance of philosophical and scientific educational treatises in French. Thus French was becoming the language of all France—just as the idioms of Latium, Florence, and Middlesex became the Latin, Italian, and English languages respectively.

And yet, in spite of the triumph of the absolute monarchy, in spite of three centuries of central and local administration which has known no language save that of Paris, in spite of the blossoming of a literature which has raised it, in the common estimation of mankind, to an incomparable height, French has not yet completed the conquest of its natural territory. Provençal is still spoken in the cities of southern France, and in the greater proportion of the country districts of the *langue d'oïl* the local patois are still employed—along with French; in the country districts of southern France the peasants know hardly anything but their patois; and the Basque and Lower Brittany regions are hardly touched. But, with military service and obligatory primary instruction, the day will come when the French of the *Ile de France* will complete its conquest of France.

Evolution of the German Language

Adapted from O. Weise: *Unsere Muttersprache,*
1897, pp. 1–21, 34–35.

THE earliest history of the German language, and the
origin of the German race, are alike shrouded in
deep obscurity. Science, indeed, tells us that the Germans
at one time occupied a common territory with the Greeks
and Romans, Celts and Slavs, Lithuanians and Armeni-
ans, and Hindus and Iranians; that their civilization was
virtually the same, and that all spoke a common language.
We are even able to form a fairly definite idea of the common vocabulary of these peoples, of their word-forma-
tions, inflections, and conjugations; but we can no more
determine the year of the birth of the German language,
than we can tell when and how the allied peoples broke
apart and went their several ways. Not until the morning glow of history penetrates the mysterious darkness
which brooded over the land of our forefathers, does
any light fall upon the word-structure of their language.

Meanwhile, several thousands of years elapsed. The
different peoples parted company and spread over Europe
and southwestern Asia. The Germans split up into
several tribes and dwelt upon the shores of the Baltic.
But, like the flowing over of boiling waters, the Germans
drove ever onward, under the overmastering impulse of

their ramble-loving natures; and the German language tore at the bonds of form imposed by remote antiquity. The consonants, especially, were radically transformed: *bh, gh,* and *dh* were lost to the aspirates; *p, k,* and *t* took the place of *b, g,* and *d,* and where we meet *p, k* and *t* in the cognate languages, German then employed *f, h,* and *th.*

The accent, also, was materially changed. In the primitive language the stress might fall upon any syllable whatsoever; in Latin and Greek it was restricted to one of the last three syllables, and might be either upon the root or the case-ending, as *Róma, Románi, Romanórum.* Our old ancestors put an end to this irresolution. They placed the accent, once for all, on the syllable most essential to the word, which is usually the stem, as *Thát, thátig, Thátigkeit, Thátigkeitstrieb.*

Thus were the independence and originality of the German language declared; but centuries had to pass before the wandering race reached its final dwelling-place. Even after it had settled down, whole bands frequently went forth to quench their thirst for war in warmer and more fruitful regions. In the second century B.C. the Cimbri left the North Sea and roved through Germany, Gaul, and Spain, down to the Italian peninsula. In Cæsar's time whole swarms of Germans passed over the middle and lower Rhine into Gaul. About 150 A.D. the Goths abandoned the neighborhood of the Vistula and wandered in a southeasterly direction to the mouth of the Danube and the shore of the Black Sea; about 300 A.D., under Hunnish pressure, they again set forth and traversed nearly all Europe, and,

Medieval Civilization

after a brief and not inglorious career, were destroyed as a separate tribe in the trituration of the peoples. Their name still survives in different parts of Europe, from Gotland and Göteborg to Gossensass on the Brenner and Catalonia (*Catalonien = Gotalanien:* Goths and Alans); and in Ulfilas's translation of the *Bible* we have eloquent testimony to the beauty and strength of their language.

Still other Germanic peoples were seized by the great forward movement. The Burgundian race blazed its burning way from the Baltic coasts (*Bornholm = Burgunderholm*) to the middle Rhine, and later to the Saône; the Lombards passed from the lower Elbe (*Bardewik = [Lango] Bardenort*) into the valley of the Po. The Alemannians and the Bavarians settled between the Alps and the Danube; the Franks located themselves on the Rhine and the Main, and the Thuringians chose middle Germany as their abiding-place. Swarms of Angles, Saxons, and Jutes swept across the Channel into Britain, or moved southward from their former seats. The territory left vacant by the Germans, east of the Elbe, was joyfully accepted for settlement by the advancing Slavs. The Frisians and the Hessians (*Chatti*) were the only considerable Teutonic tribes which were still located, after the Völkerwanderung, in the territories which they had held in the days of Cæsar and of Tacitus.

When the billows of this second great migration-flood had subsided, it was unmistakably manifest that the German language had undergone fundamental transformations. But this second great shifting of the German peoples, unlike the first, affected only a portion of

Evolution of the German Language

the German tongues. The first involved similar changes in all the cognate languages; the latter affected different ones unequally.

This newer linguistic movement had its beginning, so far as we can judge, in the sixth century, and continued its development until the eighth. It is first noticeable in the Alemannic and Bavarian territories; then it pressed northward into middle Germany, with decreasing wave-force, until finally it was shattered on the immovable rock of the Low (north) German character. It was the Saxons who so carefully protected the old language sounds against the advancing flood of linguistic innovation, and thus added to the existing tribal borders a notable language frontier. Hence, with High (south) German *Waffe* and *Staffel,* we have the Low German *Wappen* and *Stapel;* and, similarly, for *Lachen* and *machen, Laken* and *makeln,* and for *Weissenburg, Schneeweisschen,* and *Altenberg, Wittenberg, S(ch)neewittchen,* and *Oldenburg.* In fact, if the German fatherland to-day falls into two great linguistic halves, a High German and a Low German, it is due especially to the events of this early time. The linguistic frontier has shifted somewhat, in the course of centuries, to the advantage of High German; but, in the main, the possessions of each half remain unaltered. The frontier passed through Aachen, Cologne, Cassel, Duderstadt, and Aschersleben, and terminated in Barby, at the junction of the Elbe and the Saale, where it touched the old border between German and Slav.

Henceforward, the two branches of the German tongue, the High and the Low, developed in complete independence of each other. Accordingly, while we have on the one hand Old High German (up to 1100), Middle High German (up to 1500), and modern literary, or New High, German (up to the present), we have, on the other, Old Low German (Old Low Frankish [1]), Old Saxon and Old Frisian, Middle Low German and New Low German (*Plattdeutsch*). In England, where the Norman conquest mingled German and Romance, the English speech grew out of the Anglo-Saxon dialect. In the Scandinavian lands, Old Norse gave way to her daughters, Swedish, Norwegian, Icelandic, and Danish.

Of all these German sisters, High German has, next to English, enjoyed to the fullest degree the influence of Roman and Romance culture. Roman merchants and soldiers early appeared on the Rhine and the Danube, bearing with them bales of strange goods, and also more precious gifts—those priceless spiritual wares which helped to produce in those regions, quicker than elsewhere in the German lands, a more refined development of mind and heart. Here the seeds of the Christian religion were first planted, and the Irish and Scottish monks, zealous for the faith, scattered them broadcast. With the foundation of the monasteries by the missionaries, learning and poetry made their entrance into Germany. Many of the writings of this early time are, of course, lost forever; but enough survives to enable us to declare, with certainty, that virtually all who studied

---

[1] Old Low Frankish has since developed, owing to political divisions, into Middle Low Netherlandish, Hollandish, and Flemish. But in the sixteenth century the Netherlanders still regarded themselves as German (*Deutsche*), and that is the reason why Hollandish is still called *Dutch* by the English-speaking world.

Evolution of the German Language

and wrote did so in the quiet of monastic cells. To be sure, little independent work was done. The most important piece of intellectual labor performed by the Visigothic race was a translation—the translation of the *Bible* by Ulfilas. The pious monks of St. Gall and Reichenau, of Wessobrunn and Weissenburg, restricted their energies in large part to the " Book of books," and frequently limited themselves to translating or expounding, in German, what the Fathers and other Christian predecessors had written in Latin or in Greek. Even the evangelical compilations of an Otfried of Weissenburg (ca. 870) are, from the standpoint of art, only slight performances. The chief service Otfried rendered was to increase the respectability of the despised German, by employing it in poetical compositions, at a time when Latin still dominated in the Church and in ecclesiastical affairs.

Old High German, however, still lacked many expressions, especially those which involved Christian ideas, and industrious monks, like Kero, Notker Labeo, and Williram, zealously labored to enrich it. If they did not simply adopt the Latin words, as so often happened, they either translated them as accurately as possible, or else attributed the lacking meaning to native German expressions. In so doing, they often transported words from the domain of the sensual to the territory of the moral and spiritual. Their treatment of the days of the week exhibits the method of accurate translation. For example, the German *Montag* is equivalent to the Latin *dies lunae* (French, *lundi*), and *Freitag* (Old High German, *Friatag*, or *Tag der Freia*) is the Latin *Veneris dies*

Medieval Civilization

(French, *vendredi*). The influence of Christian ideas is seen in such translations as *barmherzig* (Old High German, *armhërzi*) = Latin *misericors; Ge-wissen* = Latin *con-scientia; Mittler* = Latin *mediator; Beichte* (Old High German, *bi-jiht*) = Latin *con-fessio.* Other words were translated more freely. The Latin *paganus* became the German *heidan*—modern, *Heide* (*pagus* = *Heide*); *apostolicus* was rendered by *zwelfboto*—modern, *Zwölfbote; discipulus* was translated *jungiro*—modern, *Jünger;* and *prophetia* was Germanized as *wis-sagunga*—modern, *Weissagung.* Many German words were adapted to Christian purposes, and were filled with the most moral content. Such were *Glaube, Gnade, Busse, Heil, Sünde, Schuld, Reue, Taufe, Hölle, Schöpfer,* and *Heiland.* Other words were transferred directly from the Latin, with only such modifications as were required by the laws of German speech. Examples of such words are: *Marter* (*martyrium*), *Pein* (*poena*), *Segen* (*signum*), *Messe* (*missa*), *predigen* (*predicare*), *feiern* (*feriae*), *opfern* (*operari*), and *verdammen* (*damnare*). Even the structure of the German sentence was, to a certain extent, affected by the Latin influence. By nature it was simple, and it could only be rendered stiff and awkward by being imprisoned in the strait-jacket of the Latin periods. Otfried might complain, in the introduction to his New Testament, that the barbarous German speech was rough and wild, and averse to the governing bridle of grammatical art. The German mother-tongue had, at least, one advantage over the polished Latin: it was born of sentient strength and living clearness. German words still show distinctly the stamp they received in their native mint.

Evolution of the German Language

The Old High German speech also possessed, as a result of the fullness and rich color of its vowels, a much greater euphony than its successors, Middle High German and Low High German. Various linguistic survivals, preserved through lucky circumstances, give us a certain amount of information on this subject. As the amber dredged on the coasts of Samland prove that forests, rich in resinous trees, once hemmed the cold ocean shores of to-day, so these broken fragments of old word-forms give infallible evidence of a long-vanished splendor. Exempt from the destructive influences of time, each has preserved that brilliant exterior which even now gladdens the eyes of the discoverer. The Old High German word-structure is shown here and there by proper names, which are especially reliable sources; by compound words which have, through their firm articulation, saved many word-structures from perishing; and, lastly, by technical expressions which, continually handed down in narrow circles from generation to generation, have defied the storms of thousands of years. In the names Emma, Bertha, Frida, Hulda, and Hansa we see old feminine stems in *a*. Otto, Hugo, Kuno, Bruno, and Arno are examples of the Old High German nominative of the weak declension. In *Nachtigall* (songstress of the night; compare Old High German *galan = tönen*) and *Bräutigam* (bride's man; compare Old High German *gomo,* man, = Latin *homo*) we have probably the old genitive of the singular, and in *ihro* (*iro*) and *dero* (*dëro*), the old genitive of the plural. Prefixed and affixed syllables still exhibit, now and then, vowels retaining their original color. Thus, alongside the unaccented forms *er-* (as in *erteilen* and *erlauben*) and *ent-* (as in *entgegnen*), we have retained, because they were accented, *ur-* and *ant-* in *Urteil, Urlaub, Antwort, Antlitz,* etc. The endings *-and* and *-und* in *Heiland, Weigand, Wiegand,* and *Leumund* (Old High German, *hliumunt*) correspond to the modern *-end* in *Liebend* and *Jugend; -ist* in *Obrist* shows the superlative ending of Old High German. Lastly, we discover in *hallo* and *holla* old imperatives of *halon* (*holen,* equivalent to *hol über!*).

Such was Old High German, which was current in the eighth, ninth, tenth, and eleventh centuries throughout upper Germany, in the lands of the Bavarians, Alemannians, and Franks. It had not yet developed into a uniform *literary,* or *written, language,* in spite of the mighty influence wielded by the great Charles over all the lands of German speech.[1] The great emperor and conqueror busied himself with the writing, grammar, and vocabulary of his beloved Germany,[2] but he failed to secure the acceptance of one German dialect as the universal literary language of Germans. After his death, German literary endeavor and the empire shared a common decline.

At the end of the twelfth century, the place of leaders in poetry passed from the ecclesiastics to the laymen—from the hands of the monks into the hands of the knights. Under the influence of the crusades, the

---

[1] Charles's fame extended far beyond these limits, as is shown by the use of his name, by many non-German peoples, in the sense of *king.* We have the Polish *krol,* Bohemian *kral,* Russian *koroli,* Hungarian *kiraly,* and Lithuanian *karalius.* (Compare Cæsar = *Kaiser.*)

[2] He introduced, for example, German names for the months: *Wintarmanoth,* December; *Ostarmanoth,* April; *Hornung,* February. He caused the old German folk-songs to be collected, and began to make a German grammar.

Evolution of the German Language

knightly order quickly reached a high state of development; and the ideas which flowed from wide travel
in strange countries, especially the much-praised won-
derland of the East, gave fresh nutriment to the mind
and a mighty stimulus to the imagination. Involuntarily,
men were moved to depict in poetry adventures like those
of the crusaders, and to dictate their poems to the scribes.[1]
The knights frequently found it advantageous to borrow
the material for their heroic songs from foreign sources.
French tales were generally chosen, for France was the
chief school of refined taste and the home of courtly
poetry; and the French troubadours and trouvères (from
the French *trouver,* to find or invent) took the lead in
inventing and narrating adventures. Their creations
entered Germany by various routes, but the Netherlands
—Flanders and Brabant—was the principal one. The
Low Frankish Henry of Veldeke first gave them vogue
in Germany, and Hartmann of Aue, a Swabian, was his
apt pupil. Soon the Frankish nobility of the Main country fairly rivaled the Swabian and middle Rhine nobility
in the production of heroic songs and love-songs. Ans-
bach was the cradle of Wolfram of Eschenbach; Eisak-
thal was, perhaps, the birthplace of Walther of the Vogel-
weide; the *Nibelungenlied* and *Gudrun* were given their
final form in Austria. These poets and these poetical
compositions made this the zenith of the poetical creativeness of the Middle High German period.

Scholars are not yet agreed whether this epoch saw
the establishment of a uniform literary language; that is,

[1] The German *dichten,* to write poetry, comes
from the Latin *dictare.*

whether there was an accepted norm, or model, which was followed both at the Hohenstaufen court and by the poets of upper Germany, and was even employed in song and story in various parts of the Low German lands. Lachmann, J. Grimm, Haupt, Wackernagel, Raumer, and Müllendorf are of the affirmative opinion, and hold, for the most part, that the Alemannic speech was the foundation of this written, or literary, German. Others, like Hermann Paul, contest this view, although they admit that " many-sided linguistic influences were at work upon the poets belonging to different regions, and that such influences were doubtless active in the sphere of vocabulary and syntax." It should be added, too, that certain forms of the spoken language were intentionally avoided in poetry.

This Middle High German poetical language had great and peculiar merits. It was as courtly and refined as the knights who employed it. Like the precious jewel, which must be cut and polished before its true splendor is revealed, German style first attained full beauty under the hands of the knights. Under their guidance, it turned away decisively from the clumsiness of earlier centuries, and differed as markedly from the earlier language as the worldly-wise courtiers differed in manner of life from the comfortable monks. But while the language gained mobility and suppleness, it lost much of its sensuous strength and sonorousness.

The presence of an *i* sound wrought a transformation in the full-sounding *a, o,* and *u,* and other vowels of the preceding syllable; stronger accentuation of the stem syllable wore down the sonorous endings. The former

Evolution of the German Language

process is called vowel-modification (*umlaut*); the latter, weakening. Both tendencies gained strength gradually. The umlaut took its rise in the north, and began to spread early in the fifth century. The oldest extant examples of old Norse and Anglo-Saxon exhibit the process in full operation. Old Saxon and Old High German show its effects to a limited extent. In the latter of these two it is first noticeable in the short *a*; its influence upon the other vowels can seldom be detected before the tenth century. After that time, however, the movement gradually widened, and Middle High German was the first to experience its full force. In Middle High German *a, o,* and *u, â, ô,* and *û,* and *ou* and *uo,* regularly became *e (ä), ö, ü, ae, oe,* and *iu,* and *oü* and *üe,* respectively.

These changes made the appearance of Middle High German essentially different from that of Old High German, and the gulf was widened through the weakening of the back vowels.

The more the stem syllables were emphasized, the less was the strength left for the terminal syllables; and the full-sounding *a, o,* and *u,* and the *i* sounds, either vanished completely from the latter, or gave place to the colorless *e: haba, boto, sigu,* and *burdi* became *habe, bote, sige,* and *bürde;* and *salbôn* and *lôsjan* were altered to *salben* and *loesen.* This transformation was very gradual, and its rate varied from place to place. The vowels exhibited different powers of resistance: *a* and *o* were more obstinate than *i* and *u.* Weak verbs, and the comparative and superlative degrees of adjectives, clung with especial tenacity to the long vowels; and, consequently, it is not unusual to meet in Middle High German

Medieval Civilization

poems such forms as *gemanôt* (*gemahnt*) and *oberôst* (*oberst*). But these are, after all, only exceptions to the general rule, and even here the sapless and impotent *e* soon penetrated victoriously. The unabbreviated and the abbreviated forms have but rarely survived together, as in *also* (that is, *ganz so*—Old High German, *alsô;* Middle High German, *alse*) and *als*.

And yet, in spite of these regrettable changes, Middle High German, in comparison with the language of to-day, still possessed great variety and rich diversity. The feminine nouns, which are now invariable in the singular, had then more vigor; contrary to the present practice, proper names could, in part, be made feminine, as in *Otto, Otte* (compare *Ottendorf*); the adverbs, which cannot be distinguished in form to-day from their kindred adjectives, then had usually another form; and, lastly, the pronouns possessed a richer variety; *dës, wës, dër,* and *dën* corresponding to the modern *dessen, wessen, deren,* and *denen.* This is seen in the proverb, " *Wes Brot ich ess, des Lied ich sing* " (Whose bread I eat, *his* praise I sing), and also, in such compounds as *des-halb* and *wes-wegen.*

That which gave Middle High German an especial charm, and great superiority over modern literary German (New High German), was the great number of short roots it possessed, which made it so flexible and gave it such a sprightly, lively movement. German still retains traces of the earlier pronunciation of syllables which ended in a consonant—in words of one syllable, like *an, in, bin, ab, ob, weg, doch, ich, noch, was, es, des;* and in the compounds. *băr-fuss, Vŏrteil. Hĕr-berge, Hĕr-zog,*

Evolution of the German Language

Wŏl-lust, Wăl-kyre, Wăl-halla, Schĕl-lack, Schĕll, fisch, Úrteil, and *vĭel-leicht* (Middle High German, *villĭhte*). Even to this day, one hears in many parts of Germany *Glăs* and *Grăb;* but rarely does one now hear the short vowels in open syllables: *Glăs-es, Grăb-es, Klăg-en, lĕ-ben, Wĭse, lŏ-ben,* and *Tŭ-gende.*

The sway of the German language extended as the power of the empire increased. In Old High German days, the Elbe and the Saale had formed the eastern frontier of the German fatherland, but the Saxon emperors had inaugurated the work of reconquering the old German territory upon which the advancing Slavs had settled. Their successors continued their work most auspiciously, and were energetically supported by such valiant princes of the empire as Henry the Lion. Under the protection of the cities which the dauntless knighthood of Germany built in the foreign territory, German settlers began the cultivation of the newly won lands allotted to them, and pious monks taught the heathen population the Christian faith. Henceforth, Low German was the prevailing tongue in the Baltic lands from Mecklenburg to Courland, for this region was largely settled by Saxons. In Austria, Salzburg, Steiermark, and the other adjacent territories, the settlers were Bavarians, and the language employed was, consequently, a High German one. Meissen, Bohemia, and Silesia received their new German population principally from Thuringia and the region of the Main, and so their language was Middle German, a tongue which in many respects occupied an intermediate position between those spoken in the two other groups of colonies. One effect of this

Medieval Civilization

German *Drang nach Osten* was the eastward extension of the linguistic frontier between north and south Germany. From Barby, on the Elbe, it now advanced in an easterly direction, passing through Wittenberg, Lübben, Guben, Krossen, Züllichau, and Meseritz; and, in the district of Birnbaum, on the Warthe, it entered right into Slavic territory. Some districts of Electoral Saxony which were originally Low German now passed over, gradually, to the High German camp. Merseburg (ca. 1340), Halle (ca. 1400), and Mansfeld (in the fifteenth century), and even the southern portion of the province of Brandenburg, in this way, became High German in language. In view of the mental advantages which south Germany possessed, through its writings and linguistic creativeness, and in view, also, of its political preponderance, the territorial conquests of High German cannot be regarded as surprising.

The territory south of the great linguistic frontier was, however, exposed to the invasion of a new vowel-shifting, which took its rise in the twelfth century in southeastern Germany. It consisted in the lengthening of the vowels *î, û,* and *iu* (long *ü*) into *ei, au* (*ou*), and *eu* (*äu*). *Mîn, rûm,* and *hiute* became *mein, Raum,* and *heute.* In the early thirteenth century this " linguistic phenomenon " seems to be restricted to lower Austria; by 1280 it embraced the Swabian and Frankish borders and the Tyrol and Steiermark; and in the fourteenth century it made the conquest of Austria, Bavaria, and east Franconia. Silesia accepted the innovation in the same century; upper Saxony definitely succumbed about 1470; and Mainz, Worms, and Frankfort finally gave up the

Evolution of the German Language

battle about 1500. In the meantime, the Alemannic territory was besieged, and partly surrendered when the book-publishers of Augsburg, Ulm, and Strasburg gave up using the simple letters in works for which they anticipated a wide circulation. Switzerland, alone, held out for some time longer. The Low German dialects (and some dialects of middle and upper Germany) have clung to the old pronunciation to the present day. That explains why we have to-day several expressions in literary German which, according to the district in which they are employed, appear in the old or the new form. Such are *Dune* and *Rhin,* or *Daune* and *Rhein.*

Southwestern Germany gave birth to still another sound-change. It appeared first on Alemannic-Swiss soil in the thirteenth century. It consisted in the substitution of *sch* for *sk* (*forskôn: forschen*). This change won its way in upper and middle German lands before the beginning of the age of modern literary German (New High German) ; and in these parts of Germany initial *sm, sn, sl,* and *sw* gave way to *schm, schn, schl,* and *schw,* and even *sp* and *st* had to yield partially to *schp* and *scht.* Literary German has definitely accepted the change in the cases of *schm, schn, schl,* and *schw,* but it has remained loyal to the original forms *sp* and *st.* Here again, however, the Low German dialects have remained firmly attached to their past, and they are still untouched by this whole sound-change.

North Germany and South Germany thus went their own independent ways, and developed sharp linguistic contrasts. These contrasts were reconciled, or at least dulled, in the territories along their common border—

that is, in the lands of middle Germany. The intermediate linguistic position of middle Germany was exhibited both in pronunciation and vocabulary. Here, again, she formed the bridge between north and south.

The Middle German dialects undoubtedly exhibit, on a High German foundation, a close agreement with Low German.[1] Hence, they were best fitted for the diffusion of Luther's translation of the *Bible* throughout Germany. It was, therefore, an especially clever stroke on the part of Luther to choose, as the basis for his translation, the language of the chancery of Electoral Saxony. He himself says, in Chapter 69 of his *Table Talk:* " I have not used any one, special, peculiar, German dialect, but have employed the common German tongue, in order that both High German and Low German lands might understand me. I speak after the fashion of the Saxon chancery, which is followed by all princes and kings in Germany. All imperial cities and princely courts write according to the usage of the Saxon chancery, which is that of our prince. Hence, it is the most common German language. Kaiser Maximilian and Elector Frederick, duke of Saxony, have also, in the Roman Empire, fused together the German tongues into one definite language." The rise of official—legal—languages demands a few words.

[1] Hence many expressions in Luther's *Bible* were at first unintelligible to the people of upper Germany, and different Basel, Strasburg, and Augsburg publishers of new editions of his New Testament deemed it advisable to append short dictionaries in which the more obscure Middle German and Low German expressions were elucidated in High German. Adam Petri was the first to do this, in 1523. It was done for the last time in 1532, a proof of the astonishing rapidity with which the Germans learned to understand the vocabulary of Luther.

Evolution of the German Language

When Latin, in the first half of the fourteenth century, ceased to be the almost exclusive language of official documents, the court of the Saxon electors at Wittenberg began to develop a legal style out of the Upper Saxon dialect; and this was employed in dealings with the courts of the other princes. But each of these princes had also created a "chancery German" out of the dialect of his country. Consequently, a desire was soon manifested for the joint establishment of a German for official documents which would be easily comprehended by all the parties concerned. In the work of determining what this *official* German should be, the written German of the imperial court exercised a decisive influence, for it carried with it the imperial prestige. This written German had been developed out of the Middle German employed at Prague during the rule of the Bohemian-Luxemburg house, and had been substantially fixed as early as the middle of the fourteenth century in the chancery of Emperor Charles IV. One hundred years later it was the model for the written German of the chancery of Electoral Saxony, and in all cases of doubt the practice of the imperial court was followed. At the accession of Elector Frederick the Wise of Saxony, in 1486, the reconciliation of the imperial and the electoral chancery German was, in the main, complete; and after Luther's translation the same process was carried out at the capitals of the other princes.

The influence of the imperial chancery upon the German publishers was less important, for it was not direct. It was exerted indirectly, through the chanceries of the princes and the free cities in whose territories the print-

ing centers were located. Furthermore, the publishers,
little by little, made themselves entirely independent of
these local models, and, in fact, far surpassed them in
their efforts to establish a uniform practice in literary
German. The growing self-reliance of the publishers, in
this matter of the language, is not to be undervalued;
for they had the most to say in the matter of the linguistic
form of their books, and it was incumbent upon them to
secure as much unanimity of practice as possible, if their
books were to have the most extensive circulation. The
most important publishing centers were located in upper
and middle Germany: in Swabia (Augsburg), in the
region of the upper Rhine (Basel and Strasburg), in
Franconia (Nuremberg), in the middle Rhine territories
(Worms, Mainz, and Frankfort), and in upper Saxony
(Leipzig and Wittenberg). At first the printing establishments of these cities were rather dependent upon the
manner of speech in their locality; but more and more
they broke away, and, especially about 1530, they approx-
imated to the common German language of the Saxon
chancery. The Augsburg printers came nearest, in their
publications, to the language of the imperial chancery;
the printers of middle Germany still remained more or
less firmly rooted in their dialect. And yet, as time
passed, this middle German dialect grew increasingly
influential. The special reasons for this were that the
decisions of the imperial Diet were printed at Mainz, in
the middle Rhine country; that Frankfort was then one
of the most important book-markets; and that the Protes-
tant writings, which were scattered broadcast, were, to
a very large extent, issued from the Saxon electorate.

Evolution of the German Language

The most important cause of the growing influence of Middle German was Luther's translation of the *Bible*. This mighty intellectual achievement thrilled the hearts of the whole German people, and step by step aided the written language of Electoral Saxony to obtain the victory in all Germany.

Whoever thinks that Luther's German coincides completely with the literary German of to-day makes a very great mistake. In many particulars the former is more akin to Middle High German than to the latter.[1] He also errs who is of the opinion that Luther's language was

---

[1] Luther uses *e* where *ö* is now customary, writing *Helle, Leffel, zwelf, leschen*, etc. He writes *ie* for *ü*, as in *liegen* and *triegen* (*lügen* and *trügen*), and *i* for *ü* in *wirdig* (*würdig*). He employs the suffix *-lin* where the modern form is *-lein* (*Pünktlin, Megdlin, Stündlin*, and *Gebetlin*), the suffix *-lich* for the modern *-ig* (*adellich, billich*, and *unzellich*), and *e* for *ä*, as in *Veter, Hende, teglich*, and *allmechtig* (*Väter, Hände, täglich*, and *allmächtig*). Moreover, he writes *nu* for *nun*, *rauch* for *rauh*, *Heubt* for *Haupt*, *gülden* for *golden*, *frum* for *fromm*, etc., etc. He forms the past tense in the Middle High German way: *ich, beiss, bleib, greif*, and *reit* (modern *biss, blieb, griff, ritt*), *wir schwunden, funden, drungen, hulfen* (modern *schwanden, fanden, drangen, halfen*); *stund* and *hub* are the Lutheran form of *stand* and *hob; weiste* and *preiste*, of *wies* and *pries;* and *worden, kommen, geben, funden, bracht*, and *missethan*, of *geworden, gekommen, gegeben*, etc. Luther frequently uses *zeuch, kreucht*, and *fleucht* for *zieh, kriecht*, and *fliegt*. He treats *Angel, Gewalt, Lust*, and *Sitte* as masculine words, and *Bekenntnis, Aergernis, Gefängnis*, etc., as feminines. He frequently has weak genitives in the singular, as *Gallen, Kirchen, Pforten*, and *Zungen*, and nominative plurals like *Tugende* and *Meinunge*. For the numeral *zwei* he gives three genders: *zween, zwô, zwei*. Lastly, we find archaisms in his *Bible: lecken* (to kick with the feet), *thüren* (Middle High German *turren*) for *wagen, evern* for *wiederholen, ergern* (to lead into sin), *hellig* for *ermüdet, freidig* for *kühn, ehrlich* for *ansehnlich, wacker* for *wachsam, richtig* for *gerade, Ort* for *Ende, Reise* for *Kriegszug, Fahrt* for *Reise, Elend* for *Ausland, weil* for *so lange als*, etc., etc.

Medieval Civilization

fixed from the start. In language, as in questions of religion and morals, we see him struggling and developing; and Franke has been able to discover three stages in the development of his written language, *viz.*, 1516-1520, 1521-1531, 1532-1546. The decisive factor in these periods is the diminishing use of the forms of Middle High German and the patois of middle Germany.

Luther's style, too, was a gradual development, a style which completely mirrors the blunt, kernelly personality of the mighty man, and which has contributed so much to the popularity of his translation of the *Bible*. Luther alone could wield such a style—so perspicuous, so life-giving and soul-stirring, so simple and true. He did not hesitate to visit the workshops of the artisans and to listen to the speech of the common man in the street, in order that he might fix his words in the sense and after the fashion of the people. It is true that several centuries were required before there was built upon the foundation which Luther laid a complete accord in written German, from the Rhine to the Niemen, and from the Schlei to the Alps, but the delay was due to special circumstances [with which a sketch of the medieval evolution of German has nothing to do]. The striking personality of Luther is the most prominent landmark in the whole history of the German tongue. The *Bible* has transformed and ruled the world; Luther's translation has been a transforming and ruling factor in the development of the German language. He made it German again; that is, he made it the language of the people, and renewed its strength through fresh grafts from the great tree of the life of the people. Without his trans-

Evolution of the German Language

lation of the *Bible,* Germany would have had no Goethe
and no Schiller. As the Romans for centuries zealously
studied their language from the Twelve Tables of their
law and instructed their youth therein, so the *Bible* of
Luther has been for hundreds of years the work from
which the German people have drawn their intellectual
sustenance, and on which both the great and the small
have modeled their style. A law-book was the linguistic
plumb-line of the rationalistic Romans. A religious book
was the touchstone of the nobly sentimental Germans.
The Roman sword prepared the way for the Latin language through a great part of Europe; Luther's linguistic activity prepared the way for the German sword and
for the political union of Germany. The more the material power of the empire declined, the more closely were
the spiritual bonds which united the German races
drawn together, and the more zealously did Germans seek
comfort in the intellectual wealth common to all, and
find solace in the remembrance of their great ancestors
and in the joy of their noble language. Luther began
the work which was completed by the victorious cam-
paigns of 1866 and 1870—the work of German unity.

Life and Interests of the Students

Adapted from A. Lecoy de la Marche: *La chaire
française au moyen âge*, 1868, pp. 415–427.

NOTHING in the thirteenth century is more remarkable than the zeal which incited the spirit toward
study, than the activity of the schools and the influence
of the universities. France was the scene of this great
intellectual movement; and Paris was, to use the expression of St. Bonaventure, the source whence the little rivu-
lets of science spread throughout the entire world. Medicine was studied at Salerno, magic at Toledo, and law at
Bologna or at Orléans: but it was necessary to reside at
Paris to learn the liberal arts and theology, the *summum
scientiae*. Colleges multiplied in the capital. In addition
to the university center of Mount St. Genevieve, a great
number of churches had their schools: Notre-Dame,
Saint - Germain - l'Auxerrois, Saint-Nicolas-du-Louvre,
Saint-Julien-le-Pauvre, etc.; the Dominicans, almost as
soon as they reached Paris, opened one in the rue Saint-
Jacques, which soon became, in spite of the opposition
of the lay doctors, the most flourishing of all. Robert
de Sorbon, a little later, gave to these different foundations a most opportune supplement. At Toulouse and at
Montpellier, education was also in a very active condition: Helinand and Alain de Lille found there, among the
students, well-instructed and zealous hearers.

Life and Interests of the Students

From all the countries of Europe disciples flocked to the masters who had acquired a reputation for knowledge in any branch. Stephen Langton and Robert Grosse-Tête had studied at the university of Paris before being professors and filling official positions in it. This expatriation to which love of science condemned the young men was very useful to them, if we may believe Jacques de Vitry; for, in their own country, under the parental roof, they lived in the midst of pleasure and a thousand frivolous occupations which prevented them from working. For that reason they preferred, when they were wise, to go elsewhere. In the bosom of the university they found a welcome and protection, and enjoyed independence and much-envied privileges, which, however, did not always tend to make the studies more profitable, for they were the cause of perpetual trouble and conflict. The lessons were interrupted at every moment. This caused the complaints which we find in the mouths of several preachers of sermons, who cried out, in 1273, with regard to events of this nature, of which the details are not known to us: "Let us pray for the schools at Paris, for the suppression of a single course of study leads each day to incomparable and irreparable loss. . . . There, in fact, are recruited all the men of talent and all the prelates of the universal Church." In fact, the resistance to the progress of the mendicant orders and the rivalry of the doctors contributed to these disorders. The great city resounded with the noise of vain disputes and scholastic quarrels.

"What are these combats of scholars," asks the chancellor, "if not true cock-fights, which cover us with ridi-

cule in the eyes of laymen? A cock draws himself up
against another and bristles his feathers. . . . It is
the same to-day with our professors. Cocks fight with
blows from their beaks and claws; ' Self-love,' as some
one has said, ' is armed with a dangerous spur.' "

It was necessary for the students who arrived at the
university with the intention of pursuing serious study to
shun these constant fighters, to choose good masters, and
to listen to them assiduously. The cardinal of Vitry,
among other things, recommends to them to beware of the
neophytes—that is, of the young doctors who draw
crowds by the bait of curiosity, and take all their teaching, not from their memory or experience, but from the
copy-books and the book-shelves; for some pupils are led
away by them through their prayers, caresses, and even
money, and so waste their most precious time in idle pursuits. Scholars paid by the teacher,—is not that a pretty
example of the spirit of intrigue and jealousy which
agitated these schools? . . .

Some were so fickle and careless that even under skilful professors they learned nothing. They went from
one lecture to another, changing continually their courses
and their books. They followed the classes during the
winter and went away in summer. It is evident that they
desired merely the title of scholar or the revenues consecrated by the churches to the support of poor students.
They seated themselves upon the benches once or twice
a week, and by preference went to the lectures of the de-
cretists, because these came only at the third hour, and
thus they could sleep in the morning at their ease. This
did not prevent them, however, from often carrying

enormous volumes out of pure ostentation, following the example set by the sons of the rich Romans in former times.

Another essential thing for the young student in quest of solid learning was the choice and use of a good method of work. It has often been said that at that time the whole system of teaching consisted of argumentation, but it was not, as one might suppose, only a mechanical intellectual trick put in practice. One of the most competent teachers drew up for the students a very well conceived and thoughtful plan, which informs us of their exercises and their daily occupations. The founder of the Sorbonne wrote a treatise, including the most precise details, upon the examinations set for the candidates for the license (*De conscientiâ*). This has long been known. The unedited piece of which we wish to speak is no less instructive, although abridged in form. Here is an analysis of it:

" The student who wishes to profit by his lessons ought to observe six essential rules:

" 1. Consecrate a fixed hour to each study, as St. Bernard advises in his letters to the brethren of Mont-Dieu.

" 2. Fix the attention upon what is read, and do not pass over it lightly. ' There is,' says St. Bernard again, ' the same difference between reading and study as between a host and a friend, a salute exchanged in the street and unalterable affection.'

" 3. Extract from the daily reading some thought, some truth, and grave it upon the memory with special care. Seneca has said: ' *Cùm multa percurreris in die, unum tibi elige quod illâ die excoquas.*'

Medieval Civilization

" 4. Write out a résumé, for words which are not confided to writing fly away like dust before the wind.

" 5. Discuss the matter with fellow-students in disputations or in familiar talk. This exercise is even more advantageous than reading, because it results in clearing
up all doubts and all obscurities that the reading may
have left. *Nihil perfectè scitur, nisi dente disputationis
feriatur.*

" 6. Pray; this is, in fact, one of the best means of
learning. St. Bernard teaches that reading ought to excite the movements of the soul, and it is necessary to
profit by it for raising one's heart to God without inter-
rupting the study.

" Certain students act like fools. They display their
subtlety in foolish things and show themselves destitute
of understanding in important things. In order not to
seem to have lost their time, they get together sheets of
parchment and form thick volumes, filled with leaves
blank on one side, and cover them with elegant bindings
of red leather. Then they return to their fathers' houses
with a little sack filled with knowledge, and with a mind
completely empty. But what is this knowledge that can
be stolen by a robber, gnawed by rats or worms, and destroyed by fire or water?

" To acquire learning, it is necessary to abstain from
carnal pleasures and from the embarrassment of material
cares. There were at Paris two masters, who were close
friends, of whom one had seen a great deal, had read a
great deal, and night and day bent over his books. He
scarcely took time to say a *Pater*. He had only four students. His colleague possessed a smaller library and was

Life and Interests of the Students

less given to study, but he heard mass each morning before giving his lesson and his school was full. ' How do you do it? ' the first asked him. ' It is very simple,' he replied smilingly; ' God studies for me. I go to mass, and when I return I know by heart all that I ought to teach.'

" Meditation is suitable not only for the master but also for the scholar. A good student ought to walk evenings along the banks of the Seine, not for pleasure, but for repeating or thinking about his lesson."

Robert finishes by blaming those who are satisfied with incomplete learning and do not know how to utilize what they have gotten. " Grammar forges the sword of the word of God; rhetoric polishes it; finally, theology puts it to use. But there are students who learn constantly to fabricate and to sharpen it, and by dint of too much grinding finally wear it out entirely. Others keep it shut up in the scabbard, and, when they wish to draw it, it is old, the iron is rusted, and they can no longer produce anything. As for those who study in order to get dignities and prelacies, they are very much deceived, for they scarcely ever attain anything."

This sketch is still incomplete, and it shows us only the private work of the student, without telling us of the character of the teaching. The latter took place by means of *lectiones,* simple discourses pronounced by the professors, as in our public courses, during which the listeners took notes according to their skill or their fancy. When the subject was the explanation of a text, they followed in a copy, just as can be seen in the miniature placed at the head of the sermons of Jean d'Abbeville,

Medieval Civilization

which shows students seated before the chair of the master. On Saturdays there were recitations on all the lessons given in the university during the week. These were presided over by the *magnus magister scholae*.

Such a method certainly offered great advantages. It left, above all, a large part of the initiative to the student, who was ordinarily old enough to work alone; for it was not unusual for a scholar to stay on the benches until twenty-five or thirty years of age. One was called a *scholasticus* only when he had proved that he had followed courses for a fixed time; after long evenings had been given to study, it was necessary to go to the chancellor of the university to obtain, by a public examination, the desired degree. This is the way in which the examinations for the license were conducted, according to the indications which can be drawn from the parallel related by Robert of Sorbon in his discourse upon *The Conscience:* The candidate, already a bachelor, went to the chancellor and received from him the book upon which he was to be questioned. He carried it away, read it through, then noted or studied the difficulties which he might have encountered. Thus prepared, he returned to ask for a date for his examination. Then he appeared before a jury, composed of the chancellor and several doctors, who heard him speak upon this subject. If he passed, they declared him admitted. If not, they sent him away for a year. It seems that cunning and corruption sometimes glided into these solemn judgments. The examiners voluntarily showed themselves less severe to the nobles and the great. Certain candidates who had been rejected obtained their diplomas by bribery or solicitation, and that was a new source of trouble.

Life and Interests of the Students

The subjects taught were arranged in a regular, methodical curriculum, comprising theology and the seven liberal arts,—grammar, rhetoric, and dialectics (the *trivium*), and arithmetic, geometry, music, and astronomy (the *quadrivium*). These different sciences formed a ladder, of which it was necessary to mount the rounds one after another, for it was not customary to go into a specialty. All branches of study, in the thought of the sermonizers and in the general belief of the time, had a single object and the same end,—the knowledge of God, which theology finally accomplished: "*Omnis scientia debet referri ad cognitionem Christi.*" Theology was the supreme science, for which the others were only a preparation. "*Debet scolaris ire per viam ad puteum (ut Isaac), id est per scientias adminiculantes ad theologiam.*" "Logic is good, since it teaches us to tell the good from the false; grammar is good, since it teaches us to write and speak correctly; rhetoric is good, since it teaches us to speak elegantly and persuasively; geometry is good, since it teaches us to measure the earth, the domain of our bodies; arithmetic, or the art of accounting, is good, since it is the means by which we can convince ourselves of the small number of our days; music, since it instructs us in harmony and recalls to us the sweet chants of the blessed; astronomy, since it makes us regard the celestial bodies and the virtue of the stars which shine before God. But far better is theology, which alone can be called a liberal art, because it delivers the human soul from its ills."

The chancellor of Paris blamed young men who abandoned the Holy Scriptures for the law and other faculties. In spite of all, they rushed to the lessons of the legists, and certainly it was not merely because they were

Medieval Civilization

given at a later hour. Logic, or rather dialectics, was another attractive subject, and another subject of abuse.

The student at the university presented still another aspect from that which we have just seen. He was not always a serious young man, full of zeal for study, who bent over the glosses of the *Bible* or of Aristotle. He was also, and often above everything else, a mad reveler, who "at night rushes about armed in the streets of the capital, breaks open the doors of the houses for the sake of violence, and fills all the tribunals with the noise of his misdeeds." . . . His quarrels with the powerful corporation of the citizens of Paris were incessant. The *Pré-aux-Clercs,* where some students gravely walked about with their books in their hands meditating or arguing in the Latin tongue, was also the scene of tumultuous acts.

Great liberty fortified by numerous privileges was allowed to the students. Each one lived alone, or with a comrade, in some modest hired room, where his little collection of volumes or rolls of parchment, generally his only possession, was not always safe from the thieves who roamed about the great city. The pupils of the grammar class, who were younger and generally Parisians, remained under the parental roof; and the trip to school, which they had to make, served as a pretext for running at large throughout the city. Others came from distant countries, were under no oversight, and were protected only by the chiefs of their "nation." Some were noblemen, some of the middle class, but they were not rich, for the servants of the university lightened their purses when it was necessary.

Life and Interests of the Students

In order to meet the needs, on account of this poverty, special funds were placed in certain churches. The students also aided one another. The cardinal Eudes de Châteauroux, in his sermon to the poor students, says that it is the duty of his hearers to aid their brethren liberally, as they are all equally poor. A student who was on his death-bed and wished to leave his comrades something to be given in alms for the salvation of his soul, could find nothing except his shoes. Another employed his Sundays in carrying holy water for private houses, " according to the Gallican custom," a task for which he was recompensed by small sums from time to time, and by curses and blows. Some clerks did not have money enough to attend the lessons in theology. Aside from the pious foundations destined to furnish them with means, they had, as a resource, the liberality of some doctors who wrote, for their use, treatises which might take the place in part of the official lessons. . . .

City Life in Germany

Adapted from K. Lamprecht: *Deutsche Geschichte,*
Vol. IV, 1896, pp. 211–217.

IN the glorious days of the medieval towns, say in the
second half of the fourteenth century, when a traveler
approached a large city, its very appearance suggested to
him that he had reached his journey's end. Proudly and
almost boastingly the silhouette of the city rose from the
horizon, with its turrets and towers, its chapels and
churches. Even then, from outside, the cities showed the
same elevation that is familiar to us from the great wood-
cuts which have come down from the first decades of the
sixteenth century, although in the latter the perspective
is somewhat idealized.

First of all, its strong fortifications impressed the traveler. The narrow city limits included normally the old
city market and often a much larger territory. All of this
was embraced in the fortifications. Its boundaries were
surrounded by ramparts and a wall with a ditch in front.
This was often strengthened still more by so-called hedges
and widely projecting watch-towers at regular intervals.
Even when the ramparts were less strongly fortified, there
was at least a beacon with a wide outlook. Here a guard
kept watch, and by signals communicated his information
to the garrison within the city. Frequently these beacons

were buildings of great extent and beautiful proportions
There are still some which adorn all the country round
about, like the beacon at Andernach. In the larger cities
the commander of the beacon directed an extensive system of communications that extended beyond the limits of
the city's territory, and at times assumed the form of a
secret service.

When the stranger was admitted through the barricade
at the outposts and approached the city more closely, he
might well be astonished, even in the smaller cities, by
the extent of the fortifications and mass of towers which
surrounded the city, especially at the gates. Until well
into the twelfth century the walls of even the larger cities
had been simple enough. Earlier, at least on the Rhine,
the old Roman walls had given sufficient protection, until
they were destroyed by the assault of the enemy or sacrificed to the internal need for building-space when the
city's area was enlarged. Then simple walls of earth,
crowned by palisades, with fortifications at the gate, had
sufficed. But since the twelfth century the larger, and
since the thirteenth the smaller, cities had done more.
Funds were collected everywhere " for the work of the
city." Everywhere the citizen sought permission from
the lord of the city to raise a special tax for building
purposes; sometimes they asked the monasteries in the
city to contribute. Thus they built with relatively small
means, often for generations, but almost always with
stubborn energy. From the old earthen wall rose arch
upon arch, and these arches supported the new walls,
which often reached the respectable height of twenty-five
to thirty feet. And while the walls were raised, the

ditches were at the same time deepened and broadened
and a glacis was thrown up with the dirt which had been
excavated. There were few gates in the walls, and these
usually opened only upon the chief streets. They were
considered the most dangerous points in the fortifications,
and therefore were made especially strong. The gate was
built with a pointed arch, and flanked on each side by a
strong tower. Not infrequently the whole was included
in a new defense extending to the city proper. There
were also a drawbridge and a portcullis behind its iron-
bound gate. Thus a regular castle developed at the gate,
especially in the north. When bricks were used it became a splendid building. For this reason the commanders of the several gates were called burggraves in
most cities. Paid soldiers, often nobles from the surrounding country, but always men trained to arms whose
business was war, were expressly engaged by the city
council. They furnished a small garrison for the gate:
the watchman who stood on the lead roof of the gate-
tower and in case of danger blew his horn; the gate-
keepers, common soldiers, who were always present to
manage affairs at the gate and under some circumstances
had to help the officials who collected the tolls; lastly, as
it often happened that a jail was connected with the gate,
they supplied keepers for the prisoners whom the city
councilors had lodged beneath the tower.

In addition to this regular garrison, which was remarkably small, there were usually, in times of peace, only a
few guards posted along the city wall. These were chosen
from the citizens and relieved every day. It was their
duty to make the rounds of the wall regularly, especially

during the night; for this service a path was made along
the inner side of the wall. But it was realized that such
an arrangement was very unsatisfactory. Making a path
necessitated the acquisition of expensive land, and the
guards could see, on their rounds, little or nothing of
what went on outside the walls. The idea of placing the
walk on the wall itself readily occurred to them. For this
reason they either made the wall broad enough to have
a path behind the battlements which crowned it, or else
built a wooden walk on supports at the top of the battlements.

While they thus obtained the desired security for the
watchmen on duty, careful rules were made for calling
all the citizens to arms. For military purposes most cities
were divided into quarters, each of which had its own
place of assembly in case of alarm; gathering in these
places, they hastened to defend the walls. About every
hundred and twenty feet, following the old usage of the
long hundred, the wall was interrupted by small towers
(as, for example, at Wisby) which were open on the side
toward the city and frequently had scarcely any roof; but
where the path for the guards crossed them there was a
vaulted chamber which contained a regular arsenal of
catapults, bows and arrows, as well as covered steps leading to the top of the wall. Here the troops stationed at
the different parts of the wall got their weapons, and
issuing forth, appeared unexpectedly on the battlements
wherever an attack was made.

In times of peace any one who looked out over the
country from these battlements enjoyed a very delightful
view. In the foreground of the ivy-covered walls of the

city the most intensive agriculture was practised. Here
plants grown for commercial purposes flourished, and cultivation with the spade took the place of the ruder plow-
ing. In the level country beyond, the three-field system,
employing only a small number of cattle, imposed almost
insuperable obstacles to anything more than meager cultivation. Even the largest cities still retained some traces
of cultivation in common on a large scale; everywhere
there were forests belonging to the city community as a
whole, as well as commons to which the cattle of the citizens were driven each morning; and there were city
herdsmen and field watchmen appointed by the councilors.
But as fast as individual citizens acquired a private property in the neighborhood of the city, cultivation with the
spade spread more and more. Here arose vineyards and
vegetable and rose gardens; hops, flax, and woad were
planted. And, a thing that may at first view appear remarkable, inside the city, near the walls, there was in
many parts the same prospect as outside, especially in the
most important and rapidly growing cities which had extended their walls. Within the city walls there were also
vineyards and cherry orchards, vegetable and flower
gardens; and skirting them, broad, dirty streets, with
little houses filled with the poor agriculturists, and stately
manure-heaps in front.

The aspect of the cities is explained by the fact that it
was not so very long since they had broken away from
the system of *natural economy* which had prevailed exclusively up to that time; the traces of their earlier life,
when they had been merely larger and more prosperous
villages, still clung to them. Most cities were still to

City Life in Germany

a very great extent engaged in agriculture; at Coblenz, in the second half of the thirteenth century, work on the city walls had to be given up during harvest-time, because of the lack of workmen; at Frankfort in the year 1387 the city employed four herdsmen and six field-guards, and even in the fifteenth century a strict law was enacted against allowing pigs to run about in the city streets. Even in the largest cities there are very many indications of the activities of a widely extended population engaged in agriculture. Cattle-breeding and gardening were actively engaged in along with manufacturing and trade; in fact, the former had their own location in the country before the gates, as well as in the parts of the city which lay nearest the walls.

Manufacturing and trade, on the contrary, were located near the center. Here the guilds often dwelt together in narrow lanes with shops opening upon the street; here by the river or some other road the merchants thronged to the warehouses; here little shops of the retail dealers were snuggled in every corner. In walking through this portion, in the very heart of the city, somewhere around the market and city hall, one often came upon a few streets shut off by wooden doors, with only a few entrances and very compactly built up; that was the Jewish quarter. Here the Jews' school, the synagogue, stood in the midst of the congregation; until the middle of the fourteenth century it was often a splendid Roman or early Gothic building, with peculiar Oriental traces of a mixed style; here the bishop of the Jews ruled with his elders and kept one of the keys with which the doors of the quarter were locked at night to protect from the rage of the populace the Jews, who were considered hostile to the citizens both in economic matters and because of their race.

It was no accident that, in the medieval towns, the kinds and locations of the citizens' activities were distributed in this way. The results of historical evolution can easily be recognized in the fact that the activities in trade and manufacturing, which are peculiarly characteristic of a city, were situated at the center; and that, on the other hand, agricultural occupations were carried on in the outer portion of the city's area. Until some time in the thirteenth century most of the cities had been small. In the west they were often surrounded by the walls of an old Roman city which had grown out of a camp; in the east, recently founded on a small spot of ground, they were scarcely more than large castles. This narrow area was almost the only scene of earnest industrial activity and extensive intercourse with foreign parts. But about this center, later known as the old city, religious societies established themselves very early and acquired widely extended possessions; sometimes there were more than a half-dozen monasteries and cloisters and a bishop's seat, too, which with their property surrounded and sometimes crossed the center of the city. When the development of city life began in the twelfth and thirteenth centuries, the old walls were destroyed; generally the area of the cities began to be extended; and usually the new fortifications were placed beyond the circle in which the clerical property was situated. Thus the rural population was brought into the city; it was a long time before they gave up their old occupations and mode of life; indeed, they were strong enough to create outside of the city walls new groups of fruit and vegetable gardens. In time, to be sure, the space between the walls and the center of the city, which had once been covered with gardens, was filled with streets, and again the suburbs of the city began to extend beyond the gates. But the movement in this direction no longer proceeded from the lords of the old ecclesiastical property: they had fallen long before; now it was rather the business interests of the city itself which caused a new settlement at this point. Before the gates, especially in the neighborhood of a much frequented bridge, suburbs extended in long rows of streets, with low hovels, some of which were inhabited by rough people with interests which were partly rural and partly urban; these often found expression in a special government for the community. These were by no means the pleasantest portions of the city; here were the retail trades in their most humble forms and the pawnshops; here the fortune-tellers and " wise women " lived and boasted of their occupations; here the vagabonds and criminals had come when, by the extension of the city, they had been driven out of their caves under the city walls, and with them all sorts of evil-livers; here, too, in the case of cities which made cloth on a large scale, the great mass of the poor weavers lived.

It was the dregs of the population that lived in a suburb. Its separation from the city, in the course of the fourteenth century, shows that from this time we can date the completion of one stage in the development of the city's population.

Advice of St. Louis to his Son

Adapted from *Bibliothèque de l'École des Chartes.*
Vol. XXXIII, 1872, pp. 424–442.

1. To his dear first-born son, Philip, greeting, and his father's love.

2. Dear son, since I desire with all my heart that you be well instructed in all things, it is in my thought to give you some advice by this writing. For I have heard you say, several times, that you remember my words better than those of any one else.

3. Therefore, dear son, the first thing I advise is that you fix your whole heart upon God, and love Him with all your strength, for without this no one can be saved or be of any worth.

4. You should, with all your strength, shun everything which you believe to be displeasing to Him. And you ought especially to be resolved not to commit mortal sin, no matter what may happen, and you should permit all your limbs to be hewn off, and suffer every manner of torment, rather than fall knowingly into mortal sin.

5. If our Lord send you any adversity, whether illness or other thing, you should receive it in good patience, and thank Him for it, and be grateful for it, for you ought to believe that He will cause everything to turn out for your

good; and likewise you should think that you have well merited it, and more also, should He will it, because you have loved Him but little, and served Him but little, and have done many things contrary to His will.

6. If our Lord send you any prosperity, either health of body or other thing, you ought to thank Him humbly for it, and you ought to be careful that you are not the worse for it, either through pride or anything else, for it is a very great sin to fight against our Lord with His gifts.

7. Dear son, I advise you that you accustom yourself to frequent confession, and that you choose always, as your confessors, men who are upright and sufficiently learned, and who can teach you what you should do and what you should avoid. You should so carry yourself that your confessors and other friends may dare confidently to reprove you and show you your faults.

8. Dear son, I advise you that you listen willingly and devoutly to the services of Holy Church, and, when you are in church, avoid frivolity and trifling, and do not look here and there; but pray to God with lips and heart alike, while entertaining sweet thoughts about Him, and especially at the mass, when the body and blood of our Lord Jesus Christ are consecrated, and for a little time before.

9. Dear son, have a tender and pitiful heart for the poor, and for all those whom you believe to be in misery of heart or body, and, according to your ability, comfort and aid them with some alms.

10. Maintain the good customs of your realm, and put down the bad ones. Do not oppress your people and do

not burden them with tolls or *tailles,* except under very great necessity.

11. If you have any unrest of heart, of such a nature that it may be told, tell it to your confessor, or to some upright man who can keep your secret; you will be able to carry more easily the thought of your heart.

12. See to it that those of your household are upright and loyal, and remember the Scripture, which says: *" Elige viros timentes Deum in quibus sit justicia et qui oderint avariciam; "* that is to say. " Love those who serve God and who render strict justice and hate covetousness; " and you will profit, and will govern your kingdom well.

13. Dear son, see to it that all your associates are upright, whether clerics or laymen, and have frequent good converse with them; and flee the society of the bad. And listen willingly to the word of God, both in open and in secret; and purchase freely prayers and pardons.

14. Love all good, and hate all evil, in whomsoever it may be.

15. Let no one be so bold as to say, in your presence, words which attract and lead to sin, and do not permit words of detraction to be spoken of another behind his back.

16. Suffer it not that any ill be spoken of God or His saints in your presence, without taking prompt vengeance. But if the offender be a clerk or so great a person that you ought not to try him, report the matter to him who is entitled to judge it.

17. Dear son, give thanks to God often for all the good things He has done for you, so that you may be worthy

to receive more, in such a manner that if it please the Lord that you come to the burden and honor of governing the kingdom, you may be worthy to receive the sacred unction wherewith the kings of France are consecrated.

18. Dear son, if you come to the throne, strive to have that which befits a king, that is to say, that in justice and rectitude you hold yourself steadfast and loyal toward your subjects and your vassals, without turning either to the right or to the left, but always straight, whatever may happen. And if a poor man have a quarrel with a rich man, sustain the poor rather than the rich, until the truth is made clear, and when you know the truth, do justice to them.

19. If any one have entered into a suit against you (for any injury or wrong which he may believe that you have done to him), be always for him and against yourself in the presence of your council, without showing that you think much of your case (until the truth be made known concerning it); for those of your council might be backward in speaking against you, and this you should not wish; and command your judges that you be not in any way upheld more than any others, for thus will your councillors judge more boldly according to right and truth.

20. If you have anything belonging to another, either of yourself or through your predecessors, if the matter is certain, give it up without delay, however great it may be, either in land or money or otherwise. If the matter is doubtful, have it inquired into by wise men, promptly and diligently. And if the affair is so obscure that you cannot know the truth, make such a settlement, by the counsel of upright men, that your soul, and the souls of your pre-

decessors, may be wholly freed from the affair. And even if you hear some one say that your predecessors made restitution, make diligent inquiry to learn if anything remains to be restored; and if you find that such is the case, cause it to be delivered over at once, for the liberation of your soul and the souls of your predecessors.

21. You should seek earnestly how your vassals and your subjects may live in peace and rectitude beneath your sway; likewise, the good towns and the good cities of your kingdom. And preserve them in the estate and the liberty in which your predecessors kept them, and if there be anything to amend, amend and redress it, and preserve their favor and their love. For it is by the strength and the riches of your good cities and your good towns that the native and the foreigner, especially your peers and your barons, are deterred from doing ill to you. I well remember that Paris and the good towns of my kingdom aided me against the barons, when I was newly crowned.

22. Honor and love all the people of Holy Church, and be careful that no violence be done to them, and that their gifts and alms, which your predecessors have bestowed upon them, be not taken away or diminished. And I wish here to tell you what is related concerning King Philip, my ancestor, as one of his council, who said he heard it, told it to me. The king, one day, was with his privy council, and he was there who told me these words. And one of the king's councillors said to him how much wrong and loss he suffered from those of Holy Church, in that they took away his rights and lessened the jurisdiction of his court; and they marveled greatly how he endured it. And the good king answered: " I am quite certain that

they do me much wrong, but when I consider the good-
nesses and kindnesses which God has done me, I had
rather that my rights should go, than have a contention
or awaken a quarrel with Holy Church." And this I tell
to you that you may not lightly believe anything against
the people of Holy Church; so love them and honor
them and watch over them that they may in peace do the
service of our Lord.

23. Moreover, I advise you to love dearly the clergy,
and, so far as you are able, do good to them in their
necessities, and likewise love those by whom God is most
honored and served, and by whom the Faith is preached
and exalted.

24. Dear son, I advise that you love and reverence your
father and your mother, willingly remember and keep
their commandments, and be inclined to believe their good
counsels.

25. Love your brothers, and always wish their well-
being and their good advancement, and also be to them
in the place of a father, to instruct them in all good. But
be watchful lest, for the love which you bear to one, you
turn aside from right doing, and do to the others that
which is not meet.

26. Dear son, I advise you to bestow the benefices of
Holy Church which you have to give, upon good persons,
of good and clean life, and that you bestow them with the
high counsel of upright men. And I am of the opinion
that it is preferable to give them to those who hold nothing of Holy Church, rather than to others. For, if you
inquire diligently, you will find enough of those who have
nothing who will use wisely that entrusted to them.

27. Dear son, I advise you that you try with all your strength to avoid warring against any Christian man, unless he have done you too much ill. And if wrong be done you, try several ways to see if you can find how you can secure your rights, before you make war; and act thus in order to avoid the sins which are committed in warfare.

28. And if it fall out that it is needful that you should make war (either because some one of your vassals has failed to plead his case in your court, or because he has done wrong to some church or to some poor person, or to any other person whatsoever, and is unwilling to make amends out of regard for you, or for any other reasonable cause), whatever the reason for which it is necessary for you to make war, give diligent command that the poor folk who have done no wrong or crime be protected from damage to their vines, either through fire or otherwise, for it were more fitting that you should constrain the wrongdoer by taking his own property (either towns or castles, by force of siege), than that you should devastate the property of poor people. And be careful not to start the war before you have good counsel that the cause is most reasonable, and before you have summoned the offender to make amends, and have waited as long as you should. And if he ask mercy, you ought to pardon him, and accept his amende, so that God may be pleased with you.

29. Dear son, I advise you to appease wars and contentions, whether they be yours or those of your subjects, just as quickly as may be, for it is a thing most pleasing to our Lord. And Monsignore St. Martin gave us a very great example of this. For, one time, when our Lord made it known to him that he was about to die, he set out

to make peace between certain clerks of his archbishopric, and he was of the opinion that in so doing he was giving a good end to his life.

30. Seek diligently, most sweet son, to have good *baillis* and good *prévôts* in your land, and inquire frequently concerning their doings, and how they conduct themselves, and if they administer justice well, and do no wrong to any one, nor anything which they ought not do. Inquire more often concerning those of your household than of any others, and learn if they be too covetous or too arrogant; for it is natural that the members should seek to imitate their chief; that is, when the master is wise and well-behaved, all those of his household follow his example and prefer it. For however much you ought to hate evil in others, you should have more hatred for the evil which comes from those who derive their power from you, than you bear to the evil of others; and the more ought you to be on your guard and prevent this from happening.

31. Dear son, I advise you always to be devoted to the Church of Rome, and to the sovereign pontiff, our father, and to bear him the reverence and honor which you owe to your spiritual father.

32. Dear son, freely give power to persons of good character, who know how to use it well, and strive to have wickednesses expelled from your land, that is to say, nasty oaths, and everything said or done against God or our Lady or the saints. In a wise and proper manner put a stop, in your land, to bodily sins, dicing, taverns, and other sins. Put down heresy so far as you can, and hold in especial abhorrence Jews, and all sorts of people who are

hostile to the Faith, so that your land may be well purged of them, in such manner as, by the sage counsel of good people, may appear to you advisable.

33. Further the right with all your strength. Moreover, I admonish you that you strive most earnestly to show your gratitude for the benefits which our Lord has bestowed upon you, and that you may know how to give Him thanks therefor.

34. Dear son, take care that the expenses of your household are reasonable and moderate, and that its moneys are justly obtained. And there is one opinion that I deeply wish you to entertain, that is to say, that you keep yourself free from foolish expenses and evil exactions, and that your money should be well expended and well acquired. And this opinion, together with other opinions which are suitable and profitable, I pray that our Lord may teach you.

35. Finally, most sweet son, I conjure and require you that, if it please our Lord that I should die before you, you have my soul succored with masses and orisons, and that you send through the congregations of the kingdom of France, and demand their prayers for my soul, and that you grant me a special and full part in all the good deeds which you perform.

36. In conclusion, dear son, I give you all the blessings which a good and tender father can give to a son, and I pray our Lord Jesus Christ, by His mercy, by the prayers and merits of His blessed Mother, the Virgin Mary, and of angels and archangels and of all the saints, to guard and protect you from doing anything contrary to His will, and to give you grace to do it always,

Advice of St. Louis to his Son

so that He may be honored and served by you. And this may He do to me as to you, by His great bounty, so that after this mortal life we may be able to be together with Him in the eternal life, and see Him, love Him, and praise Him without end. Amen. And glory, honor, and praise be to Him who is one God with the Father and the Holy Spirit; without beginning and without end. Amen.

Life of Gerbert

Adapted from Julien Havet's *Introduction* to the *Lettres de Gerbert,* 1889, pp. v–xxxviii.

GERBERT was born of obscure and poor parents in central France, between 940 and 945 A.D. He was educated at Aurillac, in the Benedictine monastery of St. Géraud, of which Géraud of Céré was abbot. He learned grammar there, that is to say, Latin, and had as his master the monk Raymond, who afterward succeeded Géraud as abbot.

About 967 Borel, count of Barcelona and duke of the Spanish March (a province which was then a part of France), came to Aurillac on a pilgrimage. The abbot, Géraud, asked him if there were in his country scholars versed in the sciences, and, being answered in the affirmative, begged the duke to take Gerbert and have him taught. Borel entrusted this duty to Atto, bishop of Vich. Gerbert acquired, during his stay in Spain, a profound knowledge of mathematics. Perhaps, thanks to the nearness of the Mussulmans, who held the remainder of the peninsula, something of the teaching of the Arab mathematicians had passed into the Christian schools of the Spanish March.

In 970, Borel went to Rome and took Atto and Gerbert with him. The pope remarked the mathematical acquire-

ments of Gerbert, and spoke of him to the emperor, Otto
I, who was then in Italy. Otto induced Gerbert to reside
at his court and teach mathematics to chosen students.

Gerbert was less anxious to teach what he knew than
to learn what he did not know, and said to Otto I that,
in truth, he knew mathematics fairly well, but that he
wished to learn logic, or, as we would say, philosophy.
He very soon obtained an opportunity to satisfy this desire. He had been in Italy about a year when there came
to the imperial court an archdeacon of Reims, who had
been sent on an embassy by King Lothair; this man was
a certain G——, who had a great reputation as a philosopher. Gerbert asked and secured permission to accompany him on his return to France, and they reached Reims
together about 972. Gerbert gave his companion lessons
in mathematics, and in exchange received from him lessons in philosophy. But the archdeacon found insur-
mountable difficulties in the rules of music—a study
which was then included among the mathematical
branches. On the other hand, the young monk very soon
knew as much about philosophy as his master did. Thus
he completed his instruction in all the branches of human
knowledge.

His varied attainments attracted the attention of the
archbishop of Reims, Adalbero, a pious and enlightened
prelate, who was zealously laboring to maintain order
and discipline among the clergy of his diocese. This
was the beginning of a friendship which lasted until the
death of the archbishop and occupied a large place in
the life of Gerbert.

There was at that time, in every cathedral church, a

school which was under the authority of the bishop and was directed by a clerk, who was called the *scholasticus*. Adalbero appointed Gerbert *scholasticus* of Reims. He had every reason to be satisfied with his choice. The young teacher introduced into his instruction new methods, as well as ideas hitherto ignored. His reputation spread throughout all Europe, and pupils came to him from all parts. Thus passed about ten years, the most tranquil, and probably the happiest of his life (972–982). Only one incident of this period is known to us. It redounded to his glory and hastened his good fortune.

In the heart of Germany, at Magdeburg, there was a celebrated teacher named Otric. The fame of Gerbert's teaching displeased him. He sent an emissary to Reims, with instructions to listen to the lessons of the scholasticus, and to report what he heard. The envoy performed his mission badly, and reported inexactly the instruction of Gerbert upon a scholastic detail; Otric believed that his rival had made a mistake and hastened to publish the error. But Otto II had confidence in the learning of Gerbert: he had seen and heard him in Italy several years before (971–972); he could hardly believe Gerbert capable of the error attributed to him, and resolved to put his talent to the proof. The next year he went to Italy, accompanied by Otric, and, at Pavia, fell in with Archbishop Adalbero and his scholasticus, who were going to Rome, for some purpose unknown to us (December, 980). He invited them to join his court, and, embarking upon a flotilla, they all descended the Po and landed at Ravenna. Here, by his orders, a public discussion was held between the two rivals in the presence of a great number of scholars (December, 980, or January, 981). It lasted a whole day and turned altogether upon metaphysical points. One cannot read the report of it given in the *Chronicle* of the monk Richer without being astonished at the futility of the debate over words, which at that time passed for scientific problems, and at the patience of the emperor, sovereign of three kingdoms, who could give hours to such an occupation. Richer adds that the victory rested with Gerbert, who refuted, in all particulars, the arguments of his rival. After the termination of this scholastic tournament, Gerbert, in company with the archbishop, returned to Reims, loaded with gifts from the emperor.

The most beautiful gift, however, was received by him two years later, when Otto II called him to govern the abbey of St. Columban at Bobbio, in the Apennines (983). This was one of the richest benefices in Italy. Gerbert, who was born poor, was entitled to love money, for he made a most honorable use of it. His greatest expenditures were for the increase of his library. He accepted the emperor's offer and took an oath of fidelity to him—the first in his life. Henceforth he must have ceased to consider himself a Frenchman; he recognized, as was his feudal duty, the emperor to whom he had plighted his word as his sole master and sovereign. He remained faithful to the allegiance thus contracted, and was, his life long, one of the most devoted and disinterested servants of the imperial house.

The post which Otto II had given him was one of confidence. The abbot of Bobbio was a political personage;

he bore the title of count and had vassals who owed military service. The emperor, who had only a moderate faith in his Italian subjects, required Gerbert to reside in his abbey. He obeyed this command, but he did not leave Reims without the expectation of returning. He did not even take his books with him; he left them at Reims, locked up in chests whose keys he bore with him to Italy.

He found the greatest disorder at Bobbio. The possessions of the abbey had been despoiled. His predecessor, the abbot Petroald, who belonged to an influential family, had made friends by renting the lands of the monastery at very low rates to the lesser nobility of the neighborhood. The emperor had removed him and reduced him to the rank of a simple monk; nevertheless, he had retained the enjoyment of a portion of the abbot's revenues, and Otto II advised Gerbert not to disturb him. Gerbert, a Frenchman, accustomed to the strict discipline of the monasteries of Aurillac and Reims, could not participate in these irregularities. With more vehemence than policy, he claimed the restoration of the goods of the abbey and repudiated the leases made by Petroald. He made a number of enemies; several of them had powerful protectors, and Gerbert soon found himself at loggerheads with personages of considerable importance, for example, Peter, bishop of Pavia, who some months later became Pope John XIV, and the empress Adelaide, widow of Otto I and mother of the reigning emperor. Thanks to the great power of Otto II, he gained his object, but the irritation only became greater and revealed itself in coarse sarcasms, some of which were aimed at him, and

Life of Gerbert

others at his sovereign. When Otto II died suddenly at Rome (December 7, 983) and left his throne to a three-year-old son, Gerbert, who was then at the imperial palace in Pavia, learned that the monks had renounced his authority and that Bobbio was being pillaged. Neither the pope nor the empress Adelaide, both of whom he had offended, could be expected to intervene in his behalf; the other empress, Theophano the Greek, widow of Otto II and mother of the new king, Otto III, had more pressing cares. Gerbert returned to France, carrying with him only the empty title of abbot and the memory of his abbacy (984).

He had spent less than a year at Bobbio. He had had only sufficient time to cast his eye over the library of the monastery and to find that it contained books of science which interested him much; he had not been able to have them copied, and probably had not read them. Five years later he still regretted this, and, on two occasions, he wrote to Italy to obtain copies of the precious volumes.

Returning to Reims, he resumed his duties as scholasticus. But hereafter politics occupied him as much as study. He had become the vassal of the emperor on receiving from him the abbey of Bobbio, and did not believe himself released from his duty by the loss of the benefice or the death of his lord. He thought that he owed to the little king, Otto III, and his mother, Theophano, the same fidelity which he had given to Otto II. Archbishop Adalbero was of the same opinion, although externally his position was quite different. As archbishop of Reims and grand chancellor of France, he was above all the vassal of the king of France, and was bound to recognize him as his principal lord; but as a noble, he could not, as easily as the plebeian Gerbert, forget his birth. His family was one of the first in the kingdom of Lorraine, which was one of the states at that time composing the realm of the king of Germany. His brother, Count Godfrey, was regarded as one of the best servants of Otto II. He himself had been at first a canon at Metz, in Lorraine, and even at Reims his spiritual and temporal power was not restricted to the French side of the frontier; for a part of his diocese and two of his castles, Mouzon and Mézières, were in Lorraine. He was under obligations to Otto I, and we have seen that he had been received with honor at the court of Otto II. Thus both the archbishop and the scholasticus, although dwelling in a French city, had their eyes turned to Germany, and were interested, above all, in what was occurring in the neighboring kingdom.

At that time, the throne and the life of the young Otto III were threatened by a turbulent and unscrupulous prince, Henry, duke of Bavaria, and first cousin of Otto II, who had, ten years before, been implicated in an attempted revolt against the emperor. At the news of the death of Otto II, which was not known in Germany until the last part of December, 983, or the first part of January, 984, Henry took advantage of the absence of the empress-mother, Theophano, in Italy, to demand the guardianship of the young king and to seize his person. On Easter Sunday, March 23, 984, he called together, at Quedlinburg, an assembly of some nobles devoted to his cause and had himself saluted by them as king. This criminal attempt offended the greater number of the

nobles of Germany and of Lorraine, and they combined
to defend the rights of the imperial infant and of the
¿mpress. Adalbero and Gerbert took up the cause with
ardor. The archbishop, by virtue of his rank and his
birth, had great influence in Lorraine and in Germany;
Gerbert had a talent for writing, appreciated by all his
contemporaries, a chaste and vigorous style and lofty
and winning eloquence. They united their strength:
letters written in the name of the archbishop, but drawn
up by Gerbert, were sent to various great personages of
Germany to stir up their zeal against the usurper. It is
difficult to read these letters and believe that they could
have been without effect. At the same time, Adalbero
induced the king of France, Lothair, who was married
to a sister of Otto II, to declare himself guardian and
protector of his nephew, Otto III. Henry was terrified
and yielded; he surrendered the little Otto to his mother
and his grandmother, the empresses Theophano and
Adelaide, who had been recalled from Italy in all haste
by their supporters (June, 984), and, at Worms (October, 984), he made a treaty with them, by which he
seemed definitely to give up his claims.

It was only a feint. The peace had hardly been made
when Henry entered into negotiations with Lothair, and
offered in exchange for his support to give up Lorraine
to France. The king of France, won over by such an
advantageous offer, agreed to meet Henry at Alt-Brei-
sach, on the right bank of the Rhine, on February 1, 985.
Gerbert, who had an admirably organized secret-service
system, learned of the plot and hastened to warn his
friends in Lorraine. He strove at first to gain for Otto

Medieval Civilization

III, against Henry and Lothair, the alliance of the most powerful French noble, Hugh, duke of France, whom modern historians called Hugh Capet. His attempt, which was badly supported, failed, but he at least was successful in securing the neutrality of Hugh, and this was worth a great deal. Lothair, when he arrived at Breisach, did not find Henry, whose courage had failed a second time. Nevertheless the king of France single-handed undertook the conquest of Lorraine (February-March, 985). He besieged Verdun, took it, almost immediately lost it, and then regained it. The second time that he won it, he captured the defenders of the city, the *élite* of the Lorraine nobility: Count Godfrey, brother of Archbishop Adalbero, Frederick, son of Godfrey, Siegfrid, his uncle, and others. He left a garrison in Verdun and carried his prisoners to France, where he entrusted them to the keeping of two of his vassals, who imprisoned them in a castle on the Marne (March, 985).

Gerbert obtained from these vassals permission to visit the prisoners. It is still hard to understand how he obtained this permission, for he did not take pains to hide his fidelity to the empress. However that may be, he was able to enter the castle where the Lorraine counts were imprisoned, and talked with them in private. He was commissioned by Godfrey to write on his behalf to his wife, sons and friends, and to Theophano. To all he made the same recommendation: continue the struggle unceasingly; do not worry over the lot of the prisoners: " Cause the enemy to feel that he has not captured the whole of Godfrey." Nothing is more generous than the sentiment which dictated this advice; nothing more

engaging than the language in which Gerbert knew how
to put it.

Archbishop Adalbero could not, like Gerbert, make a
public avowal of his sentiments. Although naturally attached to the cause of his brother and nephews and devoted with his whole heart to the empress, he had
officially to serve their enemy, the king of France. He
dissimulated, but only half-deceived Lothair. The latter
dictated to him letters which were to be sent to the
prelates of Lorraine; the archbishop obeyed, and then
caused other letters to be written secretly by Gerbert,
which gave the lie to the first ones. He could not avoid
furnishing to the king, his suzerain, a contingent of
troops for the garrison of Verdun, but he did not obey
the king's orders, and gave him bad advice. When he
had information to send to the enemy, Gerbert transmitted it in his own name, in order not to compromise
his master. Lothair, until the end of his life, suspected
the bishop of treason, but the latter, cleverly aided by
his scholasticus, found a way to elude the royal sur-
veillance.

Lothair died March 2, 986, and was succeeded by his
son, Louis V, who had been his associate since 979. For
the moment, Adalbero and Gerbert believed themselves
masters of the situation. Emma, mother of the new
king, and widow of Lothair, was a daughter of the old
empress, Adelaide, and aunt of Otto III; all her sympathies were with Germany. The very day of Lothair's
death she recalled the archbishop of Reims to the court,
caused or permitted several of the Lorraine prisoners to
be liberated, and took Gerbert for her secretary. She

opened peace negotiations with the imperial court. But the new king soon perceived that his mother was serving the enemies of his kingdom and broke with her and her counselors. Adalbero, threatened by the royal troops in his metropolitan city, saved his life only by giving pledges of submission. He was summoned to appear before the court of the king under an accusation of treason. In the meantime the peace negotiations were continued, and Gerbert still found it possible to employ himself actively with them, but they did not terminate in any definite result. An accident changed the situation: Louis V, while hunting, fell from his horse, and died at Senlis, May 21 or 22, 987, fourteen months after his father, leaving the throne vacant. At this epoch, coronation alone made the king, and there was no crowned king. By birth, Charles, duke of lower Lorraine, brother of Lothair, seemed entitled to the throne, but Archbishop Adalbero preferred to call to the throne Hugh, the powerful duke of France, who was a first cousin of Lothair in the female line. The coup was executed with marvelous promptitude. The day after the royal funeral, an assembly of nobles of the court—*principes*—presided over by the duke, acquitted the archbishop of the charge brought against him. Some days later, an assembly of the same nobles, presided over by the archbishop, conferred the crown upon the duke. Ten days after the death of Louis V, Hugh was crowned at Noyon (June 1, 987), and, five weeks later, was consecrated at Reims. The Capetian dynasty was founded.

This revolution was apparently the work of Adalbero, but really that of Gerbert. A word let fall by his pen two years later shows this. Adalbero had died. Charles, seeking to reconquer the throne of which he had been deprived, had taken possession of Reims. Gerbert was denounced to the angry pretender as the man who, he tells us, " deposed and set up kings." Thus the arch-bishop of Reims, in this matter, had acted, as always, in agreement with his scholasticus, and, indeed, under his inspiration.

Gerbert was, as has been seen, wholly devoted to the family of the Ottos. If, then, he thought it wise to cause Hugh to be made king of France, he must have believed that this would be advantageous to Germany. His motives are not hard to divine. Charles, who held lower Lorraine of Otto III, had not proved a good vas-sal. He had participated in the attempts of Lothair to unite Lorraine to France and to put Henry of Bavaria on the throne of Germany. If Charles became king of France, he would probably continue the war and would be all the more anxious to annex Lorraine, since this would be the means of uniting his duchy to his kingdom. Hugh, on the contrary, had given Germany pledges of his good will. During the last war, instead of aiding his sovereigns, Lothair and Louis V, in their struggle against the foreigner, he had maintained toward them a threatening neutrality. Moreover, his only son, Robert, then about thirteen years of age, was a pupil of Gerbert and the latter might well hope to influence the father through the son. In conclusion, the duke, in order to gain the throne, would undoubtedly be only too happy to make all the concessions that could be asked of him; all that would be necessary would be to dictate conditions to him. These conditions were a definitive peace with Germany, the liberation of Count Godfrey, and the abandonment of all attempts upon the eastern frontier.

Godfrey was set at liberty three weeks after the coronation of Hugh. Hostilities were terminated between the two countries. The roads were again free, and Archbishop Adalbero, released from the burden of public affairs, was able to announce his intention of making a pilgrimage to Germany. Thus the kingdom of Lorraine, which the kings of France and of Germany had been disputing for a century, was acquired by the Germans. Even the name of this kingdom was quickly forgotten, and the time came when the dwellers on the banks of the Meuse could say, in good faith, that they belonged to the " kingdom of Germany." Gerbert, in excluding from the throne of France the last descendants of Charlemagne, had done a great service to the country of his adoption. Not until three centuries after Hugh Capet, in the days of Philip the Rash and Philip the Fair, were French kings found who seriously attempted to gain for France some portion of Carolingian Lorraine.

The archbishop and the scholasticus of Reims, moreover, showed themselves faithful servants of the king whom they had chosen. Hugh made use of Gerbert's talents as a writer and entrusted to him the drawing-up of several important letters. Among those which are extant is one in which the king asks of the two emperors of Constantinople the hand of a Byzantine princess for his son Robert. Another letter promises aid to Borel, duke of the Spanish March, against the threatening Mussulmans, who, two years before, had taken the city of Barcelona from him. Gerbert, who had lived at the court of Borel and owed to him his scientific education, was probably not a stranger to the decision of the king to aid the duke. The plan could not be realized, but it gave to Hugh, who alleged that it would endanger his person, an opportunity to associate his son Robert in the kingship, and thus to assure the succession in his family. The young prince and pupil of Gerbert was crowned at Orléans, December 25, 987, and consecrated at Reims, January 1, 988.

Under these circumstances, Duke Charles resolved to make good his right or his claim to the crown (988). He was able to raise a body of troops and march upon Laon, the capital of the old Carolingian kings. The lord of this city was its bishop—a man named Adalbero (not to be confused with the archbishop of Reims), whose surname was Ascelin or Azolin; Queen Emma, widow of Lothair, also resided at Laon. The bishop and the queen were on bad terms with the duke, who had made accusations touching their morality. Charles, by a ruse, was able to capture the city. He imprisoned Emma and Ascelin, gathered a great supply of provisions, completed the fortifications of the place, and thus made his position very strong. The two kings, Hugh and Robert, after some hesitation, decided to besiege the place. Archbishop Adalbero, as lord of Reims, had to furnish his contingent and take part in the expedition. The city was besieged twice in the year 988, both times unsuccessfully. Gerbert took part in the first siege. His letters are among the documents which enable us to follow some of the incidents of this useless campaign.

Medieval Civilization

The ensuing winter, the archbishop fell sick, and died at Reims. King Hugh was present at the funeral and busied himself with the choice of a successor. In theory, the right of election belonged to the clergy and people of the diocese and the bishops of the province; but, in fact, the king's will was all-powerful. The position to be filled was one of the most important in the Church, and the post of grand chancellor of the kingdom which went with it gave its holder much political importance.

Gerbert was torn by conflicting emotions—sorrow at the loss of his master and friend, and ambition which was awakened by the prospect of the magnificent future that seemed to open before him. Adalbero had designated Gerbert, the latter said, for the archbishopric, and he might legitimately hope that the king, who had gained the throne through him, would honor this wish. Hugh was, however, maladroit and ungrateful. Notwithstanding the very sensible advice given by a nephew of the dead archbishop and inspired by Gerbert, he thought it would be good politics to give the vacant archbishopric to young Arnulf, an illegitimate son of Lothair. He hoped, in this way, to divide the Carolingian family and gain the help of Arnulf against his uncle Charles, the pretender. He was soon undeceived. Gerbert, whatever his disappointment may have been, remained master of himself. He did not show a trace of ill-will toward his rival, and remained attached to him as he had been to his predecessor. He framed the certificate of election and drew up several letters on behalf of his new master. On the other hand, having lost hope of gaining preferment at Reims, he wrote to his friends at the imperial court, re-

Life of Gerbert

calling his loyal services to the family of the Ottos, and begged for a reward, whatever it might be. He had no greater success with Theophano than he had had with Hugh. He was forced to be content with the nominal title of abbot of Bobbio and with the actual position of scholasticus at Reims. The new archbishop, Arnulf, either by premeditation or impulse, soon betrayed, for the sake of his uncle, the pretender, the kings to whom he had sworn fidelity. He was careful only to preserve appearances and to seem to be the victim of the crime for which he was really responsible. One night, in the summer of 989, Charles appeared with his troops under the walls of Reims. A priest named Adelger, at the instigation of Arnulf, took from under the latter's pillow the keys of the city and opened the gates to the duke. The city was pillaged and the archbishop was seized and carried prisoner to Laon. Gerbert, who had been denounced to Charles as the author of the revolution which placed the Capetians upon the throne, feared for his life. He thought of flight, but in vain. At this point, a curious incident occurs, and Gerbert, usually so firm in spirit and so loyal, exhibits surprising weakness. Arnulf had raised the mask and had openly declared himself a partisan of Charles, and Gerbert followed him in his defection. He continued to serve as his secretary, and, in the letters written at his command, manifests a strong opposition to the cause of the princes who had made Arnulf archbishop and whom he himself had made kings. Gerbert has not left it for another to denounce this aberration; a short time afterward, conscious of his error, he frankly accused himself of having been leader in the

most criminal enterprises and of having played the rôle
of an organ of the devil, in championing error against
the truth. Whatever may be the true explanation, he
figured for a short time among the members, if not among
the chiefs, of the rebellious party.

It was only for a short time. Even during his defection, he was tormented by scruples. Friends strove to
reconcile him with his own conscience. Some leagues
from Reims, there was a castle, called Roucy, in which
two near relatives of the last Carolingians lived. These
were Gislebert, count of Roucy, and Bruno, his brother,
bishop of Langres, who were sons of a sister of Lothair
and Charles, and therefore cousins of Archbishop Arnulf.
Bishop Bruno found himself in a very awkward situation
as the result of the treason of Arnulf, for he had been
rash enough, some months before, to guarantee the fidelity of his cousin to the kings, Hugh and Robert. He had
an interview with Gerbert at the castle of Roucy, and
pointed out to him the peril of the course he was entering
upon, and persuaded him to return to the cause of the
kings. Gerbert, relieved of a heavy weight, left Reims
and wrote to Archbishop Arnulf definitely breaking with
him, in a letter which was very honest and very clever,
for he could almost always combine these two qualities.
He went to the court of the kings, who were then living
at Senlis, and in the letters to his friends, announcing his
return to the good cause, his unmixed joy is very evident. Hugh again placed entire confidence in him. He
gave him the task of drawing up, in the name of a provincial council, assembled by royal command at Senlis,
a sentence of anathema against the accomplices of Arnulf

and Charles, as well as a letter addressed to Pope John XV, imploring intervention against the faithless prelate (summer of 990). An archbishop's treason had caused Hugh Capet to lose the city of Reims; the treason of a bishop placed in his hands, not only the archbishopric and the city, but also the chief of the whole rebellion, the pretender Charles. This new traitor was Adalbero or Ascelin, the bishop of Laon. After a pretended reconciliation with Duke Charles, and after the most solemn oaths, he betrayed him to the royal troops and opened to them the gates of Laon. This perfidy took place during the night of Palm Sunday (991). Arnulf was captured with his uncle. Duke Charles, with his wife and children, and the archbishop were imprisoned in Orléans. The civil war was thus ended at a stroke. But it may be truthfully said that Hugh Capet owed his success to his good fortune rather than to his prudence or his cleverness.

In June, a national council was assembled at Verzy to try the archbishop. Gerbert has left a detailed account, which he wrote four years later, probably composed from stenographic notes which he took during the sittings, for he had learned the system of shorthand which was used by the Italian notaries. The guilt of Arnulf was unquestioned; he himself admitted it. The only dispute was about a legal question: could a national council try a prelate without the express authorization of the pope? The bishops said that it could; but two abbots declared that it could not. They recognized that it was to the interest of the regular clergy to defend the rights of the Holy See, which had often granted the

Medieval Civilization

monasteries exemption from the episcopal authority. The bishops cited the ancient discipline of the Church, the condition of anarchy and barbarism into which Rome had fallen, and the ignorance of the popes of the time; the defenders of the papacy found arguments for their cause in an apocryphal collection, composed in the middle of the preceding century and already widely known throughout Christendom—the False Decretals. The bishops who were strong in number and had the kings on their side, insisted on the punishment of the traitor, carried the day and sentenced Arnulf to be degraded from his office. They made him abdicate in writing, tore from his person the insignia of his rank, and sent him to prison. Gerbert was elected archbishop in his place. This had been the supreme goal of his ambition for many years. It was also the beginning of the greatest tribulations of his life. His opponents made haste to denounce to the pope the injury which had been done to the papacy by the council of Verzy, in judging and condemning an archbishop without papal concurrence—an injury which had been aggravated by the very disrespectful language in which one of the bishops had spoken of the court of Rome. The Holy See at once opened a campaign of canonical litigation against the new archbishop, which lasted six years without any definite result. Gerbert, who was full of zeal for serious studies, had no taste for chicanery. He was disheartened at the time and energy he lost in defending a position which he believed he had obtained legitimately. " I would much rather," he wrote, " fight against armed men than dispute over legal questions." And yet he displays in this struggle all his clearness of thought, his correctness of reasoning, and his strength of character. In the administration of his diocese during this period of strife, he showed himself to be a prelate fully conscious of his spiritual duties, careful to maintain discipline, and to protect impartially all the faithful of every rank who were subjected to his metropolitan authority and entrusted to his pastoral care.

An Italian monk, Leo, abbot of St. Boniface of Rome, was appointed papal legate to examine the charges against Arnulf. In 992, he went, not to France, but to Aix-la-Chapelle, in Lorraine, and there summoned a council of bishops from Lorraine and Germany. It was only there, he declares, that he learned of the deposition of Arnulf. He returned to the pope and reported the condition of affairs. The sovereign pontiff summoned to his court at Rome the kings, Hugh and Robert, and the French bishops. This summons naturally had no effect. A second council was held in the territory of Otto III, at Ingelheim, near Mayence (994); the legate evidently did not dare to come into France itself and attack a sentence which had been pronounced with the assent of the king of France. The German bishops rendered a formal decision against the council of Verzy, and requested the pope to quash the condemnation of Arnulf.

Emboldened by this first success, John XV planned a decisive stroke. He excommunicated Gerbert and the French bishops who had deposed Arnulf. His measures met with a vigorous resistance. Gerbert protested against the sentence of the pope, and induced his colleagues to disregard it. A national council was assembled

at Chelles and directed by him, although presided over
by the young king Robert, and it was formally decreed
that the pope was not entitled to obedience when he gave
unjust orders, and that the condemnation of Arnulf had
been regularly pronounced and would be maintained.

John XV recognized that his authority would be
powerless against prelates who were directed and sustained by their king. He thereupon adopted a new ex-
pedient, which was to assemble upon the border between
the kingdoms of Hugh and Otto III a council composed
of the bishops of both countries. He undoubtedly hoped
to get, through the support of the prelates of Lorraine
and of Germany, a majority against Gerbert, and he expected that the French prelates would not dare to refuse
obedience to the decision of a council in which they themselves had taken part. Leo, the papal legate, returned
and summoned a council to meet at Mouzon, which was
within the diocese of Reims and in the kingdom of Lorraine, upon the French frontier. King Hugh, however,
checkmated the plan of the pope by forbidding his bishops
to obey the summons of the legate. Gerbert was the only
French prelate at the council, where he pleaded his cause.
No decision was reached, and all that was done was to
order a fresh council to assemble at Reims, July 1, 995.
They requested Gerbert, during the period before a final
decision should be rendered, to regard himself as suspended from his ecclesiastical functions. He only consented, through a spirit of conciliation, to abstain from
celebrating the mass. Whether the council sat at Reims
or Senlis or elsewhere, and whether it decided anything, is
unknown. All that is certain is that the matter was still

Life of Gerbert

in suspense in 996. In that year, Gerbert, taking advantage of Otto III's journey to Italy to receive the imperial crown, went with the monarch to explain his cause to the pope. However, while they were journeying to Italy, John XV died and was succeeded by Gregory V, a relative of Otto III. No one dared to speak to the new pope against a man who was a favorite of the emperor, a member of his suite and his secretary; in the absence of an accuser, the case remained undecided. It was referred to a new council, which was to meet, probably at Rome, in 997. Meanwhile Hugh Capet died, and thus Gerbert lost his best defender. The young king, Robert of France, was, to be sure, Gerbert's pupil, but he was also the friend of Abbo, the abbot of St. Benedict-upon-the-Loire, who had been the strenuous defender of Arnulf and the papacy at the council of Verzy. Furthermore, Robert needed the pope's friendship, for he wished to marry one of his relatives, the countess Bertha, and he naturally feared that the marriage would be attacked at Rome—as it actually was, a little later. As a matter of fact, Gerbert had already been consulted concerning the projected marriage and had formally opposed it, in the name of the laws of the Church. He now recognized that he could no longer expect the support of the French court. He appeared in France, probably for the last time, at a council held in St. Denis in March, 997; then, feelthing that he was encompassed by enemies in the very heart of his metropolitan city of Reims, he sought refuge in Germany, at the court of Otto III.

A year before, this prince had exchanged his title of king for that of emperor. He was seventeen years old, and exhibited great zeal for study. He gladly welcomed for the second time such a celebrated scholar, and made haste to attach him to himself and to give him the means to lead a tranquil and honorable existence at the court. At the end of 997, when the difficulties stirred up by the famous Crescentius called the emperor to Rome, he again took Gerbert with him to Italy. When they had passed the Alps, they learned that King Robert had yielded to the demands of the pope—of which the abbot Abbo had made himself the official interpreter—and had liberated Arnulf from prison. This event clearly indicated that he intended to restore to Arnulf his archbishopric; it was a warning to Gerbert to seek his fortunes elsewhere. The emperor did not permit the search to last very long. He gave him the archbishopric of Ravenna, one of the first ecclesiastical dignities in Italy. He thus recompensed Gerbert in a princely fashion for the services which the latter had rendered gratuitously in the days of the regency of Theophano. The pope promptly ratified a choice which so peculiarly facilitated the solution of the quarrel over the see of Reims, and Gerbert was officially installed in his new archbishopric (April, 998).

Nevertheless, it was not yet considered safe to restore Arnulf completely to his see, for that would have involved the condemnation of Gerbert and of the council of Verzy, and this was neither desirable nor feasible. Hence, by a new compromise, the pope authorized Arnulf to resume the exercise of his archiepiscopal functions until the case was settled. Gerbert was archbishop of Ravenna about a year. Little is known of his life or of his acts during this period. He reëstablished discipline in

Life of Gerbert

the monastery of Bobbio, of which he was still abbot, and, by an imperial diploma, secured the official restitution of the monastic property which had been usurped during his absence. He was always much concerned about regularity and discipline, and consequently went further than this measure, which interested him particularly; he used his influence to set limits to the waste of the goods of the Church. He recalled the extent to which he had been embarrassed, fifteen years before, through the long leases by which the abbot, his predecessor, had alienated the resources of the monastery for practically nothing. He secured a decree from an Italian council and from the emperor that, in the future, leases made by a bishop or abbot of the property of his bishopric or abbey, should be valid only during the lifetime of the said bishop or abbot. It is worthy of note that he also appended his signature, after that of Pope Gregory V, to a sentence of excommunication launched against King Robert, his former pupil, for violating the canons by marrying a relative, the countess Bertha. The following year, Gregory V died (February, 999), and Otto III, who disposed of the pontifical throne, gave it to Gerbert. It is quite certain that this piece of good fortune was unexpected. Less than four years before, in an apologetic letter to the bishop of Strasburg, he expressed astonishment at having been raised to the archiepiscopal see of Reims; such an exalted position seemed in excess of his deserts. " If it is asked how this happened," he said, " I declare that I do not know; I do not know how a poor man, an exile, without birth or fortune, was able to get the preference over so many men possessed of riches and high birth."

Medieval Civilization

No one could have foreseen at that time that he was very soon to become the first bishop of the universe and that the world would see, in his person, science and virtue seated upon the throne of St. Peter, where, he had so loudly complained, one could see only ignorance and corruption. He took the name of Sylvester, and was consecrated at Rome, probably in the presence of Otto III, on Palm Sunday, 999. He was pope until May, 1003. During these four years, the history of his life is bound up with the history of the Church, and only a few of his acts need be spoken of in this place.

Gregory V having failed to give a final decision for or against Arnulf, Sylvester II had to decide the case. His generosity forbade him to overwhelm his rival; his conscience forbade him to absolve a criminal who had been justly condemned. With his usual cleverness and honesty, he found a way to reconcile his generosity and his conscience, and, at the same time, finally to restore peace to the church of Reims. In a haughty letter to Arnulf, he declared that this prelate had been condemned " for certain misdeeds," *quibusdam excessibus,* but that the Holy See has, among other prerogatives, the right of sovereign mercy, which permits it " to lift up those who have fallen," *lapsos erigere.* By virtue of this right and showing mercy, he judged it good to come to the aid of the dispossessed archbishop; he reëstablished him in his first dignity and permitted him to resume, with the insignia of his office, the exercise of his diocesan and metropolitan authority, and forbade anyone ever to reproach him with his condemnation, " whatever the reproaches which he might feel in his conscience," *etiamsi conscientiae reatus accurrat.* In a word, the pope restored him everything save his honor; but the sentence pronounced by the fathers of Verzy remained intact. If Arnulf had any sense of honor (which is doubtful) he must have felt more humiliated to recover his archbishopric on these conditions than to have lost it. Nevertheless, he thought it wise to accept it; and he kept it twenty-two years, dying archbishop of Reims, eighteen years after the death of Sylvester II. Until quite recently the details of this whole matter were known only through the unsatisfactory reports of non-contemporary chroniclers. It was generally believed, from the evidence of these chroniclers, that Gregory V had annulled the acts of the council of Verzy, that he had deprived Gerbert of the archbishopric of Reims to give it to Arnulf, and that Gerbert had no office at the moment when Otto III gave him the archbishopric of Ravenna. It is now known that all this is false. But the impression given by the old ideas still persists, and, even now, there are Catholic writers who think that they can give the assembly of Verzy no other name than that of false council, and that they can call Gerbert archbishop of Reims only by prefacing the title with the word " intruding." If by these words the authors who employed them wished merely to express their personal opinion, well and good, but if they desired to show their submission to the decrees of the Holy See, they deceived themselves. The Holy See has never pronounced upon either the validity of the acts of the council of Verzy or the legitimacy of the election of Gerbert. These questions are still to-day among those to which the second of the three principles attributed to St. Augustine applies: *In dubiis libertas.*

The irritation which Gerbert felt when appointed abbot

of Bobbio at the irregular administration of his predecessor, Petroald the monk, has already been spoken of.
When he became pope, he showed that he knew how to
forget. He gave, or caused Otto III to give, to Petroald
the abbey of Bobbio, and an imperial diploma defined and
confirmed the rights of the new abbot.

The odious treason of Adalbero or Ascelin, bishop of
Laon, who had delivered Charles of Lorraine into the
hands of Hugh Capet, at the very time when the bishop
enjoyed the complete confidence of Charles, was not forgotten. This act of perfidy had been advantageous to
Gerbert, since it had resulted in the condemnation and
deposition of Arnulf; but the advantage which he had
derived from it did not prevent him from feeling the in-
famy of the whole transaction. During his pontificate, a
complaint made by King Robert against the bishop of
Laon furnished him an opportunity to give free course
to his indignation against the traitor. He summoned
Ascelin to Rome, and himself drew up the letter of citation. This letter has a most extraordinary tone for an
official document, which can be explained only by the
contempt that the former scholasticus of Reims must
have nourished during many years for the miserable
Ascelin. In this letter, it is stated that the complaint of
King Robert has reached the hands of the pope and of
the emperor, *apostolicis et imperialibus oblata est manibus*. It is not clear that it was addressed to the emperor, from whom the king of France had nothing to
ask. The explanation of these words is to be found in
certain chimerical projects which had been formed by a
too-youthful emperor and a too-learned pope. Impressed

by the memories of antiquity, Otto III and Sylvester II had dreamed of restoring the ancient Roman Empire, not that of the pagan Cæsars, but the empire of Constantine the Great. They wished to make the Christian world into a single monarchy, which the emperor and the pope, equal in the territorial extent of their power, should govern in common accord. The documents drawn up at this time frequently mention the common action of Otto III and Sylvester II. This explains why the pope had thought it well to submit to Otto III the complaint of Robert, as if the king had been the subject of the emperor. It is not the only case in which the pope strove to favor the encroachments of the empire upon the rights of the king of France. At another time, he caused two French subjects, Count Ermengard of Barcelona, son of his old protector, Borel, and Bishop Arnulf of Vich, the successor of his old master, Atto, to discuss their respective rights before Otto III and to humble themselves before the imperial majesty. It is commonly said that Sylvester was the first French pope; it is true that he was the first pope born in France, but he was very far from exhibiting French sentiments in his government. He had become the subject of Otto II when he accepted Bobbio and of Otto III when he accepted Ravenna; and, if Hugh Capet attached him momentarily to himself when he gave him Reims, Robert freed him when he took it from him unjustly; finally, the sole favor of the emperor had made him sovereign pontiff. Seated upon the throne of St. Peter, he showed himself as devoted to the imperial house as if he had been born in Germany.

Death soon put an end to the dreams of the prince and

of the pontiff. Otto III was carried off by a sudden illness, January 23, 1002, before he was quite twenty-two years old. Sylvester II died at Rome sixteen months later, May 12, 1003, and was buried in St. John Lateran.

Varying judgments have been passed upon Gerbert. In medieval legends he appears as an adept in Mussulman necromancy, a sorcerer, a limb of the devil. Some modern writers have spoken of him as a man without a conscience, a perverse, perfidious creature, a traitor and an enchanter, as one possessed of a demon, as barely a Christian. His learning, acquired with so much labor, has been viewed by ignorant and superstitious men as the fruit of intercourse with the powers of darkness. The foregoing sketch shows that he was not traitorous or perfidious. It is true that on one occasion his attachment to his master, Archbishop Arnulf, led him to join for a brief space the party in rebellion against Hugh. But the eagerness and quickness with which he returned to the cause of Hugh should be considered as at least a palliation. The pangs his conscience gave him, while he was in rebellion, rebut the charge of lack of conscience. He was ambitious. But he could not well avoid knowing his own value, and he never showed an unworthy haste in seeking his reward. The charges of coldheartedness and friendlessness are false. He never forgot his old teachers at Aurillac, Abbot Géraud and the monk Raymond, and kept up a steady correspondence in which he revealed to them the sorrows of his spirit. When abbot of Bobbio he shared with his poor relatives a fortune which he had inherited. When scholasticus at Reims he intervened between a too harsh abbot and an erring monk.

Life of Gerbert

When archbishop of Reims he did not hesitate to correct wrongs committed by his suffragans upon some poor clerks, although his hold upon his archbishopric was so slight that every friend counted. When pope he was famous for the liberality with which he distributed alms. He was always generous with the money he had amassed by his labors, and spent it, without stint, to purchase copies of the writings of the ancient authors, allowing the copyists to fix their own price. In short, he was always good and generous, loyal and upright. An investigation of all the charges which have been brought against him will show that there was no act done by his authority or under his influence which was not dictated solely by duty, by zeal for justice, or by care for the public good. No higher praise can be given to a prelate, a pontiff, and the favorite of an emperor.

Saint Bernard

Adapted from A. Luchaire, in *Revue Historique,* Vol. LXXI,
1899, pp. 225–242. Reprinted in Lavisse: *Histoire de
France,* Vol. II, Part ii, pp. 266–282.

ST. BERNARD, who governed Christianity in the
West from 1125 to 1153 by the mere prestige of his
eloquence and holiness, is the synthesis of his century.
He personifies the whole political and religious system
of an epoch in the Middle Ages which was dominated by
the moral power of the Church. Recounting his life
would be equivalent to writing the history of the monastic orders, of the reform movement, of the orthodox
theology, of the heretical doctrines, of the second crusade, and of the destinies of France, Germany, and Italy
during a period of almost forty years. It is not at all
astonishing that his biographers have recoiled before
such an enormous undertaking.

To the difficulty of the task is to be added the difficulty
of comprehending and defining the man. It has been
truthfully said that, of all his miracles, the most surprising was his personality itself, the inconceivable union of
two contradictory temperaments: on one side, the monk,
according to the ideal of the age, contemplative, mystical,
ascetic, who kept his body under almost to its destruction, and seemed to have lost the sense of things mate-

rial, skirting Lake Geneva a whole day without seeing it, and drinking oil for water; on the other hand, the man of action, the indefatigable preacher, the officious counselor of the high barons, kings, and popes, the real chief of the Western Church, the politician who was extraordinarily busy and active. There is the same opposition between the physical and the moral; his body had been beautiful in his youth, but was very early debilitated, exhausted by fastings and macerations, and so worn out that it was scarcely able to take nourishment; it burned with fever and was afflicted with premature infirmities; beneath this frail envelope lay an astonishingly vigorous power of soul and mind, an incredible strength for work, an energy which overcame fatigue. And, in this same soul, singular contradictions: sweetness, unction, kindness, even toward animals, even toward Jews (which is characteristic of the Middle Ages), in contrast with an impetuous, militant will, which is revealed in a thousand passages in the correspondence of Bernard, by violent excesses of language. The most profound and most sincere humility was associated with a very lively love of power, and with a contempt for humanity and the things of this world, which breaks forth in haughty expressions.

Moreover, the man is admirably depicted in his writings. In spite of his abuse of allegory, in spite of plays on words and quotations, has any author a style that is more individual, more original, and yet more disconcerting? An indefinable mixture of the serious and ironical, of calm and violence, of simplicity and elevation. On every page, familiar expressions are intermingled with the harmonies of an excessive lyricism, and the railing tone changes suddenly to apostrophes inflamed with a passion which cannot be checked. It is a style formed of contrasts, like the man himself.

" Contrasts," but not " incoherence." A secret logic in St. Bernard binds everything together, and the contradictions are only apparent. His logic was founded, primarily, upon faith, upon an absolute faith, which admitted of no qualifications and extended to the most complete contempt of human reason; and, in the second place, it was founded upon the idea which St. Bernard had of the higher interests of the Church. That was the supreme criterion, the principle to which he subordinated all his acts, to which he sacrificed, without pity, his own inclinations, his dearest affections, the private interests of his friends and allies, social usages, and even the outward coherence of his thought and conduct. It is because he had faith, and because in his opinion everything must yield to the general good of the Church, that his rough frankness did not consider anyone, that he attacked vigorously the same institutions and the same men to whom he had formerly been devoted, and that those who benefited by his apostolic zeal, became, in turn, its victims.

The undeniable influence which this extraordinary man exercised over his contemporaries sprang precisely from these very contradictions. He mastered and guided them according to his will, because his complex nature offered something which satisfied their most divergent aspirations. Some were astonished and enraptured by his monastic virtues, his holiness, and his miracles; he pleased others by his militant zeal and his power as an agitator; still others, by the disinterestedness which he

Saint Bernard

showed in the midst of circumstances most fitted to intoxicate a man's ambition. We divine, rather than know, the secret of the power of his eloquence, which irresistibly carried away the multitude when Bernard wished to lead them to conversion, to the cloister, or to the crusade. Contemporaries describe little except the effect, of a physical rather than moral kind, due to the contagious force of a vibrating nature formed to act upon temperaments which were impassioned and impressionable to excess.

The historical work of St. Bernard may be summed up in a few words. He continued, in every way, the reform of the Church, directed the papacy, in order to save it from schism, fought for the unity of the faith, and caused a second movement of Europe against Asia. The Middle Ages do not offer another example of an activity so prodigious, and of a moral power so universally accepted.

Bernard was born at Fontaines, near Dijon, of a family of the higher nobility, and as a mere youth attempted to convert his own kinsmen and the people about them. In his retreat at Châtillon, " he became the terror of mothers and of young women; friends were frightened when they saw him accosting their friends." He was an impassioned evangelist and could comprehend no life except that of the cloister, and he induced his brothers, in succession, to follow him into the abbey of Cîteaux (1113–1114).

He was an admirable monk, it might be said the ideal monk, working at the same time with mind and body, wielding the sickle with a skill which won him the reputation "of an excellent harvester. But he was determined to create a peculiar system of monastic life, and, on June 25, 1114, he settled in the uncultivated and wild valley of Clairvaux. "The cell which he occupied in the new monastery resembled," in the words of his most recent biographer, "a prison. A corner was left under the curving stairway. In this angle he placed his bed, on which a bit of wood, covered with straw, served as his pillow. Under the mansard roof, in the wall which supported it, was cut the only seat in the cell, elevated a foot from the floor. When he wished to sit down or get up, he had to bend his head in order not to hit the beams. A tiny opening formed the window." The ruler of Christian Europe lived there more than thirty years, and died there.

The greatest work of St. Bernard is the Cistercian Monk and the rule of Cîteaux.

The Cistercian monk ought to have the least possible contact with the outer world. An abbey of this order is constructed by preference far from cities, in a wild spot difficult of access. Clairvaux cannot, like Cluny, own all kinds of property. The rule forbids the acquisition of churches, villages, serfs, ovens, mills, in short, everything that constitutes a feudal domain and a source of political authority. A Cistercian abbey legally exploits only property useful for the manual labor of the monks, fields, vineyards, meadows, and woods. The monks are absolutely interdicted from carrying on business and selling at retail the products of their lands. They are not less rigorously interdicted from taking the cure of souls, that is to say, from officiating in a church or parochial chapel. As they did not desire the presence of laymen, the Cis-

Saint Bernard

tercians were careful not to open a school and admit students. Here again there is a striking contrast to the Cluniac system. They were afraid of everything which directed the mind toward the outer world and toward profane things. They were suspicious of books, literature and science. A monk guilty of making verses was sent to another house. The servants, who were not, however, true monks, could not have books in their hands. The Cistercians were satisfied to have the servants learn by heart the Lord's Prayer, the Creed, the *Miserere* and the *Ave Maria*. Faith is enough for pure souls.

A return to asceticism characterizes the rule of Clairvaux, just as it does the rules of the other congregations which sprang from the reform movement. Chastity, obedience, silence, individual poverty, are inviolable obligations. One of the most heinous crimes that a Cistercian monk can commit is to be a proprietor; the monk who is a proprietor, like the incendiary or the thief, is subject to excommunication. At Clairvaux, not merely was meat prohibited, but vegetables fried in fat were not permitted, and even the sick did not eat meat in Lent or on Saturday. No white bread, no spices, fish only occasionally, and very little wine were allowed. The first associates of St. Bernard often ate beech leaves. They lived on peas, lentils, and other vegetables, without seasoning; and these poor meals were prepared by the monks themselves, each one in his turn serving as cook. The additions to the repasts or the pittances, which were customary at Cluny on certain days of the week, were formally forbidden. When they retired, the Cistercians threw themselves upon their beds, all clothed, in a dor-

Medieval Civilization

mitory without cells, and which, of course, was not warmed. The bed was composed of a pillow, two covers, and a straw tick. The mattress was a Cluniac institution: at Clairvaux, it was allowed the sick, in exceptional cases.

The garment of the Cistercian differs from the black robe of the Cluniac: it is gray, the natural color of wool which has not been dyed. The Cistercians were absolutely forbidden to wear furred robes, woolen shirts, hoods, gloves and boots, as so many of the abbots and monks of the older congregations did. The same severity of principles extends to the ceremonies of worship. The Cistercians chant in unison without an organ. In their churches, there is a pitiless proscription of everything which appeals to the eyes or the senses, of everything which may distract the monk from contemplation and prayer. The walls are bare; there are no ornamented pavements, no mosaics, no colored-glass windows, no mural paintings; there are no statues, and only the cross is tolerated, and even then no large gilded or silvered crosses. Silk ornaments are prohibited, even for the grand ceremonies. On the exterior, stone towers are forbidden: they must be built of wood and be of small size. Little bells alone are authorized. Finally, in abbatial churches, no outsiders are to be buried except kings, queens, archbishops, and bishops.

Fundamentally, Clairvaux in its early days was a living satire on Cluny. Clairvaux is the model abbey, the new creation opposed to the ancient monastic system. Moral preponderance and religious prestige soon passed from the Cluniacs to the Cistercians. Bernard contributed to Clairvaux's victory by the fervor of his propaganda, working with all his might to drive out strange monks, and filling the episcopal seats with Cistercians. After all, it was a legitimate rivalry; he acted in this, as always, merely under the sway of his Christian conviction. His partisanship, which at times became somewhat heated in the struggle against the rival abbey, brought out so much the better the sentiments of friendship which he did not cease to profess for its chief, Peter the Venerable, a reformer of practical sense and mild manners. The mutual affection of the two monks triumphed over the incidents which seemed almost certain to alter it.

Peter had kept at Cluny a young cousin of St. Bernard, whom the latter loved with special tenderness. St. Bernard complained vigorously, but revenged himself by taking the bishopric of Langres from a Cluniac and giving it to a Cistercian after a bitter struggle. The conflict became more intense when the Cluniac monks of Gigni in Burgundy destroyed by arms a priory of Cîteaux. Nevertheless, the chiefs of the two orders continued their friendly correspondence; a meritorious amity due less to the moderation of Bernard than to the uncommon patience of Peter the Venerable. "Who will ever be able to stifle the tender affection of my heart for you," wrote the latter, "since so many storms have not been able to do it, up to the present time, and since our friendship has resisted both the flood of the rivalry of our orders and the tempest of Langres? . . . I have always attempted to maintain harmony between my brethren and yours, and if possible, to bring all hearts together in perfect charity. In public, in private, in our great capitulary assemblies, I have never ceased to endeavor to destroy this feeling of

Medieval Civilization

jealousy and animosity which secretly gnaws at our entrails."

Bernard wished to show, in his turn, that he was not animated by any unkind feeling against Cluny, and, between 1123 and 1125, he wrote the *Apology,* in which he protests his love for all the monastic rules. He characterizes as "pharisees" the monks who speak with disdain of the other observances, and himself celebrates in magnificent phrases the unity of the regular Church, "the seamless coat of many colors." But the subject carries him away, and he cannot help scourging, with his sarcastic heat, the soft and luxurious habits of the Benedictines. He does not attack their morality, but their manner of religious life, their repugnance for mortifications and manual labor, and their ideas upon the external conditions of worship, so profoundly different from his own. The Cluniacs are condemned by this pitiless judge, even for their zeal in ornamenting their churches, and consecrating art to the service of God: "The Church," he said, "is resplendent in its walls and is wholly lacking in its poor. It gilds its stones and leaves its children naked. With the silver of the wretched, it charms the eyes of the rich." What is the use of pictorial representations, statues, and paintings? All that stifles devotion and recalls the Jewish ceremonies. Works of art are idols, which turn man from God, and, at best, serve only to excite the piety of feeble and worldly souls.

The fiery apostle, who spoke with so much violence against the abuses of the rival congregation, had no more indulgence for the independent monasteries of the old order of St. Benedict. He was particularly severe on

Saint Bernard

the royal abbey of St. Dennis, where the Capetian monarch, his courtiers, and his soldiers felt almost at home, and prevented the monks from yielding to the new ideas. He termed it " a garrison, a school of Satan, and a den of thieves." When the abbot Suger, at his instigation, had reformed the monastery, Bernard heaped praises upon him with as much ardor as he had formerly shown in reproaching him for the scandals. " The wounds made by a friend," he said, " are better than the kisses of an enemy."

From Clairvaux, the breath of monastic reform had already passed over the secular Church itself; it was necessary to induce the bishops to change their life and breathe in the Cistercian spirit. One of the most striking conversions was that of the archbishop of Sens. In adopting reform and the new manner of life which it involved, he brought upon himself the hostility of the king of France and his courtiers (1130) ; but Bernard defended the archbishop, and even went so far as to say of Louis VI, the eldest son of the Church and the protector of the papacy: " This new Herod no longer pursues Christ in his cradle, but he prevents Him from triumphing in the churches."

The reform of the bishoprics was a part of his ideas as well as the reform of the abbeys, and he was indignant at obstacles. With as much boldness as he had shown in denouncing the vices of the monks in the *Apology,* he stigmatizes the vices of the episcopacy in his *Treatise on the Duty of Bishops,* 1126. No one has painted in more lively colors the unworthiness of these prelates, who believed that they were doing honor to their ministry by the pomp of their clothes, the luxury of their horses and equipment, " and who spend the property of the poor in useless extravagance." He was frightened when he saw " unbearded boys elevated by family influence to the highest dignities of the Church. They have barely escaped from the teacher's ferule when they are provided with important places and preside over assemblies of priests." He reproaches them with wearing " female toilets " and concludes that " a good bishop is a rare bird."

He thought that the fault was in the selection of the bishops, always vitiated by lay influences. He has not said anywhere exactly what his opinion was on the weighty question of episcopal elections; but, from all his writings and all his conduct, the idea emerges that bishops can be canonically instituted only by the choice of the clergy and the people, and by the consent of the bishops of the province. It was a return to the practices of the primitive church. In St. Bernard's opinion, the nomination of prelates was an ecclesiastical matter; the king had no right to delay an election, to interfere with it for his own profit, and, still less, to impose his own candidates. Thus the religious party of which Bernard was the soul and organ, after having first condemned simony, and then investiture, finally rejected all interference of the lay power in elections. This was the third phase in the reform movement. The abbot of Clairvaux never hesitated, any more than the popes of the eleventh century, who were his models, to enter into a struggle even with the French monarchy, when the principles of reform were in question.

And why should he have hesitated? Exclusively

dominated by the religious ideal, he never considered the point of view of the progress of the Capetian dynasty, nor even the special interests of the French nation. Those who have believed and said the opposite, have been deceived.

In 1891, the eight hundredth anniversary of St. Bernard was celebrated in the ruins of the old castle at Fontaines-lès-Dijon, and one of the orators, claiming this great man was the most national and the most French of all the saints (almost equal to Joan of Arc), spoke " of his incessant preoccupation with the interests of France and the Church, married together." In reality, Bernard represents no special nationality; he personified merely the universal Church of the Middle Ages, regenerated by the monks. He is above dynastic and national ideas and acts only for the supreme good of Christianity and reform. All else is wholly indifferent and strange to him. Thus, his standpoint is opposed to that of Suger, who was so closely bound to the reigning family and to the nation.

In certain passages of Suger's *Vie de Louis le Gros,* a vague sentiment of the unity of French patriotism begins to appear. There is nothing like this in the writings of the founder of Clairvaux. If their acts are studied, the same difference comes out. When the Capetian dynasty was beginning to identify itself with the country, St. Bernard preferred the count of Champagne to the king of France. When Louis VII was guilty of desiring to name an archbishop of Bourges, when the court of Rome refused, St. Bernard opposed him in the most vigorous manner, and supported passionately Thibaud IV of Champagne, the ally of the pope and the enemy of the

Medieval Civilization

king. He also favored, at least indirectly, the impolitic divorce of Louis VII and Eleanor of Aquitaine. It would be as puerile to deny that the celebrated abbot acted thus, as to condemn him in the name of principles which were not his. Both he and Suger acted, each in his own sphere, conformably to his situation and his ideas, and the two were very different. To nationalize St. Bernard would be equivalent to belittling him.

He showed himself a reformer even against the papacy, and this is perhaps the most original side of his apostolate. In the time of St. Bernard, the omnipotence of the Holy See had become an indisputable fact. But then the spirit of reform began to turn against the pontifical monarchy itself, and tried to render it wholly unworthy of the absolute authority which it exercised. A party with advanced opinions was already murmuring against the abuses which had become notorious: the excessive multiplication of exemptions, the exaggerated extension of appeals to Rome, the luxury of the Roman court, its attachment to temporal interests, and the venality of the cardinals. The most ardent of the reformers condemned the policy of compositions, of compromises, of opportunism, which was followed by the successors of Gregory VII and Urban II. On the other hand, those who did not desire the traditional hierarchy to be too greatly weakened were already disquieted by the very extent of the pontifical power, by the enormous sovereignty devolved upon a single man, which was very apt to turn the most sensible head.

Of all these griefs, of all this discontent, of all these fears, St. Bernard composed the woof of his treatise upon

418

Saint Bernard

the *Consideration* (1149–1152), a strange work, which has been called " the catechism of the popes." It is a singular catechism, in which the papacy, in the person of Eugenius III, receives as many reprimands and blows as marks of affection and friendly counsels.

In order to warn Eugenius III against pride, St. Bernard reminds him, in biblical terms, that a foolish king upon his throne resembles " an ape upon a roof," and that the dignity with which he is clothed does not prevent him from being a man, " that is to say, a poor, miserable, naked being, made for work and not for honors." There is neither poison nor sword which Bernard fears as much for the pope as the passion for dominating. Ambition and cupidity, in the Roman Church, are the sources of the most deplorable abuses. The cardinals are " satraps " who prefer grandeur to truth. And how can anyone justify the unheard-of luxury of the Roman court? " I do not see that St. Peter has ever appeared in public laden with gold and jewels, clothed in silk, mounted on a white mule, surrounded by soldiers and followed by a boisterous cortège. . . . From the pomp which surrounds you, you would be taken rather for the successor of Constantine than for the successor of St. Peter."

In presenting to the papacy the " mirror in which it could recognize its own deformities," Bernard hoped to make it better. He relied upon the services which he had rendered to the institution to secure pardon for this severe language.

Services that were as immense as they were disinterested! The spectacle at which the West looked for eight consecutive years, from 1130 to 1138, has remained

Medieval Civilization

unique in history. Two popes, Anacletus II and Innocent II, had been elected at the same time, and Bernard, in order to end the schism, made himself supreme judge in an infinitely complex and delicate case. He declared with remarkable boldness for Innocent II, the candidate whose election had been less legal in form. But Bernard recognized in him a superior moral value, and thought that, in the choice of a pope, votes should be weighed and not counted. Not content with imposing his candidate on the clergy and on Christian opinion, he forced kings and high barons to receive him: Louis VI at the council of Étampes and Henry Beauclerc at Chartres solemnly ratified the judgment of the abbot of Clairvaux. During the long voyage of Innocent through France, Normandy, Lorraine and the lands of the empire, Bernard accompanied his protégé, cleared all obstacles from the path, lavished his eloquence, and converted or confounded opponents. At Liège, the emperor Lothair wished to abuse his position as protector of the new pope, to repudiate the Concordat of Worms, and to put the Church again under the yoke of the State. Everything would have been lost if the eloquent intervention of the monk had not saved Innocent II from this great peril. The emperor prostrated himself at the feet of the pope of St. Bernard (1131).

The man who thus imposed his will upon Europe was only at the beginning of his task. Anacletus remained master of Rome and of Italy.

It was necessary to persuade Lothair to cross the Alps in order to open Rome to Innocent II. While awaiting the imperial army, the indefatigable Bernard traversed upper Italy with his pope, and reconciled the Genoese

Saint Bernard

with the Pisans. He was very proud of this new victory:
" How rapidly this marvel happened," he said; " the same
day I have sown the seed, reaped the harvest, and loaded
upon my shoulders the sheaves of peace." Finally Lothair
and Innocent entered Rome together, and the emperor
was crowned by the pope (1133), while Anacletus and
his defenders barricaded themselves in the castle of St.
Angelo. But, almost as soon as the imperial forces had
departed, the anti-pope succeeded in again driving out
his rival, who took refuge at Pisa. In order to repair
this breach, Bernard went to Germany. He bore his
aid to a political work of high importance: the reconciliation of Lothair with his rivals, Frederick and Conrad of
Hohenstaufen, heirs to the duchy of Swabia and perpetual pretenders to the empire. Causing them to enter
into alliance with the emperor was taking from the German opposition every pretext for revolt and from the
anti-pope useful protection. Bernard appeared at the
assembly of Bamberg; he spoke, and the rivalries of the
German princes were again appeased, as if by a miracle.
Lothair gave up Swabia to the Hohenstaufens, and the
latter promised to take part in a new expedition to Italy.
Then the saint hastily recrossed the Alps and went to
Pisa, where he was triumphantly received. A council
was held in this city (June, 1135); it was necessary again
to excommunicate Anacletus and his partisans, to affirm
the authority of Innocent, to reform the abuses, and to
fortify the discipline of the Church. The abbot of Clairvaux directed the action of the council, unraveled all the
difficulties, dictated all the resolutions, and gave life to
everything with his powerful breath.

When he had converted Milan, the stronghold of the

Medieval Civilization

schismatics, to the cause of Innocent II, the enthusiasm became delirium. The abbot of Clairvaux alone, by his presence, his preaching, and his miracles, broke successively every obstacle against which the combined efforts of the pope and the emperor had failed. The crowd thronged about him, acclaimed him, kissed his feet, and cut bits from his garments for relics. At Milan, every day, the sick filled the presbytery of St. Lawrence, where he was stopping, and paralysis, possession by the devil, and epilepsy disappeared under the touch of this incomparable doctor. Passive in the midst of the popular intoxication, he utilized his prestige to found or reform religious establishments, refusing the bishoprics which were offered him and thinking only of again living in his dear little cell, surrounded by his brethren of Clairvaux.

Sickness tortured him without intermission, and still more did his scrupulous conscience, which made him consider "monstrous" the life to which the Church condemned him. "I do not know what kind of a chimera of my age I am, neither clerk nor laic, wearing the habit of a monk and not keeping the observances." Nevertheless, he was obliged, for the third time, to leave his abbey, and to make a last journey to Italy (1137), when Lothair and Innocent came to open strife with Roger I, king of Sicily, the obstinate partisan of Anacletus. The defeat of the Normans at Palermo, the urgent reproofs of Bernard, and above all, the death of the anti-pope, at length put an end to the schism.

At the news of the disappearance of Anacletus, the joy of the abbot of Clairvaux broke forth: "Thank God, the wretch who has led Israel into sin has been swallowed up by death and cast into the bowels of hell. May all those who are like him undergo the same chastisement!" The unity of the Church was saved, and the papacy owed its victory to the devotion and heroism of a simple monk. Such a work might well astonish and make enthusiastic a century of faith: "Here I am," Bernard wrote to the prior of Clairvaux: "I no longer say to you: 'I am going to return'; I return; I am here; and I bring with me my reward, the triumph of Christ and the peace of the Church."

Bernard found his reward also in a prodigious increase of moral influence and in the fact that a monk of his order, Eugenius III, came to the throne of St. Peter (1145). At bottom, the cardinals and the Roman curia did not pardon him easily for being what he had become, a private man more powerful in the Church than the pope and the bishops, and holding this power by his own personal prestige. They even went so far as to make him feel that he was too much inclined to substitute his own action for that of the official and regular government of Christianity. "The affairs of God are mine," he said, with imprudent naïveté to his friend the cardinal Aimeri, "and nothing which concerns Him is foreign to me." The cardinal replied: "In the Church there are divers vocations. All is at peace when each one remains in his own office and rank, but all is confused and disorganized when anyone oversteps the bounds of his professional position. What ought a monk to have in common with courts and councils?"

He was reproached especially for his disapproval of the irresistible evolution which was pressing Rome on to

Medieval Civilization

desire the undivided rule of Catholic Europe. If the struggle over investitures had ended, the rivalry between the pope and the emperor still continued. It was the eve of the furious war which was about to break forth between the priesthood and the empire. It was important to know whether pope or emperor should be master of Rome and Italy. And the opinion of St. Bernard on this weighty question was known. He wished the maintenance and the union of the two powers. He recognized the temporal right of the emperors over the city of Rome, since in a letter to Conrad III, he called Rome the capital of the empire. On the other hand, he resisted energetically the tendency which was leading the Holy See to busy itself with terrestrial things. Not that he condemned the temporal power of the popes in precise terms, but what he wrote and what he did, prove that this power appeared to him little in harmony with the spiritual mission of the papacy and dangerous to the future of the institution. Was anything more needed to render the abbot of Clairvaux an object of suspicion to the statesmen who directed the Roman Church and who aimed, by it, to govern the entire world?

The man who knew how to reëstablish unity in the religious government of the Christian peoples, had to work also to maintain it in the domain of faith. Bernard strove with the same zeal against the attempts which human thought was already making to shake off the yoke of the Church and to free itself from tradition. At all times, he showed himself the convinced defender of the ancient faith, and the natural enemy of the novelties introduced by theologians and philosophers. We may well think that this man, who corrected his friends so sharply, did not hesitate to enter into strife with the enemy. He had the unreflecting and powerful faith of simple souls. Sometimes he pretended that instruction in the great school of nature was enough: " The trees and the rocks in the forest will teach you more than books "; sometimes he recognized the apostles as his sole masters: " They have not taught me to read Plato and to pierce through the subtleties of Aristotle, but they have taught me to live, and that is no small knowledge."

Nevertheless, he knew theology, but he profoundly despised scholasticism and its adepts: " There are some," he added, who wish to learn only for the sake of knowledge, and this curiosity is unworthy of a man; others wish to learn only to be regarded as skillful, and this vanity is shameful; others learn only to make gain of their knowledge and to acquire money or offices, and this traffic is dishonorable." Accordingly, he would wish to dissuade young men from coming to Paris to seek knowledge, and, by knowledge, pleasure and fortune. " Flee from Babylon, and save your souls," he wrote in a sermon delivered before the students in 1140, and twenty of them followed him to Clairvaux.

In reality, learning displeased him above all because he found it dangerous to religion, and he complained bitterly of the boldness of his century: " Men laugh at the popular faith; they lay bare the divine mysteries; they rashly discuss the most important questions; they turn to derision the Fathers who have preferred to quiet these quarrels rather than to decide them. The human mind usurps everything and leaves nothing to faith."

Medieval Civilization

He combated the scholastic heresy (which he calls *stultilogia*), in the person of Abélard and of Gilbert de la Porrée, and the purely religious and social heresy, in the person of Henry of Lausanne and Peter of Bruys.

Political heresy was represented by Arnold of Brescia, a popular agitator and a dangerous tribune, who denied to the clergy the ability to possess fiefs, and left them only religious authority. No more regalian rights for the bishops, no more collective property for the monks: the tithe was enough for the members of the Church. Absolute separation of the temporal from the spiritual is necessary; priests can govern only conscience: they have no rights over land and money. Such a doctrine was not in very great disagreement with the ideas of certain apostles of ecclesiastical reform. The Christian ideal to logical minds would have been that the clergy should renounce territorial possessions and the pope his sovereignty. The thesis of Arnold of Brescia finally excited the people in large cities to cast off the rule of the bishops, and made legitimate the communal movement which the Church had condemned.

The abbot of Clairvaux hastened to denounce Arnold of Brescia as a man who was so much the more to be feared, since, as he lived an austere life, " he had the form of piety without its spirit."

A papal legate, who loved philosophy and philosophers, was imprudent enough to offer his protection to the heresiarch. The reprimand was prompt: " Arnold of Brescia is a man of amiable and seductive conversation, but his teaching is poisoned; he has the head of a dove and the tail of a scorpion, a monstrous creature, whom the city of Brescia has vomited out, whom Rome has rejected, whom France has repulsed, whom Germany hates, whom Italy is no longer willing to receive, and it is said that you have given him an asylum? Protection to such a man is infidelity to the pope, or, rather, to God Himself." The Roman curia understood St. Bernard's indignation better when it saw the Roman people putting in practice the theories of Arnold, emancipating themselves by pillage and murder, and proceeding under his direction to an unintelligent reconstruction of the forms of the ancient Latin republic (1143–1145).

Bernard violently reproached this populace with making Rome " the laughing stock of the whole universe." Since the schism, he had for the Roman people a contemptuous antipathy which he did not conceal. " What is to be said of this people? " he wrote, in his *Consideration,* " it is the Roman people; there is no term more brief and more expressive for indicating what I think of it." But elsewhere he made his idea more clear: " Let us pardon the thieves; they are Romans and money is too great a temptation for them." He was but little interested in the cause of urban liberty. At Reims, where he attempted to calm the effervescence of the citizen body (1140), all his eloquence failed before the obstinacy of those who wished to establish the commune. In his opinion, as well as in the opinion of the whole Church, Louis VII, in putting down these insurgent rascals by force, only fulfilled his duty as king.

The monk of Clairvaux could not admit that anyone should dare to rise against the established powers and attack a social order of which religion was the very foundation. He preached charity, he pitied the wretched and he condemned the luxury of the rich, because he would have desired to give the poor the necessaries of life; but democratic tendencies, or a socialistic theory, in the modern sense of the word, would be sought for in his writings in vain. He does not flatter the peasants any more than he cajoles the kings, the bishops, and the popes. He reproves in the peasants the grossness of their manners, their spirit of gain and robbery and their belief in sorcerers. He desires the people to continue, as in the past, to pay the taxes to the lord and the tithes to the curate.

This man who, by dint of energy, barely succeeded in keeping in his body the life which was always ready to vanish, found means, before his death, to arouse the whole West by calling it anew to the holy war. Bernard was the son of a soldier and a great partisan of the crusade. He had contributed more than anyone else to the foundation of the order of the Templars, the knight-monks, whose rule was very largely his work (1128). His *Eulogy of the New Militia* was inspired by a breath which was wholly military, full of hatred for the Saracen, and intended to justify religious wars and to inflame the zeal of the crusaders. This clerk avows that there are some circumstances which make it necessary and even glorious to shed blood: "Undoubtedly," he said, "it would not be necessary to kill the pagans if there was any other means of stopping their invasions and preventing them from oppressing the faithful; but to-day it is better to massacre them than to leave the rod of sinners suspended over the heads of the just. Come, let the children of the faith draw the two swords against the enemy! . . ."

Saint Bernard

"Christ's knight," he says elsewhere, "kills conscientiously and dies more tranquilly: in dying, he secures salvation; in killing, he labors for Christ."

The second crusade was his work, and he led into it kings, of whom there had been none in the first. His apologists to-day, seeing that this enterprise failed, have undertaken to show that he was not the author of it; that the initiative really belonged to King Louis VII, the incendiary of Vitry, and to Pope Eugenius III; that Bernard followed the movement as the orator of the Roman Church, charged with preaching to the Christian people. The distinction at bottom is subtle. If it is true that the king of France was the first to think of the crusade, St. Bernard alone brought it about, because he alone could enlist the nobility which had not yet forgotten the disasters of the preceding expedition. Everyone knows the succession of fatalities by which the second crusade terminated in a catastrophe, in such a veritable scandal for religious souls, that even the popularity of the saint was shaken. He underwent this new trial with the serenity of the believer who lives only for celestial things. The sickness which was consuming him did not prevent him, however, from again going to Metz, a few weeks before his death, in order to put an end to the bloody quarrels of the nobles and the citizens, who were engaged in mutual slaughter. This last effort wore him out. August 20, 1153, he died surrounded by his brethren of Clairvaux, in this peaceful asylum, where the Church and the world had not let him repose as much as he would have desired.

He did not die soon enough to avoid seeing the lamentable end of his crusade; but how many other disappointments was he spared by death! This peerless orator lost most of the causes for which his powerful voice had resounded. Fifty years after his death, France and Europe saw his dearest hopes destroyed and his most generous dreams dissipated.

He had made of Clairvaux the *chef-d'œuvre* of monastic asceticism. In the course of the thirteenth century the congregation, corrupted by the very liberality of the faithful, had no longer any reason to reproach Cluny. It had descended to the same point, and with a still more rapid fall. The very life of its founder had contributed to its destruction. It was by a continuous miracle that the first abbot of Clairvaux had been able to reconcile the rôle of chief of a monastery with the general government of the Christian Church. Absorbed in business foreign to their true functions, his successors did not have, as he had had, the strength to remain truly monks in the midst of politics and courts.

As a reformer of the episcopacy, he had wanted to prevent the interference of kings in elections. The French church, becoming more and more monarchical, and submitting, on the other hand, to the will of the popes and the cardinals, lost the liberty which remained to it. In combating heresy in all its forms, Bernard had attempted to make faith prevail over reason, and to fetter the flight of independent thought. But such a current was irresistible. Heresies multiplied, and southern France had to be drowned in blood in order to reëstablish unity of belief. At the same moment, scholasticism triumphed in the schools, and the University of Paris was founded.

Saint Bernard

. He had feared that the Catholic Church would become a monarchy, occupied especially with terrestrial interests and excessively centralized. The whole Middle Ages tended to this end. It was pursued in spite of him; and the pontificate of Innocent III, a preparation for that of Boniface VIII, in certain respects made a reality of the theocratic idea.

Finally, Bernard had proclaimed the necessity of concord between the priesthood and the empire, and the equality of their rights over Rome. Ten years after his death, war raged between these two powers, and the pope was chased from Rome and from Italy. Europe entered upon that troubled and bloody period, which was terminated only after a century of violent strife by the fall of the German Empire.

What, then, was the work of St. Bernard? The useless opposition of a man of genius to the currents which were bearing his century on. Perhaps it might be said that the great monk of Clairvaux appears as an accidental cause of trouble in the normal development of Catholicism and of the general institutions of the Middle Ages. The isolated attempt of this admirable dreamer was condemned in advance. Nevertheless, he gave new vigor to Christian feeling, raised morality for a time, exalted idealism, and left to the world the example of an energy and of a virtue which was superhuman.

Southern France and the Religious Opposition

Adapted from A. Luchaire: *Innocent III, la croisade des Albigeois*, 1905, pp. 1–33.

SUNNY southern France,—Gascony, Languedoc, and Provence,—in the twelfth century was the home of a lovable people. They talked a charming language, had light hearts and easy manners. Religion, wholly an external form, troubled them little. The troubadours sang of their gallant intrigues, or of the amusements which they sought from castle to castle, or of the lords whom they beguiled into giving largesses. Whether they were noble or not, the heroes of this brilliant world were interested chiefly in poetry, and the cult which they preferred was the worship of woman and pleasure. Narbonne, Montpellier, Arles, and Marseilles had their consuls and agencies in distant countries and were marts for the whole known world. The exchange of merchandise and ideas, the diversity of races and religions, and the mixture of oriental and occidental elements, brought wealth and also the mobility of disposition and the taste for novelty which favor all kinds of changes.

There were shadows on the picture. First of all, there was political anarchy, because the counts of Toulouse, high suzerains of the district, had not been able to use their feudal rights in such a way as to obtain the mastery. Barons waged war against one another, cities against their lords, the laity against the clergy; and brigands infested the land. In 1182, Bishop Stephen of Tournay, a man of letters and a diplomat, was sent on a mission to Toulouse by Philip Augustus. He returned from the South very badly frightened. Everywhere he had seen nothing but " the image of death, churches in ruins, villages in ashes, human habitations become the abiding-places of wild beasts." He exaggerated. The Middle Ages overdid oratorial effects and rarely gave exact statements of facts. The same scourges were devastating to a greater or less degree other parts of France. Everywhere the people were suffering from the same troubles. As a whole the South was superior to the North in its culture, in its sonorous language, and in its legal customs in which the Roman law was still influential. Its social constitution was more merciful, its cities more free, its barriers between the classes less difficult, and its serfdom less rigorous. In addition, and this was the side where its originality was greatest, the South was tolerant.

Jews could live there without being persecuted or oppressed. They were permitted to hold public office. The lords and even the prelates willingly confided to them the management of their finances and the administration of their domains. Commerce and industry enriched them in broad daylight. Narbonne then contained nearly three hundred Jewish firms, represented by branch establishments at Pisa and Genoa. Almost everywhere the synagogue rose freely side by side with the church.

Medieval Civilization

Is it astonishing that heretics profited by this mental attitude of the southerners? Preachers of new doctrines made proselytes, held meetings, and defied bishops without any protest from the multitude or any interference from the authorities.

An impartial and well-informed historian, Guillaume de Puylaurens, states that the knights in Languedoc could with impunity belong to any sect which they chose. Heresiarchs were not persecuted at all; they were venerated. They had the right to acquire land, and to cultivate their fields and vineyards. They possessed large houses where they preached in public and private, and cemeteries where they solemnly interred their followers. In certain cities, they even enjoyed special privileges; the municipal or seigniorial administration exempted them from serving on the watch and paying the *taille*. Those who traveled with them had no attacks to fear, and were protected by the respect which the heresiarchs inspired. At the moment of death very many proprietors and citizens bequeathed to the heretical ministers who came to assist them, their bed, their clothing, and their money. Religious etiquette varies in vain; customs do not change. One day the bishop of Albi was called to the bedside of one of his kinsmen, who was a noble. " ' Is it better to divide my property between my two sons or to leave it undivided?' asked the dying man. 'Division is better, in order to maintain peace between your heirs,' replied the prelate. The sick man promised to follow this advice. Then the bishop asked him in what monastery he wished to be buried. 'Don't concern yourself about that,' was the answer, 'my arrangements are made.' 'But tell me,' insisted the bishop. 'I want my body taken to the home of the Good Men' (the heretics). The bishop was indignant and declared that he would not allow it. 'Don't trouble yourself,' continued the other, 'if my wishes were opposed, I would crawl there on all fours.' The bishop left this man as one abandoned by God, but knew that it was not possible to prevent him from doing just as he pleased. By this you see how powerful heresy was among us. A bishop was not in a position to check it even in a kinsman subject to him."

"At Lombers, near Albi, dwelt a famous heresiarch, Sicard the Cellarer. The same bishop was in this town, and the knights and citizens begged him to hold with Sicard one of the debates in which the representatives of the two religions argued on the truth of their doctrines. At first the bishop refused, alleging that the hardened sinner would never acknowledge his mistake. But the inhabitants insisted and the bishop consented, in order not to be accused of shunning the combat. As a matter of fact, the people of Lombers thought that he, and not his adversary, would be worsted.

"'Sicard,' said the bishop, 'you are in my diocese, you live in my territory, you ought then to render me an account of your belief. Answer the questions that I am going to ask by a simple yes or no.' 'All right,' replied Sicard. 'Do you believe,' asked the bishop, 'that Abel, the victim of Cain, Noah, who survived the flood, Abraham, Moses and the other prophets before Christ, can be saved?' 'No one of them is saved,' responded the heresiarch. 'And how about my kinsman who has just died?' the bishop continued. 'Yes, he is saved because

he died in our faith,' answered the heretic. Then the
bishop said: ' Sicard, the same thing has happened to you
that befell a doctor in my diocese who had recently come
from Salerno. When he saw two sick men he prognos-
ticated that one would die the following night and the
other would get well. Just the opposite happened. " I
see," said the doctor, " that I have read my books all
wrong. I am going back to the university to study again
what I have studied badly." You are in the same position, Sicard, you have read our books badly, for you condemn those whom the Scriptures and God have absolved,
and promise salvation to a man who has always lived by
crime and robbery. Accordingly, it is necessary to send
you back to school to learn to read correctly.' Having
said this, the bishop went away and Sicard was left silent and in confusion. Nevertheless the bishop's authority was powerless to prevent him from living where he
was."

These disputations between theologians made the same
impression on the people as a heated tournament. They
followed the events with curiosity and marked the
blows. In 1204, at Carcassonne, Catholics and Cathari
engaged in a prolonged joust in the presence of the
papal legate and King Peter II of Aragon, who ad-
judged the victory to the champions of the ancient faith.
Can one imagine such a scene in northern France?
There bishops and people, instead of discussing heresy,
hastened to put an end to it. The South allowed it to
speak, to act, and even to organize its religion. In 1167
heresy had held its solemn council, a reunion of Albigensian and foreign bishops, at Saint-Felix-de-Caraman.

Under the presidency of a personage from the Greek Empire, and without being disturbed, it regulated questions of internal discipline and of administrative forms.

After this time it seemed as if the cities and country districts were filled with sectarians. In 1177 Raymon V, count of Toulouse, sends out a cry of alarm and informs the Chapter General of Citeaux of the terrifying development of the new religion: " It has penetrated everywhere. It has brought discord into every family, dividing husband from wife, son from father, daughter-in-law from mother-in-law. The priests themselves yield to the contagion. The churches are deserted and are falling into ruin. For my part, I do everything possible to arrest such a scourge, but I feel that my own strength is insufficient for this task. The most important personages in my land have suffered themselves to be corrupted. The crowd has followed their example and has abandoned the faith, so that I neither dare nor can repress the evil."

The question of the number of dissidents on the eve of the Albigensian war is one of the questions which history will never answer with exactitude. Catholics have designedly exaggerated the number in order to justify the work of proscription; their opponents, in order to render the persecutors more odious, regard the heretics of Languedoc as an insignificant minority. If they had been such a negligible quantity, the papacy would not have let loose one half of France upon the other; it is necessary to measure the danger by the effort made to remedy it. Perhaps the Albigensians were in a majority in certain maritime towns of Languedoc whence the sect had sprung. But the ardor and the rapidity of their propaganda, the inertia of the public authorities, and the support which they found among the upper classes, rendered them everywhere so redoubtable that the Church finally believed action imperative and defended itself.

Two currents of religious opposition, one native, the other foreign, had converged upon southern France.

Certain doctrines, spontaneously born in the French environment, were the natural result of reflection and reason, of the need of asceticism, and of the desire to make the religious system harmonize with the scruples of moral conscience. As these reforms were directed toward a more elevated Christianity, they added nothing positive and manifested themselves by negations. They did not desire to destroy the Church, but to purify it by leading it back to its beginnings. Such was the dream of Peter Waldo, a merchant of Lyons, whose followers were popularly called " Poor Men of Lyons."

Their earliest belief contented itself with preaching poverty and reading the Bible. For a long time the clergy in the South tolerated this faith and even allowed its adherents to read and sing in the churches. They were allowed to beg from door to door and the tender-hearted people, while remaining good Catholics, gave them hospitality. These disciples of voluntary poverty, who went about almost bare-footed and wore a monk's robe, excited nothing but sympathy. But, little by little, radical tendencies in their preaching were emphasized; by dint of simplifying Catholicism they came almost to the point of suppressing it. They were destined to end

by denying the worship of saints, purgatory, transub-
stantiation, and the necessity of a priesthood and an
episcopacy, of a hierarchy constituted by ordination and
consecration. They desired to reduce worship to preaching, prayer, and the reading of the Gospel and sacred
books, which were to be put within the reach of all by
translation into the vernacular. Finally they attributed
to every believer who was in a state of sanctity, the
power to confess and absolve others.

Although the Waldenses took from the Church its
wealth and political power, the material covering in which
the Middle Ages had clothed and, as it were, stifled it,
nevertheless they intended all the more to remain Christians and even thought that they alone possessed true
Christianity. Far from wishing that their belief should
be confused with that of the Albigenses, they were at first
the declared opponents of the Cathari. " The heretics
were not agreed among themselves," wrote Guillaume de
Puylaurens; "all, however, were united in supplanting
the Catholic faith; but the Waldenses in particular
preached violently against all the others." The historian
of Simon de Montfort and the orthodox of his age also
knew very well how to distinguish one from the other.
" The Waldenses were bad but, by comparison, very much
less perverse than the others. Their doctrine was in
many respects the same as what we profess; it differed
only in a few points."

This explains why the faith of the Waldenses, during
the last thirty years of the twelfth century, spread so
quickly and so far from the place of its origin. It was
found in the Rhone valley, in the Alps, in Lorraine, in

the maritime and mountainous regions of Languedoc, in
Lombardy, in Catalonia, and even in Aragon where it
was in rivalry with Catharism. Very many Catholics
joined the Waldenses, because they thought they were
deviating only very slightly from the ancient religion. It
is true that in practice the adversaries of heresy rarely
took the trouble to distinguish one from the other. In
time of war and before the funeral pyre, the differences
in the hostile religions disappeared. In the mass of victims due to the crusade of Innocent III there were perhaps as many Waldenses as Cathari or real Albigenses.

Catharism came from afar. Originating in the Orient,
it had taken shape among the Greco-Slavs of the Balkan
peninsula, and especially among the Bulgarians. From
there it had spread to Bosnia, to Dalmatia, and through
the Adriatic ports, to northern Italy. Since the beginning
of the eleventh century it had been brought into France
by students and merchants, the usual intermediaries of
heresy. Italians frequented the great French schools and
the fairs at Champagne, Picardy, and Flanders. Through
them the new belief filtered in, at first sporadically in
most of the populous cities of northern France, Orléans,
Châlons, Reims, Arras, and Soissons. But it also won,
by more considerable numbers, the region of Lower Languedoc and of Provence. The first groups of preachers
in the sect were formed at Montpellier, Narbonne and
Marseilles. Thence they went from market to market,
from castle to castle, and spread out as far as the Pyrenees and to Toulouse and Agen. Introducing their belief
along with their wares they converted lords, citizens and
peasants. Luc, bishop of Tuy, one of the most violent

opponents of heresy, launched against them this mocking apostrophe: " Do you find in the New Testament that the apostles rushed from fair to fair in order to trade and make money? "

The religion thus peddled was not a system of purified Catholicism, but a positive belief which was founded upon a principle radically different from that of the Christian doctrine. It was dualism instead of monotheism: a good god who was the creator of everything which is spirit, and of everything which is good, over against a bad god who was the author of bodies and matter and of physical and moral evil. Everything which is material is detestable to the Cathari. Contact with the flesh constitutes impurity, loss and mortal sin. In such a belief, acting as a pure spirit is perfection. The belief theoretically condemns marriage, procreation and the family. Carried to its logical conclusions it admits only of individuals of whom each is his own center and his own end. In fact these essential principles were applied by the logical spirits of the sect, by those who directed it and were called " the perfect." These undoubtedly were a small minority, but active and convinced. This élite furnished to Catharism its bishops and its priests, who were clad in black. It maintained enthusiasm for the faith among the mass of believers.

There can be no doubt that such a religious system, a survival of ancient Manicheism, was inferior to Christianity from a philosophical point of view. The dogma of divine dualism, on which everything rested, settled in far too simple a manner the questions of the relations of soul and body and of the existence of evil. Christian speculation attempts to reconcile what is really bound together, *i. e.,* the idea of perfection and absolute power with the existence of evil, and the spirit with matter. Catharism, on the contrary, finds it more convenient to separate them completely. From the practical point of view it rather weakened the social bond, for it exaggerated the excessive tendencies of the Middle Ages still more; namely, abuse of self-mortification, absolute contempt for the flesh, and admiration for the life of the anchorite or of the cloistered monk.

In the accounts of inquisition trials drawn up in the middle of the thirteenth century, but which often refer to much earlier facts, it is not merely the fanaticism of the inquisitor which astonishes us, but also the fanaticism of the accused; the opposition of the Catharin apostles to the most powerful instincts of human nature is astounding. Those whom they admit to an active rôle in their sect ought to abandon parents, children, husband, or wife. Obliged to follow a male or female companion selected for them they are condemned to perpetual celibacy and abstinence. They leave social life and come in contact with it only for preaching and propaganda. Very many of " the perfect " maintain without pity that to belong to their church is necessary to salvation; that those who remain outside are demons; and that this is true even of mere infants, even of those who are in the mother's womb, the impure product of sin. Sometimes is heard the outcry of a mother's heart. " Why have I lost all my children? " a witness asked of two heretics who had told her that they were friends of God, *i. e.,* " perfect." " Because all your children were demons," they replied. And after that the woman did not want to listen to their preaching. Again, a husband reproached his wife for not becoming a heretic as everyone was doing in their village, and he vainly attempted to compel her. She was obstinate in avoiding the heretics; had they not said that she was bearing a demon in her womb? She told the inquisitors, " My husband has often abused and beaten me because I was unwilling to love them."

Albigensian fanaticism manifested itself in another excess: the aspiration of the believer for death, when he had received, by the solemn act called the *consolamentum,* the kind of baptism *in extremis* which ensured him salvation. Then the sick, happy to be in a state of grace, let themselves die of hunger, of their own volition or by the advice of a minister. And when the instinct of self-preservation revolted against this, the kinsmen were at hand to overcome it. A woman who was called as a witness said: " For two days my daughter refused me food or drink, because she did not wish me to lose the benefit of the sacrament which had been conferred upon me. Only on the third day was I able to procure food for myself, and I recovered."

This religion, s ofundamentally different from Catholicism, so productive of violations of human instinct, was foreign in every way to the sensual and tolerant temperament of the Southerners. How did it make so many proselytes among them? The rigorous asceticism which sprang from the principles of Catharism was obligatory only upon the small number of " the perfect." For good reasons it was not imposed upon the mass of adherents. The latter undoubtedly ought to imitate the leaders as

Medieval Civilization

much as possible, and to approach their ideal, but by tolerance they were allowed to marry, to found a family, and to lead the common life. It sufficed for their salvation that they should receive the *consolamentum* at the hour of sickness or danger. A simple imposition of hands, a *Pater Noster,* and they had paradise. This is the way in which the monk of Vaux de Cernai explains the success of their propaganda while at the same time calumniating the sectarians whom he detests. " The heretics who are called believers continue to live in the world. Although they do not succeed in leading the life of ' the perfect ' they hope, nevertheless, to be saved by their faith. These believers abandon themselves to usury, theft, homicide, perjury and all the vices of the flesh. They sin with all the more security and zest, because they have no need of confession and penitence. It suffices if in the article of death they are able to say the Lord's prayer and receive the Holy Ghost."

Moreover, the Cathari appealed to certain sentiments which are always strong in the multitude, by arousing among the poor an aversion to a clergy which was rich and indifferent to social misery. The heretical school of Périgord taught that almsgiving was worthless, " because no one ought to have any private property." They took care to recall that in the primitive Church no Christian could be richer than any other, and that everything was put into a common stock for the benefit of all. In certain respects the community of " the perfect " among the Albigenses did not recognize individual property. Money received from the faithful by donation or legacy was put into a common fund and consecrated to the relief of the

444

disinherited. " Do you wish to escape from your wretched condition? " they said to the poor. " Come to us. We will take care of you, and you shall lack nothing."

Catharism had other means of seduction: no purgatory (prayers can do nothing for the dead) and no hell. Hell, to the Albigenses, the place of penitence and of punishment, was this earth, the bodily life in the visible world. After a more or less lengthy passage through various human bodies, all the souls are finally saved. It is easy to see how attractive such a perspective was to the multitude. They did not ask how the theory of eternal happiness reserved for all could be reconciled with the belief in demons and with the denial of salvation for those who did not belong to the sect. They were satisfied to think that in becoming Cathari they escaped an eternity of punishment and spared their reason the torment of insoluble mysteries. The religion of the Albigenses did not admit the Trinity. Christ was for them only a creature, an angel of the first order, and the Holy Ghost the chief of celestial intelligences. Dogmatic difficulties, such as incarnation, the resurrection and the ascension of Christ, disappeared, since Jesus was not made flesh and had only an apparent humanity. The Virgin also was only an angel and not the veritable mother of the Son of God. Finally, the Cathari did not have to inquire into the manner in which, at the last judgment, bodies which had been dissolved and destroyed could find themselves again intact. They believed that only souls were to be resurrected.

Even the least Christian element in the new religion, the existence of a bad god, was not so repugnant to the intelligence of the Catholic masses as one might suppose. We know how great a place the devil occupied in their imagination, what powers they attributed to him and how easily they believed in his frequent intervention. The propagation of Catharism was so much the more rapid because its preachers, instead of dwelling upon the exotic characteristics in their belief, strove to bring out its relations with the ancient faith. They clung to Christianity with all their might and protested against the accusation of heresy. From their accounts it was Catholicism which went astray from the true Christian tradition; they, for their part, were merely reëstablishing the worship and doctrines of the primitive Church. In fact, it would be difficult to deny the striking analogy between the Catharian ceremonies and those of the Christian liturgy of the first centuries. The sectarians relied upon the New Testament in combating the degenerate Catholicism; they practised Christ's morality and thought that they too had been sent on earth to deliver souls. Although they saw in the Old Testament chiefly Satan's work, they took from it whatever suited them and interpreted it symbolically; thus they preserved the sacred books of the Catholics. They also kept the great religious festivals, Christmas, Easter, and Pentecost; they practised a kind of confession, the *appareillamentum,* which was merely the public confession of the early Christians; they had even formed for themselves a hierarchical organization of priests and bishops, with diocesan boundaries almost identical with those of the ancient clergy. They lacked only a pope. The adept in the Albigensian religion might have an illusion that after all, in abandoning the faith of his fathers, he was not making such a complete change in environment, traditions and habits.

Add the impression made upon the multitude by the austere life of " the perfect," and the comparison which was inevitable with the kind of life led by the prelates of the Roman Church. Undoubtedly, however elevated its ideal, every human society has its tares, its scabby sheep and its bad shepherds. The reports of inquisition trials show that certain ministers of Catharism abused their position in order to extort money from the sick or to seduce their parishioners. But these reports never mention the nocturnal orgies with which the multitude was wont to reproach the partisans of heresy. On the contrary they establish beyond a doubt the rigid chastity of the Catharian apostles and their over-scrupulous precautions for shunning even the appearance of contact with women. The contemporaries who were not blinded by hatred have themselves recognized the high morality of the sect. One day after hearing the bishop of Toulouse preach a knight, who was a Catharian, cried out: " We would never have believed that the Roman Church had such strong reasons for opposing our ministers ! " " Why," replied the bishop, " do you not see that they cannot answer my objections ? " " Yes, we see it," said the knight. " Then why don't you drive them out of your land ? " asked the bishop. And the other replied: " We cannot. We have been brought up among them; several of our kinsmen are living with them and we are obliged to admit that they act very honorably."

The spread of Albigensian heresy, accordingly, is explained by its very nature and by the character of those who propagated it. But the social condition of the country was remarkably favorable to the work of the preachers; the land was ready when the seed was sown.

The first favorable circumstance for the heretics was that they had only to contend with a clergy which was destitute of moral influence and profoundly discredited. "The laymen," says Guillaume de Puylaurens, "had so little respect for their priests that they put them on the same footing as the Jews. When they swore, instead of saying: 'I had rather be a Jew than do that,' they said, 'I had rather be a priest.' When priests appeared in public they took care to hide their tonsure. Knights in our country very rarely dedicate their sons to a clerical life. In churches where they receive the tithe (by virtue of their right of patronage), they present the son of a tenant or of an official for the rectorship, and thus bishops are obliged to ordain the first-comer."

Bishops and abbots led a scarcely more regular life than those who were merely priests. Councils in southern France ordered them to wear the tonsure and the garb of their order. They forbade them to put on luxurious furs, to use decorated saddles and gilded bridles, to play games of chance, to hunt, to curse and suffer others about them to curse, to have actors and musicians at their tables, to hear matins in bed, to chat about frivolous matters during the service, and to excommunicate at random. They ought not to leave their diocese; they ought to convoke their synod at least once a year; in their episcopal visitations they ought not to take with them too numerous a suite, as it was an oppressive burden for those who received them. They were forbidden to take money for conferring orders, for tolerating the concubinage of priests, for dispensing with marriage bans, or for freeing the guilty from ecclesiastical penalties. Finally they were forbidden to exact payment for celebrating unlawful marriages and breaking legal testaments.

This list of abuses which were prohibited is in itself a tableau of customs. When we add to it the confessions of a monastic chronicler, Geoffrey de Vigeois, the sarcasms of certain troubadours, and above all the accusations contained in the letters of Innocent III, we are in a position to judge the usual conduct of the prelates of Languedoc. It is sufficient to see the terms in which this pope spoke of the clergy in the diocese of Narbonne and of its chief, the archbishop. " Blind men, dumb dogs who are no longer able to bark, and simoniacs who sell justice, who absolve the rich and condemn the poor. They do not even observe the laws of the Church; they accumulate benefices and entrust sacerdotal and ecclesiastical functions to unworthy priests and illiterate children. That is the cause of the insolence of the heretics, and of the contempt felt by lords and people for God and His church. Prelates in this region are the laughing stock of the laity. But the archbishop of Narbonne is the root of all the evil. This man knows no god but money; he has only a purse instead of a heart. During the ten years that he has held his office he has not visited his province once, not even his own diocese. He extorted five hundred sous of gold for consecrating the bishop of Maguelonne, and when we asked him to raise subsidies for the safety of the Christians in the Orient, he refused to obey us. When a church becomes vacant, he neglects to name an incumbent, in order that he may profit from the revenues. He reduces by one half the number of canons in Narbonne in order to appropriate the prebends to himself and also keeps vacant archdeaconries in his own hands. In his diocese monks and canons regular cast their frocks aside, take wives, live by usury, and become advocates, jongleurs or doctors."

Compromised by the unworthiness of its own members, the southern Church was still more enfeebled by the constant attacks of the barons who were rabidly determined to plunder it. The war which the nobles made on the clergy, the continuous plague of the Middle Ages, had taken on in this region a character of malevolent harshness. Feudalism dared to do anything against bishops and abbots who were not protected by the respect of the multitude.

At Toulouse the bishop is so harried by the nobles in the neighborhood that he implores safe-conducts from them in order that he may make his diocesan rounds. His mules can not go to the river or horse-pond without an escort, so that the attendants are often reduced to giving them drinking water from the well within the bishop's house. What can the count of Toulouse do to defend his bishop? He himself represses with great difficulty these vassals who are incessantly rebelling; and, moreover, this high suzerain does not act any differently from the others. He persecutes the abbey of Moissac and gets himself excommunicated in 1196 by Pope Celestine III because he has destroyed several churches dependent upon St. Gilles, has put the men of this monastery to ransom and has built a fortress which menaces the abbot.

Southern France

From one end of Languedoc to the other the church was suffering from the same attacks; Roger II, viscount of Béziers, sacked an abbey (1171), threw the bishop of Albi into prison and found it amusing to make a heretic his gaoler (1178). In 1197 the monks of Alet elected an abbot who was not acceptable to the guardian of the new viscount of Béziers, and the latter put the abbey to fire and sword and imprisoned the abbot. Then, animated by a ghastly whim, he had the corpse of the dead abbot installed in the abbot's pulpit until he had forced the monks to elect one of his own creatures.

At Pamiers the followers of the count of Foix, Raymond Roger, cut in pieces one of the canons of an abbey and put out the eyes of another brother in the same house. The count arrived soon after with his knights, jesters, and courtesans, shut up the abbot and his monks in a church, where he left them for three days without food, and finally drove them out, almost naked, from the territory of their own city. This "very cruel dog," as Pierre des Vaux de Cernai calls him, besieged the church of Urgel and left only the four walls standing. With the arms and legs from the crucifixes, the soldiers in his company made pestels for grinding their food. Their horses ate oats from the altars; they themselves, after having dressed up the images of Christ with helmet and shield, practised piercing these with their lances, just like the manikins used for the quintain.

Highwaymen's amusements! The war of which the clergy were the victims was made more outrageous by the employment of these hordes of brigands. It did no good to excommunicate them. They took special pleasure in polluting holy places and in giving to their ravages a flavor of sacrilege. In spite of the prohibitions and the threats of the Church, the counts and viscounts could not get along without the brigands. In their lands the bond of vassalage was so weak or so little respected that the military obligations regularly due by the feudal law would not have sufficed to procure for them the necessary troops for offensive and defensive war. The free-booter was a necessary evil. The Church did not understand this and saw, in these robbers hired by the nobles, only heretics paid to destroy it. In this respect it was deceived. In every part of France where he happened to be, the free-booter, impious by profession, went straight for the churches and convents, attracted by their treasure.

The noble with his brutal passions was not the only enemy of the clergy. How could the burgesses thrive and become independent without dispossessing the seigniories which held the cities, bishoprics, chapters and abbeys? The conflicts with the Church over their respective jurisdictions and interests led to equally violent crises. In 1167 the inhabitants of Béziers, after assassinating their viscount, threw themselves upon their bishop and knocked out his teeth. In 1194 the burgesses of Mende expelled their bishop. In 1195 the people of Capestang were excommunicated for imprisoning the bishop of Lodève and demanding a ransom of him. Three years later, the burgesses of Lodève pillaged the bishop's palace and with a knife at his throat compelled the same bishop to give them their liberties.

Wherever lords and burgesses were warring against the clergy, they received enthusiastically those people who

came, in the name of a new religion or with an ideal of
higher morality, to combat Catholicism and to attempt to
supplant it. The Catharian of the Waldensian preacher
was an unexpected auxiliary. Very soon, interest in
the unknown and dilettanteism had an influence and it
became the fashion in the feudal world and in the cities
to show a contempt for the ancient worship and to favor
the new. The count of Foix remained on horseback, with
his head up, in the presence of a procession which was
passing with some relics. He lived surrounded by sectaries. His wife and one of his sisters were Waldenses.
In 1204 he was at the castle of Fanjeaux, a stronghold
of heresy, surrounded by a group of knights and citizens.
In his presence his other sister and four other noble ladies
were initiated into Catharism by the bishop. They promised in the future to eat no more meat, eggs or cheese,
but only oil and fish. They also bound themselves not to
lie or swear, to maintain perpetual chastity, and to practise the new religion as long as they lived. The heretics
had them recite the *Pater Noster,* laid their hands upon
them, and then placed a Gospel on their heads. Afterward all who were present prostrated themselves before
the ministers who had just officiated, and exchanged the
kiss of peace. Forty years later the scene was described
by a witness of the inquisition.

The collection of scandal carefully gathered by the
monk of Cernai, is not silent about Raymond VI,
count of Toulouse. " I want to have my son educated
among you," he said to the heretics at Toulouse. He
affirmed that he would gladly give a hundred marks of
silver to have one of his knights converted to their belief.

He accepted with pleasure presents from the sectaries; he was seen to prostrate himself before their ministers, to ask their blessing and to embrace them. One day when he was impatiently awaiting some soldiers who did not come, he said, " It is evident that it is the devil who created the world, for nothing is done as I would like it." He protested to the bishop of Toulouse that the monks of Citeaux could not be saved, " because the people subject to them were consumed with luxury." He dared to invite the bishop to come to his palace one night and be present at the preaching of the Albigenses. One day when he was in a church during mass he ordered his court fool to mimic the gestures of the priest at the moment when the latter turned toward the people and chanted the *Dominus vobiscum.* Speaking of an ill-clad and frightfully crippled heretic, he said, " I would rather be that man than be named king or emperor."

More serious facts were related. A heretic of Toulouse had polluted the altar in a church and committed unclean sacrilege. He said out loud that when the priest officiating at the mass partakes of the Host his body absorbs only a demon. The abbot of Grandselve asked Raymond VI to punish the heretic for all these scandalous acts. The count replied: " I would never prosecute a compatriot for such deeds." Pierre des Vaux de Cernai thought that he was in a position to declare that the count had actually become a heretic. In his military expeditions the count took with him Albigensian bishops dressed in lay costumes. If he had been severely wounded he would have immediately received from them the laying on of hands.

All vices were freely attributed to these abettors of

heresy. The monk of Cernai believed Raymond VI was
a rascal whose immorality did not hesitate even at incest,
and he poured upon him a stream of invectives: "Limb
of the devil, son of perdition, hardened criminal, warehouse of all sins." These Southerners were certainly no
saints. Raymond, like the others, had concubines and
bastards, to say nothing of his five legitimate and successive wives. But did the lords in the North lead a
more edifying life? They also made rude war on the
Church; only when stealing its temporal property they
respected its religious power, its traditions and its dogmas. The state of mind of the barons of Languedoc remained an insoluble enigma to the Catholic multitude.
They were profoundly astonished at their toleration, at
their refusal to act vigorously against the sect, and at their
motley following, in which Jews, Cathari, Waldenses and
the orthodox elbowed one another. They thought conversion to Catharism was the only possible explanation
of such extraordinary conduct. As a matter of fact, the
promoters of the crusade against the Albigenses made a
mistake in thinking that because this feudal society
patronized the heretic, it had embraced heresy.

In the scene at Fanjeux, all present took part in the
ceremonies of initiation except the count of Foix himself
—a significant exception. He allowed his people to affil-
iate with the sect, but he did not enter it. Raymond VI
always denied that he was a heretic and no one (we may
believe Innocent III) has ever been able to prove that he
was one. He loaded the religious congregations with
presents; he was especially friendly toward the Hospitalers of St. John of Jerusalem, and even associated himself

with their order in 1218, declaring " that if he ever entered religion he would choose no habit but theirs." Authentic evidence proves that he had made his daughter Raimonde a nun in the convent of Lespinasse and that even when he was excommunicated, he remained at the doors of the churches, in order to be present at the holy ceremonies, although afar off. If he met, on his way, a priest bearing the eucharist to the sick, he dismounted, adored the Host, and followed the priest. When the first Franciscans reached Toulouse he gathered them together, on Holy Thursday, in the house of one of his friends, served them at table with his own hands, and carried his respect for Christian tradition so far that he washed and kissed their feet.

The contradictory actions of these lords of the South may be explained by their hereditary instincts, their indifference, their eclecticism and their anti-clerical passion. Following the example of their fathers and grandfathers, they pillaged and robbed the property of the Church, but this did not prevent them, any more than their fathers and grandfathers, from enriching convents, founding chapels, and wearing drugget when seriously ill and expecting death. Between times, according to circumstances and their own interests, they listened to the preachers of heresy and aided their mission. None the less, in external matters, they remained attached to the religion of their ancestors. Even if they no longer had the faith, they always practised the works, and this was the essential thing in the Middle Ages. Very many of these so-called heretics kept up the Catholic observances until the last day of their life.

Southern France

Their equivocal attitude seemed only the more dangerous to those who saw the new religion gradually winning the whole South. Guillaume de Puylaurens throws part of the responsibility for this situation upon the carelessness of the sovereigns of Toulouse who had suffered the evil to spread and to become almost irremediable. But he especially incriminates the negligence of the prelates of the country, their intentional inertia or even their secret complicity. Whether they felt themselves powerless or whether they too were penetrated by ideas repugnant to religious persecution, the fact is that the bishops refused to make inquests and to proscribe their diocesan subjects. " The shepherds who ought to watch over the flock have fallen asleep," says Puylaurens; " that is the reason why the wolves have ravaged everything."

The Intellectual Movement of the Thirteenth Century

Adapted from C. V. Langlois, in Lavisse: *Histoire de France*, Vol. III, Part ii, 1901, pp. 387–416.

TWO facts are dominant in the history of the intellectual activity of the thirteenth century: the decadence of idealism and of artificial literature, and the development of the scientific spirit.

In the schools of the twelfth century, there had been a renaissance of letters, which is not without some analogy to the later Renaissance which was more celebrated, more complete, and more fruitful. Most of the men in the twelfth century, who wrote in Latin, were scholars, humanists, and rhetoricians, adorned with the spoils of antiquity; even those who treated abstruse questions, Abélard and Gilbert de la Porrée, for example, wrote with due attention to style; in the vernacular, on the other hand, the chanson and the " court " romance flourished in the twelfth century. All of this courtly literature was worldly, agreeable, and refined, but had neither depth nor sincerity.

A hundred years after St. Bernard and Crétien de Troyes came the age of St. Thomas and Jean de Meun, when everything was changed. It is difficult to imagine

The Intellectual Movement

a more complete contrast. From that time, among the
clergy there were no more elegant orators or poets, that
is to say, makers of Latin verses, like Gautier de Châtillon or Hildebert de Lavardin, whose works are imitations so perfectly insipid and without color or date that
modern humanists, by mistake, have attributed some
fragments to ancient authors. " If you look for a poet
among them," says Hauréau, " you will find none. The
hexameter has passed out of fashion, as well as the
pentameter; little rhythmical pieces, sometimes pious
and sometimes obscene, make up the whole [clerical]
poetry of that day." Theologians and philosophers
spoke a technical jargon that the logicians of the preceding century would have had difficulty in understanding, and they treated problems that were wholly new.
Moreover, in the lay world, *courtoisie* had had its day.
The idealistic conceptions of the preceding century were
no longer taken seriously, and sometimes were derided.
The characteristic works of this age are pompous, pe-
dantic poems full of grossness and life.

The twelfth century, at its close, had seemed to despair of human reason: never had the mystics, who
despised science and scientific curiosity, been more numerous than in the time when the theological school of the
monastery of St. Victor of Paris was in its glory. The
thirteenth century, on the contrary, the most intellectual
of the Middle Ages, had a passionate confidence in reason; it attempted to know; it wished to prove everything.

The event which gave the initial impulse to the
philosophical and theological evolution of the thirteenth

century was the appearance of hitherto-unknown works of Aristotle, and commentaries on these works, which were brought from Spain about 1200: the Physics, and the Metaphysics, and almost the whole body of Aristotelian learning.

At the very moment when the new Aristotle and his Moslem commentators were introduced at Paris, the philosophical-theological system which was reigning in the schools was Platonic idealism or pseudo-Platonic, on the model of St. Augustine. Although St. Augustine had been almost dazzled by Greek metaphysics, yet he was one of the most violent contemners of reason: he subordinated the True to the Good, the Intelligence to the Will, and prostrated human thought in the dust. The disciples of this somber genius continued to maintain his fundamental theses, which were satisfactory to spirits inclined to obedience, to religious and mystical souls, to born defenders of orthodoxy, and to rhetoricians. For these reasons, Augustinianism has never ceased to have numerous partisans. All-powerful in the twelfth century, it was taught in the thirteenth century by many doctors. However great the differences between them, and although they all had undergone, to a greater or lesser degree, in spite of themselves, the influence of Aristotle or of the Aristotelian terminology, most of the secular and Franciscan theologians of the thirteenth century,—and even some celebrated masters among the Dominicans,— were Augustinians.

The rationalistic philosophy of Aristotle was received with distrust by theologians who followed the Augustinian tradition, because they judged it dangerous; but

The Intellectual Movement

most scholars fell upon this new food with an avidity which is comparable only to the intoxication of the first humanists in the presence of the resuscitated Antiquity. Such a vigorous fermentation immediately set in that the ecclesiastical authorities attempted to stop it, in 1210 and 1215: "The books of Aristotle on metaphysics and natural philosophy are not to be read." Nevertheless, prohibition pure and simple could not be maintained. April 13, 1231, Pope Gregory IX gave absolution to the masters and students who had been excommunicated for having disobeyed orders by reading or interpreting Aristotle; in principle, he confirmed the prohibitive decrees of 1210 and 1215, but "provisionally, until the books of the Philosopher had been examined and expurgated." The task of expurgation—"cutting out the erroneous, doing away with the suspected"—was confided by Gregory XI to three lay masters at Paris. As such an enterprise was, naturally, chimerical, the three masters gave it up. There is no evidence that they ever even attempted it. The absolute prohibitions of 1210 and 1215 were never removed, but they were forgotten. An official decree of the faculty of arts in the University of Paris, March 19, 1255, mentions, among the books which the professors in arts ought to "read" publicly, the Physics and Metaphysics and other treatises that were written by Aristotle or attributed to him. The Philosopher accordingly remained in full possession of the freedom of the schools, and Aristotelianism became, in spite of the Augustinian party, the prevailing mode of thought.

Now, in all the religious circles where the Aristotelian philosophy was known and tolerated in the Middle Ages, whether Arabic, Jewish, or Latin, the same phenomena occurred. Among the admirers of Aristotle, there were two parties: one, filled with respect for dogma and also with veneration for the Philosopher, attempted to reconcile the two by subtleties of interpretation; the other, after having taken the precaution, which was indispensable, and perhaps ironical, of declaring that what is true according to the faith is not always true according to reason, and that, in case of any contradiction, the solution according to the faith ought to be preferred, very freely drew the most extreme conclusions from the doctrine of the Master.

A Franciscan, Alexander de Hales, apparently was the first to bring within the bounds of orthodoxy this Aristotle whom ecclesiastical authority had not succeeded in banishing or restricting. But two disciples of St. Dominic, Albert the Great and Thomas Aquinas, are entitled to the glory of having accomplished the Christianization of Aristotelianism. Albert "conceived and carried out the plan of adopting Aristotle to the usage of the Latins . . . and also of correcting him, so that he might enter into the thought of the Church." His disciple, Thomas Aquinas, with greater care, and under the auspices of the Holy See, undertook the task a second time, substituting the most exact method of literal exegesis for that of paraphrase, in order to accomplish "the fundamental problem of the interpretation of Aristotle and the correction of his errors." The Dominican order was officially designated by the Holy See, in the thirteenth century, to correct the text of the Bible (Hugues de Saint-Cher) and to revise the *Corpus juris canonici* (Raymond de Peñafort)—the two "texts" in the teaching of theology and law. In addition, the order accomplished a similar, but still more important, task: the preparation of the philosophical encyclopedia of Aristotelian thought for the use of the schools in general. In this way, the Dominicans played, in the thirteenth century, a rôle very analogous to that played by the Company of Jesus three hundred years later. They turned Aristotelian rationalism to the profit of orthodoxy, just as the Jesuits, in the interests of the Church, confiscated triumphant humanism.

The work of Albert and Thomas, which was a colossal effort and demanded rare ability, especially in Thomas, was very much valued by most of their contemporaries. Godefroy de Fontaines says that the new Dominican philosophy is the "salt of the earth"; the faculty of arts at Paris compared it, in 1274, to the light of the sun. But it was also attacked very vigorously, on one wing, by Augustinians who were absolutely opposed to Aristotelianism, such as, for example, William of St. Amour and John Peckham; on the other wing, by the irreconcilable Aristotelians and by a small group of thinkers, who "had despaired of Aristotle," after having conscientiously attempted to profit by his teaching. It is only in our own day that men have ventured to say that "the *Summa Theologiae* embraces all the science and all the philosophy" of the thirteenth century, and some have even said "of the Middle Ages," and that the encyclopedic philosophy of St. Thomas, so clear and so prudent (*prudentissime*), qualities which have made its extraordinary fortune, is classic in the Church.

Medieval Civilization

Nothing was more difficult than to reconcile Aristotle with dogma, as Avicenna did among the Mussulmans and Albert the Great and Thomas Aquinas among the Christians, for the Augustinians were not wrong in stating that the philosophy of Aristotle is incompatible with the necessary postulates of a revealed religion. The writings of the Philosopher imply, even if they do not formally state, that there is no creator, no first man, no anthropomorphic God, no providence, no survival of individual souls after death. In fact, Avicenna and Thomas Aquinas, out of profound respect for the Master, have, as far as possible, attenuated, excused, distorted, or charitably passed over in silence, his malodorous opinions. Most frequently they denied that he intended to say what he seemed to say; but in the presence of too-manifest errors, they did not fail promptly to condemn him. St. Thomas never hesitated between Aristotle and " sound philosophy," that is, between Aristotle and the Faith: *Amicus Aristoteles, sed magis amica Fides.*

Among the Arabs, this had not been the attitude of Averroès. This commentator never tired of repeating that he proposed to " state the opinion of the Philosopher," without being responsible for it. His rule in explanation of obscure texts and the determination of doubtful points was to follow the general spirit of the Master's teaching. Servile, but faithful, interpreters, the Averroists emphasized, in place of concealing, the contradictions which exist between Aristotelianism and theological " truths; " and some appeared to enjoy this game under the protection of the authority of the great man. It is natural that Averroism—that is, Aristotelianism carried to its ex-

The Intellectual Movement

treme conclusions—had its disciples at Paris, as well as in
Mussulman Spain and in the synagogues of Languedoc:
there were some from the first years of the second half
of the thirteenth century, if not earlier.

The protagonist of the sect, in the schools of Paris,
was a certain Siger de Brabant. He first appears in
1266, as the cause of the disorders which broke out that
year among the four " nations " of the faculty of arts. In
1270, he wrote a manifesto, the *De anima intellectiva,* to
which Thomas Aquinas replied; and the bishop of Paris
condemned the most striking of the Averroistic propositions. For three years after December, 1271, the faculty
of arts was divided into two factions, each of which
elected its rector. One of these two factions, the smaller
numerically, is designated as the " faction of Siger." It
was composed, doubtless, in great part of the masters and
students who professed Averroism. In 1275, the cardinal
of St. Cecilia (later Pope Martin IV) put an end to this
schism by a ruling which contains the most direct and
vigorous threats against the " satellites of Satan, who
have, for a long time, been sowing discord in the *Studium*
of Paris." Two years later, the bishop of Paris, Etienne
Tempier, ex-chancellor of the University, excommunicated the authors of two hundred and nineteen propositions taught in the faculty of arts. Etienne Tempier, in
this instance, carried out the wishes of the lay doctors
of the faculty of theology, who had Augustinian tendencies. In his condemnatory decree of March 7, 1277, he
considers not merely the characteristic theses of pure
Averroism, but, also, some theses of the moderate Aristotelianism of the Dominican school, taught by Thomas

465

Aquinas. Lay theologians would have been well pleased to crush all Aristotelianism under the same condemnation; but this partisan attempt failed, because of the activity of the brethren of Thomas (who had died in 1274) and the intervention of Rome. The crisis of 1277 was disastrous to the Averroists alone.

The influence of Aristotle manifested itself, at that time, in two ways: first, Aristotelian metaphysics led the western philosophers astray, as it had already done the Syrians, the Jews, and the Arabs, by inviting them to endless controversies over questions of existence, quality, and form, out of which nothing has ever come; secondly, the Aristotelian encyclopedia rendered great pedagogical services. Not only is it full of instruction, true and false, upon the things of this universe, and historical facts which are very well fitted to awaken curiosity, but it is arranged in conformity with rigorous logic, and the methods of argumentation of the Philosopher are of such a nature that they furnish the instrument, or the illusion, of a scientific method. In short, Aristotle has inculcated or developed not only the taste for abstract speculation, but also the desire to learn—that lust for knowledge which St. Augustine placed among the most dangerous of the lusts—and the habit of reasoning. Albert the Great, had the temperament and the desires of the scholar. Thomas Aquinas, Duns Scotus, William of Ockham, and their rivals, were, if not rationalists, at least consummate reasoners and learned men, after their fashion. Even the most exalted mystics, in those days, paid tribute, as far as they could, to the scientific method.

The Intellectual Movement

Raymond Lull, of Majorca, who wandered for thirty
years through all the lands bordering on the Mediterranean, and often displayed at Paris his luxuriant beard,
his poetic effusions, and the extraordinary fancies of a
partially deranged intellect, invented a scientific mech-
anism for solving all problems and reaching the truth
in everything: an *Ars major,* which ought to serve for
ideas as the table of Pythagoras for numbers.

THE preachers who were contemporaries of St. Louis
and of Philip the Fair did not at all resemble those of
the preceding age, who were rhetorical gourmands. In
the thirteenth century, preachers, who addressed audiences of the clergy and consequently wrote or spoke in
Latin, generally followed the "scholastic" method, that
is, they attempted to demonstrate laboriously, after the
manner of the schools, points in morals or doctrine, by
bringing together a great number of authorities and
distinctions. Others, who spoke in the vernacular before
lay audiences—although nearly all of their sermons
which have been preserved are in Latin or Latin mixed
with French—abandoned the lofty style and the ingenious allegories which formerly were the fashion. "The
sharpened sword of argumentation," says the cardinal
Jacques de Vitry, "has no power over the laity; to the
knowledge of the Scriptures, without which one cannot
take a step, it is necessary to add refreshing, and sometimes edifying, stories."

An experienced preacher, according to the ideal of the
thirteenth century, ought to have in reserve a store of
anecdotes and experiences, a bric-à-brac of instructive

teaching, of adages, and of repartee. The popular orator in the time of St. Louis knew his flock; he knew that, if he tired them, he would see them "leaving for the shows of the jongleurs." Accordingly he sacrificed himself, but voluntarily, for he was the first to be amused at his own stories. Most of the itinerant preachers, whether regular or secular, were from the ranks of the people, and they shared the popular tastes; they also shared the popular passions, and that is why their sermons are often so astonishingly free. "It is our duty," they said, "to bark in the house of the Lord." They "barked," in fact, very willingly, especially against the rich, the powerful, and the dignitaries of all the hierarchies. Without caring at all, they provoked the hatred of the aristocrats, of the office-holders, and of the clergy who had prebends and did nothing; and they even violated the proprieties. They also had a confused idea of a social justice which did not exist. "The rulers in our time," said one of them, "are like blind men who have dogs to lead them. The dogs are called counselors, bailiffs, provosts, etc., and they are, strictly speaking, dogs who always wag their tails and fawn upon their masters, and chase strangers, especially people of humble rank and the good, to bite and tear them." "It is the fashion," said another, "to have a festival when a son is born to the king. I have seen that in France. Much more should there be feasting on Christmas day over the birth of the Son of the King of Paradise. Princes come into the world, not to give us anything, but, on the contrary, to take our goods from us, while the Son of the Celestial King came to pay our debts." "All riches," said a third, who was a bishop, " come from theft. I consider the saying entirely true that every rich man is a thief or the heir of a thief." An anonymous writer even ventured to censure God himself: " A jongleur, summoned by a priest to make his will, said: ' I have two horses; I give one of them to the king and the other to the bishop; as for my clothes, they shall be given to the barons and other rich men.' ' But,' cried the priest, ' and the poor?' ' Do you not preach to us every day,' replied the jongleur, ' that we should imitate God? I imitate Him, for He gives everything to the rich, and nothing to the poor.' "

THE paucity of details relative to the artists of the thirteenth century renders invaluable the " album " of Villard de Honnecourt, a book of sketches and mementoes, which has been preserved by chance. This document of the age of Louis IX is unique in its class. It is a small volume of thirty-three sheets of stitched parchment and is covered with sketches and explanatory notes in the dialect of Picardy. On the first page there is a note: " Villard de Honnecourt salutes you, and asks all those who work at the different trades contained in this book to pray for him, for in this book can be found great aid and instruction in the fundamental principles of masonry and carpentry. You will also find in it the method of draughting, as commanded and taught by geometry."

Honnecourt is a village on the banks of the Scheldt, in the *arrondissement* of Cambray, where there was, in the thirteenth century, a priory of the order of Cluny. Six kilometers away, in the days when Villard was young,

the great Cistercian abbey of Vaucelles was finished;
probably the author of the album got his education and
did his first work in the work-shops of Vaucelles (closed
in 1235). Then he traveled. " I have been in very many
countries," said he. At Laon, he sketched one of the
towers of the cathedral—" the most beautiful tower in
the world," in his opinion. At Reims, he studied the
cathedral which was in process of construction. In his
memorandum, he has recorded the plan of St. Étienne de
Meaux, the design of the great western rose window of
Notre-Dame de Chartres, and the details of the cathedral
at Lausanne. When he traveled through Lausanne, he
was going to Hungary. In Hungary, he saw, as he says,
certain church pavements, of which he reproduced the
plans. The Cistercian monks of Hungary, who probably
came from Cambrésis and Artois, and possibly from Vaucelles, were at that time building a great number of
abbeys. It is almost certain that he was sent to these
distant lands to enter the service of the Cistercians. However that may be, some of the numerous Cistercian edifices which were built in Hungary between 1235 and
1250 were probably his work. It would be interesting, in
the ruins that remain, to seek for his builder's mark.
This builder's mark is seen in the collegiate church of
St. Quentin (Aisne), which was consecrated in 1257. In
fact, the interior and exterior elevations of the choir of
St. Quentin are modeled upon those of the cathedral of
Reims, noted in the album; the Hungarian motive of the
album is found in the pavement of the narthex of St.
Quentin; the plan of one of the chapels of St. Quentin
is like that of the chapels of Vaucelles; and the incorrect

The Intellectual Movement

drawing of the rose window at Chartres, which is in the album, is reproduced in that chapel. The methods of work of the architect and decorator can be grasped here: he combined the details of various edifices which had pleased him. This method was very common: hence the extraordinary likenesses which are noted now among buildings which are sometimes very distant from one another. Villard was not content, however, with imitation. He had thought out, in collaboration with an associate named Pierre de Corbie, the plan for a church, where square chapels alternated with apsidial around the deambulatory. This arrangement, which was very uncommon, has been carried out in the cathedral at Toledo, of which the architect, who died in 1290, is designated by the name of " Master Peter." It is not impossible that this architect at Toledo was the friend of Villard de Honnecourt.

Although we know that he built several great edifices, Villard de Honnecourt was not an artist of the first rank. The protégé of the monks of Vaucelles has no right to be placed by the side of the masters at Paris, Amiens, Reims, etc., or of those who worked for the kings, princes, and bishops of northern France. He had, as it were, a provincial talent. His style, which is a composite of the styles of the Ile-de-France, of Champagne, and of the Rhineland, was not pure. He drew rather badly; his figures are commonplace, laboriously and heavily draped, in the German fashion. His " vademecum " can give no adequate idea of the skill of the great masters; but, on the other hand, he furnishes sufficiently precise notions of the general culture of an architect in the thirteenth century. Villard de Honnecourt was an educated man; he knew Latin, but not at all well; he was interested in the tales which made up, in his day, zoölogical science; he indicates the method of making an herbarium, and he sets down some recipes for a depilatory, and some cures for wounds so common in the work-shops. He was an engineer: the album contains the plans of several machines: a saw-mill run by water, a screw-jack, and a gin; and the author flattered himself that he had discovered perpetual motion, by suspending movable weights on the circumference of a wheel. Several elementary problems of practical geometry are set and solved in the album: finding the center of a circle; determining the circumference of an imbedded column; measuring the width of a river without crossing it. As for cutting stones and calculating the resistance of materials, we do not need the statements of Villard in order to know that the builders of the Middle Ages were very expert in such matters. But it is not superfluous to state that questions of carpentry and joinery occupied the author of the album just as much as questions of masonry. He speaks of the method of setting up a bridge, props, and a roof. Then, he teaches the method of designing for ornamentation, and for the human figure as used by sculptors. For portraying the figure, " the procedure," says M. J. Quicherat, " consisted in reducing attitudes to simple lines. . . . Thus the sculptors acquired the art of reproducing the various attitudes by remembering certain conventional symbols, . . . and the positions which his method would reproduce, and the routine, indicated in his album, are exactly those which the contemporary sculptors and miniaturists followed with marked predilection. . . ." In a word, Vil-

The Intellectual Movement

lard de Honnecourt was well versed in the scientific and artistic knowledge of his age. The great masters of the thirteenth century were, like him, architects, sculptors, decorators, geometricians, and military and civil engineers.

The Antecedents of the Renaissance

Adapted from E. Gebhart: *La renaissance italienne et la philosophie de l'histoire*, 1887, pp. 6–27.

THE Middle Ages, which were so frequently disturbed by violent explosions of individual passion, made a remarkable effort to discipline the souls of men. From Carolingian times onward, a few exalted notions, a few mighty institutions, the prestige of certain traditions and the mystical ascendency of authority, determined the organization of society and regulated the interests and consciences of men. The idea of Christendom was the first and most general of these notions; next came the theory, which was both religious and political, of the empire and the papacy; then the feudal régime, which gathered the weak around the strong and bound them together by the oath of fidelity and the duty of protection, and thus founded the social hierarchy; then the communes, which established the independence of the cities organized as corporations. In the bosom of the Church monasticism united the purest of the Christians under the sway of a more austere law of renunciation and obedience. Finally scholasticism placed knowledge under the tutelage of theology, and caused thinkers, even the most high-spirited, to join in a common work of dialectics. In all this, the medieval era displayed

474

The Antecedents of the Renaissance

its profound idealism, its feeling of God's rights over
humanity, its pity for the isolated man, lost in his feebleness, and the anguish which it had learned from the
dreams of solitary souls. In these stiff moulds of social
or religious life, and in the restricted area of the school,
supervised by the Church, the reason of the individual
and the will of the individual were imprisoned. In
whatsoever direction he turned, he was confronted by a
master: the pope, the emperor, the count, the bishop, the
text of the holy books, or the charter of his commune.
And he felt his weakness all the more since he saw,
under these visible forms of authority, the power of
God. God was the universal suzerain. The ideal seat
of His authority was Rome, upon the tomb of the apostles, in the holy city toward which Western Europe
gravitated. Thence issued the commands of the two
infallible vicars of God: the pope, whose rights were
derived from Jesus Christ, and the emperor, the de-
scendant of Cæsar. Every case of political disorder
was consequently a criminal attempt against the peace
of Christendom: "Remember God and your Christianity," wrote Charles the Bald to the rebellious barons of
Aquitaine. Later, even when the empire represented
less grandly the notion of Christendom, the primacy of
God still dominated society. The kings, the counts and
the bishops still invariably issued their decrees in the
name of the Holy Trinity. But in the eyes of the Middle Ages the perfect community was monasticism, which
keeps man in perpetual contemplation of things divine.
"Let the monk," wrote Arnulf of Beauvais in the
eleventh century, "be like Melchisedech, without father

or mother or kinsmen. Let him not speak of father or mother upon this earth. Let him regard himself as alone, and God as his father. Amen."

It is manifest that the peculiar trait of the Middle Ages was the absolute submission of the individual conscience to an inflexible discipline. The individual disappeared in the political edifice which the Church and the doctrine of the world-monarchy had erected for the peace of the world and the exaltation of the kingdom of God. He disappeared in the feudal policy, where the suzerain was the vassal of a greater lord and the subject was a serf, bound in his person to the land of his master. The collective work of the crusades was accomplished, most fittingly, in the times when the interests of individual men and of the greatest of kingdoms were effaced before the superior interests of Christendom. The social revolution of the cities was also a collective work in which the individual accepted the yoke, often the very heavy yoke, of the communal law. In France these little republics were quickly absorbed by the monarchy. In Italy they destroyed one another and from their ruins arose the tyranny. However, the tyranny of the fourteenth century was one of the first signs of the Renaissance. Scholasticism lasted longer than the universal empire, feudalism or the communes; and it may well be that, in the countries where it was in the ascendant, it left the strongest impress upon the minds of men. Originally it had been, in a sense, a movement toward liberty, exhibiting the first opposition of the spirit of criticism to authority. But it was doomed to fail from the very start, by the extravagance of its method. It believed that interpretation is the foundation of philosophy, that the art of reasoning is knowledge itself, and that a regular syllogism is the sole instrument of certitude. Logic was to it the whole of philosophy. And, as it had made up its mind as to the proper method, so it determined the problems which it judged best fitted for the play of that method. It declared Aristotle the master *par excellence,* and forced the whole series of the experimental sciences to pass under the yoke of the false Aristotelianism of the Arabs. Scholasticism was thus condemned to the deadly regimen of abstraction. The Church, which was always uneasy about the doctrine of the Trinity, unceasingly brought scholasticism back to the idealism of Scotus Erigena and William of Champeaux. The greatest doctors—Abélard, Peter Lombard, and Albert the Great—were powerless to restore to scholasticism the sense of reality and of life, the art of analysis, and the freedom of experience. At the beginning of the fourteenth century Ockham demonstrated the foolishness of the Gothic wisdom, and by a last evolution recalled the doctrine to the point where Abélard had placed it—to the simple notion that ideas are not beings. Scholasticism had died, but scholastic routine and the superstitious worship of the syllogism, sheltered by the University of Paris as in a fortress, lasted until the time when the France of Rabelais and of Ramus welcomed the Platonic traditions of Florence and the rationalism of Italy.

The concert of three countries—Italy, Germany and North and South France—formed the civilization of the Middle Ages. All three accepted the feudal régime.

Medieval Civilization

Italy created the spiritual primacy of the Holy See, and Germany the supreme suzerainty of the empire. Italy and France founded communes. Scholasticism was peculiarly a product of France. All the nations sent their masters and scholars to Paris for instruction. Generally speaking, one might say that in these three countries every effort to enlarge or break the rigid bonds of the Middle Ages was marked by the most severe crises. Let a doctor, Abélard, attempt to base knowledge upon reason; let a province, Languedoc, attempt to break away from Christianity; let a pope, Gregory VII, wish to free his Church from the grip of the empire; let an emperor, Frederick II, assault the political activity of the Church; let a tribune, Arnold of Brescia, endeavor to reduce the pope, in Rome, to the mere position of first of the bishops;—in each case a terrible explosion immediately resulted. Whosoever dared to touch any part of the sacred edifice of medieval authority was a brigand, an apostate, a heretic, a type of Anti-Christ. Almost without exception it was a church council which launched the thunderbolt that struck down the innovator. Nearly all these martyrs might in their last hour have repeated the dying words of Gregory VII, for they sought justice and died for liberty.

Thus, in the Middle Ages tradition repressed personal initiative. The whole moral life of man was wounded by the rigor of its discipline, and its effects are shown in the works of the mind. France, whose medieval period was prolonged until the sixteenth century, saw, from the fourteenth century on, the decline of her genius; her earlier civilization, so full of promise, suddenly languished, as if attacked by a secret disease. On the other hand, from the twelfth century onward, Italy little by little shook from her shoulders the crushing garment of the past, and already a morning glow of renaissance illuminated her, when the twilight of the old ages seemed to be settling down thicker and thicker upon France.

It is well known that the original creations of the North of France, between the eleventh and the thirteenth centuries—the *chanson de geste,* the romance of chivalry, and Gothic architecture—had a tremendous vogue throughout Christendom. From the French trouvères the whole civilized world got Charlemagne and the heroes of the Round Table. The lyric poetry of the Provençals had almost as great success throughout Latin Europe. The French troubadours carried their lyres into Sicily, Tuscany, Catalonia and Portugal. Italy exhibits, in her earliest lyrical works, the Provençal influence. Toward the year 1200 the first literature of the Italian peninsula appeared, and it was really Franco-Italian. The Lombard troubadour, Sordello, wrote in *langue d'oïl.* As late as the fifteenth century Italy translated, recast and compiled the French romances which Dante read; she mingled the matter of France and of Brittany in popular books which later gave inspiration to Pulci and Ariosto. Such astounding success may be explained by a variety of reasons. The figure of Charlemagne was always the most august memory of history. He had accomplished three things which made him sacred to the Middle Ages: he had established justice, raised the Church, and beaten back the pagans. Moreover, he had reanimated the

Medieval Civilization

image of the Roman Empire, and had caused the earth to tremble beneath the hoofs of his horse. Christendom really begins with Charlemagne. Behind him marched his peers—Roland, Turpin and Renauld,—transfigured by his glory and lending themselves, even better than their master, to the fantasies of poetic imagination. The historical reality of the personages of the Round Table was much more vague; but the medieval era rediscovered in them all its dreams and all its tears; rediscovered, too, mystical love, the worship of woman, the feeling of the vanity of life, the maternal voice of nature and of fairies, the vision of the terrestrial paradise. Arthur, Merlin, Launcelot, Perceval, Tristan, knights, prophets and justiciars, fed with hope the peoples bent beneath the burden of feudalism, crusaders going to the Holy Land, and delicate souls whom the charm of a love stronger than death consoled for the miseries of the age. From the poets of the South of France, Europe asked the same emotions—songs of love and battle cries. France still had leisure, before the hour of her decline, to give to several of her neighbors the old mocking epopee of Reynard —the parody of the feudal world, the revenge of villains on their lords, of mediocre souls on the *prud'hommes,* of laymen on the Church.

French literature in these centuries expressed in a marvelous degree the thoughts, regrets, and wishes of all Western Europe. And this literature, with its adolescent grace, had nothing about it which could disconcert the nations to whom, in the order of civilization, France seemed an elder sister. It was exquisitely frank, and most intelligible to youthful minds. It could, without difficulty, become popular in foreign lands. If it had been more perfect it would have remained more strictly national. Its very naïveté made it European. It would be unjust to consider this trait a defect, for it was characteristic of its age. The consciousness of the old French poets was but a half-opened flower. The gifts of moral maturity, the ripe fruits of reflection, interest in the mysteries of the heart, the art of imagining, with the aid of one's own emotions, the passion of another, and the still more difficult art of creating narrative upon the basis of the emotion of others, and of touching the reader with the *nuances* of the composition, were beyond the powers of the trouvères. Their imagination was the impersonal imagination of the Middle Ages. They gave to their era and to the world the legends of love and of battles which filled the memory of the multitude. Their experience was after all very restricted, and they made only slight efforts to disentangle the history of the confused traditions which came down to them. The Carolingian *chansons de geste* embody the memories of the Merovingian epoch. Consider now the troubadours. Their form is very varied, even skilful, but their inspiration is altogether juvenile— timid sensuality, ingenious rather than touching tenderness, tears quickly dried-up, infantile gusts of anger which are immediately dissipated or which lose their force by being directed simultaneously against all those whom the poet hates—such is the genius of the Provençals. They sing passion as the poets of the medieval West, French or German, sing nature; the latter are interested in flowers, the heath, sunbeams; they have foreground, but no background: they paint in striking colors the object under their eyes, the fugitive sensation which stirs them; there was as yet no one who could see and measure the profound depths of nature and of the human heart.

Could the North of France have produced a Dante or an Ariosto, and the South of France a Guido Cavalcanti or a Petrarch? The Albigensian crusade did not leave the South the leisure to bear all its fruits; a noble civilization, quickly blotted out, carried with it the secret of its future. On the other hand, the literature of the *langue d'oïl* pursued untroubled the course of its destiny. In the twelfth and thirteenth centuries France read and apparently understood the Latin writers, and classical culture slowly aided the growth of literary consciousness. Nevertheless, in the age of St. Louis, when the French nationality already recognized itself clearly, every effort to create a literature of reflection was still premature. Compare with graceful feebleness of the understanding of Joinville with the intellectual health of his Italian contemporary, Marco Polo! Already the old chivalrous vein was exhausted; compilers were recasting, abridging, translating into prose or lengthening beyond all reason the ancient works. Don Quixote's library had begun. Powerless to rejuvenate the literary tradition, the writers were seeking a new one. They show to what an extent three centuries of scholasticism had worn out the elasticity of the French mind. And, just as men could no longer reason about real things, so they were no longer capable of creating living beings. Scholasticism had arrested science and had dried up the springs of poesy. The era of abstractions and versified chimeras had come. Charle-

magne, Roland and Merlin were now pure accidents,
literary quiddities which men rejected; henceforth uni-
versals alone had the right to move and speak—one cannot say to act: vices and virtues, the species and the
genera which already peopled the first part of the *Roman
de la Rose,* are joined in the second part, by two high
quintessences, *Reason* and *Nature,* who find it no effort
to sermonize to the length of three thousand verses. A
subtle preaching invaded the whole poetic field. Theological allegory glided into the romance of Reynard and
extinguished its gaiety. Symbolism envelops this doc-
toral literature as with a fog; only the wholly middle-class
and mocking forms of literature—the fabliau, the mystery, the tale and the farce—maintained themselves with
joy. But what a gulf between all this and the Song of
Roland!

Gothic architecture, the supreme French art, perished
from the same disease which slew poetry. During a long
period it had remained true to sedate Romanic traditions
—solid pillars, grand lines, and proportions which tran-
quilize the eye. It respected the laws of matter. But
now it passionately carried lightness to the point of folly.
It exaggerated heights and voids, rarefied the stone, reduced the walls to the utmost degree of thinness, and
played with pillars and vaults as if these masses were only
geometrical figures; weight and equilibrium were laws
it no longer regarded. The object now was to raise to
the skies the chiseled dream of spires and towers; detail,
refined beyond measure, and multiplied in pointed tri-
angles, in order to support the aerial whole, steadily increased, and absorbed not only the horizontal lines but all

the great lines. The cathedrals, maintained erect against all probability, supported by thousands of buttresses, veritable sophisms in stone, remind one of the syllogisms of the school, where reasoning, deprived of reason in the premises, totters and would give way were it not sustained by the adjacent sophism. Architecture, tortured and diseased, killed the other arts; the severe statue of the twelfth century would in this age have found no place in the edifice in which to stand upright; the delicate statuette of the thirteenth century was reduced to the rôle of embroidery; sculpture degenerated into imagery; the Madonna and the Child lost all nobility; the Child became " only a bourgeois child whom they were amusing "; impudent gargoyles, fantastic flowers, and grotesque imps more and more changed the mystic form of the churches; and painting upon glass was corrupted by the pursuit of detail and the search for effect.

The historical experience of the Middle Ages was, then, completed for France. Her civilization was unable to prolong or rejuvenate its originality. The earliest civilization of the West had produced its last results in France. Italy, which had early rebelled against this civilization, had a different experience. Her Middle Ages bore the most fruitful germs of her Renaissance.

In the concert of Christendom Italy always played a unique part. Invaded successively by Goths, Lombards, Arabs, and Normans, and ruled by Byzantines, Franks, Hohenstaufens and Angevins, she received from her masters only that which pleased her, and arranged her civilization, her public life and her religion in accord with her own likings. From the history of Rome she had

The Antecedents of the Renaissance

chosen to preserve only traditions of liberty, maintained by the continued existence of her corporations of artisans, and an ideal image that served as a norm by which to judge the régime of the double universal monarchy and feudalism. This triple yoke she bore more lightly than any other people because she had early learned the art of playing off the emperor against the pope, and thus causing them to weaken each other. She knew how to prevent, through the resistance of the Church, the absolute primacy of the empire; through the support she lent the emperors, and through the obstinate pretensions of the commune of Rome, she unceasingly checked the progress of the temporal primacy of the Church; and very cleverly she employed first the pope and then the emperor to enfeeble the counts and protect the municipal republics. When she had emancipated herself from the despotism of the feudal lords, it was found that she had at the same time weakened both the Holy See and the empire, by destroying the hierarchy which supported them; and thus her hands were freer to deal with either of them. Henceforth they had to deal with an Italy of communes which, whether Guelf or Ghibelline, could, through her military leagues, exhibit the views of a truly national policy. Italy had, in truth, a more tragic history than any other people, because the crux of all the problems which agitated Christendom was at Rome, and yet, at bottom, this history was perfectly self-conscious. With the exception of the Two Sicilies, which were always falling under some foreign dominion, Italy sought a new social order, founded on the autonomy of cities, and then on that of provinces—a régime in which the suzerainty of emperor and pope had become fictitious, in which the Holy See, until the fifteenth century, had seen itself continually dispossessed of its temporal royalty by the commune of Rome, but in which the Roman Church, as the master-creation of Italian genius, always preserved its prestige. Italy harassed the popes; during three centuries she saw them flee, proscribed and outraged, along her highways, and felt no remorse; but she never consented to rally to the support of the anti-popes—generally Germans—whom the emperors gave her. In the days of the Avignonese papacy she resisted the seductions of a schism; in the days of the Great Schism she knew how to reserve apostolic legitimacy for her own pontiffs.

It was indeed natural that the greatest efforts of the Italians were directed to maintaining their religious independence. It would have profited them nothing to escape the control of the empire and of feudalism if they had submitted to the domination of the Holy See. A sort of tacit concordat was established between the Church and Italy in which reciprocal leniency was the principal element. The Church permitted the Italians to pass without austerity or sadness through this vale of tears. The popes granted the Italians ecclesiastical liberties which they had refused to foreigners; the Church at Milan, whose archbishop was a sort of sovereign pontiff, was conceded liturgical autonomy; Venice, a patriarchate almost independent of Rome; Sicily and the Neapolitan South were permitted an astonishing likeness to the Greek communion, and the use of the Greek language in worship. The best Christians of Italy, the monks and the anchorites, unceasingly raised their voices against the abuses of the Roman pontificate, corrupted by secular power. Peter Damiani, the friend of Gregory VII, deplored that the Church had the temporal sword in her hands. Dante's furious invectives against Rome are well-known, as is the insolence shown by the monk Jacopone toward Boniface VIII. But in all this, political passion rather than religious emotion is to be seen.

Italian Christianity is a singular creation. It has in it much of the primitive faith. Narrow dogma, rigid morality, strict practices, and the hierarchy, trouble its independence but little. Individual inspiration and direct communion of the faithful with God, which form the basis of the Franciscan religion, are perhaps the most essential traditions of the Italian spirit. One thought frequently appears in their first writers, as, for example, in Dante, that true religion is a matter of the heart. Dante puts King Manfred in purgatory, though the Church had cursed him and Clement IV had his body torn from its sepulcher and thrown on the banks of the Garigliano. " No," exclaims the son of Frederick II in Dante's verse, " their curse cannot damn us." *Per las maledizion si non si perde.*

Italy was not far from thinking that all religions lead to the kingdom of God. The proximity of the most diverse faiths—of Islam and the Greek Church—had saved her from religious egotism, and toleration led her to entertain a liberal notion of orthodoxy. The story of the three rings was familiar long before Boccaccio. This explains why the Italians, very free within the precincts of their Church, never thought seriously of leaving it. They have never had a national heresy: the Lombard *pataria,* oriental Catharism, and the affiliation with the Waldensian sect, between the eleventh and the thirteenth centuries, were only brief experiments at revolt and were more social than religious. The doctrine which sprang up from the predictions of Joachim de Flore, appeared for a short time more threatening; it disturbed the Franciscan world with the hope of a third revelation—the eternal Gospel of the Holy Spirit. The Holy See treated this outburst of Italian mysticism with tenderness; it authorized Joachim's liturgy and worship in the dioceses of Calabria; it condemned John of Parma, the general of the Franciscans, then offered him the cardinal's hat, and finally canonized him; it allowed the little sects of *Fraticelli* and *Spirituals,* which perpetuated Joachimism, to multiply, and it canonized in his turn Jacopone, the most fiery of all these sectaries. It was well understood between the Church and Italy, that, according to the words borrowed by Joachim from St. Paul, " Where the spirit of the Lord is, there is liberty." A free conscience in a free city was the law of Italian civilization in the great medieval centuries.

In the domain of thought the Italian of the Middle Ages was no less master of himself. He thought freely and very sanely. It is a most significant fact that scholasticism was never firmly rooted in the peninsula. Italy gave to the school of Paris several of its greatest doctors —Peter Lombard, St. Thomas, St. Bonaventura, Gilles de Rome and James of Viterbo; but those of them who returned to Italy, dazzled rather than won over their compatriots. St. Thomas explained his doctrines before Urban IV, " by a singular and novel method," wrote a contemporary. Scholasticism was accepted docilely in Italy only by the theologians and the monks. In the fourteenth century, Petrarch, and Cino da Rinuccini, in his *Paradis des Alberti,* ridiculed the *trivium* and the *quadrivium.* The first moralists, Brunetto Latini and Dante, might preserve in their works, as they did, the divisions and the logical appearance of scholasticism; in reality they proceeded by experience in their descriptions of nature and of the human heart. The national science of Italy, at Bologna, Rome and Padua, was not dialectics, but the written law of Rome, that is, reason applied to the things of actual life; it is also the Aristotelianism transmitted by the Arabs, but absolutely freed from theology, that is, Averroism, with which the revival of the natural sciences and of medicine was connected. This great school, whose center was Padua, mightily disturbed the Church. The religious painters, for example Benozzo Gozzoli, willingly depict Averroës prone upon the ground, as Anti-Christ, beneath the feet of St. Thomas. The Averroists attempted in medieval Italy, a reconnaissance of the purely rational order which Descartes will resume for France. Their more or less declared adherents went very quickly to the extreme limit of incredulity: they denied the immortality of the soul and the soul itself. When the common people, *gente volgare,* saw Guido Cavalcanti pass musingly through the streets of Florence, they asserted that he was thinking up reasons for disbelieving in God. Even in the beginning of the twelfth century, as Villani reports, Florence had epicureans who scoffed at God and the saints, and lived according to the flesh. As all these free spirits belonged to the Ghibelline

party, it is perhaps well to accept only with reservations
the charges made against them by Guelfs and monks.
One cannot, with certainty, measure the extent of their
scepticism, but it is necessary to mark well their possession of this trait of the modern man. They had, in their
unbelief, that pride natural to consciences which scorn the
faith or the illusions of their age. Dante condemns them,
as heretics, but one feels that he admires them, for they
are of his race. Farinata degli Uberti, the most haughty
of all, placed upright in his burning sepulcher, with disdainful forehead, seems, Dante says, to hold hell in the
greatest scorn. But have we not already lost sight of the
Middle Ages in the West? While France halts in the
work of civilization, Italy, a more backward worker, is
quite ready to devise a new civilization. She holds in her
hands the instrument of all progress—the art of thinking
clearly; she knows how to oppose to the authority of
tradition, the rational worth, and the energy of the individual. She passes almost imperceptibly from the
Middle Ages to the Renaissance.

St. Louis

Adapted from C. V. Langlois, in Lavisse: *Histoire de France,*
Vol. III, Part II, 1901, pp. 18–40.

NOTHING is known about the youth of Louis IX
except what the king later chose to relate to his
friends. His mother, Blanche of Castile, told him many
times that she would rather see him dead than have him
commit a mortal sin. Her words made a vivid impression upon him. He also remembered with pleasure that,
when he went to play in the woods or along the river
bank, he was always accompanied by his tutor, who
taught him his letters and from time to time thrashed
him. He was brought up " like a nobleman," as was fitting for a prince, but very piously, after the Spanish
fashion. Every day he heard mass, vespers, and the
canonical hours. He was a very good and sweet-tem-
pered child. He shunned noisy games and did not care
for playthings. He had no intimate companions; he
did not sing the popular songs, and he made one of his
squires who did sing them learn instead to sing the an-
thems of Notre Dame and of the *Ave, maris stella,*
" although it was very difficult." From his childhood
he was charitable: Stephen of Bourbon reports that
" according to the popular tradition, one morning, while
he was still very young, a number of poor people were

Medieval Civilization

assembled in the court before his lodging awaiting alms. Taking advantage of the hour when everyone was asleep, he left his room, accompanied only by a servant, carrying a large number of pennies, and he distributed these to the poor. He was returning when a monk, who had perceived him from the corner of a window, said: 'Sire King, I have seen your misdeeds.' 'Very dear brother,' replied Louis, 'the poor are in my service. They bring upon the kingdom the benediction of peace. I have not paid them all that I owe them.'"

Old portraits of Louis IX are numerous enough, but indefinite and contradictory. We know, however, that from his grandmother, Queen Isabella, he had inherited the renowned beauty of the princes of the house of Hainault, which was perpetuated, through Philip the Rash and Philip the Fair, in the last Capetians of the direct line. "The king," says the Franciscan, Salimbene, who saw him in 1248, "was tall and graceful, *subtilis et gracilis, convenienter et longus,* with an angelic air and a very gracious countenance." Joinville says, in his account of the battle of Mansourah: "Never have I seen such a beautiful armed man, for he towered above his knights by a whole head. He wore a gilded helmet and held a German sword in his hand." When he was young, he must have had thick blond locks. Later, and early in life, he was bald and a little bent. His body, which he subjected to excessive mortifications, was more shapely than strong. All who saw him agree in saying that his appearance was frank, affable, and thoughtful. He had the "eyes of a dove." His costume was simple. His apologists, the monks, exaggerate when they say that after his twentieth year he entirely renounced the magnificent costumes to which Queen Blanche had accustomed him during his infancy, because of his rank. But, after his return from the crusade of 1248, a notable reform was seen in his manner of dress, as well as in the whole conduct of his life. He gave up costly furs, the vair, and the gris. After that, his robes were trimmed with lamb, rabbit, or squirrel; he renounced striking colors: in winter, he wore garments of dark wool, and in summer, of brown or black silk. The equipment of his horse was white, unadorned; his spurs and stirrups were of iron, ungilded. We shall always think of him just as Joinville saw him one summer's day in his garden at Paris, " clad in a coat of camelot, a surcoat of linsey-woolsey without sleeves, a mantle of black sendal about his neck, very well combed and without coif, and a hat with a white peacock's feather on his head." This almost clerical costume undoubtedly helped as much as the reputation of the holiness of his person, to inspire the ill-natured description attributed to the count of Gueldre's messenger: " This miserable devotee, this hypocritical king, with a wry neck and a cowl on his shoulders."

The envoy of Gueldre was not the only one who accused Louis IX in his lifetime of hypocrisy. Among his subjects, who were, in general, little devout, very many, lords and common people, smiled or were indignant at the extreme piety of the king. They called him " brother Louis," *frater Ludovicus.* The same idea is expressed by the well-known anecdote of the woman named Sarete de Faillouel, who saw the king one day just as he was

Medieval Civilization

leaving his apartments, and addressed him in these terms: " Fie! Fie! Are you the man to be king of France? It would be better that another should be king in your place, for you are only king of the Minorites and of the Dominicans, of the priests and of the clergy. It's an outrage that you should be king of France. It's a great marvel that they don't put you out." Were these popular sarcasms and the more discreet criticism of well-educated persons justifiable? Is it true that St. Louis was better adapted for the cloister than for the world, as has been said, both in his own day and ours?

The clerks who were the biographers of St. Louis or the witnesses who testified during the process of his canonization, certainly tell remarkable stories about the devotion of this prince. The biographers, Geoffrey of Beaulieu and William of Chartres, give the schedule of the hours which Louis passed daily in prayer. At midnight he dressed, in order to take part in the matins in his chapel; he went back to bed, half-dressed, and, for fear lest he might prolong his sleep too much, he told his attendants to wake him for prime when the candle had burned a certain distance; after prime, each morning he heard at least two masses: a low mass for the dead, and the mass of the day, chanted; then, during the rest of the day, the offices of tierce, sext, and none, vespers and compline; in the evening, after fifty genuflections and as many *Ave Marias,* he went to bed, without drinking, although it was then customary before going to bed. Even when traveling, he did not interrupt the regularity of these observances. " When he was riding on horseback, at the hour prescribed by the Church,

tierce, sext, and none were chanted by his chaplains, on
horseback about him, and he himself with one of the
company said them in a low tone, as if he were in his
chapel." Often, kneeling, without cushions, on the pavement of a church with his elbows upon a bench, he became absorbed in such long meditations—such extremely
long ones—that his servants, who were waiting at the
door, grew impatient. Then, he asked God with so much
fervor for the " gift of tears " that he sometimes rose all
confused, seeing only obscurely, and saying, " Where
am I." On special festivals he had the divine service
celebrated with so much solemnity and slowness that, as
the Confessor of Queen Marguerite naïvely avowed,
everyone was tired.

The chapter on his abstinences and mortifications, in
the biographies written by the clerks, is no less edifying
than the chapter on his prayers. Louis IX, from a feeling of penitence, deprived himself of things which he
loved: early vegetables, large fishes, particularly the
pike. He detested beer, as was clearly shown by the
face which he made when he drank it; nevertheless he
drank it, during the whole of Lent, precisely because he
wished " to bridle his appetite for wine." Very few
people, moreover, put as much water in their wine as he
did, and he put water even in the sauces, when they were
good, so as to make them insipid. Of course, he fasted
frequently and severely. Shortly before his death, one
Saturday, he refused to take the mulled egg recommended by the doctors, because his confessor was not
present to grant him permission. He never laughed on
Fridays, or, if he began to be cheerful, forgetting what

day it was, he stopped short as soon as he remembered. On that day, in memory of the crown of thorns, he did not wear any hat, and he forbade his children to wear garlands of roses, as was the custom of the time. He who, in the words of Geoffrey of Beaulieu, committed no mortal sin, confessed every Friday, and had the discipline administered to him by his confessors with five little chains of iron; he was heard to say smilingly that some of these ecclesiastics did not have the " dead hand." In vain did brother Geoffrey attempt to show him that the use of haircloth was not fitting to his position; he wore it and he made presents of similar instruments of penitence to his friends, his kinsmen, and his daughter, the queen of Navarre.

What is to be said of his charity? " His liberality toward the unfortunate," a contemporary declares, " passed all bounds." Every day, wherever the king was, more than a hundred poor received their pittance. His almsgiving, abundant and continual, cost him dear, for it sometimes extended to entire regions and often took the form of lasting foundations. " One year, when famine desolated Normandy, the hogsheads bound with iron that the wagons ordinarily brought to Paris filled with the receipts of the treasury, were seen making the journey in the opposite direction." The hospital foundations of Louis IX, at Paris and in the neighborhood, are celebrated. Among them were the *Filles-Dieu,* for the prostitutes, the *Quinze-Vingts,* for the blind, the hospitals of Pontoise, of Vernon, of Compiègne, etc., for the sick. " As a writer who has made his book," says Joinville, " illuminates it with gold and azure, the king

496

illuminated his kingdom . . . with the great quantity of *maisons-Dieu* that he built there." But, if we must believe some of his clerical associates, this man, who was naturally charitable, was not contented with doing well. In an ascetic spirit of humility, as if eager for mortification, he preferred, among good works, the most repugnant, not because they were the most useful, but because they were repugnant. Thus, when he invited beggars to his royal table—which happened very often —he had the dirtiest seated by him; he served them, and cut their meat and bread. That is not all: he ate the remnants they left, out of the plates they had held with their unclean hands, *cum manibus ulcerosis et immundis.* Even that is not all: he washed their "scabby and disgusting" feet, and, after drying them, he kissed them. The hagiographers, full of their subject, record details which are sickening. More brutal and more disgusting still are their stories about lepers. Louis IX assisted the lepers,—frightful objects—with his own hands every time he met them. "Now there was at the abbey of Royaumont a brother named Leger, who had been isolated because he was so consumed with leprosy that his nose was eaten up, his eyes gone, and his lips cracked open; running with pus, he was abominable. This brother Leger became the favorite of the king, who begged the abbot to go and see Leger with him. The abbot, as he declared later, was terrified enough in doing so. Louis kneeled before the leper, and fed him." Louis also entered the hospitals, in spite of the "corruption of the air" and the odor of infection which inconvenienced his attendants, and there he felt it necessary, from time to time, to perform the most disgusting offices. At Sidon, in Palestine, he aided in burying the putrified remains of the Christians.

When we read the list of good works, abstinences, and observances attributed to Louis IX, even admitting that the witnesses at the process of canonization embellished the truth (and they surely embellished it involuntarily in representing certain exceptional acts of the saint as customary), we can understand well enough the invectives of Sarete.

Louis IX understood perfectly that the excess of his devotions and certain forms of his charity would tend to displease his people: Sarete taught him nothing. Consequently, as he was devoted to his task as king, he did not surrender himself unreservedly to the exercises of humility. One day, when he manifested a desire to wash the feet of the monks, the abbot of Royaumont, who was a prudent man, dissuaded him, saying, " People would talk about it." " And what would they say? " replied the king. But he knew well what they would say, and he refrained from doing it. During his frequent sojourns at the abbey of Royaumont, he often visited the infirmary, and, with the doctors, inspected the sick; but, " when he did these things, he desired that few people should be present, and only those who were his trusted companions." The poor whose feet he washed every Saturday were blind. He had them gathered with great care and " brought very privately to his closet," and " it was thought that he chose the blind more willingly in order that they should not recognize him and tell about it outside." Louis IX attempted, then, to conceal, from modesty, and from a desire not to lessen the royal dignity, such of his good works as he judged—not without reason—might shock the public. His subjects certainly did not have any suspicion about most of his macerations, which were revealed after his death only by his most intimate confidants.

Nevertheless, he did not have any fear of the world. " There are some noblemen," he said to the Sire de Joinville, " who are ashamed to do right, by going to church and hearing the service of God. They are afraid that people will say: they are hypocrites." For his own part, he bore it cheerfully when his conduct was blamed. When the nobles murmured at seeing him pass so much time at the religious services, he said that, if he lost twice as much time playing dice or hunting, no one would find fault. To those who reproached him with spending too much in charity to the poor, he replied: " Be silent. God has given me everything that I have. That which I spend thus is best spent." Or else: " I prefer that my excessive expenditures should be in alms for the love of God rather than in luxury or in the vainglory of this world." Robert de Sorbon recounts that a certain prince dressed modestly and that it displeased his wife. " Madam," he said to her, " you wish me to wear costly garments. I agree; but, since the conjugal law is that the husband must seek to please his wife and *vice versa,* you are going to give me pleasure by laying aside your beautiful ornaments. You shall conform to my habit, and I to yours." When Louis issued his ordinance against blasphemers, there were protests; but he declared that he was better pleased with the curses thus brought upon him than with the benedictions which certain works of public utility won for him at the same time. To Sarete he replied, without getting angry: "You tell the truth, assuredly. I am not worthy to be king, and, if it had pleased our Saviour, another would have been in my place, who would have known better how to govern the kingdom."

Prudence without false shame, good humor, and smiling irony are some of the traits which have nothing in common with the exalted mysticism that the pious folly of his attendants saw exclusively in Louis IX. In fact, the holiness of this excellent man was not at all monastic, and, although posterity has often been deceived concerning it, just as the crowd was in his own day, never was any saint less ecclesiastical (*papelard*) and more laic than he. This king, who did not love beautiful garments for his personal use, did not forbid others to wear them: "You ought," he said to his son Philip and his son-in-law Thibaut, "to dress well and neatly, because your wives will love you better, and because people will think more of you, for, as the wise man said, one ought to wear such a costume and arms that the best men of this age shall not say that he is overdoing it nor the young people that he is deficient." This king, who was so generous to the poor and to the churches, thought that Thibaut, his son-in-law, who was in debt, was spending too much for the convent of the Dominicans that he was building at Provins; he did not like to have people "give alms with another's money." This king, who was so passionately devoted to pious exercises, sometimes preferred chatting to edifying reading: "When we were together in private," Joinville recounts, "he sat down on the foot of his bed, and, when the Dominicans and the Cordeliers, who were there, mentioned the books which he loved to hear, he said: 'You shall not read to me at all, for reading, after a meal, is not as pleasant as *quolibet*, that is, when each one says what comes into his head.'" This king, although his manners were simple, was careful about the dignity of his court: "In spite of the great sums that the king spent in almsgiving, he expended as much each day on his household. He was magnificent and liberal in his dealings with the *parlements* and with the assemblies of barons and knights. He had his court served bounteously and luxuriously—more so than had been the case for a long time in the court of his predecessors." Joinville, who was a connoisseur in such matters, is not the only one who attests this. Geoffrey of Beaulieu, also, states that the household establishment of Louis IX was more brilliant than that of the former kings. Finally, this pretended *papelard* made fun quietly of the devout, and, to tease Master Robert de Sorbon, he pretended, when he was gay, to prefer the virtue of the knights (of the gentlemen), *prud'homie,* to the virtue of the clerks. "Seneschal," he said to Joinville, "tell me the reasons why a *prud'homme* is better than a *béguine."* Then Master Robert and Joinville disputed, and, when the quarrel had lasted long enough, the king gave his decision in these terms: "Master Robert, I would prefer to have the renown of a *prud'homme,* and to be so truly, and that all the rest should remain for you; for *prud'homie* is such a great thing and such a good thing that even in naming it it fills the mouth."

The works of charity and penitence of Louis IX would not be enough to distinguish him from a host of other medieval princes who were exemplary Christians; not even from his contemporary, King Henry III of England, who also waited on lepers, who frequented churches even more assiduously than his brother-in-law of France, and yet was a fool. That which renders Louis IX preëminent is his bright, refined, pure nature as a moralist and as an honorable man.

The "saintly king" can be known truly by hearing him speak. He spoke well, easily, and wittily. Joinville and the witnesses at the inquest concerning his canonization fortunately have preserved many of his sayings. Why has no one ever thought of collecting these and uniting them to the *Instructions* that the saint dictated, toward the end of his life, for his son Philip and for his daughter Isabel? These sayings of St. Louis, compared with the *Thoughts* of Marcus Aurelius, would illustrate the differences which separate these two great and excellent men, who have so often been compared. It would be Louis IX painted, so to speak, by himself, with his simple virtues, in no way superhuman, and also with his faults, his weaknesses, and his mistakes.

The most marked trait in the character of Louis IX was the intensity of his religious and moral preoccupations. Throughout his life, he conscientiously sought truth and justice, with the fixed idea of making his beliefs and acts conform to them.

His religious beliefs were, up to a certain point, the

result of thought. Everyone about him noticed that in the matter of spiritual exercises he preferred sermons, the reading of the sacred texts, and theological discussions to the observance of rites. "The king," wrote the Confessor of Queen Marguerite, "heard the word of God very gladly and very often; when he took a ride, if an abbey was near the road, he turned aside and had a sermon preached there, while he himself sat upon the straw and the monks in their stalls." On his return from the Holy Land, while he was at Hyères in Provence, a Cordelier named Hugh, who was a popular orator, happened to pass. The king asked him for a sermon, but this brother Hugh was no courtier; he began rudely in these words: "My lords, I see too many monks in the court of the king and in his company who ought not to be there—first of all myself." He spoke, however, so well that Joinville advised his master to keep this bold adviser near him. "But the king said to me that he had already asked him and that brother Hugh was unwilling. Then the king took me by the hand and said, 'Let us go and ask him again.'"

Not only did he like sermons and desire that others should like them, but he was a connoisseur and distinguished the good from the bad. For a layman, Louis IX was very well versed in the Scriptures and in the early Christian literature. "Each day after compline he went to his room; a candle, three feet or thereabouts, was lighted, and, as long as it burned, he read the Bible or some other holy book." While he was in the Orient, he was struck with the richness of the Saracen libraries, and accordingly gathered one at Paris in the treasury

of his chapel and opened it freely to his friends. There
were gathered together, above all, " the original works
of Augustine, Ambrose, Jerome, and Gregory, and of
other orthodox doctors." For he read by preference
" the authentic books of the saints rather than those of
the masters of our own time." His sacred learning,
thus drawn from the sources, sometimes enabled him to
confound arrogant scholastic erudition: " A learned
clerk," Robert de Sorbon relates, " often preached before
the king of France. He had just said the following:
· All the apostles, at the moment of the passion, abandoned Christ, and faith was extinguished in their hearts;
the Virgin Mary alone preserved it; in memory of this,
in the holy week, at the matins all the lights are extinguished except one, which is kept for lighting the others
at Easter.' An ecclesiastic of high rank then rose to
question the orator and to lead him to affirm only what
was written: the apostles, in his opinion, had abandoned
Jesus Christ with their bodies and not with their hearts.
The clerk was at the point of being compelled to retract
publicly, when the king, rising in his turn, intervened.
' The proposition is not false,' he said, ' it is in the
Fathers. Bring me the book of St. Augustine.' He
was obeyed, and the king showed a passage in the commentary upon the gospel of St. John, where, in fact,
the illustrious doctor expresses himself thus: *Fugerunt,
relicto eo corde et corpore. . . .*" Such was his appetite
for apologetics that, in company with grave and orthodox persons, Louis IX discussed the faith even at table.
He often invited to share his repast some " religious or
even seculars, with whom he could speak of God, and

this is the reason why he did not often dine with his barons."

It is certain that Louis IX was sometimes tormented by the antinomies which exist between reason and faith. According to the testimony of Joinville, he strove with all his might " to have his barons believe very firmly " and to put them on their guard against these temptations of the enemy (he avoided naming the devil) which sometimes caused doubt. " The devil is so subtle! It is necessary to say to him: ' Avaunt; you shall not tempt me not to believe firmly all the articles of the faith; you can cut me in pieces: I wish to live and die in this condition.' " Nevertheless, why is it necessary to believe? On this point the king one day asked Joinville what his father's name was. The seneschal replied, " Simon." " And how do you know it? " " I told him that I believed it to be certain because my mother had told me. Then he said to me: ' Then you ought to believe firmly all the articles of the faith that the apostles bear witness to, as you hear it chanted on Sunday in the creed.' " It is evident that the good king's critical ability was not very strong. Nevertheless it was awakened. Did he not say repeatedly that there is more merit in believing when doubt has arisen than in believing peaceably, like a brute, without combat? He had himself sustained the combat; he had issued from it victorious; and, although sure of the triumph, he did not laugh at new proofs. He loved to hear those who justified the faith, not those who attacked it.

He was not partial to the discussions of Christians with Jewish rabbis, which the doctors of the thirteenth century enjoyed so much. Above all, he disliked such discussions for laymen, who risked being defeated by the dialecticians of the synagogue. " He told me," says Joinville, " of a great dispute between clerks and Jews at the monastery of Cluny. A knight, who was a guest at the monastery, rose and asked the greatest Jewish master if he believed that the Virgin Mary was mother of God. The Jew replied that he did not believe it at all. ' Then you are a fool,' answered the knight, ' to have come into her house without believing in the Holy Virgin and without loving her.' And he knocked down the Jew with a blow on the head from his stick. Thus ended the dispute. . . . ' And I tell you,' added the king, ' that no one, if he is not a very good clerk, ought to dispute with these people ; the layman, when he hears the Christian law calumniated, should defend it with his sword, with which he ought to give as many blows in the belly as he can get in.' "

Louis IX felt infinitely more at his ease in the domain of morals than in that of the historical and rational foundations of dogma. From his early youth he had had a taste for moralizing. When he was afflicted with a malignant fever at Pontoise, while still young, and believed that he was going to die, he " called his associates and admonished them to serve God." " When he was in his room with his suite," reports the Confessor of Queen Marguerite, " he said holy and discreet words and told beautiful stories for the edification of those who were conversing with him." " Before going to bed," says Joinville, " he summoned his children, and reminded them of the deeds of good kings and good emperors, and told them to follow these examples, and he told them also the deeds of bad, wealthy men who, by their luxury, rapine, and avarice, had lost their kingdoms." During the expedition to Egypt and Syria, he had made of Joinville one of his catechumens. Nevertheless, he did not speak to him willingly concerning matters of the faith, for the " subtle sense," that is, the good common-sense of the seneschal of Champagne frightened him. But with a greater abundance he showered on him advice in practical morals. The seneschal was certainly not a bad man, but he had his faults, and rather grave ones. He drank his wine undiluted, and "always the best to be had." Alive to the joys of life, he cared for money which procures them, and, although perfectly brave, he exposed his person only when circumstances were propitious. Proud of his rank, he had some difficulty in thinking of villains as his brethren in Christ. Finally, a faithful but lukewarm Christian, he said unhesitatingly that " he would prefer to have committed thirty mortal sins rather than to be a leper." The king, who had taken a liking to him because of his amiable and frank character, exhorted him to be temperate, polite, patient, to shudder at sin, and to profit by the warnings of God. The triteness of these maxims was atoned for by the acuteness of their expression. If he said that one must not take the goods of others, even to give them to God, the king added: " for rendering them is so painful that, even in saying the word, render excoriates the throat, because of the r's in it, which signify the rakes of the devil, who always draws backward toward himself those who wish to render property wrongly acquired." William of Chartres has also recorded a rather amusing anecdote. It was during the sitting of a *parlement*. A lady, formerly beautiful, but of ripe age, very carefully dressed, entered the king's chamber, in the hope, as they thought, of attracting his attention. " But the king, preoccupied," as William of Chartres said, " with the salvation of this lady, called for his confessor and said to him very quietly: ' Sit there and hear what I am going to say to this woman, who wishes to speak to me in private.' When the three were alone, Louis IX went on: ' Madam, I should like to have you think of your salvation. Formerly you were beautiful, but that which is past is past. *Sicut flos qui statim emarcuit, et non durat.* You will not resuscitate that beauty of yours; exert therefore all your efforts to acquire the imperishable beauty, not of the body, but of the soul.' "

This severe and playful moralist had more simple, natural goodness than moralists ordinarily have. The Confessor of Queen Marguerite says that his heart was " transpierced with pity for the wretched " and that he had a predilection for the weak. We read in his *Instructions* to his son: " If a poor man contends against a wealthy, support the poor rather than the wealthy until the truth has been made known." But, still better than by these general statements, the goodness of the man truly good, good and gay, is often shown by a common act, by a gesture which leaves no doubt. His contemporaries have drawn from life incontrovertible sketches of some typical scenes. As always, Joinville has left the prettiest anecdotes, those of Corbeil and Acre.

At Corbeil, in Pentecost, the seneschal and Robert de

Sorbon had fallen into a dispute in the presence of Louis IX. Master Robert, accusing the seneschal of being too well-dressed, had drawn upon himself this retort: "Master Robert, begging your pardon, I am not to blame if I dress in vair, for this costume was left to me by my father and mother, but you are to blame, for you are the son of peasants and you have abandoned the costume of your father and are dressed in richer *camelin* than the king is." "And then," adds Joinville, "I took the skirt of his coat and of the king's coat, and said to him, 'See if that is not true'; and then the king strove to defend Master Robert with all his might." But the good king, seeing the sadness of the seneschal, was not slow to ask him to sit down so near him, "that my coat touched his," and admitted, to console him, that he had been wrong in defending poor Master Robert: "But I saw that he was so confused that he had great need of my aid."

At St. Jean d'Acre, in a council held to discuss the question whether they should return to France or remain in the Holy Land, Joinville, almost alone, spoke against returning. "When the session ended, the assault on me began from all sides: 'The king is foolish, Sire de Joinville, if he listens to you against the council of the whole kingdom of France.' When the tables were set, the king made me sit beside him to eat, as he always did if his brothers were not there, but he did not speak to me while the meal lasted, which was contrary to his custom. And I truly thought that he was angry with me because I had advised him to spend his money freely. While he heard grace, I went to a barred window, which was in a distant corner near the king's bed, and I rested my arms upon the bars of the window and thought that, if the king returned to France, I would go to the prince of Antioch, my kinsman, until our companions who were prisoners in Egypt had been delivered; and, while I was there, the king came to lean upon my shoulders and placed his two hands upon my head. I supposed that it was my lord Philip of Nemours and said: 'Let me alone, my lord Philip.' But, by chance turning my head, the king's hands glided over my face and I recognized the emerald which he had on his finger. And he said to me: 'Keep quiet, for I wish to ask you how you, although a young man, were so bold as to dare to advise my remaining here, in opposition to all the nobles and wise men of France, who advised me to return.' 'Do you say,' he asked, 'that I would be wrong if I went away?' 'Yes, indeed, sire,' I replied; and he said to me, 'If I remain, will you remain?' And when I said yes: 'Now be at ease, for I am much pleased with your advice; but do not tell anyone this week.'"

So much goodness, so much juvenile and charming delicacy is often united to feebleness. According to Geoffrey of Beaulieu, certain people were afraid, in fact, that such a good man would be a weak man; but these fears were not well-founded. Not only was St. Louis an accomplished knight in war, but, in addition, he always gave proof of unusual energy in the conduct of his private and public life.

Joinville saw him and depicts him during the campaign in Egypt and the stay in Syria, at first as rash as a young man and then heroic in adversity. Before Damietta, "when the king heard that the standard of St.

St. Louis

Denis was down, he ran across the bridge of his vessel with great strides, and, in spite of the legate, in order to save the standard, he leaped into the sea when the water came to his armpits, and with his shield around his neck, his helmet upon his head, his sword in his hand, he went to his men who were on the shore. When he saw the Saracens, he asked who they were and was told that they were Saracens. Then, with his sword under his arm and his shield in front of him, he would have rushed upon this mob, if the *prud'hommes* who accompanied him had not prevented it." During the lamentable retreat which followed the battle of Mansourah, his conduct was exemplary, although he was suffering from the epidemic which was ravaging the army. "Sire," his brother, Charles of Anjou, said to him, "you are wrong in not following the advice which your friends gave and in refusing to go on shipboard, for, while you are on land, the army's march is dangerously retarded." "Count of Anjou, Count of Anjou," he replied, "if I am a burden to you, get rid of me; but I will never abandon my people." When a prisoner of the sultan and then of the emirs, he surprised them by his coolness. Facing the bloody sword of Faress-eddin-Oct-aï, he did not experience the indescribable fright of Joinville, when he saw the huge Danish axes which the followers of this emir bore. When he was returning, the vessel on which the king was, ran on a shoal near Cyprus. The sailors advised him to get on board another vessel. He refused, with a calm intrepidity which was not shared by the famous Olivier de Termes, one of the most valiant knights of his time, who, "from fear of drowning," was absolutely determined to disembark. " My lords," said the king to the masters of the vessel, ' I have heard your advice and that of my people. Now I 'll tell you mine, which is this : if I leave this vessel, here are five hundred persons and more who will remain in Cyprus for fear of their life (for everyone values his life just as much as I do mine) and who never, perhaps, will see their country again. I prefer to place my body and my wife and my children in the hands of God rather than to do such damage to the people here."

Magnanimity in the presence of danger is one form of energy; it is not the least common. Louis IX, who, in grave circumstances, naturally rose to heroism, gave proof, on every occasion, of a strong will. There is no doubt that he had the imperious disposition of his mother, of his father, and of his grandfather, Philip Augustus. The mawkish legend of the angelic benignity of St. Louis is contradicted by positive facts. Joinville, the clear-seeing and talkative confidant, does not leave us in ignorance of the fact that the king was apt to get angry. Joinville said gayly to him at Caesarea, when it was a question of prolonging the engagement which bound the seneschal of Champagne to the royal service : " As you get angry when anyone asks something of you, agree that, if I demand something this year, you will not be angry, and, if you refuse, I shall not be angry." The king laughed very merrily; but the seneschal had hit the mark. Many anecdotes bear witness to this. During the journey from Egypt to Palestine, " the king complained of the count of Anjou, who was in his vessel and did not keep him company. One day he asked what the count of Anjou was doing, and was told that the latter was playing at tables with my lord Gautier of Nemours; and he went there all in a tremble, because of his feebleness from sickness, and took the dice and threw them into the sea, and he was very angry with his brother because the latter had gone back to shaking dice. But my lord Gautier got the best of it, for he gathered up all the pennies that were on the board (of which he made a great harvest) and carried them off."

Everyone knew so well that Louis was irritable that, when Queen Marguerite gave birth to her first-born, a daughter, and they thought that the king was hoping for a son, no one dared to be the messenger to tell him the news. It is true that the witnesses heard during the process of canonization eulogized his indulgence to his domestics, but Joinville saw him at Hyères in Provence "very hotly attack" Pons the squire, an old servant, because he had not brought the king's horse on time. The king was aware, moreover, of the violence of his own character, and he often succeeded in overcoming it. The anecdotes about his clemency show that it astonished his people, and that the king's patient demeanor was the fruit of internal struggles.

Louis IX, accustomed to command, was imperious. When Joinville intervened in order that Pons the squire should not be corrected so sharply for such a small fault: "Seneschal," Louis replied to him, "King Philip, my ancestor, said that it was necessary to reward people according to their merits." And he added, *ad hominem:* "King Philip also said that no one can govern his land well if he does not know how to refuse as boldly and as rigorously as he knows how to give. And I tell you these things because the world is so greedy in asking that few people consider the salvation of their souls or the honor of their bodies, provided they can get possession of other people's property, rightly or wrongfully." He knew, in truth, how to refuse and how to punish sharply, as well as, or even better than, his ancestors, and, if he was certain that he was in the right, either in great matters or small, nothing moved him. "Be strict," he counsels his son, "strict and loyal in doing justice and right to your subjects, without turning to the right or to the left." And everyone felt the effect of his decisions—his family, his friends, his barons, his bishops, for, following the expression of the Confessor, he was no respecter of persons.

Charles, count of Anjou, had imprisoned a knight, who had appealed, as was his right, from the court of Anjou to the court of France. Louis summoned Charles and said to him: "There ought to be only one king of France, and do not think, because I am your brother, that I shall spare you, contrary to strict justice." Enguerran, sire of Coucy, had hanged three young people who were hunting in his woods. Louis condemned him severely and shut him up in the Louvre. Thereupon a noble, John of Tourote, furious at such contempt for the privileges of the nobility, cried out: "The king will be hanging us next!" The king heard him and although he had paid no attention to similar remarks from a humbler person, he sent officials to arrest the offender. When the latter was kneeling, he said: "What do you say, John—that I will have my barons hanged? Certainly I shall not hang them, but I shall punish them if they do wrong." In this affair of the sire of Coucy, the king of Navarre, the count of Brittany, the countess of Flanders, and very many others, prayed the king in vain to release the guilty person. He, " indignant because they appeared to be forming a conspiracy against his honor, rose without replying to them."

Another time, Guy, bishop of Auxerre, in the name of all the prelates of France, declared to him that " Christianity was perishing at his hands." The king crossed himself when he heard this, and said, " How is that?" " Sire," replied the bishop, " to-day people mock at excommunications. Command your provosts and bailiffs to compel under penalty of confiscation of their property, all those who remained under the ban of excommunication for a year and a day to get absolution." The king responded to this, without taking counsel of anyone, that he would willingly grant this request, on condition that he should be permitted to ascertain whether the sentence of excommunication had been pronounced justly. And he said, " I give you, as an example, the count of Brittany, who, an excommunicate, has pleaded seven years against the prelates of Brittany. It has finally resulted in the pope's condemning the prelates. If I had compelled the count to get absolved at the end of the first year, I should have done wrong to him and in the sight of God." He often received the requests of the bishops in the same way. " At a *parlement*," recounts Joinville, " the prelates asked the king to come all alone and speak to them. When he returned, he told us, who were waiting for him in the chamber of pleas, the torment that he had had. First the archbishop of Reims had addressed him thus: 'Sire, what will you give me in return for the guardianship of St. Remi of Reims, which you have taken from me, for, by the saints of this district, I would n't wish to have committed such a sin as you have done, for all the kingdom of France.' 'By the saints of this district,' said the king, 'you would do it willingly for Compiègne, because of the greed which is in you.' The bishop of Chartres, in turn, had been put down in these terms: 'He required me to give back to him his property which I held. I said to him that I would not do it at all until I had been paid; that he was my vassal; and that he was conducting himself neither well nor loyally toward me when he wished to disinherit me.' Finally, the bishop of Châlons had spoken, in order to complain of Joinville. 'My lord bishop,' said the king, 'you have agreed among you that an excommunicated person ought not to be heard in a lay court, and I have seen letters sealed with thirty-two seals, that you are excommunicated; accordingly, I shall not listen to you until you have been absolved.'" "And I tell you these things," adds the seneschal of Champagne, "in order that you may see clearly how he delivered himself all alone, by his own good sense, of that which he had to do."

The good sense of Louis IX, which Joinville also called his wisdom, was, in fact, as strong as his will. His attitude toward his councils and counselors is re-markable. " Never was anyone so wise in his council as he. . . . When they spoke to him of anything, he did not say, ' I will consider it;' but, when he saw the right perfectly clearly, he responded without his council, unhesitatingly." It was not because he wished to act as an autocrat without consulting anyone. On the contrary, like a true feudal king, he often asked the advice of his barons and of his suite. But he did not restrict himself to following their advice. In suits to which he was a party, he guarded himself against the probable complacency of his followers. In his *Instructions* we read: " If anyone has a quarrel against you, be always for him and against yourself until the truth is known, for thus your counselors will judge more boldly, according to right and truth." The history of Matthew of Trie brings out his scruples in this respect very clearly. " My lord Matthew of Trie brought the king a letter, a donation made recently by the said king to the father of the countess of Boulogne of the county of Dammartin-en-Goële. The seal of the letter was broken, and he showed it to us, who were members of his council, so that we might aid him with our advice. We all declared that he was in no way held to recognize the validity of this letter, but he said to us, ' My lords, this is a seal which I used before I went beyond the seas. It is clear that the imprint of the broken seal is like the entire seal; here is a copy; therefore I would not dare conscientiously to retain the said county.' Then he called my lord Matthew of Trie, and said to him, ' I restore the county to you.' "

Joinville has vividly depicted the great council held at Acre, in 1250, to consider returning to France, where he himself, supported only by the sire of Chatenai, opposed the opinion of the majority. The king listened attentively, called those who interrupted to order, and said: " My lords, I have heard you very carefully, and I shall reply, on such a day, what it is pleasing to me to do." Then he gave his answer, with his reasons, without considering the votes. He often intervened without delay to settle or redress a matter: " Many a time it happened that he went and seated himself in the forest of Vincennes, in summer, after mass, at the foot of an oak, and had us sit around him, and all who had business came to speak to him without any hindrance from officials or anyone else. He said, ' All be silent. Your matters will be attended to one after another.' And he called my lord Pierre de Fontaines and my lord Geoffrey de Villette, and said to one of them, ' Finish up this business for me.' And when he saw something to amend in the speech of those who spoke for him, he corrected it with his own mouth." Moreover, although obstinate, he was a man who allowed himself to be convinced. It seems that he renounced the project of abdicating and entering a monastery when he was shown its inconveniences. Sometimes, even, he accepted lessons gracefully; and Joinville had the chance to give him some very clever ones. " While the king was staying at Hyères, attempting to procure some horses for the return to France, the abbot of Cluny made him a present of two palfreys, which to-day would certainly be worth five hundred livres—one for him and one for the queen. The following day this abbot returned to speak of his business to the king, who heard him very diligently and at great length. When he had gone, I said to the king: ' I want to ask you, if you please, if you have heard the abbot of Cluny more courteously because he gave you those two

palfreys yesterday.' He thought and said, 'To be sure.'
'Sire,' said I, 'do you know why I asked you this question?' 'Why?' replied he. 'In order, sire, that when
you return to France you may forbid all your sworn
council to take anything from people who have cases
before you. For be sure that, if they take anything, they
will listen more willingly and more diligently to those
who give, just as you did to the abbot of Cluny.' Then
the king called all his counselors and told them what I
had said, and they said I had given him good advice."

To sum up, Louis IX can be held responsible for the
policy he followed. He did what he wanted to do. But
what did he want to do? What were his political ideals?

Certainly no man charged with governing men ever
had more upright intentions. "The great love which he
felt for his people," says Joinville, "appears clearly in
what he said to my lord Louis, his eldest son, during a
very severe sickness at Fontainebleau: 'My dear son, I
pray you that you make yourself loved by the people of
your kingdom, for, truly, I should prefer that a Scot
should come from Scotland, and govern the kingdom
well and loyally, rather than that you should govern it
badly.' "

What he meant by governing well, Louis IX himself
has declared in his spiritual will, addressed to the future
Philip III: Retain nothing from the goods or rights of
another; watch that your subjects live in peace and uprightness; make war on Christians only in the last extremity; appease quarrels, "as St. Martin did"; prevent
sin and heresy in your presence. For the royal dignity
was, in his eyes, according to the expression of William

Medieval Civilization

of Chartres, a true "priesthood." He guided himself thus by the light of two ideas: that of right and that of salvation. "More preoccupied than one would believe with the eternal salvation of souls," it appeared to him natural to punish as crimes public sins: blasphemy, usury, prostitution and heresy, and to sacrifice everything, in spite of the evident repugnance of his people, to the crusades beyond the seas. Imbued with the notion, more feudal still than Christian, "to teach one his own," he did not think that encroachment upon the acquired rights of the neighbor, spoliation and theft, which were forbidden to private persons by common morality, were made legitimate by reasons of state. To unjust pretensions, that is to say, the illegal and novel pretensions, either of the emperor or of the pope, he knew how to set up a barrier quietly in defense of his own right, but every conquest, in his eyes was odious. So greatly did he esteem the blessing of peace that, in several cases, he consented to sacrifices in order to procure it for his own country and for his neighbors. It was a principle with him to reconcile his adversaries instead of profiting by their quarrels. "With regard to these foreigners whom the king had appeased, some of his council said to him that he did not do well, that he ought to let them war, for, if he allowed them to impoverish themselves, they would not attack him as they could do if they were very rich. And the king said that his counselors were wrong. "For, if the neighboring princes saw that I let them war, they would attack me because of the hatred which they had against me, so that I might well lose, without taking into account that I should deserve the hatred of God, who has said, ' Blessed are the peacemakers.' "

Practised two hundred years earlier, the charitable policy of St. Louis might, perchance, have kept the French monarchy in its original mediocrity, but, in the thirteenth century, the Capetian dynasty was already strong enough to afford the costly luxury of an idealistic prince. Louis IX has no reason to repent having procured for France, between the terrible ages of Philip Augustus and Philip the Fair, the repose of a pacific and just reign. He was honored and he was feared. " They feared him," said William of Chartres, speaking of the barons of France, " because they knew that he was just." He is perhaps the only king, who was an honorable man, and was respected in his own lifetime, and yet has been placed, after his death, in the list of great kings.

It is certain, however, that, by his simplicity, by his ingenuousness, and by his ignorance, resulting from his perfect sanctity, he committed grave faults.

The whole campaign in Egypt was planned for and carried out with remarkable maladroitness. King Haakon, of Norway, who Louis hoped to lead across the sea, deceived him. At Cyprus, in 1248, there arrived in the camp of the Franks the ambassadors of the khan of the Tartars, the emperor of China and an enemy of the Mussulmans, who offered to help the Christians vanquish the sultan of Egypt and conquer Syria. The king received them " very debonairly," and thought of no better plan than sending to the khan, by the monk, Rubruquis, " a scarlet tent, made in the shape of a chapel, in which were displayed, by images, the annunciation of our Lady and all the other matters of the faith; . . . a chalice, books, and everything necessary for chanting mass:" he wished this "to lead the Tartars to our belief," and the monks, bearers of this chapel, were charged to show the khan "how he ought to believe." By this action, he brought upon himself a very cavalier response, and Mussulman Syria was saved. Between Damietta and Mansourah, and during the retreat, the chief of the army constantly made mistakes. The accounts of witnesses like Joinville, show it clearly. Louis IX never understood the Orient or Islam at all: when he was captured by the Mussulmans, the absurd rumor spread among the crusaders that the emirs were going to elect the French king, their prisoner, to the office of the defunct sultan. When asked by Joinville if he would have accepted the "kingdom of Babylon" if he had had the chance, he declared that "truly, he would not have refused it." But it was in 1269 especially, that the zeal of Louis IX for propaganda blinded him and that the excess of his ingenuousness was clearly revealed. "Those who advised him to make the voyage to Tunis," says Joinville, "committed a mortal sin." The expedition to Tunis, this second crusade attempted against the advice of the wise men, without any chance of success, was, in fact, disastrous both to France and to the cause of the Holy Land. Now, Louis IX went to Tunis because he believed, in good faith, that the prince of that country, El Mostanssir, wanted to become a Christian. He said: "Oh! that I might be the godfather of such a godson!" In the presence of the envoys of this barbarian potentate, who were presented to him at Paris, he said effusively: "Say to your master that I desire so strongly the salvation of his soul that I would willingly consent to stay in the prisons of the Saracens all the days of my life, without ever seeing the clear sky, if he might be converted, if only your king and his people might become Christians." It is generally agreed that St. Louis was, in this matter, " too credulous."

The Relation of Antiquity to the Renaissance

Adapted from Carl Neumann: *Byzantinische Kultur und Renaissancekultur*, in *Historische Zeitschrift*, Vol. XCI, 1903, pp. 215–232.

JACOB BURCKHARDT'S celebrated book, *The Civilization of the Renaissance in Italy,* which was first published in 1860, has done much to color our views on the Renaissance. Since its appearance the opinion has quite generally prevailed that the Renaissance was the mother of modern civilization, that the Italians were the first-born people of a modern world, and that all this was due to the passionate zeal with which they overleaped the Middle Ages and sought, with success, to link themselves again to the ancient world. The way had long been prepared for this opinion by the neo-humanism of the late eighteenth century. There is a remarkable work in German, written in 1785, which is saturated with the purest spirit of the Renaissance. In this book, better than in any historical romance of later date, in which the costume may be truer, but not the characters or events, there lives the unfettered, daring, voluptuous and unscrupulous spirit of the Italian Renaissance, which strove, with titanic energy, to bring down happiness and enjoyment and everything good to this earth and hold them fast.

Relation of Antiquity to Renaissance

This book is Wilhelm Heinse's romance, *Ardinghello und die glückseligen Inseln*.

Then came Goethe's well-known interest in Benvenuto Cellini, and his translation of the artist's autobiography. Finally, the young Germany of Gutzkow and Heine appeared, with its manifesto of sensuous joy and the emancipation of the flesh, its new transfiguration of things Hellenic, its loathing of asceticism, the Middle Ages and the Worship of the Nazerene.

A study of the civilization of Constantinople reveals remarkable parallels with these ideas. In spite of the incense and the candle gleam of church ritual, the city on the Bosphorus was still, in the full tide of the Middle Ages, an oasis of unaltered antiquity. In its union of Christo-ecclesiastical usages with a strong heathen spirit, it had something which inevitably suggests the Renaissance.

Constantinople had a glittering court, at the apex of a State which was, throughout, the product of reason. It had a bureaucracy functioning with great efficiency, and a policy of the purest Machiavellianism. In these respects, it was as essentially alien to the romantic world of the crusades as was, let us say, the very medieval spirit of adventure of Charles the Bold of Burgundy to the Renaissance. From this point of view the emperor Frederick II, whom Burckhardt regards as the prototype of the modern ruler, is seen to bear a suspicious resemblance to Byzantine personages. There was, in Constantinople, a cultivated, sociable upper class which wrote Attic Greek as the men of the Renaissance wrote Ciceronian Latin; a cloud of humanists who made verses and field phrases,

Medieval Civilization

begged and were unashamed, and looked down with a true hidalgo's pride on every barbarian; Platonists, like Psellos in the eleventh century, who associated with the emperors as tutors and counsellors, and, versatile and unprincipled, dabbled in politics. Pretty gestures and a fine style were worth something. This had always been so, and consequently the antique elements had not, as in fourteenth century Italy, been suddenly borne to power, but operated as natural forces in the regular flow of intellectual tides.

Even in the externals of daily and holiday customs the antique was retained. If they desired to honor and amuse a noble visitor, they conducted him to the circus, and a Turkish sultan could there witness, as could a Mauretanian or Parthian prince in old Rome, the chariot speeding through the stadium and around the spina. While scenic theaters, mimes and pantomimes had fallen victims to clerical zeal, the circus retained its place, and its opponents had been answered that the prophet Elias himself had ridden to heaven in a chariot, and that the sport was therefore legitimized by the classical authority of the Old Testament. Imagine the appearance of the city, and the impression it made upon a foreign medieval visitor, with its altars and shrines, to be sure, filled with the priceless relics of old Christendom, the crown of thorns and the true wood of the cross, the veil of the most blessed Virgin and the hair of John the Baptist. But, in the sunshine, in the porticoes and on the forums and squares, stood pillars with imperial statues just as Marcus Aurelius and Trajan in Rome, a growing forest of antique works of art, brought together and increased since the art thefts of Constantine the Great. On the forum of Constantine stood the colossal form of the goddess Hera, and in the circus a colossus of the reclining Hercules and the group of Paris offering an apple to Venus, figures which with the melodious curves of their bodies seemed still to sing the siren's song of vanished beauty. The picture inevitably suggests the parallel between the capture and plunder of Constantinople by the crusaders in 1204 and the sack of Rome in 1527.

Along with manifold similarities between Byzantine and Renaissance civilization there are obvious differences. It is easy to speak of the barrenness of Byzantine civilization, and there is some truth in the charge. There was no barrenness in politics; these were productive enough to leave behind, after the vanishing of the Byzantine State, a fearful gap which has never been filled. The Eastern Question is the specter which reproachfully cries out for revenge for the destruction of this State and can find no peace. Nor was the political history of Byzantium (before 1204) unfruitful, but rather those other realms of life which, away from the world of affairs, draw sustenance from the deeper reserves of man's nature, and flourish in the pure air of the spirit. In a word, Byzantium did not produce a Leonardo, a Raphael and a Michelangelo. As a consequence, Byzantine civilization lacks, for the favorable judgment of posterity, that nimbus which genius and the profoundly creative power of the recollection of vanished eras bestow, through which past ages endure for posterity and are felt as living and present.

One who is confronted by problems of this sort cannot

Medieval Civilization

usually free himself from their spell. Why is it that the strong antique element which was fundamental in Byzantium, as in the Renaissance, produced such entirely different consequences? May it not be that in the final analysis the results in the two cases rest on different foundations, and that the share and influence of antiquity has been overvalued?

Let us then make an effort to analyze the bases of Byzantine civilization. If we succeed in comprehending its essence and in contrasting it with the Renaissance, the reflex light which falls from Byzantium upon Italy may so sharpen our observation and so illuminate the object observed, that perhaps we may also gain a clearer understanding of the Renaissance.

BYZANTIUM, the new creation of Constantine the Great, had, as its first and supreme task, to fuse the Roman State and Christianity. One would naturally think that this needful combination could have been consummated more easily on the fallow soil of the new city of Constantine than in the old Rome on the Tiber, where the great traditions of paganism, and the pagan State which had had its center here, were still prominent and tremendously potent, and could have made the new goals of the time unattainable and have created obstacle after obstacle.

In truth, the Roman State was too firmly articulated to be bound up in one particular capital. Men were already accustomed to the division and change of residences. Christianity was therefore face to face with a Roman State which was by no means uprooted or weak-

Relation of Antiquity to Renaissance

ened. At the same time Christianity itself had already departed widely from its origins: it had become a Church and had long since got accustomed to the world and its affairs. It had been called by Constantine to share the government, and the great question now was, would it transform this joint dominion into its own sovereignty? If it had succeeded, then the entire civilization would have required to be renovated and Christianized. Let us consider first of all one of the most important spheres, that of law. Did Christianity succeed in Byzantium in placing a new law alongside of or above the Roman law?

It may be answered, no; such a thing is a chimera; such a juristic innovation would be impossible and has never occurred. Yet Islam proves the contrary. When the Mohammedans invaded lands of highly developed civilization—Persia, Palestine, Syria and Spain, it might have happened that the civilization and law of the conquered should, by their own strength, vanquish the conqueror. Certainly there were tendencies in this direction. But the memorable thing historically is, that the Koran could actually develop and foster a peculiar jurisprudence. True, the Koran itself, a collection of speeches which grew out of simple relations and was not intended for complicated civilizations, had, from the standpoint of law, more gaps than content. But these gaps were filled by a very remarkable growth of new law. It grew out of a tradition of oral decisions of the prophet which were not fixed in the Koran, but could, nevertheless, be carried back through trustworthy witnesses to the prophet. This tradition had a double origin: first, the saying, the decision itself; and secondly, the so-called *Musnads,* that is, the " genealogical chains " of the companions and confidants of the prophet, and their descendants, who handed down the sayings by word of mouth. These oral declarations of the prophet now form a most comprehensive literature, the so-called *Hadith* literature, which supplemented the Koran. On this territory, which was prodigiously extended, there grew up the religious jurisprudence of Islam. Just as there was in Roman law a rivalry between the Proculians and Sabinians, so here, different legal schools arose. From one point of view, these occupied themselves mainly with casuistry and debates over the genuineness of the traditions; but they realized that they could not succeed without certain general principles. and hence systematized the legal material deductively. This legal material may have been and often was taken, in part, from the Greco-Roman law or other national laws of the conquered countries and travestied to fit the faith: the decisive fact is that the religious form gives its stamp to the material and that this form is wholly and entirely peculiar to Islam.

Christianity was not able, in Byzantium, to create a similar religious *corpus juris*. It did not produce, as did Islam on the basis of Koran and Sunna, a new public and civil law based on the material of the Old and New Testaments or other sources. It did make occasional theoretical efforts to parallel and harmonize Roman and Mosaic law. But the power of pagan Roman legal tradition was not shattered. Naturally, after the recognition of Christianity by the State, new legal spheres were added; for example, the laws concerning heresy and non-Catholic sects; Church law, which in the Theodosian code

was only an appendix, stood, under Justinian, at the head
of the law book; and other legal spheres, like the law of
marriage, were transformed. But great demands, based
upon principle, above all, perhaps, the suppression of
slavery, got no foothold; it was possible only in practice,
and through practice, to soften its rigors. The State law
—the Roman law—remained in force, and the Church
law, as it was developed through the Councils, remained
by its side without subordinating the State law, in case
of conflict with it.

From our school-days we have got the impression that
Byzantium was above all religion-ridden, and that relig-
ious-dogmatic questions were by far the most urgent interests of the State. Our ears still ring with Arianism,
monophysitism, monothelitism and all other possible sec-
tarian shades, with fanatical religious persecutions, for-
mulæ for settling Church differences and Councils with
their marvellous vagaries; all this was externally so. But
it should be remembered that in an absolute State religious opposition was the only possible opposition, and that
only on theological grounds could words be found, and
battle-cries formulated, behind which the self-consciousness and opposition of rich provinces, exploited by heavy
taxation, could make a stand against the capital city and
the government. Hence the fact remains that while in
these struggles the opposition was frequently real, the
point at issue was accidental. After all, the result of
century-long struggles over questions of dogma was, to
modern religious perception, quite a matter of accident.
Greek love of disputation and Roman juristic subtlety
had this effect, that the whole sphere of religion was

reduced to paragraphs and that one knew as exactly what men might believe and might not believe, as what in the juristic field a delict or an obligation was. One might therefore speak of a secularizing of religion. Moreover, religion was not given over to the zealous protection of a priestly class, outside of which the rest of the world had to keep silence in Church affairs. On the contrary, theology was an element of general education; it was associated with military, political, legal, scientific and literary education, and the laymen, above all the emperor, were fully trained to understand religious-theological questions, to have an opinion and to express it. The great Photius, who is especially dear to all philologists for his classical studies, and is well-known to historians as the originator of the great schism with the papacy in the ninth century, was a layman, and was raised, after being hurried through all the consecrations and spiritual dignities within a few days, to the patriarchate. Cases of this kind also occurred in the West; but they did not bridge over the enormous gulf between clerics and laymen and did not disturb the self-consciousness of the clerical class, which was recognized as the first estate. Neither this gulf nor this hegemony existed in Byzantium. As a result, men in old Byzantium were occasionally fanatical from political motives, but they were not fanatical in their hearts, and more than one emperor endeavored, with some Mohammedan doses, to transform Christianity into a martial religion which should find joy in worldly things. But where, one may ask, were the true idea and spirit of Christianity in the presence of all this half-antique rationalism?

Relation of Antiquity to Renaissance

To this question the iconoclastic controversy gives a decisive answer. It made a complete separation between secular clergy and monks. Since it was not possible to destroy the monks, as hurtful to the State—if all the world ran into the cloister, if the cloisters exerted an ever-increasing attractiveness, whence would come the recruits and soldiers for the army?—the Church was cleansed from their influence. The secular Church renounced the religious ideal and became an organ of the State. The patriarch was transformed into a species of minister of public worship. In the vicissitudes of the struggle over the images the high dignities of the secular Church were so irremediably compromised that great hierarchical figures like Athanasius and John Chrysostom of glorious memory henceforth vanish and never reappear. On the other hand, monasticism, condemned to a Robinson Crusoe existence, realized the ideals of asceticism and mysticism. It goes without saying that the highest type of Greek monasticism always remained the hermit, and not the coenobite, as in the West. The Benedictines and Franciscans fled out of the world for the sake of others, and thus gained strength to affect the world; the Greek monks, since the iconoclastic strife, had no influence upon society; they had been driven out. Hence Byzantine Christianity either became an organ of the State, or, in the realm where it could develop its peculiar life, saw itself doomed to sterility through artificial isolation.

After all, and in spite of all transformations, the profane Roman State, with its pagan kernel, remained supreme; it had settled Christianity in its own way. The

Medieval Civilization

same is true of the whole range of Byzantine civilization. Another example may be given, in a brief discussion of a curious effort to construct a new Christian geography.

In the sixth century there lived a monk on Sinai who had formerly been a merchant and who, because of his travels or those of his intimates, was known, even in the monastery, as Kosmas the Indian traveller. Kosmas had written a book which he called *Christian Topography*. He began the book because he discovered a contradiction between the accounts given in the Bible, which he could not but accept as inspired and therefore unimpeachable, and the Ptolemaic system which places the earth in the center of the universe and ascribes to it a spherical shape. Under these circumstances the error could only be on the side of the Ptolemaic system, and he had to try to combine the declarations of the Scriptures into a clear picture of the world. (He used in his studies a Greek translation of the Septuagint and constructed on its errors a system which even if the premises were accepted would fall to pieces before the simplest text emendations. This, however, does not concern us here.) He had also read that the tabernacle of Moses was the model for the whole universe, and, connecting this with passages out of Isaiah and Job, he constructed his representation of the world as a great chest with a vaulted roof and a floor which divided it horizontally into two stories. Below is the earth; on its side walls rests the firmament which, like a strong partition, divides off the mansions of the blest, which are above. The earth itself is flat and, like the bottom of the chest, is of rectangular shape. On the north it is bounded by a high mountain chain, around

Relation of Antiquity to Renaissance

which the sun and stars move. When the sun is behind
the mountains, it is night. The earth is surrounded by
the ocean and has four great gulfs, the Roman, Caspian,
Erythrean and Persian. On one side of the earth and
on the other side of the ocean there is still another bit of
land, and behind it is Eden and its garden. Thence flow
the four rivers of paradise through the land in front and
the ocean, which again appear as the great rivers of the
earth, the Nile, Euphrates, etc. A precious manuscript
of Kosmas in the Vatican library shows all this graphi-
cally by colored miniatures, and enables us to see with
perfect clearness the elaboration of this system of Biblical cosmography, into the scheme of which geography is
made to fit.

Science may, from its experimental but one-sided
standpoint, smile at these things. Nevertheless Kosmas's
effort remains a very interesting one. Every endeavor of
the human spirit to escape from the accustomed ruts is
worthy of the highest respect and consideration. It aimed
to find a new, a Christian, standpoint, and to establish
science afresh on the foundation of the revealed books.
Efforts of this sort in the West became more fruitful
and pregnant of results, although they have not strikingly
enriched science, or what is more, the human spirit.
While for a time intelligence, critical skill, etc., declined,
the free imagination could develop, and what the soul
of mankind thus gained in perception and depth cannot
even be expressed or estimated. The topography of
Dante's *Divine Comedy*, with its richness and life, is
unthinkable without precursors of the kind just mentioned. A widely imaginative and religious-symbolic ten-

Medieval Civilization

dency was thus developed in the medieval West. How could the Gothic cathedral and Christian painting have been so completely developed without these previous mental and spiritual tendencies and dispositions?

In the East, in Byzantium, such a bent was not established; it never got beyond the beginnings and remained in fetters, because the classical spirit and rationalism formed a counterpoise of a strength unknown in the medieval West until the Renaissance.

If it is the case, then, that in Byzantium the antique biases and traditions were maintained almost all along the line, and that a productive permeation with the new elements of world-history was lacking, the same holds true of the relations of Byzantium with the barbarians, the other great factor in the Middle Ages.

The soil of the kingdom was thoroughly penetrated by non-Greek and unhellenized peoples. But the State was a Greek minority, which operated the State machine according to the ancient political rules. The bureaucracy was not racially exclusive: a Mohammedan renegade, a Bulgarian, an Armenian or a Slav could gain full admission to it, although always at the price of disowning his origin and becoming a Greek-speaking and Greek-thinking Byzantine. The individual barbarian, provided he were trained in the State political and military discipline, could, just as in imperial Rome, see the road to the highest office open before him; but Byzantium never became a barbarian State. The Bulgarians, non-Slavic in origin, had been Slavized in the midst of the Slavs of the northern Balkan peninsula, but had not been Hellenized. Basil II had waged a murderous war against them and had subdued them; but no Bulgarian Odoacer or Charles the Great was able subsequently to seat himself on the throne of the Caesars. The difference lies in this, that Charles the Great conquered the Saxons and punished them in as bloody a fashion as Basil II the Bulgarians; but one hundred and twenty years after the death of the great Charles a Saxon prince won the German and soon afterward the imperial crown, and it is well-known that Otto the Great never sacrificed the peculiar Saxon accent of his mother tongue. To the Roman-Byzantine, the West was ruled by a barbarian emperor and incurred the heart-felt scorn of the true Caesars, the same scorn in which the Italians of the Renaissance, later, indulged themselves over the " barbarians of the North," just as if they themselves were the true sons of antiquity. Byzantines and Italians, in this matter, overlooked one thing. These northern barbarians brought original elements of civilization with them, above all a law which was their peculiar heritage. It must never be forgotten that the German laws had a mighty influence in Italy. How many hundreds and thousands of times does one read, in medieval Italian sources, the declarations: I am subject to Lombard law, *legem profiteor Langobardicam!* These so-called barbarians, then, supplied an incalculably large amount of juristic, political and military material to the civilization of the West. They had their own mythology and their own poetry, and when, from the twelfth to the thirteenth century, the Latin-clerical culture was rent like a thin veil, and the might of the national talent and the ripening national language revealed themselves, what an astonishing richness, full of promise, was disclosed! The

Medieval Civilization

Franco-Celtic poetry found tongues, and the paladins of Charles the Great, Tristram and Isolde and Perceval appeared as if borne up from the depths. The Nibelungenlied announced a different love and hate from that which the pathetic hexameters of Virgil's Dido know, and still different from that which fills the thirteenth chapter of the first epistle to the Corinthians. Everyone knows that the most sonorous names of Italian history, Dante Alighieri and Garibaldi, are of Lombard stock.

The barbarian and plebeian lower classes had no such rise in Byzantium. There were, of course, in Byzantium a spoken Greek and a literature in the Greek vernacular. But how poor and needy it is! It did not attain prominence because it could not surmount the wall of Attic Greek, which had never ceased to be regarded as superior and alone worthy of literature. The Greek *volgare* was used but it was scorned just as if it were a barbarous language. Even to the present day this condition endures. The modern Greeks have inherited it from the Byzantines. When, some time ago, a translation of the Bible into vernacular Greek was projected, it was hindered in every way as if it were a sacrilege against both the Greek classical and the Christian antiquity. Friends and enlightened portions of the Greek people regarded this opposition of a proud caste, clinging to the classics and legitimacy, as a national misfortune. For so long as in Byzantium the renewal from below, the natural rise of the sap, remains checked, that small, aristocratic upper class will remain condemned to powerlessness and unproductiveness. The same opinion still prevails, as in the thirteenth century, when a historian of the conquest of Constantinople in 1204 broke off his narrative and said he would not so far dishonor the music of Clio as to tell and accompany the deeds of the barbarians.

WE shall endeavor to draw together the threads of our argument.

Between all ancient and modern history, beginning with the Middle Ages, there is one great distinction. The peoples of antiquity enjoyed a sort of natural growth. Their political creations, their law, religion, language, literature, art, all grew from one root, at least in essentials. With the progress of time, however, mankind becomes older, it has inheritances, it is weighed down by its history. The Middle Ages were made up of barbarians filled with the strength of youth, of an ancient political, literary and artistic heritage, and of the Christian religion, which had arisen under very singular circumstances. The situation was this, that on a promising stem foreign shoots were engrafted. Its destiny depended upon the combinations between elements and forces which at first were fundamentally foreign to one another. Law and State grew from one root, religion, perhaps, and art from a very different one. These universal premises were absolutely similar in Byzantium and in the West.

In our opinion, what men call an advance in the history of the world always came, when, in the combination of fundamental factors and powers, one of the new elements so preponderated, materially and spiritually, that it, as it

were, digested the others and thus strengthened itself.
It is in this way that the great and decisive conquests and
advances have been made.

No such great solution took place in Byzantium. An
old element, the Roman inheritance, remained master
and was always strong enough to prevent Christianity
and the barbarian element from developing freely, and
working out their peculiar strength. At most one can
say that the great factors remained in a state of aggrega-
tion which prevented a vital fusion. As far as Christianity is concerned, it was alloyed in the Church with the
State, and in monasticism it was cut off and isolated from
life and free activity. The pagan heaven was more than
a succession of beautiful pictures and metaphors: it stood
near the Christian heaven like a special kind of old dis-
pensation near the new. The barbarian element did not
triumph over the social exclusiveness of an aristocratic
governing upper class which spoke a different language.
The routine of an old traditional political wisdom, the
habit of old traditional culture, strengthened themselves
every hundred or hundred and fifty years through a
renaissance of the antique. Here one may lay his finger
on what such renaissances or restorations could accomplish of themselves: they could withhold liberty from
Christianity and the barbarian elements; they could crip-
ple; but of themselves they produced nothing new and
promising.

Let us henceforth turn our attention briefly, but, let us
hope, with fresh light, upon the Italian Renaissance.

The Renaissance embraces the last centuries of the

Relation of Antiquity to Renaissance

Middle Ages and rests upon the tremendous new forces which the Christian education of the Middle Ages created. Christianity and barbarism enjoyed quite a different freedom in the West to what they had in Byzantium, and it may be called one of the greatest facts in history that in the West, alongside of despotism and lay coercive force, a structure of higher freedom arose, a Church which at first won independence for itself as a whole, an independence which then became, although against the wishes of the later Church, the point of departure for all the freedom in the world. This is what Ranke means when, in the third volume of his *Weltgeschichte* (pp. 161 ff.) he says that the most important and most pregnant words of Jesus were the direction to render unto Caesar the things which are Caesar's and unto God the things that are God's. With these words a free state was founded in man which cannot be reached or injured by any outer coercive force. This possibility of a new man, uncontrolled by a city or a Caesar, and in the long run by a pontifex, this freedom of the new Christian man, was met by the barbarians' love of freedom. In the Middle Ages, a new soul was born, arose, grew up, and was educated.

But enough of generalities! Let us open Dante's *Divine Comedy* and read the first two terzets of the eighth canto of the Purgatory:

" It was now the hour that turns back desire in those that sail the sea, and softens their hearts, the day when they have said to their sweet friends farewell, and which

pierces the new pilgrim with love, if he hears from afar
a bell that seems to deplore the dying day." [1]

The mood of parting, the feeling of loneliness, the
voice of evening, the sound of bells, longing, the breath
of the transitory, the eternal and boundless, in a word:
Soul.

Dante could not have taken that from antiquity. Let
us see how Homer depicts the mood of evening (Odys-
sey, XIII, 31 ff.).

" And as when a man longs for his supper, for whom
all day long two dark oxen drag through the fallow field
the jointed plow, yea and welcome to such an one the
sunlight sinketh, that so he may get him to supper, for
his knees wax faint by the way." [2]

This is the antique feeling of what may be called the
animal man; out of Dante speaks the soul of a new spiritual man. No one can read Dante's *New Life* without
thrilling in his inmost being at the depths which are here
for the first time disclosed, at the music of chords and
accords which sound in it and accompany all humanity
into a new life. The new humanity sees with new eyes.
It does not try to cover reality with the beauty-cosmetic
of antique artistic feeling, nor to deck the rough reality
with a dream-like beautiful veil; a new race boldly looks
reality in the face, and realism begins, that realism which
shapes things and art. It is the same with the Italians
of the *Quattrocento* as with the Van Eycks in Flanders,

[1] [Translation of C. E. Norton.]
[2] [Translation of Butcher and Lang.]

Relation of Antiquity to Renaissance

as with the Germans and the French, and thus it is most clear that this realism does not first come from an awakening of antiquity—there can be no question of this latter in the North in the beginnings of the movement—but from a ripening of medieval civilization, which now opens its magnificent blossoms. Everywhere, the spiritual soul of the Middle Ages looks out of the eyes of the new art. Why should we call Leonardo da Vinci's Mona Lisa, with her mysterious look and her alluring smile, why should we call the Madonna of the young Raphael, *renaissance,* when the *New Life* of Dante speaks from them, the Middle Ages in all their heights and depths?

The word Renaissance was invented in Italy by a clique aping things Byzantine, who, in using it, gave expression to their hatred for the barbarians and their arrogance, as if they, the Italians, were of the pure blue blood of antiquity. According to the opinion of these people and in their propaganda the word *rinascimento,* that is, rebirth of classical antiquity in art and life, was a disavowal of the Middle Ages and a protest against the migrations. They invented the appellation " Gothic " as an insult to the northern art; they named the antique architecture " the good." The wish which Filarete expressed in 1460 was already famous: "Accursed be he who devised this wretched Gothic style of building; only a race of barbarians could bring it into Italy!" Thus, by these deluded Italians, the whole Middle Ages were viewed only from the standpoint of the devastation of the external civilization, which was accordingly laid to the charge of the barbarians of the migrations, the Goths. These were believed to have ruined everything noble, and to have destroyed civilization, which had been the creation of antiquity and had now to be restored in the spirit of antiquity.

The more the doctrinaire tendency was accentuated in Italy, the more that arrogant Byzantine feeling of legitimacy won footing—a feeling which cannot be called progressive and modern but rather thoroughly reactionary—all the more did Italian civilization actually become a renaissance civilization and depart from the spirit of the fifteenth century and the pure and great medieval tradition. The Italians now consciously took, in life and morals, the ancient examples as models; their art lost soul in the effort to acquire the great monumental style, the "correct" gestures of antiquity, and was diverted into a striving after formal virtuosity. They went to absolutely absurd lengths, and would even blame or wish otherwise such a uniquely great genius as Michelanglo, in whom so many medieval and Dantesque traits still lived. One may still venture to imagine what Italian art might have become, not if it had remained at the artistic point of development of such bloodless people as Sandro Botticelli, but if it had advanced farther in the path of Leonardo. One could dispense with Raphael's sibyls in Santa Maria della Pace and Michelangelo's Christ in Santa Maria sopra Minerva without sorrow. Italian renaissance culture, thus transformed in the spirit of antiquity—the culture, in part, of the High, and certainly of the Late Renaissance—was extremely well-fitted for cosmopolitan adaptation. It forced its way over the Alps and was taken up with enthusiasm by the aristocratic societies of the northern counties. Since that time

Relation of Antiquity to Renaissance

Machiavellianism and an unscrupulous paganism in politics, and a conventional so-called art of beauty which was severed from national feeling, rose to power. I can not see that we have great reason to thank the Italians for this dowry.

The difference between the actual Renaissance and the pretended Renaissance lies, one may say, in the proportions. As long as the Middle Ages in Italy were living and conscious, when to Francis of Assisi and Giotto the realism of the fifteenth century was added as the last word of the matured medieval man, antiquity operated most beneficently as an ingredient, as a vitalizing element. Its practical results in the discovery of the world, in the broadening of the knowledge of the exact sciences, its feeling for beauty in the direction of simplification, in contrast with grotesque bad taste—all these gifts of antiquity gave Italian civilization an advantage which caused the other peoples to seem slow and backward. But as soon as antiquity was changed from a root or an ingredient into the flesh and blood of Italian culture, as soon as it seized the mastery, it became a danger to all modern civilization.

In my opinion, the consideration of Byzantine culture and its barrenness can free us from the delusion that antiquity was the real productive element in the great Italian advance in civilization which came at the close of the Middle Ages. We must shift the accents, which were arbitrarily fixed and distributed by the hands of the humanists. We must firmly grasp the idea that the medieval-Christian training and the so-called barbarism were the life-strength of that which is traditionally called

Medieval Civilization

the Renaissance, and that the revival of antiquity was a productive and beneficial element only as long as it remained contented with the rôle of companion, with its pedagogical rôle.

IF our ideas are correct, true modern individualism has its roots in the strength of the barbarians, in the realism of the barbarians, and in the Christian Middle Ages.

The French Army in the Time of Charles VII

Adapted from G. Roloff: *Das französische Heer unter Karl VII,*
Historische Zeitschrift, Vol. XCIII, 1904, pp. 427–448.

IN the fifteenth century a momentous change took
place in the art of war. As a result, the armies of
the sixteenth century were obviously different in tactics
and composition. In the earlier army the cavalry was
the chief thing; in the later it was the infantry, equipped
with long pikes and fire-arms. The size of the armies
increased considerably. The nobles ceased to be the all-
important class on the battlefield; the burghers and peasants became quite as important. The fifteenth century,
which witnessed this transformation, was also the epoch
in which France secured her liberation from English
rule. The question suggests itself whether there is a
causal connection between these two events, and whether
Charles VII perchance transformed his army in order
to expel the English. It is constantly asserted that such
a causal connection exists and that Charles made two
innovations. He is said to have been the first to maintain troops in time of peace in order to be prepared for
instant war, and, what is still more important, to have
been the creator of French national infantry. But a

moment's reflection makes it clear that there was no real innovation in the establishment of a standing army, for such had existed for centuries: ever since the development of feudalism the feudal lord had at his castle or on his lands warriors who could take the field at a moment's notice, and the continuous wars of the Middle Ages compelled the king to keep a larger number of troops constantly under arms. The significance, then, of Charles's alleged innovation is much slighter than has been supposed. There are other questions, however, which cannot be answered so easily. By what means did Charles conquer the English? Was he really the founder of French infantry? The answers demand a consideration of all his military reforms.

The French army, like all medieval armies, was composed of knights, *i.e.*, of heavily-armed individual fighters who preferably fought on horseback. There were also infantry for the hand-to-hand conflict, and long-range fighters, such as archers and crossbowmen, but these played only a small rôle. At Beneventum and Tagliacozzo, for example, they took no part whatever in the battle; at Courtrai and Crécy they were present, but their importance was much less than that of the knights. In the earlier centuries the army had consisted of assembled vassals, but by the beginning of the Hundred Years War it was made up very largely of mercenaries. The cause of this transformation may be briefly indicated. The vassals' obligation to serve was in France, as everywhere, strictly limited; they fought for their suzerain only for a fixed period and for certain objects; they were not repaid the cost of getting ready for the field, etc. It is clear that the suzerain had a vital interest in increasing his military strength, and also that he could not do this without making equivalent concessions to his vassals, and these concessions took the form of pay. This new method also enabled the suzerain to enlist foreign warriors, who were under no feudal obligations to him. There were plenty of such men, who regarded war as their occupation, and were ready to fight for any cause in return for good pay. But the introduction of military pay, a custom which had been in use since the Crusaders, did not weaken the vassals' obligation to serve, and they were called out repeatedly during the fourteenth and fifteenth centuries, and thus there were two different elements in the army. But the value of the military service of the vassals fell rapidly. A military commander who relied entirely upon the obligatory service of his vassals would not be a dangerous foe to an opponent who had numerous mercenaries and was therefore less restricted in his operations. The possession of paid knights was therefore a necessity, whether the lord secured them by lengthening the military service of his vassals, or by enlisting foreign troops. As a rule, then, since the fourteenth century the armies of the French king and of his great vassals consisted exclusively of paid warriors; the vassals themselves appeared only as auxiliaries, as extraordinary reinforcements of the paid army. Even at this early period, the number of vassals who followed their lord to the field as a part of their feudal obligation must have declined more and more; many of them had already entered his paid service and therefore were not affected by his summons of his vassals to the field. Hence the feudal bond ceased to regulate the relations between warriors and commanders, or to determine the character of the army; its place was taken by private contracts of enlistment.

This change in the method of raising an army had an important influence upon its organization. As long as the army was made up of vassals, feudal principles necessarily determined its structure. The vassal led his vassals to his suzerain and the army was organized by banners, and, corresponding to the loose structure of the feudal state, each contingent of the whole army, and each knight in a contingent, asserted a far-reaching independence. Even the administration of the feudal army was only slightly centralized. Much of this disunion, however, ceased of itself with the coming of the régime of hired soldiery.

The paid knights, of course, were not attached to the contingents of the vassals, but formed independent sections under the special captains who had enlisted them. The commander-in-chief did not himself undertake the business of enlistment, but entrusted it to persons in whom he had confidence; sometimes the necessary money came directly from him, sometimes it was advanced on his behalf by those actually enlisting the troops; not infrequently warlike captains raised troops without any commission, on their own account, and led them to the main army in the hope of receiving pay for them or gaining booty. Since all these middlemen commanded the troops they enlisted, the whole army naturally fell into a number of bands of varying strength and quality, to which the name of *companies* gradually came to be given.

The French Army

The form of the old feudal army was thus destroyed, but its characteristic lack of cohesion was inherited by the new army. It would be easy to say that the hiring of the troops should have enabled the commander-in-chief to introduce stricter discipline and better organization. It did not result in any great improvement. It is true that the leaders of the companies, the " captains," were commissioned by the commander-in-chief, and swore obedience to him, but this was, as yet, no guarantee of proper subordination. The first condition for this was that the commander-in-chief should keep his promise to pay wages, punctually, and this he was seldom able to do. The revenues of a medieval territorial lord were too irregular and too small to enable him to provide steady pay for a considerable body of men; and even if the Estates of France allowed themselves to be forced to make considerable grants to the king, he never could keep out of the pit of chronic deficit. As soon as the pay of the enlisted troops was not forthcoming, obedience vanished, and with it the possibility of improving the discipline of the army. However, from the beginning, the attempt to make any far-reaching change in this matter had been abandoned. For it was tacitly understood at the time of enlistment that the pay alone would not satisfy the needs and demands of the troops: a share in the booty, especially the ransom of prisoners, was expressly conceded to them. This introduced an anarchical element into the military organization. The interests of the commander-in-chief and of the hired troops, of necessity, frequently clashed; for example, he might favor an undertaking of military importance but of slight booty value, while the army preferred to plunder a rich city or district, although it would injure the enemy but little, and perhaps even aid him through the consequent postponement of military operations. Thus the authority of the commander over the companies was very unstable, and at times entirely lacking.

It was also impossible to change the tactics. The hired knights, like the vassals before them, were individual fighters and did not form tactical groups. Like them, also, they possessed a strong self-respect as warriors of quality and insisted on utilizing their individual ability, instead of obliterating it in a group in which mass-tactics prevailed. They had in form, to be sure, sold their independence in accepting the contract of enlistment, but, as the commander generally failed to pay the purchase money, the troops also did not keep the contract, and preserved their freedom. Furthermore, *esprit de corps,* which facilitates the formation of tactical groups, was still weaker in these paid troops, coming as they did from far and near, than in the vassals. To the vassals a common feudal obligation and especially a common native country furnished a certain bond of union.

The companies retained still another characteristic peculiarity of medieval tactics: even the smallest bands were made up of men differently armed. The heavily-equipped knight (*hommes d'armes*), in hiring out, contracted for others beside himself; he associated with himself horse and foot soldiers who were armed with long-range weapons, or weapons for hand-to-hand fighting, and these supported him in the fight and formed his attendants. The number and quality of his followers varied

The French Army

with the means of the knight. There was still another class of soldiers, usually members of the lower nobility, who lacked a full military equipment, and therefore had to be content with lower wages than the knights received. Usually they were divided among the knights as attendants. Among these subordinates, even if they were not fully-equipped as knights, good warriors were to be found, but the mass of the long-range and hand-to-hand fighters were of little value. It is in the nature of long-range troops that they are capable of rendering substantial service only if they are in a large mass, are handled as a unit and, in addition to technical skill, possess confidence in themselves and their comrades. All this was lacking in France. For the long-range fighters divided among the separate knights had no closer bond of union than the knights themselves; they too were individual fighters, they knew no common evolutions and therefore could not fight together in any considerable masses. As a rule they advanced to the fray individually and were consequently condemned to comparative uselessness from the very start. But the long-range soldiers who attended upon the knight were not the only representatives of their kind. The cities, too, had their marksmen, and since the beginning of the fourteenth century frequently enlisted foreign archers and crossbowmen. The city contingents also accomplished little. Their mercenaries were usually undisciplined and too few; their own marksmen were not accustomed to fighting outside the walls, and therefore lacked dexterity and self-confidence. The bow and crossbow were not French national weapons, so that it would have required laborious pre-

553

paration to create a body of marksmen of real value. As a result of the inefficiency of the native marksmen the bow and crossbow were little esteemed, and this disesteem hurt the prestige of the foreign marksmen and naturally discouraged their use. It was, moreover, a common opinion that infantry who were not equipped with missile weapons were almost useless; if they were light-armed they could accomplish little against either knights or marksmen. The decisive part in the battle, then, belonged to the knights; in most of the sources where numbers are calculated, the infantry are seldom mentioned. In the English army conditions were very different. The scheme of hiring knights was made effective in England much earlier than in France; and since the English king had usually more ready money than the French king, his control over his hired troops was greater, although even he had not succeeded in making a tactical group out of the knights. In contrast with the French, the English marksmen received excellent training and their deeds won them well-merited esteem. The bow had been domesticated in England for generations, and in the wars with Wales and Scotland the lower class had had abundant opportunity to use it. Hence, in the English army there were always large bodies of archers who fought in conjunction with mounted or dismounted knights. It was by virtue of this tactic of united arms, which requires a firm organization, a certain discipline of the parts of the army, and consequently regular pay, that the English victories under the Black Prince and Henry V were won.

The military hierarchy in France was as yet only slightly developed. The commander-in-chief, under the

The French Army

king, was, since the thirteenth century, the constable, who was named by the king. The marshals and the grand master of the marksmen were subordinate to the constable. The marshals had to attend to the payment of the companies and to lead the greater divisions of the army; they had to see that discipline was preserved in the companies, that these were kept at their full strength, and that their military equipment was in good order. They had the right to appoint other officials to aid them in the exercise of their functions. The supervision of the long-range fighters was placed in the hands of the grand master of the crossbowmen, whose office had been established by St. Louis in order to improve this arm of the service. At the beginning of the fourteenth century, the regulation of the pay of the troops was entrusted to a central office, the treasury of war, and it was from this source that the marshals obtained the funds for the payment of the troops. All these arrangements were largely illusory. The marshals might in the most emphatic language impress upon the captains the necessity of keeping their troops together; if the pay gave out, the knights and their followers scattered in order to extract it, by plundering friend and foe. Even in more favorable times the authority of the marshals was frequently paralyzed through the bad disposition of the captains: they retained the pay of their troops and thus drove them to excesses, or they exaggerated the strength of their companies and required pay for men who did not exist. These dishonesties lasted in all mercenary armies well into the eighteenth century. Inspections, regularly and unexpectedly made by the marshals, could not correct the evil.

Medieval Civilization

The companies were rarely near together, but were customarily divided among several widely-scattered garrisons, and thus a contemporaneous control of all these parts was difficult or quite impossible. The resulting damage had to be borne in the first place by the peaceful population; they had to suffer the bitterest oppressions at the hands of the unrestrained soldiers and therefore had to fear their own army no less than the enemy. The troops were at their worst when war came to an end, and they, being disbanded, were without the means of subsistence. Neither the knights nor their followers had any inclination toward peaceful occupations; they preferred to gain their living by robbery and plunder. In war and in peace, therefore, during the age of the English wars, undisciplined bands, augmented by riff-raff, poured through the land. The French government, unable to repress, sought to induce the unbidden guests to embark in foreign wars, in order to free the land from their presence. Thus, after the peace of Brétigny (1360), Constable Du Guesclin led the troops he had used against the English, over the Pyrenees in order to give them employment in the Spanish wars of succession. A great portion of the disbanded English mercenaries threw in their lot with the French and accepted without question the command of a man who had always been their deadly enemy. The thought that war was a gainful occupation had already thrust all other considerations into the background.

After most of the mercenaries had thus departed, Charles V sought to organize the remaining troops more rigidly after the English model, but he did not get beyond the division into companies, above described. What he did accomplish was lost under the rule of his weak successor, and, when the war with England was renewed, France was abandoned to an army powerless against a foreign foe and ruinous to its own people. The battle of Agincourt (1415) and other defeats gave the English possession of more than half of France; the name *flayers,* which the abused people gave to the troops, adequately expresses the characteristics of the French army. Nevertheless, Charles VII finally succeeded in driving out the English with these troops. For the English army degenerated and the French army improved somewhat, after Agincourt. The rigid organization which had hitherto marked the English army declined under the weak government of Henry VI, and the conduct of the war lost in energy and unity. Under Edward III and Henry V the English long-distance troops had been far superior to the French. True, the French did not develop a national corps of marksmen worth mentioning, but they corrected their deficiences by hiring more foreigners than before, especially Genoese crossbowmen and Scottish archers, who could hold their own against the English. In addition, the French were strengthened by a sort of national exaltation; Charles VII received from his provinces more notable support than his father; and the English more and more lost the help of those portions of France which were in their possession. Popular risings even took place, and, although naturally they could not destroy the rule of the English, they divided the English forces and wore out their strength. Thus the French army gradually equaled the English in quality and surpassed it in numbers. The revolution naturally took place slowly and therefore the French did not capture their lost provinces from the English in stormy battles, but gradually, step by step. There are no more decisive struggles like Agincourt, and only toward the end, when the decline of the English was far advanced, did the French gain a success in the open field (Formigny, 1450). But the final victory of France was assured much earlier than this; when the Truce of Tours was made (1444), the English had already been compelled to abandon a large part of their former possessions.

With the turn of military luck the internal condition of the French army also improved, although slowly, and with many relapses. The willingness of the Estates to give money, which resulted from the patriotic upheaval, placed at the disposal of the king at least sufficient means to organize a small trustworthy body of troops, and every success of the French arms knit this force more closely to the throne. But it must not be forgotten that this improvement affected only a small part of the army. Most of the troops, lacking regular pay, were as unrestrained as before; captains often renounced obedience to the constable and the king, seized and plundered cities when the pay was not forthcoming, or refused to deliver up to the king cities which they were defending against the enemy. Nor was it always the worst warriors who distinguished themselves by disobedience and deeds of violence; men of achievement, like La Hire, partly through need, partly through love of gain, had recourse to the most frightful extortions. Only with the greatest caution could the king venture to oppose the most terrible excesses, for the bands which were living by plunder and robbery were much more numerous than the better disciplined mercenaries. Usually there were more troops marauding in the interior of the country than fighting on the borders against the English. The incessant commands of the king, that the troops should move to the frontier, were ignored; the captains negotiated, like independent powers, with Estates and provincial authorities, and frequently all that these could do was to induce the tormentors, through the payment of great sums of money, to move into a neighboring province. The improvement of discipline was hindered by the circumstance that many captains were enlisted by great vassals, and did not believe that they owed obedience to the king. The great vassals themselves were untrustworthy in their political attitude and had a natural interest in opposing the efforts of the king to extend his effective authority over the troops. The first signs of improvement appeared, perhaps, in the half generation after the battle of Agincourt, and in 1439 the king believed himself strong enough to take a decisive step.

Two forces hampered the development of an organized army: the plundering bands and the feudal powers. Both of these were ultimately reduced with the help of the national representatives. The way to end the war was discussed at the meeting of the Estates in Orléans, and the result was the so-called Grand Ordinance of November, 1439. By this it was decided that the king alone had the right to appoint captains and enlist troops; the only concession to the feudal vassals was that they might maintain garrisons in their fortresses. Emphatic orders were afterwards given to the captains to keep exactly within the number of troops allowed to them and to avoid any increase. The greater part of the troops then in arms were to be discharged and only the most competent were to be retained. In this way the captains would be attached exclusively to the interests of the crown, and the land would be freed from the excessive weight of plunderers who pretended to be soldiers. The magistrates received full authority to punish marauders, and even the people were empowered to repel the attack of plundering bands by force. The intimate relation between discipline and pay demanded that financial measures should accompany these reforms: in addition to the privilege of raising troops the king secured from the Estates the right to levy taxes; the feudal vassals were forbidden to diminish the royal receipts or to lay more than the customary burdens upon their vassals. The military and financial resources of the king were therefore to increase while those of his vassals declined.

It was inevitable that the two elements which were attacked—the princes and the mercenaries—should make common cause in opposing the plans of the king; they joined in a conspiracy, the *Praguerie* (1440) and won over the dauphin to their side. Through the demand for a speedy peace they hoped to gain the support of the nation, weary of war, to dethrone the king, and to establish their chief, the duke of Bourbon, as regent of the young dauphin. Their effort failed because of the energy of Charles and his constable, Count Richemont, and because of the prestige which the crown had just acquired in the nation. The royal army received reinforcements from some mercenary leaders who hoped to be rewarded for their assistance, the sympathies of the nation stood unmistakably on the side of the king, and the conspirators themselves ceased to be united. They had to submit and accede fully to all the demands of the king. Other royal successes followed. As the English were now less dangerous, Charles could lead his best troops against the plunderers; he had some captains of particularly evil repute executed, and dispersed their bands, and so made at least a beginning of carrying out the Grand Ordinance. But these were only slight rays of hope. When the Truce of Tours was made, thousands of marauding troops were still traversing the land, and it was to be expected that the troops which had hitherto been fighting on the frontiers and were now to be disbanded would follow their example. The problem of putting an end to marauding and to the pseudo-soldiery was by no means solved.

In this predicament Charles and Richemont fell back upon the device which Du Guesclin had already used—to get the troops employed abroad. By this they gained time to frame new regulations; perhaps the barbarous mercenaries would be destroyed abroad; and, at any rate, France would be freed from plundering for a time. The international situation facilitated the carrying-out of the plan. On the northeast frontier of France war was raging between the German emperor and the Swiss, and in Lorraine there was a feud between the city of Metz and the duke of Anjou. As an ally of the emperor and of the duke, Charles took a hand in the war and himself led a part of the army against Metz, while his son led another part into Alsace against the Swiss (summer of 1444). We shall not follow the details of the struggles, which lasted until the following New Year; they are of moment only so far as they are connected with an advance in the organization of the army. The success of the royal authority in leading east considerable masses of men out of the western and central regions shows of itself that the monarchy had gained in the last generation. The commands of the king, who was now freed for a time from concern about the English, could no longer be simply ignored. Certainly his power was not yet so great that he could have forced the collected soldiery to depart; several greater and smaller bands continued to ravage in the provinces, but the bulk of them disappeared and the land could breathe again. The army which went to Alsace was, according to the accounts of contemporaries, 25,000 to 30,000 strong. Of these, six to seven thousand were soldiers—a clear example of the smallness of the military value of the bands in proportion to the cost of supporting them. The Lorraine army, concerning which exact reports are not available, cannot have been very different from the Alsatian.

The king and the crown prince participated in the war for only a short time. Charles left the army at the beginning of the siege of Metz and established his headquarters at Nancy (September). Louis followed a few months later, as soon as the army in Alsace had gone into winter quarters. The hopes which Charles had placed on the campaign were not disappointed: the tedious siege of large and small cities, the fights with the Swiss and later with the peasantry, cold, bad supplies and the resultant sicknesses, rapidly reduced the numbers of the troops. Contemporary estimates of the losses of the

The French Army

Alsatian army alone fluctuate between 10,000 and 20,000, without reckoning the sick who encumbered them on their return. Without placing too much confidence in these figures, it can be accepted as certain that they returned to France weakened numerically and morally, and also that the losses must have been particularly severe upon the best portion—the fighters. Consequently Charles saw no difficulty in disbanding the troops who returned, although many of his trusted counselors were anxious and advised him not to take any steps against the still numerous bands. During his winter stay he had made all necessary preparations in common with Richemont. He had provided himself with a reliable body of picked troops, had negotiated with the most important leaders of mercenary bands and drawn them into his service with promises—the same means by which he had previously conquered the *Praguerie*. To the captains thus won over, the king entrusted the task of selecting and organizing the best men in their companies; the remaining officers and troops were to be disbanded and sent home under an escort. The discharged troops were to receive a sum of money, which should extinguish all their claims for pay; they were to be given a general amnesty which should assure them against legal prosecution for the excesses they had committed during their soldier life and facilitate their return to peaceful labor.

The plans were soon carried out. The constable went first to Lorraine and took into the service of the king (April, 1445) the troops that they desired to keep; and immediately after the troops streaming back from Alsace underwent the same treatment. The bands, which were thus split into two classes, were entirely unprepared for this measure, and the secret understanding with the useful elements excluded only the undisciplined rabble, and forced its members, willingly or unwillingly, to follow the path homeward which had been marked out for them. That this would entirely prevent disorder was not to be expected, but there was no armed opposition to the king's plans, as many of the king's counselors had feared. It was a great success; the possibility of establishing a real army was for the first time won. The king now had a body of troops no greater than he needed or than he could continue to support. It was reasonable to expect that insubordination and unreliability would henceforth disappear. The impression which the dissolution of the great bands made upon contemporaries is shown by the reports of the historians. Most of them praise the cleverness of Charles and Richemont, in finishing with the vagabonds without a battle; almost everywhere one reads that now the time of suffering had passed by, the people recovered confidence in the future, and trade and commerce prospered. In an ordinance, a few years later (April 28, 1448), Charles was able to point with pride to his success in putting an end to the plunderings of the soldiers.

The next task was to organize the troops which had been retained. They were divided (May 26, 1445) into fifteen companies, and the captains of these were named by the king; they were assigned to definite garrisons and subdivided into small groups of twenty to thirty lances, so that, as d'Escouchy remarks, they might not be able to use force against the burghers. Concerning the strength

of the new " Companies of the Ordinance," as they were
named because they had been established by royal ordinance, we have no statistics. According to the accounts
of the chroniclers, they amounted to fifteen hundred
lances, and on this basis the average strength of a company would be one hundred lances. It is uncertain how
far this ratio was carried out at that time, for by the next
year Charles was maintaining a much larger number of
troops. In tactics and organization, the new company
remained the same as the old, being reckoned by lances.
According to rule the lance should consist, after 1445, of
six men—a heavy-armed horseman, two mounted marksmen, and three mounted followers; but certainly there
must have been many variations. Whether the Companies
of the Ordinance were intended for a temporary arrangement, to last only so long as the war with England was
not definitely ended, or whether they were to remain after
the peace, it is impossible to state. As a matter of fact,
Charles did keep them after the war was over, because
he required to be constantly prepared for trouble with
Burgundy and with domestic enemies. It may well be
that he had this in mind from the beginning, but had said
nothing about it, in order not to furnish to the Estates
new ground for complaints about the high military taxes.
Charles, then, made no real innovation but only expanded
and regulated anew what had long been customary.

The king did not succeed in putting an end to the confusion of weapons in the smallest bands: the mounted
marksmen continued to be an appendage to the heavily-
armed close-range fighters. As a natural consequence the
marksmen could accomplish little; at Formigny they were

not equal to the English bowmen and had to be saved by the knights. Thus the new organization had as little effect in improving the execution of the long-range weapons as in producing a tactical unit. To fuse the lances of a company into a tactical group was absolutely impossible by reason of its heterogeneous composition, but even the idea of forming a tactical unit out of the heavily-armed horsemen alone was unthought of. The division of the knights into numerous small groups prevented this; and as a consequence regular exercises in larger bodies—a condition precedent to the formation of a cavalry corps —were rendered impossible.

Under this organization the national French army was composed almost exclusively of mounted men; for infantry, in the future as in the past, it had to rely upon Scotch and Italian bowmen, because of the slight value of the native marksmen. Charles hoped to remedy this defect and to popularize the use of bow and crossbow more than in the past. By several ordinances he decreed that in every community of about fifty hearths the local authorities should always select one able-bodied man (1448). On all feast days the man thus chosen must practise the use of the bow or the crossbow and must pledge himself by oath to take the field whenever called out by the king. In return he was freed from all taxes save the salt-tax and extraordinary war taxes (hence the name free archers, *francs archers*), and when in service the king paid him a specified wage. It was soon recognized that the militia of free archers could accomplish nothing without a fixed organization: they were therefore, like the lances, divided into companies and placed under captains (1451); the captains had to muster the archers and, at the appointed times, put those residing near each other through common exercises. At first the free archers were required to supply their own offensive and defensive weapons, and as a result only well-to-do burghers were chosen; after a few years it was decided (1451) that poor but capable men should also be enrolled in the companies of archers and that the community should supply them with arms.

In this arrangement the French historians usually see the most significant innovation made by Charles—the foundation of a national French Infantry, which the army had hitherto lacked. Here, again, it must be said that the free archers were no more of an absolute innovation than the Companies of the Ordinance. At an earlier time the king, as above mentioned, had led citizen marksmen into the field, and the organization of free archers was really grafted on to the existing communal gilds of archers, upon whom the defence of the city rested. The only new feature was the great extension given to the use of archers and the pledging of a number of burghers to serve the king as mercenaries at any time. And from the purely military standpoint, the innovation was of very slight importance. In Charles's last war with England, bodies of this kind were employed on foot, but foreign mercenaries were associated with them, and the French infantry archers accomplished as little as the mounted archers. In the battle of Castillon (1453), where they appeared in great numbers, they soon took to flight, and the burden of the battle fell, as formerly, upon the knights. The cause is clear: the time had been much too short and the force, organized on a peace footing, too weak; it was impossible in a moment to transform citizens, unacquainted with service in the field, into a body the equal of the English archers. Moreover, the free archers could not revolutionize the army; in spite of them the strength of the French army still rested upon the heavy cavalry. The importance of the free archers erroneously attributed to this period came much later.

The troops organized during the truce were designed to form the kernel of the royal army, but they alone were not sufficient for carrying on a great war: two thousand lances were not a match for the English. Accordingly, as soon as the war broke out again (1449), the army had to be increased, and the increase was made just as before: through the union of obligated feudal service and enlistment. However, there was more system than before. Special commissioners were sent into the provinces to find out the number of noble and non-noble vassals and their resources; they carried to the vassals a command to appear at specified places within six months, armed according to their wealth, in return for which they were promised regular pay during service. These orders were not issued for the whole kingdom when the war again began, but only as need arose; now only in the threatened provinces, now in others also; now in larger or smaller numbers, as the danger from the enemy was more pressing, and as the royal treasury prospered. These vassals, who were summoned and paid, together with the foreign mercenaries who sold their services, were divided into lances and companies and subjected to a discipline like the Companies of the Ordinance; the latter, however, drew a somewhat higher pay, as the name given to the newly-raised lances—*de petite paye*—indicates. The summons of the vassals had not the same success everywhere; here and there nobles sought to avoid service in arms, but they were the exception. In general, the nobility responded to the call of the king; and the lances *de petite paye* were just about as numerous as the lances supplied by the Companies of the Ordinance. Moreover, only a few of the former were disbanded after the war was over, so that it is certain the standing army of Charles always numbered some thousands of knights. Naturally, most of them were nobles, who even before the reforms had formed the bulk of the fighters. But even the non-noble vassals were called in, though it would seem that the Companies of the Ordinance were specifically reserved for the nobility. To be sure, this was not expressly stated, but a later ordinance, to be mentioned presently, which referred exclusively to the Companies of the Ordinance, speaks only of the nobility. Moreover, there could have been few non-noble vassals rich enough to provide themselves with the expensive equipment required by the ordinance.

It is not clear whether the summoning of the vassals through the use of a list of the holders of fiefs, and their classification according to the completeness of their armament, had been prepared in time of peace, or whether it was first begun after the outbreak of the war; these measures at all events were completed only after the close of the war. All the nobles were commanded, by an edict of January 30, 1454, to appear in arms before the royal official of their district, the seneschal or *bailli;* according to their means they might come either heavy-armed or light-armed, and they were to be divided into several classes, according to their efficiency. Those who had the equipment of a man-at-arms or marksman of a Company of the Ordinance received the same pay as if they had belonged to it; and those who were not so well equipped received correspondingly less. Every group receiving the same pay had to have prescribed offensive and defensive weapons and mounts. In this way, a certain unity in military equipment, hitherto lacking, was secured, and mobilization was materially facilitated through the classification of those owing service. The vassals' obligation to serve, even that of the poor vassals who could secure only a partial equipment, was sharply emphasized; those in the lowest class, composed of men inadequately equipped for long-distance or close-range fighting, were to find employment as attendants of a man-at-arms.

The effort to increase the numbers of the troops was accompanied by an improvement in administration. The number of lances each captain had to maintain, in war and in peace, was specifically prescribed; commissaries verified, by means of musters, the strength of the companies, before they turned over the pay to the captains; the garrisons were frequently inspected in order to maintain discipline and protect the population from oppression. Every excess was to be swiftly and severely punished by the regular courts of the garrisons. All these regulations would have been useless had not the underlying evil of the old army, inadequate pay, been corrected. The growth in the income of the king, through the enlarge-

The French Army

ment of his domanial possessions, through the greater
productiveness of indirect taxes from expanding trade
and commerce, and through the increase of the *taille,* had
sufficed for the regular payment of the troops ever since
the establishment of the Companies of the Ordinance.
Naturally, it was impossible to cleanse the army, in a
trice, from all the evils of lack of discipline. Complaints
against the misdeeds of the soldiers, against plunderings
in war and peace, were still frequent, but a great step in
advance had nevertheless been taken. The increased
authority of the king over the troops and the dismissal of
the useless rabble had so improved the fighting qualities
of the army that the success of the last campaign was
quickly achieved, and systematic plundering of the provinces ceased.

A survey of the life-work of Charles VII shows that
the army, after its reform, still bore in every respect the
medieval imprint. He had developed all the existing
elements, but had not created a new army. The royal
authority had assuredly made the feudal powers much
more serviceable than formerly, but the military organization was still based entirely upon the feudal conception
of the State. The nobility formed, from the standpoint
of taxation as well as of military organization, a privileged fighting class, and contributed the bulk of the first-
class warriors; the fate of the army depended on whether
the nobility kept their feudal fidelity to the monarchy or
whether the king was strong and rich enough to compel
them to fulfil the service they owed, and to pay them
their wages. As before, only a small fraction of the city
burgher class appeared on the field of battle as close-range

fighters, and the mass of the nation—the lower class of the city folk and the peasantry—remained, as can easily be seen, outside the army. No proof is required to show that, from the standpoint of the art of war in the fifteenth century, peasants and city-folk could have been used in masses only as infantry armed with knife or pike. The French army had no such arrangement. Nowhere do Charles's ordinances throw any light on the organization of such masses of soldiers, and when his son Louis later on followed the example of the Swiss, and formed some bodies of French infantry for hand-to-hand fighting, he was regarded as a very great innovator. The question arises, why did not Charles try to utilize citizens and peasants in this way for military service? What infantry in close rank, armed with pike and halbert, could accomplish, the Swiss had shown for a hundred years against Austrians and Italians, and even at St. Jacob against the French companies. The truth is that Charles did not require any such force.

In political life it is not the possibility of attaining the abstract best which leads to reforms, but the necessity of solving concrete problems. Charles's task was to conquer the English; to attain this end, he sought to reform his army upon the model of his successful enemy and, if possible, to surpass his teacher. And, as the English possessed no infantry armed with knife and pike, Charles had no immediate cause to create such a force. With the Swiss, who might have shown him in practice the need of such a force, he came into contact only casually. If one goes further and considers how slowly and labor-

The French Army

iously the formation of such a new military type is completed, and what unfortunate experiences the German princes had at this very time with their improvised infantry, it will not be hard to understand why Charles made no effort to create an infantry force for the hand-to-hand conflict, but concentrated his strength exclusively upon the improvement of the existing organization.

The decisive importance of the feudal element in the French army is shown quite clearly in the time of Louis XI. As soon as the princes dared again to oppose the king with independence, the foundations of the army and of the royal power tottered; the vassals placed in the field, as before, large bodies of troops, and their vassals aided them, unconditionally, against the king, so that the nobles' obligation to serve the king was illusory. The king was not absolutely sure even of the Companies of the Ordinance, since captains and knights sympathized in part with the rebellious vassals. The misfortunes of Louis throw light, not only upon the political, but also upon the military character of the army. The knights of the Ordinance vindicated, in spite of many deficiencies, their former worth, but the marksmen were as complete a failure as they had been under Charles and before his time. This experience led Louis to organize an infantry force, hitherto unknown in France—the pikemen, upon the Swiss model, out of which our modern infantry has developed. It is an error, then, to laud Charles VII as the founder of the standing army and of French national infantry; the standing army was in existence before him and the infantry he had was also an old institution and fell to pieces shortly after his death, without the possibility of anything new developing from it. The foundation of modern French infantry was first laid by his son, Louis XI. Charles's historical service is that he strengthened the power of the feudal monarchy through improved organization and thus was able to expel the English and carry forward the process of weakening the great vassals.

List of Works from which the
Selections have been Drawn

Bibliotheque de l'École des Chartes. Revue d'érudition consacrée spécialement à l'étude du moyen âge. Paris: A. Picard, 1839–.

Cunningham, W.: Western Civilization in its Economic Aspects. 2 volumes. Cambridge: University Press, 1898–1900.

Darmesteter, A.: Cours de grammaire de la langue française. Paris: C. Delagrave. Fourth edition.

Devic, Dom. Cl., et Vaissete, Dom. J.: Histoire Générale de Languedoc, avec des notes et les pièces justificatives. 15 volumes. Toulouse: E. Privat, 1872–1892.

Diehl, Ch.: Justinien et la civilization byzantine au VIᵉ siècle. Paris: E. Leroux, 1901.

Dozy, A.: Recherches sur l'histoire et la littérature de l'Espagne pendant le moyen âge. 2 volumes. Paris: Maisonneuve et Cⁱᵉ, 1881.

Esmein, J. P. H.: Cours élémentaire d'histoire du droit français. Paris: L. Larose, 1901.

Flach, J.: Les origines de l'ancienne France. 3 volumes. Paris: L. Larose, 1886–1893.

Garreau, M.: L'Etat social de la France au temps des Croisades. Paris: E. Plon, Nourrit & Cⁱᵉ, 1899.

Gebhart, E.: La renaissance italienne et la philosophie de l'histoire. Paris: L. Cerf, 1887.

Graf, A.: Roma del medio evo. 2 volumes. Torino: E. Loescher, 1883.

575

List of Works

Havet, J.: Lettres de Gerbert. Paris: A. Picard, 1889.

Historische Zeitschrift. Founded by H. von Sybel. München: R. Oldenbourg, 1859–.

Lamprecht, K.: Deutsche Geschichte. To be completed in 14 volumes. Berlin: H. Heyfelder, 1894–.

Lavisse, Ernest: Histoire de France, despuis les origines jusqu'à la Révolution. Publiée avec la collaboration de MM. Bayet, Bloch, Carré, Coville, Kleinclausz, Langlois, Lemonnier, Luchaire, Mariéjol, Petit-Dutaillis, Pfister, Rébelliau, Sagnac, Vidal de la Blache. To be completed in 8 volumes, each published in two parts. Paris: Hachette et Cie, 1900–.

Lavisse et Rambaud: Histoire Générale du IVe siècle à nos jours. Ouvrage publié sous la direction de MM. Ernest Lavisse et Alfred Rambaud. 12 volumes. Paris: A. Colin & Cie, 1893–1901. The collaborators of the first two volumes are: MM. Bayet, Bémont, Berthelot, Blondel, Cahun, Chénon, Coville, Denis, Desdevises du Dézert, Haumant, Langlois, Lavisse, Lavoix, Levasseur, Luchaire, Malet, Müntz, Novakovitch, Petit de Julleville, Pinguad, Pirenne, Rambaud, Tannery, Wahl, and Xénopol.

Lecoy de la Marche, A.: La Chaire française au moyen âge. Paris: H. Laurens, 1886. Second edition.

Luchaire, A.: Innocent III, la Croisade des Albigeois. Paris: Hachette et Cie, 1905.

Luchaire, A.: Manuel des institutions françaises. Paris: Hachette & Cie, 1892.

Martroye, F.: L'Occident à l'époque byzantine. Goths et Vandales. Paris: Hachette & Cie, 1904.

Recueil des historiens des Croisades. Paris: Imprimerie Nationale, 1841–.

Revue des Deux Mondes. Paris: Bureau de la Revue des Deux Mondes, 1831–.

List of Works

Vaublanc, M. le Vte de: La France au temps des Croisades. 4 volumes. Paris: Techener, 1844–1849.

Viollet, M.: Droit public; Histoire des institutions politiques et administratives de la France. 2 volumes. Paris: L. Larose, 1890–1898.

Voigt, G.: Die Wiederbelebung des classischen Alterthums. Berlin: G. Reimer, 1893.

Weise, O.: Unsere Muttersprache. Leipzig: B. G. Teubner, 1897.

Index

Index

Index

Index

583

Index

Index

Index

Index

Index

588

Index

Lord high justiciar, 165, 166, 182, 195

Lordship (*seigneurie*), 159, 163–166, 173, 175

Lorraine, 382–388, 561, 563

Lothair, of France, 377, 383, 384, 385, 387

Lothair II, of Germany, 420, 421

Louis the Debonnaire, 134–135

Louis the Fat, 184, 185

Louis d'Outremer, 138

Louis V, 385, 386; VI, 415, 420; VII, 206, 417–418, 427, 429; XI, 572–574

Louis, St., 179, 180, 185, 319, 322, 366–375, 482, 491–523, 555

Loup, St., 66

Low German, 329 ff.

Lucan, 277, 279, 296, 297, 298, 305, 306

Lucian, 221

Lucretius, 298, 310

Luther, 342, 343, 345–347

Luxeuil, 116

Lyons, 10

Macrobius, 306

Maghrebins, 260

Magic, 348

Magister memoriæ, 11

Mainz, 126

Majolus, abbot, 145, 148

Mamelukes, 251

Manfred, 487

Manicheism, 441

Mansourah, 492, 511, 522

Marco Polo, 482

Marcus Aurelius, 502

Marie of France, 299

Marseilles, 9–10

Martin I, 115; IV, 465

Martin, St., 67–69, 76, 372

Masonry, 469, 472

Mathematics, 376–377

Maximilian, 342

Mechanics, 293

Menander, 15

Merchants, 213, 215, 250, 253, 262, 267, 330, 433

Merovingians, 60, 62, 63, 75, 82, 84, 134. See also Franks

Metropolitan, 60, 62

Michelangelo, 527, 544

Migrations, influence of, 44–49, 50–59

Milan, 486

Miles, 240

Mirror of Nature, 209

Mirror of True Penitence, 290

Missionaries, services of, 119. See also Monasteries

Missions, in Gaul and Germany, 114–128

Modjam, 238

Mohammed, 238, 254, 266

Mohammedans. See Mussulman

Monasteries, economic influence of, 129–136, 158. See also Missionaries, and names of monks, monasteries and orders

Monasticism, 474–475; Greek, 533, 540

Monks, preservers of literature, 282, 288, 290–291, 330–331. See also Monasteries, Monasticism, and names of monks and orders

Monte Cassino, 124, 282

Moors, 224

Mortmain, 26, 197, 205. See also Amortissement

Moslem civilization, 224–239

Moslem jurisprudence, 529–530

Motacim, 225–239

Mummolin, 319

Mundium, 203

Mundus, 109, 111

589

Index

Index

Index

Index

Index